Michael R. Chernick
15 Quail Drive
Holland PA 18966

MONOGRAPHS ON
STATISTICS AND APPLIED PROBABILITY

General Editors
D. R. Cox and D. V. Hinkley

Probability, Statistics and Time
M. S. Bartlett

The Statistical Analysis of Spatial Pattern
M. S. Bartlett

Stochastic Population Models in Ecology and Epidemiology
M. S. Bartlett

Risk Theory
R. E. Beard, T. Pentikäinen and E. Pesonen

Residuals and Influence in Regression
R. D. Cook and S. Weisberg

Point Processes
D. R. Cox and V. Isham

Analysis of Binary Data
D. R. Cox

The Statistical Analysis of Series of Events
D. R. Cox and P. A. W. Lewis

Analysis of Survival Data
D. R. Cox and D. Oakes

Queues
D. R. Cox and W. L. Smith

Stochastic Abundance Models
S. Engen

The Analysis of Contingency Tables
B. S. Everitt

Finite Mixture Distributions
B. S. Everitt and D. J. Hand

Population Genetics
W. J. Ewens

Risk Theory

THE STOCHASTIC BASIS OF INSURANCE

R. E. BEARD

O.B.E., F.I.A., F.I.M.A., PROFESSOR

Leicestershire, England

T. PENTIKÄINEN

PHIL. Dr, PROFESSOR h.c.

Helsinki, Finland

E. PESONEN

PHIL. Dr

Helsinki, Finland

THIRD EDITION

LONDON NEW YORK

CHAPMAN AND HALL

First published 1969 by
Methuen & Co. Ltd
Second edition 1977
Published by Chapman and Hall Ltd
11 New Fetter Lane, London EC4P 4EE
Third edition 1984
Published in the USA by
Chapman and Hall
733 Third Avenue, New York NY 10017
© 1969, 1977, 1984 R. E. Beard,
T. Pentikäinen, E. Pesonen
Printed in Great Britain at the
University Printing House, Cambridge

ISBN 0 412 24260 5 (hardback)
ISBN 0 412 25980 X (paperback)

British Library Cataloguing in Publication Data

Beard, R.E.
  Risk theory: the stochastic basis of
  insurance.—3rd ed.—(Monographs on statistics and
  applied probability)
  1. Risks (Insurance)
  I. Title   II. Pentikäinen, T.
  III. Pesonen, E.   IV. Series
  368   HG8782
  ISBN 0-412-24260-5
  ISBN 0-412-25980-X Pbk

Library of Congress Cataloging in Publication Data

Beard, R. E. (Robert Eric)
  Risk theory.
  (Monographs on statistics and applied probability)
  Bibliography: p.
  Includes indexes.
  1. Insurance—Mathematics. 2. Risk (Insurance)
  3. Stochastic processes. I. Pentikäinen, Teivo.
  II. Pesonen, E. (Erkki) III. Title. IV. Series.
  HG8781.B34   1984   368   83-25180
  ISBN 0-412-24260-5
  ISBN 0-412-25980-X (pbk.)

Contents

Preface

The theory of risk already has its traditions. A review of its classical results is contained in Bohlmann (1909). This classical theory was associated with life insurance mathematics, and dealt mainly with deviations which were expected to be produced by random fluctuations in individual policies. According to this theory, these deviations are discounted to some initial instant; the square root of the sum of the squares of the capital values calculated in this way then gives a measure for the stability of the portfolio. A theory constituted in this manner is not, however, very appropriate for practical purposes. The fact is that it does not give an answer to such questions as, for example, within what limits a company's probable gain or loss will lie during different periods. Further, non-life insurance, to which risk theory has, in fact, its most rewarding applications, was mainly outside the field of interest of the risk theorists. Thus it is quite understandable that this theory did not receive very much attention and that its applications to practical problems of insurance activity remained rather unimportant.

A new phase of development began following the studies of Filip Lundberg (1909, 1919), which, thanks to H. Cramér (1926), C.O. Segerdahl and other Swedish authors, became generally known as the 'collective theory of risk'. As regards questions of insurance, the problem was essentially the study of the progress of the business from a probabilistic point of view. In this form the theory has its applications to non-life insurance as well as to life insurance. This new way of expressing the problem has proved fruitful. In recent years the fundamental assumptions of the theory, and the range of applications, have been significantly enlarged. The advancement of the general theory of stochastic processes and its numerous sub-branches and applications has been reflected in the development of risk theory. The explosive development of computers has made it feasible to treat problems which previously could not be handled because of their complicated structure. For example, it is now possible to create models to describe the insurance business as a whole, and the interactions between its sectors, instead of limiting the consideration to isolated sub-problems like the range of risk fluctuations, reinsurance, safety loadings, reserve funds, and so on.

Today the theory of risk generates an interesting and far-reaching field for research. The development of the theory is still far from complete, as is demonstrated by the many papers which continue to be published on the subject. A defect, as in so many other new and rapidly developing branches of human knowledge, is that the theory has become difficult for practising actuaries to follow. This is regrettable, because a knowledge of this theory deepens actuarial intuition and helps towards an understanding of the insurance business as a process characterized by varying progress and fluctuations from year to year. The modern theory of risk can also give an actuary concrete assistance in the form of practical applications. It is true that many problems in this field, for example, problems of a company's solvency, reinsurance requirements, safety loadings in premiums and many others, are such that risk theory alone is incapable of providing a definite solution. This is because in practical work it is often necessary to take into consideration many aspects with which risk theory is not competent to deal. In reinsurance arrangements, for example, attention has to be given to many political aspects of insurance such as reserves, reciprocity and liquidity. In spite of this, when choosing a form of reinsurance and calculating suitable net retentions and safety loadings, and in business planning in general, risk theory provides effective tools to estimate the fluctuations in the business retained by a company; such fluctuations should obviously always be kept within the limits of the company's resources. Thus the theory of risk can facilitate important considerations of financial interest and be useful in making final decisions.

To disseminate knowledge of the theory of risk it seemed essential to provide an introduction to the theory based upon the elements of probability theory which form part of actuarial study and which provide some of the basic ideas concerning risk theory. Furthermore, there is a need for a summary of the results of the present theory, easily available for practical application.

For this reason, one of the authors, Pentikäinen, published an elementary textbook of risk theory in the Finnish language in 1955, primarily designed for the use of Finnish actuaries as an introduction to the theory. Many participants at meetings of ASTIN (Actuarial Studies in Non-Life Insurance – a section of the International Actuarial Association) expressed a wish for a concise book of this kind in English and devoted primarily to practical applications. The authors attempted to produce such a book. The first edition was completed in 1969. The basis of compilation was that the Finnish authors rewrote and brought up-to-date the earlier Finnish textbook and passed it to the English author, who, for his part, worked it into shape, taking into consideration British circumstances and paying special attention to general actuarial education in English-speaking countries.

Since the publication of the first edition there has been a continued growth of interest in the subject. ASTIN now has well over a thousand members, and there are few actuarial societies which do not include some aspects of risk theory in their education and training. A number of universities and technical institutions now have courses of study and, on the application side, the growth in the concept of risk management, namely the technique of total financial management planning, has emphasized the important part played by the theory of risk.

The present and essentially renewed third edition has been worked very much along the same lines, taking into account recent developments of theories and applications. The compilation of the text was mainly made in connection with the university lectures of Pentikäinen, and many of the new approaches were developed and tested in a comprehensive research work concerning solvency and the reserve technique (Pentikäinen 1982, Rantala 1982).

Since the first edition was published several other textbooks on risk theory have become available, for example Bühlmann (1970), Gerber (1979) and Seal (1966b and 1978). The existence of these excellent presentations of risk theory has very much facilitated the compilation of the third edition of this book. Because the other authors have followed more strictly mathematical lines, it has been appropriate to assume a more pragmatic approach here. The authors hope that all these books will complement each other and give the interested reader a more comprehensive view of the theory than would be possible in any single monograph.

To prevent the book becoming too large and developing beyond the limits of a primary textbook, it has been necessary to limit the subject matter. This has been a very difficult task, due to the very abundant field which the theory and its applications cover today, and from necessity many interesting aspects of the theory have been omitted. Furthermore various alternatives, lines and methods of presentation are possible. Our aim has been for simplicity – the more so because the main purpose of this book is to serve as a first introduction to the theory of risk, since there are several publications dealing with advanced aspects of parts of the theory. On the other hand, the authors have been quite conscious of the danger of over-simplification, which could reduce the theory to 'pseudoscience'; moreover, ignorance of the basic assumptions of the theory could lead to serious mistakes when applying the theory to various actuarial problems. For this reason the basic foundations of the theory have not been omitted. The main lines, the practical one and the theoretical one, are unfortunately not easy to fit together, and in the present state of the theory a firm bridge between the practical problems and exact theory is often not fully developed. Bearing in mind that our main purpose is practical, we have also been obliged to present formulae which are based on approximations without well-mapped confidence limits. We have also attempted a compromise between accuracy and simplicity, transferring some cumbersome considerations to the appendices, which can be omitted at a first reading.

We sincerely hope that this book will prove to be only a first step for each reader in his introduction to the theory, and that sufficient interest will be stimulated to provoke a more extensive and profound investigation. An extensive bibliography has been included to assist the reader in this direction.

The book has been written on the assumption that the reader has a knowledge of the elementary aspects of probability theory. On the other hand, familiarity with the axiomatic theory of probability and stochastic processes is not assumed and the text is compiled accordingly, not covering, for instance, strictly axiomatic existence proofs of the processes concerned, as they are irrelevant to the aims of the book.

In order to render the book more readable, as far as possible, for those with different interests and different degrees of familiarity with probability calculus, the parts of the text that utilize special techniques, or consider details of limited interest only, are marked ** or referred to appendixes. These sections as well as many of the proofs, can be omitted on the first reading and the reader can proceed directly to the final formulae.

Martti Pesonen, PhD, participated in the final collation of the text.

The authors are grateful to the numerous experts in various countries for the generous donation of very helpful criticisms and advice.

The typing of the manuscript for printing, taken from numerous texts and formulae, was undertaken by Brita Aalto, to whom we owe our special thanks for accurate work requiring great patience.

Last but not least, we wish to thank Chapman and Hall Ltd and in particular Mr Richard Stileman and Ms Mary Ann Ommanney for their generous cooperation in the preparation of the book and for the final linguistic checking of the text.

Leicestershire and Helsinki
April, 1983

Robert Eric Beard
Teivo Pentikäinen
Erkki Pesonen

We are sorry to announce that our co-author and colleague of long standing Professor Robert E. Beard passed away in November, 1983 without having witnessed the completion of this new edition of *Risk Theory*.

In grateful recognition for his life-long work in the development and advancement of non-life insurance mathematics we dedicate this book to the memory of Professor Beard.

T.P.
E.P.

Nomenclature

Equations in parentheses, items without parentheses.
For principles of the notations see Section 1.5.
Many of the variables may be both stochastic or deterministic. For brevity this feature is not specified, i.e. bold face letters are not used.

$A(v)$ discounted claims (8.2.7).
a_j zero-moments of claim size (3.3.1).
B gross premiums $= P_\lambda/(1-c)$ (6.2.8).
$B(t_1, t_2)$ gross premiums from period $[t_1, t_2]$ (6.4.6).
b_j zero-moment of loss degree (3.6.16).
C loading for expenses of administration $= cB$ gross or net 6.5(a), (8.1.2), 10.2(f).
c loading factor for expenses 6.2(f), (6.5.4).
c_i factor synchronizing inflation (7.6.2).
c_1, c_2 control coeff. (7.7.1).
$D(t)$ dividends 6.5(a), 10.2(g); time lag function (6.6.7).
$d = D/B$ (10.2.8).
$d(t)$ number of deaths (8.1.4).
d.f. distribution function
$E(\ )$ expected value.
E_u equilibrium level of u (6.6.9).
e base of nat. logarithms $= 2.718282$.
$F(k) = F(k; n)$ d.f. of the claim number (2.4.1).
$\bar{F}(k)$ mixed d.f. of the claim number (2.7.4).

$F(X)$ d.f. of aggregate claims (3.2.3).
$F(X; t_1, t_2)$ d.f. of aggregate claims for period $[t_1, t_2]$ (6.1.23).
$\bar{F}(x)$ d.f. of the standardized aggregate claim (3.9.4).
$f(X)$ density of X (3.11.18).
$f = X/B$ claims ratio (6.5.4).
$f(1, t)$ accumulated claim ratio (6.6.5).
G utility d.f. 10.4(d).
$G(u_0, u; t_1, t_2)$ (6.6.17a).
$G_t(u)$ d.f. of $u(t)$ (6.6.17b)
GNP gross national product
$G(r)$ loss degree d.f. (3.6.13).
$G(x)$ Edgeworth expansion (3.10.1)
$g = \gamma/6$ 3.11(h).
$H(q)$ structure d.f. (2.7.1).
h. Polya parameter (2.9.1) or $\gamma_2/24$ 3.11(h).
$I(t)$ investment income 6.5.(a), 10.2(d).
i growth rate specified by suffices
i_g growth rate 6.1(c).
$i_{igp} = i_i/r_{gp}$ (6.5.8a)
i_i interest rate 6.3(a).
i_p rate of premium inflation 6.2(a).
i_x rate of claim inflation 6.1(j).
J number of sections or classes 3.7(a).

j current index, section index 3.7(a).

K error factor (4.3.5).

k number of claims 2.1(a).

$L(s)$ Laplace transform (1.6.9).

$l(t)$ cohort size (8.1.1).

M net retention 3.6.

$M(s)$ moment generating function (1.6.1).

m mean value of one claim $= a_1$ (3.3.2).

m.g.f. moment generating function 1.6.

$m(t)$ mean value of claim for year t 6.4(b).

$m(Z)$ measure of tail (3.5.25).

$N(x)$ normal d.f., mean 0, st. dev. 1 (3.9.3).

$N_y(x)$ NP d.f. (3.11.10).

n expected number of claims 2.4(a), (6.1.2), 6.4(b).

$n(1, t)$ expected number of claims for period $[1, t]$ (6.1.24).

$O(t)$ run-off error (10.2.7b).

$P = E(\mathbf{X})$ risk premium (3.3.7), (4.1.1).

P_{SL} risk premium of stop loss reinsurance (4.8.1).

$P_{X/L}$ risk premium of excess of loss reinsurance (4.7.1).

$P_\lambda = (1 + \lambda)P$ safety loaded premium (6.2.5).

$p_\lambda = P_\lambda/B$ (6.5.14).

$P(t_1, t_2)$ risk premium from period $[t_1, t_2]$ (6.4.7).

$p(k; t)$ claim number probability of period $(0, t]$ (2.1.1).

$p_k(n) = \text{prob}\{\mathbf{k} = k | n\}$ claim number probability (2.2.1), (2.4.2).

$\bar{p}_k(n)$ claim number probability of mixed d.f. (2.7.2).

$p(t)$ termination frequency (8.2.3).

Q insured sum 3.6.4(a); moving expenses 10.2(f).

q claims number intensity (2.6.5), structure variable 2.7(c).

q_i discrete claim size frequency (3.8.2).

$q(t)$ mortality (8.1.1).

R insolvency coefficient (9.2.1).

$R(r)$ rectangular d.f. (6.8.1).

$R(t)$ discounted income (6.6.5).

R_1, R_2, R'_1, R'_2 control limits (7.7.1), (7.7.2).

r growth or accumulation factor specified by suffices, degree of loss (3.6.12).

$r_2 = a_2/m^2$ risk index (3.3.8).

$r_3 = a_3/m^3$ (3.3.8).

$r_g = 1 + i_g$ 6.1(c).

$r_{gp} = r_g \times r_p$ (6.5.7).

$r_{gx} = r_g \times r_x$ (6.1.18).

$r_{igp} = r_i/r_{gp}$ (6.5.8b).

$r_p = 1 + i_p$ (6.2.1), (8.3.6).

$r(t_1, t_2)$ (6.6.1a).

$r_x = 1 + i_x$ (6.1.10).

$r(Z)$ extinction rate (3.5.26).

S sum insured 8.2.

$S(Z)$ d.f. of claim size (3.1.1).

S^{k*} k:th convolution of S(Z) (3.2.2).

T time period, planning horizon.

T_z length of a cycle (6.1.4).

t time

t_p time lag (6.2.2).

U risk reserve, solvency margin (4.1.5), often the initial minimum capital $U(0) = U_0$ which satisfies the solvency conditions.

U_r ruin barrier (4.1.5), 6.7(a).

u solvency ratio $= U/P$ or U/B (6.5.4).

$u_r = U_r/B$

$V = \text{var}(\cdot)$ variance

$V(t)$ premium reserve (8.1.2).

v cycle phase (6.1.3); discounting factor $1/r_i$ 8.2.

$v(y) = v_y(y)$ NP transformation

(3.11.1), (3.11.17a).

W technical reserves 6.5(c).

W_k waiting time of the k:th event, exercise 2.6.2.

$W(Q)$ d.f. of sums insured (3.6.14).

$W_T(U)$ conditioned survival function (6.7.2).

$w = W/B$ (6.5.4), maturity age (8.1.3).

$w(t)$ exogenous impulse (6.1.6).

X aggregate claims 3.2(a).

$\mathbf{X}(t)$ aggregate claims assigned to year t (6.1.1).

$\mathbf{X}(t_1, t_2)$ aggregate claims assigned to years $t_1, t_1 + 1, \ldots, t_2$ (6.1.1).

$x = (X - \mu_{\mathbf{X}})/\sigma_{\mathbf{X}}$ (3.9.1), also (3.3.13).

$x(1, t)$ (6.6.15).

x_ε = confidence coefficient defined by the NP function $\varepsilon = N_\gamma(-x_\varepsilon)$.

$Y = P_\lambda - X$ = underwriting profit

$Y(t), Y(0, t)$ profit (8.1.6), (8.1.7a), (8.3.1), (10.2.7a).

y standardized normally distributed variable 3.11(b).

$y(0, t) = Y(0, t)/B(t)$ (8.1.7b).

y_0 discounted random profit (8.2.1).

y_ε confidence coefficient, $\varepsilon = N(-y_\varepsilon)$.

Z size of one claim (3.1.1), credibility coeff. (4.10.3).

$Z(t)$ risk sum (8.2.4).

z cycle variable (6.1.3).

z_m cycle amplitude (6.1.3).

α Pareto parameter (3.5.20) or $4/\gamma_{\mathbf{X}}^2$ (3.12.1).

α_j moment about zero of the claim number (2.4.3), (1.5.5a).

$\bar{\alpha}_j$ moment about zero of the mixed d.f. (2.8.1).

β_j moment about zero of aggregate claims (3.3.3).

$\Gamma(h)$ = complete gamma function

2.9(a).

$\Gamma(x, h)$ incomplete gamma function (2.9.1).

γ skewness 1.5(g).

$\bar{\gamma}$ skewness of mixed d.f. (2.8.6).

γ_2 kurtosis 1.5(g).

$\bar{\gamma}_2$ kurtosis of mixed d.f. (2.8.6).

$\gamma_{\bar{\mathbf{x}}}$ skewness of aggregate claims (3.3.7).

$\gamma_{2\bar{\mathbf{x}}}$ kurtosis of aggregate claims (3.3.7).

$\gamma_{\mathbf{q}}$ skewness of the structure function (2.8.5).

$\Delta\mu_{\mathbf{u}}$ 7.9(c).

ε ruin probability.

$\varepsilon(t)$ noise (6.1.5).

$\varepsilon(x)$ unit step function (1.5.3).

η auxiliary variable (3.5.18).

λ safety loading (4.1.4), (6.5.12).

$\lambda_{\mathbf{b}}$ gross premium B adjusted safety loading (6.2.10).

$\lambda_{\mathbf{p}}$ risk premium adjusted safety loading (6.2.9).

$\lambda_{\text{tot}} = \lambda$ = total safety loading (6.5.12)

$\mu_{\mathbf{f}}$ mean value of the claim ratio f (6.6.6).

μ_i = ith central moment (1.5.5b).

$\mu_{\mathbf{u}}$ mean value of the solvency ratio $\mathbf{u}$ (6.6.8).

$\mu_{\mathbf{X}} = \mu_{\mathbf{X}}(1, t)$ mean value of aggregate claims $\mathbf{X}$ (3.3.7), (6.1.13).

$v_j = n_j/n$ (3.7.3).

$\pi_j = m_{\mathbf{X}j}/m_{\mathbf{X}}$ (3.7.8).

ρ risk intensity parameter (2.2.1), see also (3.3.11), relative mean risk, exercise 5.2.2.

$\rho(t)$ lapse ratio (8.3.2).

σ standard deviation.

$\bar{\sigma}$ standard deviation of mixed d.f. (2.8.6).

$\sigma_{\mathbf{q}}$ standard deviation of the structure function (2.8.5).

σ_u standard deviation of the solvency ratio **u** (6.6.10).

σ_X standard deviation of aggregate claims **X** (3.3.7).

$\sigma_X(t_1, t_2) =$ standard deviation related to $X(t_1, t_2)$ (6.1.19).

φ_c (6.9.5).

φ_{cc} (6.9.7).

$\varphi(u)$ characteristic function (1.6.8).

$\varphi(t)$ ruin state probability (6.6.19).

$\Psi_T(U)$ ruin probability related to period $(0, T]$ (6.7.1), (9.2.1).

ω cycle frequency $= 2\pi/T_z$ (6.1.4).

Some conventions

x^+ or $(\ )^+ = x$ or $=$ the expression in the parentheses if x or the expression ≥ 0, otherwise $= 0$.

$[x] =$ the integer equal or next smaller than x.

$A \cup B$ union of sets A and B = a set consisting of all the elements of A and B

$A \cap B$ intersection of sets = a set consisting of the joint elements of A and B

$A \supset B$ B is a subset of A.

$\forall x_i$ valid for all x_i

$\exists x_i$ valid at least for one of the x_i.

$*$ e.g. $F * G(X)$ convolution (1.5.8).

$**$ mark for technically detailed section or paragraph which can be passed on first reading.

f^{-1} is the inverse of f.

-1 as a subscript relates to the preceding year, e.g. u_{-1} (6.5.2).

CHAPTER 1

Definitions and notation

1.1 The purpose of the theory of risk

(a) Deterministic versus probabilistic approach Conventional actuarial techniques are largely based on frequencies and the average amounts of claims. For example, if an insurer has a portfolio of N policies at risk and if the expected mean value of the claim frequency for these policies during a specified period is q and the expected average size of the claim is m, then the expected total amount of claims is Nqm. However, the actual amounts arising from several successive periods will differ from this expected figure and will fluctuate around it. In probabilistic terms, the actual amount of claims is a random variable. Conventional actuarial techniques are in fact based on a simplified model of an insurance portfolio in which random variables are replaced by their mean values, i.e. the fluctuation phenomenon is disregarded. Whilst for many purposes this simplified model is sufficient in the hands of experts, it is undeniably an oversimplification of the facts and it is both useful and interesting to develop the principles of insurance mathematics on a more general basis, in which both the number and size of claims, as well as possibly other key quantities, are considered as random variables. Studies of the different kinds of fluctuation appearing in an insurance portfolio which start from this point of view constitute the branch of actuarial mathematics termed the theory of risk.

(b) Gradual introduction of stochasticity Of course, the financial structure of an insurance company depends on management costs and investment of capital in addition to the claim aspects, but these two factors are not subject to random fluctuation to the same extent as are claims. Therefore the analysis is first restricted to claims and to that part of premiums which remains when the loading for expenses for management has been deducted, i.e. risk premiums increased by a safety loading. These restrictions are then relaxed, leading gradually to the construction of a comprehensive model (see Chapter 10).

In particular, the high rates of inflation prevalent today cannot be ignored in practical work. To provide a satisfactory basis for development it is assumed that, when the horizon under consideration is longer than one year, the size of the claim will be corrected by a factor depending on the assumed value of money.

(c) Claims as stochastic process The claim process can be described graphically as in Fig. 1.1.1. Every occurrence from which a claim arises is represented by a vertical step, the height of the step showing the amount of the claim. Time is measured to the right along the horizontal axis and the altitude **X** of the stepped line shows the total amount of claims during the time interval $(0, t]$. The process is, in fact, a *compound stochastic process* in the sense that the time of occurrence and the number of occurrences are random phenomena

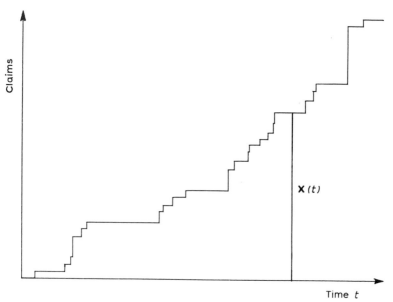

Figure 1.1.1   *A sample path of claim process.*

and the size of each claim is also a random variable. Any particular realization consisting of an observed flow like that in Fig. 1.1.1 is called a *sample path* or a realization of the process.

If the observation time t is fixed, then the corresponding outcome, $\mathbf{X}(t)$ in our example, is a *random variable* having a distribution function (abbreviated d.f.) $F(X; t) = \text{prob}\{\mathbf{X}(t) \leq X\}$. Random variables will be denoted by bold-face letters (see Section 1.5). If the stochastic process is well defined, then F is uniquely determined for every t of the observation range. On the other hand, however, mere definition of F, even if it were valid at every t, is not sufficient to determine a stochastic process. In addition, transition rules are needed to describe how the $\mathbf{X}(t)$ values related to different times t are correlated. Hence some care is necessary when the terms 'stochastic processes' and 'stochastic variables' or their distributions are used.

(d) Underwriting process If the whole risk business of an insurance portfolio is considered, this can be illustrated graphically as shown in Fig. 1.1.2. For the sake of simplicity the yields of interest and of

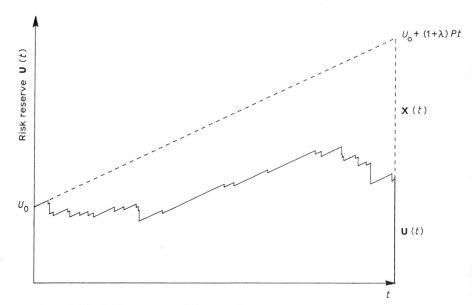

Figure 1.1.2 *Risk process as difference of incoming premiums and outgoing claims.*

many other relevant factors are omitted in this connection (they will be incorporated into the model in later chapters). The risk premium P together with a safety loading λ is continuously flowing in; this is accumulated in a risk reserve $\mathbf{U}$ of an initial amount U_0, so that the income is represented by a line sloping upwards to the right. The claims, which can be regarded as negative income, are paid out from this reserve and are represented by downward steps. The difference

$$\mathbf{U}(t) - U_0 = P(1 + \lambda)t - \mathbf{X}(t),$$

gives the net gain (positive or negative) arising during time t.

(e) Risk reserve The concept of risk reserve is closely related to or possibly identical with the concepts *solvency margin* or *net worth*, frequently used in current general practice. All these terms can be defined as the difference between the values of assets and liabilities, even if the definitions diverge in detail, for example whether or not to regard the assets as book values or as current market values. Also, in the latter case the underestimation of the book values, as 'hidden reserve', is included in the risk reserve. In the following, the risk reserve is understood to be a 'reservoir' or 'basin', where the underwriting gain is flowing in if positive or draining out if negative. When risk-theoretical models are constructed and operated, the decision as to whether the risk reserve is composed of the whole solvency margin (understood in the wide sense), or possibly only some part of it, can be left open and to be determined in each application.

In some cases it may be advisable to take $\mathbf{U}$ to mean only that part of freely allocable resources which can be used to cover adverse fluctuations of the underwriting gains or losses without too great an inconvenience. In some other contexts it may be necessary to suppose that $\mathbf{U}$ consists of the whole actual solvency margin.

(f) Parameter uncertainty There is still an important feature to be mentioned. For numerical calculations the risk models always need the assignment of numerical data for a number of model parameters and for initial values of the variables to be analysed. The derivation of these from statistics and other available experience is mostly done by well-known *estimation procedures* from the mathematical theory of statistics. This topic is outside the scope of this book. Instead it is mostly supposed that the initial values are readily available. The problems caused by parameter uncertainty are not only a feature of risk-theoretical considerations. In essence the same problems are always present and are even more critical in premium rating and in evaluation of technical reserves. In fact some of the basic data underlie both risk-theoretical and rating calculations or can be derived from the same basic files. Premium rates are ultimately based on past experience and more or less reliable prognoses of future trends, cycles, inflation and other relevant factors, and they are understandably subject to inaccuracies and errors. They affect the trading result, which makes it possible to evaluate their order of magnitude but not until after a time lag, which in practice may be two or three years and even longer for some particular classes of insurance. The rates and reserves can and should be then corrected (within limitations imposed by competitive market conditions or statutory regulations, if legally controlled). This control mechanism, which is inherent just from the uncertainty in the parameters, is one of the important causes of the underwriting cycles which will be described in Section 2.7 and incorporated in the model in Chapter 6. In fact the effect of the parameter uncertainty will be regarded in this indirect way in the risk-theoretical considerations discussed in Section 6.2.

The effect of parameter inaccuracy can also be investigated directly if necessary. The technique of sensitivity analysis, which will be developed in Section 7.6, can be useful for this purpose. Simply, variations in the initial data can be fed into the risk-theoretical models and the sensitivity of the outcomes can be used for evaluation of the effect of inaccuracies arising from the uncertainty of the initial data.

Even if the estimation inaccuracy is not considered, it must always be kept in mind as a relevant background factor. For example, it may be meaningless to apply very laborious techniques to get very accurate results if the initial data are uncertain. The selection of approaches, if alternatives are available, should thus be consistent with the environment under consideration.

1.2 Stochastic processes in general

The theory of risk is essentially a special case of the theory of random or stochastic processes which has grown rapidly in recent years and now constitutes a large branch of probability theory. Other examples of such processes are waiting time in a queue, level of water in a dam, the number of calls in telephone systems, the emission of radiation from radioactive substances, the movement of equity prices on stock exchanges, or the different kinds of 'random walks'. These and other processes have similarities with the risk process of an insurance portfolio and a number of textbooks are now available for those who wish to study the subject more deeply (e.g. Chung, 1974; Cox and Miller, 1965).

1.3   Positive and negative risk sums

Figure 1.1.2 represents a realization or a *sample path* of a general type of insurance risk process in which any occurrence giving rise to a downward step represents a loss, this being the case in classes such as fire, marine and life (death risk only). A different situation arises in the case of immediate annuity business, since the initial fund is continuously depleted until an annuitant dies, when the reserve

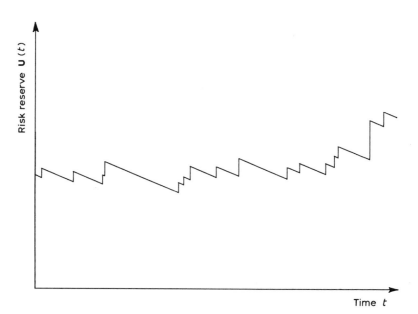

Figure 1.3.1   *Negative risk sums. A portfolio of current annuities. The death of an annuitant is reflected as a step upward.*

released gives rise to an upward step. This latter type is called a risk process with negative risk sums (see Fig. 1.3.1). In this book, positive risk sums only are dealt with as their applications are of greater interest, and because in this way the considerations could be kept simpler. However, most of the results are valid both for negative and mixed sums.

1.4 Main problems

(a) Model building Risk theory can be applied to a wide variety of situations. Before the procedure can be described the problem has to be well defined in terms of the necessary variables as well as the rules and distributions which determine their behaviour. In conventional terms it is stated that a *model* will be constructed to describe the insurance business or some particular function thereof to be analysed. A simple example is given in Fig. 1.1.2, where the model consists of incoming premiums and outgoing claims, the difference of which is accumulated into the risk reserve. In more advanced models the number of variables involved can be quite great. Some of them are usually target variables, the behaviour of which is to be examined under given conditions. Generally it is the business outcomes, such as the values of the risk reserve U in the above simple example, which are sought when the initial conditions and policy alternatives (the so-called *business strategies*) are given. The analysis is usually of the 'what...if...' type, i.e. meaningful answers are looked for to such questions as what would happen if the initial conditions and strategies were as given. Before going on to more sophisticated developments it is advisable to distinguish the following types, (i) and (ii), and to pose the relevant questions:

(i)   What is the result of the business at the *end* of a certain time period $(0, T]$ as illustrated in Fig. 1.4.1? This type of problem will be considered in Chapters 3 and 4, generally taking T to equal one year.

(ii) What is the result if the observations are extended to a certain set of times $t_1, t_2, \ldots, t_v$ of a (prolonged) interval $(0, T]$? This period can be called a planning horizon. This approach will be taken in Chapters 6 and 7, where the check points $t_1, t_2, \ldots$ are usually the end points of the calendar years included in the planning horizon, i.e. 1, 2, ..., T. Figure 1.4.2 illustrates this case.

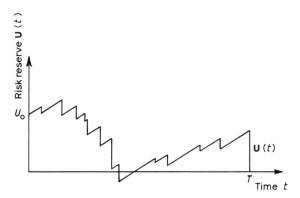

Figure 1.4.1   *A simple risk process. The state of the process can be checked either at the end of the period* (0, T] *or continuously as in item* (b).

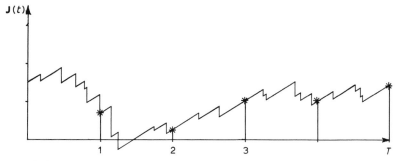

Figure 1.4.2   *Checking at points* $t = 1, 2, ... T$ *during the observation period.*

In terms of Fig. 1.4.1 the first question is equivalent to finding the probability for different values that the risk reserve $U(t)$, or any other target variable, can assume at time $t = T$. Of particular interest is the so called *ruin probability*, i.e. the probability that the risk reserve $U(t)$ may become negative or, more generally that it will fall below some given limit, usually called the *ruin barrier* and denoted by $U_r(t)$. In the case of the extended problem setting (ii), the ruin probability is defined as the probability that U is negative at one or more of the specified time points $t_1, t_2, ...$. This latter concept can be called 'finite time ruin probability' as distinct from the simple 'ruin state probability'.

(b) Discrete and continuous procedure A modification of the second problem arises when observations are taken at each point of time period $(0, T]$; i.e. what is the probability that ruin will occur during this period, while checking is performed continuously at every time point of the period? The former approach is called *discrete*, the latter *continuous*. Both of them are applied in risk theory, often depending on which of them may be more convenient for the special technique under consideration. In practice the incoming and outgoing money flows are followed continuously, but the valuation of assets and liabilities may generally be carried out completely only at the end of each accounting year. Consequently, the financial status is usually checked only at discrete time points, which suggests the discrete analysis approach. There is, of course, some difference in the outcomes resulting from the selection of this problem setting. The discrete approach ignores the possibility that the status, i.e. the risk reserve U, may be negative between the checking times t_i, t_{i+1} but then recovers to a positive level. Consequently it gives a somewhat lower ruin probability. Note that the continuous testing would consider the example plotted in Fig. 1.4.2 to be a ruin, but discrete testing would not.

In the following, the discrete problem setting is mostly assumed to take the checking interval equal to one year. However, the same technique can be used without need of modification for any other interval length, e.g. if the checking of status is made monthly or at each quarter of the year.

(c) Finite or infinite time-span Another modification, very central in the earlier development of collective risk theory, is to ask what is the result if the time T tends to *infinity*. Chapter 9 will be devoted to this case.

(d) Claim number and compound processes The analysis of risk processes begins in Chapter 2 by considering the number of claims and the process related to it, which is called the *claim number process* or often the *counting process*, the well-known Poisson and negative binomial processes being treated as special cases.

The general case where the individual amount of a claim, *claim size*, may vary forms the subject matter of Chapter 3 and later parts of the book. This process, where both the claim number and claim size are random variables, is called the *compound process*.

(e) Break-up and going-concern basis One way to define the solvent state of an insurer is to require that at the end of each fiscal year the assets should be at least equal to the total amount of liabilities (possibly increased by some legally prescribed margin). This situation may be tested by assuming that the activity of the insurer would be *broken* at the test time point and the liabilities, such as those due to outstanding claims, would be cleared up during a liquidation process. Then assets should be available in step with the time of claim and other payments. The risk factors that are involved and which are to be evaluated are the uncertainties of the magnitude of the claims, including those claims which have already occurred before the test time point but which may be notified later. Furthermore, realization of the assets is affected by changes in market value and the whole process is subject to inflation. In other words, this 'break-up basis' is involved with uncertainties arising when both the liabilities and assets go into hypothetical liquidation. The problem is to evaluate these inaccuracies and to find a minimum solvency margin in a way which still gives an adequate guarantee for the fulfilment of the commitments of the insurer.

Another possibility is to assume that the business of the insurer will *go on*. Then, in addition to the errors and inaccuracies concerning gradual liquidation of the assets and the outstanding claims and other liabilities that have arisen in the past fiscal years, i.e. the risks involved just with the break-up situation described above, the continual flow of new claim-causing events and other business transactions gives rise to further fluctuations. Because this 'going-concern' basis, by definition, includes the 'break-up' risks as a partial element, it generates a larger range of fluctuations and leads to demand for a greater solvency margin and safety loading than does the break-up basis alone. This assumes, of course, that consistent principles are followed in the two bases. It may be remarked that if, for example, the break-up basis is defined conventionally, such as by statute, there may be incompatibility with the practical reality of the going-concern basis.

The going-concern basis was tacitly assumed in the previous items and it will be followed in this book generally. The problems involved with the outstanding claims, which constitute the most important break-up risks, will be discussed in item 3.1(c). Asset risks will be considered in Section 6.3.

(f) Life and general insurance An insurance contract normally covers an insurer's liability to indemnify losses caused by specified events like fire, accident, death etc. An insurance contract can, in addition, include more than these pure risk elements; in particular, life and pension insurance schemes may also provide savings for future years. Risk theory is most appropriate to deal with the risk elements and it will be considered in detail in Chapters 1–7. The presentation is formulated, as far as possible, to cover generally all kinds of risk businesses, including the risk elements of life and pension insurance. Special features of life insurance will be discussed in Chapter 8.

1.5   On the notation

The following conventions will be applied:

(a) Stochastic variables and processes are denoted by bold-face letters, e.g. $\mathbf{X}$. If $\mathbf{X}$ is a stochastic process, then the state of $\mathbf{X}$ at time t is denoted by $\mathbf{X}(t)$ or $\mathbf{X}_t$.

Some of the variables, such as the safety loading λ, may be stochastic in some applications but deterministic in others. Then ordinary typeface is generally used, without indicating that stochasticity may sometimes occur; i.e., λ is used for $\boldsymbol{\lambda}$.

(b) Monetary variables and rates Variables directly representing monetary qualities like claims, $\mathbf{X}$, premiums, P, or risk reserves U are denoted by capital letters, they are of dimension one (or more) in terms of the monetary unit, e.g. £, $, etc.

If a dimensional monetary variable is transformed into a non-dimensional 'relative' variable, then the corresponding small letter is used, e.g. $u = U/P$ or $\mathbf{x} = (\mathbf{X} - E(\mathbf{X}))/\sigma_{\mathbf{X}}$.

(c) The (cumulative) distribution functions $(= \text{d.f.})$ are denoted by capital letters and densities by small letters. For example,

$$F(X) = \text{prob}\{\mathbf{X} \leqslant X\} \text{ and } f(X) = F'(X),$$

define the distribution function F and the density f (if it exists) of a random variable $\mathbf{X}$.

(d) Stieltjes integrals A number of different distribution (or other) functions F will be employed. Some of them are assumed *continuous*, having a continuous derivative $f = F'$ (possibly with a finite number of exception points). Some others are *discrete*, i.e. the variable X under consideration may take only values $X_1, X_2, \ldots$ by given probabilities $p_1, p_2, \ldots$. Also functions of *mixed* type are needed, being continuous except at a set of discrete points $X_1, X_2, \ldots$ (Fig. 1.5.1). These steps may for example be caused by reinsurance limits.

In the subsequent development, integrals of the type

$$\int_a^b g(X)\,dF(X), \tag{1.5.1}$$

are often needed, where g is some auxiliary function. For the types of distribution functions mentioned, this becomes

$$\int_a^b g(X)f(X)\,dX \qquad \text{(continuous case)}$$

$$\sum_i g(X_i)p_i \qquad \text{(discrete case)} \tag{1.5.2}$$

$$\int_a^b g(X)f(X)\,dX + \sum_i g(X_i)p_i, \qquad \text{(mixed case)}$$

where the sums are to be taken for $a \leqslant X_i \leqslant b$. It is convenient to make a convention that (1.5.1) will represent all the types (1.5.2). Readers who are familiar with the concept of *Stieltjes integrals* will realize that the notation of this integration theory is being used and they can regard the integral (1.5.1) as a Stieltjes integral. Readers

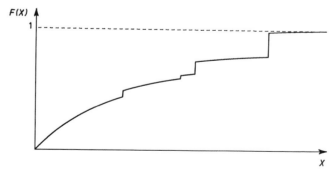

Figure 1.5.1   *A mixed type d.f.*

who are not familiar with this topic can regard it as an abbreviation and replace any such integral by the last form in (1.5.2), since for our purposes the mixed case, as defined above, is general enough.

This extended integral has the same general features as the conventional integral.

(e) **Unit step function** It is often convenient to use the unit step function $\varepsilon(x)$ defined as follows

$$\varepsilon(x) = \begin{cases} 0 & \text{for } x < 0 \\ 1 & \text{for } x \geqslant 0. \end{cases} \tag{1.5.3}$$

It can be interpreted as the d.f. of a 'degenerated' variable, where the whole probability mass is concentrated at the origin.

An example of the application of the step function in integration is as follows (see the previous item)

$$\int_{-\infty}^{+\infty} F(x) \, d\varepsilon(x - x_0) = F(x_0), \tag{1.5.4}$$

i.e. the step function picks up a selected value of the integrand.

(f) **Rates and factors** The time-dependent change of numerous quantities is required in a number of circumstances, for example reserves and assets are increased by interest, volume variables by inflation and real growth of the portfolio and risk exposure. The (mostly annual) growth *rates* will be denoted by i and distinguished by a subscript; for example, i_i, i_g, i_x, and i_p are the rates of interest, real growth of the volume variables, claims inflations (x for **X**, the notation of claim amount), and premiums, respectively. The corresponding (accumulation) *factors* will be denoted by r with the same subscripts as for the rates, e.g. $r_x = 1 + i_x$. If the change is caused by two or more factors, then the subscripts are composed of the corresponding symbols, e.g. r_{gp} is the growth factor representing the joint effect of real growth and premium inflation (this and other component combinations will be defined in the appropriate parts of the text).

To avoid inconvenient notation, the subscripts of the factors and rates are always printed by lower-case letters and without indicating whether the quantity concerned is stochastic or not, e.g. i_x for claims ($= $ **X**) inflation.

The factors and the rates may be time dependent.

(g) Characteristics of distributions The jth moment about zero of a random variable $\mathbf{X}$, defined as the expected value of the power of $\mathbf{X}$, will be denoted by α_j or alternatively by a_j

$$\alpha_j = \alpha_j(\mathbf{X}) = E(\mathbf{X}^j) = \int_{-\infty}^{+\infty} X^j \, dF(X). \qquad (1.5.5a)$$

Most random variables concerned in the sequel are non-negative, in which case the integration in (1.5.5a) can be taken from 0 to $+\infty$. The central moments μ_j of $\mathbf{X}$

$$\mu_j = \mu_j(\mathbf{X}) = E\{(\mathbf{X} - E(\mathbf{X}))^j\} = \int_{-\infty}^{+\infty} (X - E(\mathbf{X}))^j \, dF(X), \quad (1.5.5b)$$

are obtained for $j = 2, 3$ and 4 from the moments about zero as follows

$$
\begin{aligned}
\mu_2 &= \alpha_2 - \alpha_1^2 \\
\mu_3 &= \alpha_3 - 3\alpha_1\alpha_2 + 2\alpha_1^3 \\
\mu_4 &= \alpha_4 - 4\alpha_1\alpha_3 + 6\alpha_1^2\alpha_2 - 3\alpha_1^4.
\end{aligned}
\qquad (1.5.6)
$$

Recall that, for instance, in the case of discrete $\mathbf{X}$, (1.5.5a) becomes simply (see item 1.5(d))

$$\alpha_j = \sum_k X_k^j p_k \qquad \text{where } p_k = \text{prob}\{\mathbf{X} = X_k\}. \qquad (1.5.7)$$

The most important characteristics, the *mean* $E(\mathbf{X})$, *variance* $\sigma^2 = \sigma_{\mathbf{X}}^2 = \mu_2$, *skewness* $\gamma = \gamma_{\mathbf{X}} = \mu_3/\sigma^3$, and *kurtosis* $\gamma_2 = \gamma_2(\mathbf{X}) = \mu_4/\sigma^4 - 3$, can be expressed using the above moments. It should be noted that all the characteristics of $\mathbf{X}$ depend only on the d.f. F of $\mathbf{X}$. If necessary $\mathbf{X}$ will be given in connection with the characteristic either as a 'normal' argument, for example as $\mu_2(\mathbf{X})$ or $\sigma_{\mathbf{X}}$, as a subscript. The latter practice (even though inconsistent with the former) is used for common symbols like σ and γ which have no subscript related to the concept itself. Furthermore the skewness, which is one of the parameters frequently used in the following, is denoted by γ instead of the conventional notation γ_1.

(h) The convolution Let F and G be distribution functions. Their convolution $F * G$,

$$F * G(X) = \int_{-\infty}^{+\infty} F(X - Y) \, dG(Y), \qquad (1.5.8)$$

is also a distribution function. It is well known that if X and Y are *independent* random variables with distribution functions F and G, then the d.f. of their sum $X + Y$ is $F * G$. Hence, $F * G = G * F$ and the convolution of several distribution functions does not depend on the order in which the convolutions are taken.

If, for example, G is continuous with $g = G'$, then (1.5.8) can be written as

$$F * G(X) = \int_{-\infty}^{+\infty} F(X - Y)g(Y)\,\mathrm{d}Y, \qquad (1.5.9)$$

which is a continuous function of X. Thus the sum of two independent random variables has continuous d.f. if at least one of the variables has continuous d.f.

(i) A list of symbols and notation has been given after the Preface for the convenience of readers.

1.6 The moment generating function, the characteristic function, and the Laplace transform

(a) Three auxiliary functions In this section three well-known operational functions of probability calculus are introduced. They transform a given d.f. into a form from which it is, for example, easy to see the characteristics of the distribution. These transforms are of particular interest because they facilitate the handling of convolutions and some other operations.

The moment generating function, introduced in item (b), is somewhat simpler than the characteristic function (item (c)) but has the disadvantage of being not always defined, whereas the characteristic function, which is defined as a complex integral, always exists. The characteristic function also has an important continuity property.

In order to avoid the use of complex integrals, only the moment generating functions will be used in this book, except in Appendix B where the characteristic function is needed.

(b) The moment generating function (m.g.f.) of a random variable X (or of its d.f. F) is

$$M(s) = E(\mathrm{e}^{sX}) = \int_{-\infty}^{+\infty} \mathrm{e}^{sX}\,\mathrm{d}F(X). \qquad (1.6.1)$$

In the case of continuous d.f., (1.6.1) becomes

$$M(s) = \int_{-\infty}^{+\infty} e^{sX} f(X)\, dX, \tag{1.6.2}$$

and for a discrete d.f.

$$M(s) = \sum_k e^{sX_k} p_k, \tag{1.6.3}$$

where s is an auxiliary real variable; for notation see item 1.5(d).

It will be assumed that for the distributions dealt with in this section $M(s)$ exists at least in some neighbourhood of the origin, i.e. for $|s| < s_0$ for some positive s_0. This condition must be verified for each actual application, of course.

The moment generating function has the following important properties which are derived in standard textbooks and are given here without proof.

(i) The m.g.f. can be expressed by the *moment expansion*

$$M(s) = \sum_{h=0}^{\infty} \alpha_h s^h / h!, \tag{1.6.4}$$

where α_h are the moments (1.5.5a) about zero. If $M(s)$ is known, they can be obtained in terms of derivatives

$$\alpha_h = M^{(h)}(0). \tag{1.6.5}$$

(ii) The d.f. is *uniquely determined* by its m.g.f. (if the m.g.f. exists), i.e. if two distributions have the same m.g.f. they are identical.

(iii) *The linear transformation* $\mathbf{y} = a\mathbf{x} + b$ transforms the m.g.f. into the form

$$M_y(s) = e^{bs} M_x(as). \tag{1.6.6}$$

(iv) If $\mathbf{x}_1$ and $\mathbf{x}_2$ are two independent stochastic variables, then the m.g.f. of sum $\mathbf{x}_1 + \mathbf{x}_2$ is obtained by multiplication

$$M(s) = M_1(s) M_2(s). \tag{1.6.7}$$

In terms of distribution functions this means that the m.g.f. transforms convolutions of distributions into products of m.g.f.s.

(c) The characteristic function of **X** is obtained by replacing the variable s by an imaginary variable iu in the m.g.f., where $i = \sqrt{-1}$

$$\varphi(u) = E(e^{iu\mathbf{X}}) = \int_{-\infty}^{+\infty} e^{iuX} \, dF(X). \tag{1.6.8}$$

The characteristic function φ has properties similar to (i)–(iv) of the m.g.f. Owing to the fact that $|e^{iuX}| = 1$, the convergence in (1.6.8) does not cause problems. In addition, it has a special benefit in that the inverse transformation $\varphi \to F$ can be expressed explicitly in form of a Fourier integral, which is sometimes convenient for the calculation of F or for derivation of some of its properties.

One more important property of the characteristic function is the continuity property: if a sequence of d.f.s converges to a d.f., then the corresponding characteristic functions converge to the characteristic function of the limit function. Conversely, if a sequence of characteristic functions converges to a limit function which is continuous at the origin, then the limit function is the characteristic function of the limit d.f. of the d.f.s corresponding to the sequence of characteristic functions.

(d) The Laplace transform belongs to the same family of auxiliary functions. The Laplace transform of a *non-negative* random variable **X** is

$$L(s) = \int_0^\infty e^{-sX} \, dF(X), \tag{1.6.9}$$

where s now assumes complex values. The Laplace transform also has basic properties similar to properties (i)–(iv) of the m.g.f. Furthermore, its inverse can be given in the form of a complex integral. Extensive tables are available in a number of standard mathematical texts.

The integral (1.6.9) converges when the real part of s exceeds some number called the abscissa of convergence. If the real part of s is zero, the characteristic function (1.6.8) is obtained as a special case of the Laplace transform of non-negative random variables.

CHAPTER 2

Claim number process

2.1 Introduction

(a) Definition of the problem As already mentioned, the simplest problem is considered first. This is to find the probability function of the number of claims arising in a risk collective, i.e. a function $p(k; t)$ which gives the probability that the number of claims $\mathbf{k}_t$ in time t is equal to k. In terms of conventional symbols

$$p(k; t) = \text{prob}\{\mathbf{k}_t = k\}. \qquad (2.1.1)$$

In the following analysis the collective concerned can be the whole portfolio of an insurer or some special part thereof.

(b) The individual and collective approaches The problem can be solved in a number of different ways. One method is to start by regarding the portfolio in question as made up of a number of individual policies, each of which has a certain probability of claim (e.g. in life insurance it is assumed that the probability that a life aged x dies within a year is q_x). Then the total number of claims is the sum of the contributions from the individual policies and the probabilities (2.1.1) can be derived by means of the addition theorem of probability calculus from the primary probabilities. Basically the probabilities are binomial in character but to carry out this 'addition' in a rigorous way leads to rather intricate calculations and involves some restrictive assumptions.

An alternative approach, which has led to fruitful development, is to follow the collective method adopted by Lundberg. In this method the individual policy structure is disregarded and instead the portfolio is considered as a whole, i.e. a 'process' is considered in which only times and the number of events (claims) are recorded and in which no attention is paid to the particular policies from which the claims have arisen. By starting with some general conditions which the random process has to obey, it can be deduced that the process takes the well-known Poisson form.

The Poisson process is often referred to in probability calculus as the theory of rare phenomena and is well known, for example, in the theory of disintegration of radioactive atoms. However, as it is necessary in practical problems to know in which cases the Poisson function is applicable and in which cases it is not, some discussion of the assumptions underlying this probability distribution is essential. More general number processes are considered in Sections 2.7–2.10.

2.2   The Poisson process

It is now assumed that the claim number process satisfies the following three conditions

(i) Events occurring in two disjointed time intervals are independent (*independence of increments*).

(ii) The number of events in a time interval (t_1, t_2) is dependent only on the length of the interval $t = t_2 - t_1$ and not on the initial value t_1 (*stationariness of increments*).

(iii) The probability that more than one event will occur at the same time and the probability that an infinite number of events will occur in some finite time interval are both zero (*exclusion of multiple events*).

In Appendix A it is shown that with these conditions the probability function $p(k; t)$ is represented by the well-known Poisson law

$$p(k; t) = p_k(\rho t) = e^{-\rho t}\frac{(\rho t)^k}{k!},$$

(2.2.1)

for every $t > 0$, where $\rho \geq 0$ is a parameter indicating, as will be seen later, the average number of claims in a time unit. The process $\mathbf{k}$ is called a *Poisson process*. The occurrence of an event of claim depends on both the number of cases (risk units) exposed to risk and also the risk intensity, i.e. the chance that a particular case gives rise to a claim. The Poisson process arises as a product of these components.

2.3 Discussion of conditions

(a) Independence of increments Condition (i) means, in fact, that an event (e.g. a fire) cannot give rise to any other events (exclusion of 'chain reactions'). In practice, however, a fire can often spread from one risk to another in contradiction to this condition.

Condition (i) can, however, often be met by defining a risk unit, as is customary in reinsurance practice, as a combination of all those risks lying near to each other, between which contamination is possible (e.g. all property in a building irrespective of whether it is formally insured by one policy or by several or being under single or multiple ownership). In the same way a ship and its cargo are considered as one risk unit, and so on. However, it is not always possible to build up risk units in such a way that outside contamination would not occur. Such is the case with contagious diseases in sickness insurance or epidemics in life insurance. The Poisson function is not then applicable, at least not without suitable modifications. These kinds of cases will be treated in Section 2.7 where condition (i) is replaced by a more general one.

(b) Stationariness of increments This condition means that the collective flow of the events is stationary, i.e. neither steadily increasing or decreasing nor oscillating more than would be caused by normal random fluctuation. In other words, the intensity of the claims is constant. This is the usual case in insurance, particularly during short periods, when the numbers of policies or other circumstances are not subject to marked changes. This condition implies that the portfolio is so large that the exit of individual policies by reason of claims or from other causes and the entry of new cases cannot affect the collective flow of the events to any significant degree.

Quite often, however, there are situations where the stationarity does not strictly apply; for example, there may be seasonal variations in claim intensities. Then the time interval concerned can be divided into subintervals in such a way that the corresponding sub-processes have (at least approximately) constant intensities and are therefore Poisson processes. It will be shown in Section 2.6 that the sum of independent Poisson variables is again a Poisson variable. Hence, the total number of claims during the whole interval is Poisson distributed. So, if only this total number and its behaviour are of interest, as is most often the case, then the seasonal variations can be disregarded, providing that the changes in the claim intensities are deterministic, i.e. they recur in such a way that their prediction is possible through experience.

The above is also applicable to cases where the risk intensities are changing, according to some trend, in a way which is deterministically predictable. The total number of claims still remains Poisson distributed but the parameter ρt, which will be later denoted by n, is to be calculated as a sum of the parameters related to the subintervals as will be shown in Section 2.6. Another method often used in risk theory literature to derive the same result is to introduce the concept of 'operational time'. This approach is presented in Appendix A.

However, there are often other circumstances arising in practice where conditions (i) and (ii) cannot be met. For example, fire insurance can be greatly affected by weather conditions and a long, dry, sunny period can give rise to numerous abnormal fires; in some countries, hurricanes or other natural catastrophes can cause an enormous increase in claims. It is also well known that economic conditions have considerable influence in many classes of non-life insurance. Times of economic booms or recessions give rise to a considerable increase or decrease in the number of traffic or work accidents, as well as influencing credit insurance business. Such circumstances are so general that the application of the elementary Poisson function is greatly limited, and so there is a need for a development of the theory omitting the conditions concerning independence and stationarity. This will be done in Section 2.7. In spite of these limitations, the Poisson function often gives at least a good first approximation, particularly for short time intervals. It is also the basis of more generalized distributions. Furthermore, the risk of changes and of variations disturbing stationarity can often be dealt with by simply adding a precautionary amount to the parameter ρ.

(c) Exclusion of multiple events At a first glance it would appear that condition (iii) does not always hold. For example, in motor insurance, two vehicles may collide, giving rise to a double event. Similar incidents can occur in marine insurance and in some other branches. This difficulty can, however, be circumvented by a suitable choice of definition, for example by regarding the case of collisions between two cars as a single claim. This means, however, that the sum of the claims of both parties is used when building up the statistics of the distribution of the size of one claim, which is regarded separately as another random variable, considered in Chapter 3 and later. The exclusion of an infinite number of claims is no restriction from the point of view of applications.

2.4 Some basic formulae

(a) Distribution function Since the state $\mathbf{k}_t$ at time t of a Poisson process obeys the Poisson distribution law with the parameter $\rho t = n$, it is necessary to be familiar with a number of basic characteristics of the Poisson distribution function.

Let us suppose that $\mathbf{k}$ is a Poisson-distributed random variable with Poisson parameter n. Then the d.f. F of $\mathbf{k}$ is

$$F(k) = F(k; n) = \text{prob}\{\mathbf{k} \leqslant k\} = \sum_{i=0}^{[k]} p_i(n), \qquad (2.4.1)$$

where

$$p_i(n) = \text{prob}\{\mathbf{k} = i\} = e^{-n}n^i/i! \qquad (2.4.2)$$

To facilitate the technical handling of the formulae, non-integer values for k will also be allowed. By convention, $[k]$ means the rounded-down integer value of k defined by $[k] \leqslant k < [k] + 1$.

In the following, p_k is often used for $p_k(n)$ and $F(k)$ for $F(k; n)$.

(b) Characteristics Making use of the standard formulae given in item 1.5(g), the moments of the Poisson distribution can be obtained either by direct summation or by means of the m.g.f. (see exercises 2.4.1 and 2.6.1). The lowest ones are

$$\begin{aligned}
\alpha_1 &= n & (\mu_1 &= 0) \\
\alpha_2 &= n + n^2 & \mu_2 &= n \\
\alpha_3 &= n + 3n^2 + n^3 & \mu_3 &= n \\
\alpha_4 &= n + 7n^2 + 6n^3 + n^4 & \mu_4 &= n + 3n^2
\end{aligned} \qquad (2.4.3)$$

from which the basic characteristics of $\mathbf{k}$ are immediately derived (see item 1.5(g))

$$\begin{aligned}
\text{mean} \qquad & E(\mathbf{k}) = \alpha_1 = n \\
\text{variance} \qquad & \sigma^2 = \mu_2 = n \\
\text{skewness} \qquad & \gamma = \mu_3/\sigma^3 = 1/\sqrt{n} \\
\text{kurtosis} \qquad & \gamma_2 = \mu_4/\sigma^4 - 3 = 1/n.
\end{aligned} \qquad (2.4.4)$$

(c) Inter-occurrence time For some applications it is useful to note that the interval between consecutive events (claims) of the Poisson process, the so-called inter-occurrence time, is exponentially distributed, i.e. the length t_k of the time period between $(k-1)$th and kth events satisfies

$$\text{prob}\{t_k \leqslant t\} = 1 - e^{-\rho t}, \qquad (2.4.5)$$

where ρ is the expected number of claims in the time unit applied in the relevant application. (For proof see Bühlmann, 1970, for example.)

A rather more general basis for the development of risk theory is to assume some d.f. for the inter-occurrence time instead of using p_k as the basic concept. This is essentially the basis of the so-called *renewal processes* in the theory of stochastic processes. The application to risk theory was first suggested by Sparre-Andersen (1957) and the resulting processes when applied in risk theory are commonly called *Sparre-Andersen processes* (see also Thorin, 1971).

Exercise 2.4.1 Derive the expressions for α_1 and α_2 by direct summation from (2.4.1).

2.5 Numerical values of Poisson probabilities

(a) Exact values If n is not large the value of the probabilities p_k and F can be calculated directly from (2.4.1). There are also fairly extensive tables of numerical values, e.g. General Electric (1962), and values can also be derived from tables of the chi-square distribution.

Programmable calculators can be used to determine p_k and its cumulative values F, using

$$p_0 = e^{-n}, \qquad (2.5.1)$$

as a starting value and applying the recurrence formula

$$p_{k+1}(n) = p_k(n)n/(k+1). \qquad (2.5.2)$$

Owing to the wide range of values of n some special technique may be necessary to avoid problems from overflow (e.g. e^{-n} escapes from the range of numbers acceptable to the computer). It may help either to use logarithms or to start with a smaller auxiliary n', putting $p_0 = e^{-n'}$ and afterwards correcting the p_k and $F(k)$ by multiplying them by $e^{n'-n}$. Another computational difficulty may arise from the accumulation of rounding-off errors when the probability $1 - F(k)$ that **k** is greater than k is calculated for large k. Then a sum of terms of considerable magnitude is needed and the rounding-off error of the largest terms is too close to the order of magnitude of the target value $1 - F(k)$. This can easily be controlled by continuing the calculation up to the k-values where p_k vanishes from the range of the desired accuracy. If the calculation is exact, $F(k)$ should equal 1 (because $F(\infty) = 1$). The possible deviation of the computed value from 1 gives the rounding-off correlation for the upper tail of $F(k)$.

(b) The shape of the Poisson distribution for three small values of n is depicted in Fig. 2.5.1.

(c) Normal approximation If n is large, use may be made of the *central limit theorem* of probability theory, according to which F tends asymptotically to the normal distribution function when $n \rightarrow \infty$, i.e.

$$F(k) \approx N((k - n)/\sqrt{n}), \qquad (2.5.3)$$

where N denotes a normal distribution function with zero mean and unit standard deviation. The central limit theorem is applicable because of the additivity of Poisson variables, i.e. the Poisson

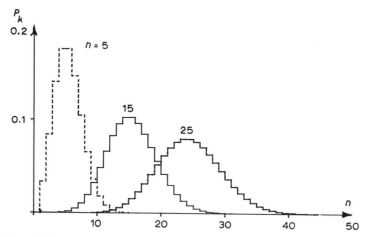

Figure 2.5.1   *Poisson probabilities* p_k. (*To help visual shaping of the distributions the discrete probability values are linked as step curves.*)

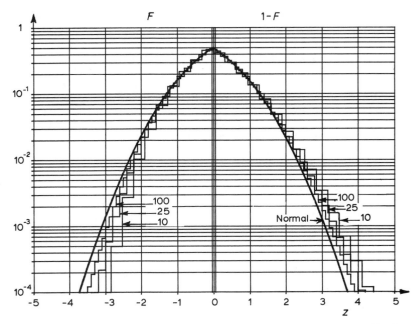

Figure 2.5.2   *F or* $1 - F$ *for the normalized Poisson distribution* (step lines) *of some values of n and for the normal approximation* (2.5.3) (logarithmic scale).

variable with parameter n can be expressed, for example, as a sum of n independent Poisson-distributed variables with the same parameter value one (see Section 2.6) (providing that n is an integer).

Figure 2.5.2 demonstrates the accuracy of this approximation for some values of n. It can be seen that the Poisson d.f. tends closer and closer towards the normal d.f. as n increases.

(d) Wilson–Hilferty approximation   A much closer approximation is provided by the following formula

$$F(k) \approx N(\kappa - 1/\kappa - C\kappa^{1/3}), \qquad (2.5.4)$$

where

$$\kappa = 3\sqrt{(1 + k)} \quad \text{and} \quad C = (9n)^{1/3},$$

(see Johnson and Kotz, 1969; Section 4.7).

This is again an asymptotic approximation but will be found to give satisfactory values for n as small as 10, as is shown in Table 2.5.1.

Table 2.5.1 *Comparison of the Wilson–Hilferty approximated values with exact Poisson values. For $k \leqslant n$ values of F are given and for $k > n$, values of $1 - F$.*

$n =$	10			25			50	
k	*Exact*	*Approx.*	k	*Exact*	*Approx.*	k	*Exact*	*Approx.*
1	0.00050	0.00058	10	0.00059	0.00061	29	0.00092	0.00093
4	0.02925	0.02920	15	0.02229	0.02232	36	0.02376	0.02377
7	0.22022	0.21974	20	0.18549	0.18529	43	0.17980	0.17969
10	0.58304	0.58341	25	0.55292	0.55303	50	0.53752	0.53756
13	0.13554	0.13527	30	0.13669	0.13656	57	0.14486	0.14479
16	0.02704	0.02715	35	0.02246	0.02250	64	0.02360	0.02363
19	0.00345	0.00354	40	0.00204	0.00206	71	0.00201	0.00203

(e) Gamma formula The d.f. of the Poisson variable can also be expressed in terms of the incomplete gamma function as will be shown in Exercise 2.9.7.

Exercise 2.5.1 A friendly society has 1000 members. In the event of death a fixed sum $S = £1000$ is paid. The mean value of the rate of mortality is 0.01, the premium $P_\lambda = (1 + \lambda)S\,E(\mathbf{k})$, where $\lambda = 0.1$ is a safety loading and $\mathbf{k}$ is the number of deaths. The actuarial status of the society is examined every year. How large a security reserve U_0 should the society have to be sure, at a 99% probability level, that the balance does not show any deficit?

Make use first of (a) the exact Poisson formulae, then (b) the normal, and (c) the Wilson–Hilferty approximations. Hint: Poisson values can be computed starting from values given in Table 2.5.1.

Exercise 2.5.2 How many members should the society of exercise 2.5.1 have for no security reserve to be necessary under the conditions mentioned? Use the normal approximation.

Exercise 2.5.3 A friendly society grants funeral expense benefits on the death of a member, the benefit being fixed at £100. The expected number of claims $n = 1$. The society has a stop loss reinsurance in accordance with which, if the number of deaths exceeds two, the reinsurer pays the third and subsequent benefits. What is the risk premium (= expected amount of claims) for the reinsurance?

2.6 The additivity of Poisson variables

(a) The m.g.f. of the Poisson d.f. can be calculated by substituting the Poisson probabilities $p_k(n)$ in (1.6.3)

$$M(s) = \sum_{h=0}^{\infty} e^{sh} e^{-n} n^h / h!$$

$$= e^{-n} \sum_{h=0}^{\infty} (ne^s)^h / h! \qquad (2.6.1)$$

$$= e^{-n} e^{ne^s} = e^{n(e^s - 1)}.$$

(b) Additivity of Poisson variables It follows from (2.6.1) that the m.g.f. for the sum of two independent Poisson variables having parameters n_1 and n_2 is

$$M(s) = e^{n_1(e^s - 1)} e^{n_2(e^s - 1)} = e^{(n_1 + n_2)(e^s - 1)}. \qquad (2.6.2)$$

This is again of the form of (2.6.1); hence according to property (ii) of item 1.6(b) the sum variable is also Poisson distributed with the parameter

$$n = n_1 + n_2, \qquad (2.6.3)$$

i.e. the Poisson distribution is *additive*: the sum of mutually independent Poisson variables is again a Poisson variable having the parameter n as the sum of the original parameters.

The additivity is a very important feature. It makes it possible to divide the risk portfolio into sections, indexed $j = 1, 2, \ldots$, according to the classes and sub classes of the insurance concerned, for example. It is often advisable to evaluate the Poisson parameters n_j, the expected number of claims, separately for each section and then to determine the parameter for the whole collective by summation

$$n = \sum n_j. \qquad (2.6.4)$$

It is also possible to divide the time-span into adjacent intervals, e.g. in months, evaluate n_t for each interval, and then to sum the n.

This makes it possible to apply the Poisson law to cases where the risk exposure, measured by n_t, may vary in some defined way, such as by following a cycle or a trend. This aspect has already been discussed in item 2.3(b).

(c) As an example consider a life insurance portfolio. The insured persons have the probability of death during one year q_j $(j = 1, 2, \ldots, J)$. Then the expected number of deaths in the whole collective, the Poisson parameter, is

$$n = \sum q_j. \tag{2.6.5}$$

This equation is, in fact, a link between the individual risk theory, which primarily focused attention on the individual risk units, and the collective risk theory, which takes the collective itself as the primary issue. A more detailed discussion of the special features of life insurance will be pursued in Chapter 8.

**(d) The additivity of the Poisson processes The additivity considered in item (b) concerned the Poisson *variables*, i.e. in the present context the number of claims during a *fixed* period $(0, t]$. If the time t is allowed to vary and the growth of the claim number $\mathbf{k}_t$ is followed, a realization of the claim number *process* is obtained. The distinction between these concepts was emphasized in item 1.1(c). It can be proved on the basis of conditions (i)–(iii) of Section 2.2 that additivity also holds for the sums of independent Poisson processes related to the same time interval (Exercise 2.6.3).

Exercise 2.6.1 Calculate the moments α_j $(j = 1, 2, 3, 4)$ of the Poisson d.f. by means of the m.g.f.

**Exercise 2.6.2 Let $\mathbf{W}_k$ denote the waiting time of the kth event of a Poisson process $\mathbf{k}$, i.e. the time of kth event. Then $\mathbf{W}_k > t$ implies that less than k events occurred during the time interval $(0, t]$. Prove that

$$\mathrm{prob}\{\mathbf{W}_k \leqslant t\} = \frac{\rho^k}{(k-1)!} \int_0^t z^{k-1}\, e^{-\rho z}\, dz \qquad (t > 0).$$

**Exercise 2.6.3 Prove that the sum of two independent Poisson *processes* related to the same time interval is again a Poisson process i.e. also that the sum process satisfies the conditions (i)–(iii) of Section 2.2.

2.7 Time-dependent variation of risk exposure

(a) Experience of the applicability of the Possion law As mentioned in Section 2.3, the simple Poisson law frequently fails to provide a satisfactory representation of the actual claim number distribution. This feature is demonstrated by Figs 2.7.1 and 2.7.2, which are typical curves taken from a portfolio of motor cycle insurances and illustrate the various types of fluctuation.

The observed data of Fig. 2.7.1 are the monthly claim frequencies of motor cyclists over the years 1960 to 1962, during which period the exposures increased from about 19 000 to about 27 000 policies. The smoothed curve is derived by a system of moving weighted averages, the weights being (1, 2, 3, 2, 1), i.e. a double summation in 3s. The maxima occur in the autumn months and the minima in late winter, a reflection of the fact that when conditions are unpleasant the motor cyclist reduces his exposure. The trend line suggests a declining tendency over the three years.

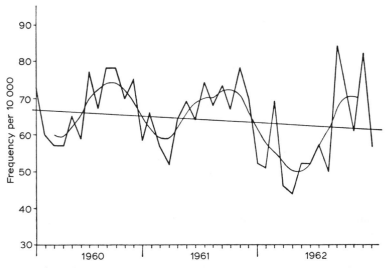

Figure 2.7.1   *Motor cycles. Four-weekly claim frequency* 1960–62.

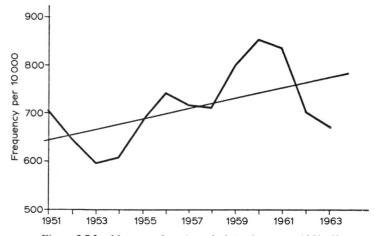

Figure 2.7.2   *Motor cycles. Annual claim frequency 1951–63.*

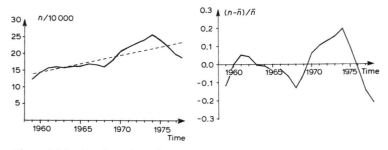

Figure 2.7.3   *Number of accidents in workers' compensation insurance in the period 1958–79 (joint data of Finnish insurance companies). The right-hand graph exhibits the relative deviations from the trend-adjusted midline $\bar{n}$ of the left-hand figure.*

Figure 2.7.2 gives the annual claim frequency for the period 1951 to 1963, the exposure increasing from about 7000 to 27 000 over the period, and shows a long-term periodic effect, with a probable trend upwards over the period. This longer period shows that the declining tendency in Fig. 2.7.1 was a downward phase of one of the longer-term variations and shows the need to look at fairly long series of values.

The workers' compensation time series depicted in Fig. 2.7.3 shows a similar behaviour. Further analysis shows that the cycles are strongly correlated with general economic booms and recessions. During a boom, industry is at full capacity and overtime working is frequent. As would be expected, the number of accidents increases accordingly. On the other hand, during a recession working hours are reduced, which is immediately reflected in the claim frequencies.

Results like these show that fluctuations observed in the actual flow of claims number processes may be much greater than would be expected if the data conformed strictly to the Poisson law. This observation, which is of the utmost importance for the applicability of risk theory, has been confirmed by research in various countries, e.g. McGuinness (1970), Helten (1977), Becker (1981), Bohman (1979), and James (1981). This phenomenon was widely considered in the Finnish solvency report (Pentikäinen, 1982).

(b) Four categories of fluctuation To elaborate the theoretical model it is necessary to analyse the different types of fluctuation in the number of claims.

(i) *Trends* These emerge as a slow moving change of the claim probabilities which must be properly defined as the ratio of the number of claims in a specified time interval to an appropriate index of the number of risks exposed to the chance of a claim. Examples are the improvement in mortality rates or the changes in frequency of fire due to changes in methods of building construction or changes in materials used. Trends in the overall experience from an insurance portfolio can also arise from changes in its constitution, for example, the proportion of newer type houses may increase in relationship to older houses so that the overall frequency will reflect any differences between the two groups. Of course, besides changes in risk intensities, the growth of the number of risks contained in the portfolio is another reason for an increase (or decrease) of the expected number of claims parameter n. This arises from the normal changes in the number of policies as well as from the internal growth of risk units under old policies, e.g. in the number of employees, vehicles, plants and facilities.

(ii) *Long-period cycles* An example of this type of variation is provided by the association of accidents with general economic conditions. The results of consecutive years are not mutually independent and a cycle period can thus have a length of several years.

(iii) *Short-period oscillations* These can be caused for example by meteorological changes or by epidemic diseases. Thus a long dry summer is almost certain to give rise to a marked increase in the frequency of fires, and the incidence of severe wind storms in certain parts of the world has a pronounced effect on the results of non-life business. Epidemic diseases, in addition to affecting the results of sickness insurance, may also be of significance in life insurance, giving rise to fluctuation in the mortality experience.

(iv) *Pure random fluctuations* like those considered in previous sections of this chapter are, of course, always present.

In addition to the four main types mentioned there may be seasonal fluctuations of which the variation in claims frequencies between summer and winter months in motor insurance may be instanced. These can, however, generally be disregarded when consideration is being given to results based on calender years, as mentioned in Section 2.3.

(c) Introduction of a structure variable In this chapter, the model is extended to incorporate short-period oscillations. These are supposed to be so short that oscillations of consecutive years can be regarded as independent.

A natural way of developing such a model is to assume that n, the expected number of claims, is itself a random number, $\mathbf{n} = n\mathbf{q}$. Here $\mathbf{q}$ (≥ 0) is an auxiliary random variable which indicates the relative deviation of $\mathbf{n}$ from its average value n whereby $\mathbf{q}$ is normed to have mean value 1. Hence this variable represents disturbances which cause the short-term oscillations beyond the range that can be explained by means of the Poisson d.f. In the following chapters, the longer term fluctuations or dependences are incorporated in other variables; this is unlike the treatment often encountered in the published literature. These variations are often assumed to be deterministic; the increments of the risk process during consecutive years will then be mutually independent. It can be interpreted that $\mathbf{q}$ has a constant value during each year but varies randomly from year to year, the values related to consecutive years being mutually independent and equally distributed. Often the behaviour of the process within the year needs no attention, and thus $\mathbf{q}$ can be considered to be a stochastic process whose state remains unchanged within each year, as illustrated in Fig. 2.7.4. Equally, one can consider that each year t has its own variable $\mathbf{q}_t$. To keep the notation simple

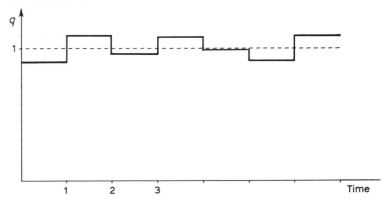

Figure 2.7.4 *A process where the risk parameter q related to consecutive time periods varies at random.*

the subscript t is mostly omitted. Since the states of $\mathbf{q}$ related to different years are equally distributed this does not usually lead to any misunderstandings.

Now let

$$H(q) = \text{prob}\{\mathbf{q} \leqslant q\}, \qquad (2.7.1)$$

be the d.f. of $\mathbf{q}$. Then the conditional probability of k claims in a year by condition $\mathbf{q} = q$ is the Poisson probability $p_k(nq)$. The unconditional probability $\bar{p}_k(n) = \text{prob}\{\mathbf{k} = k\}$ is obtained by means of the addition and multiplication rules of probabilities as 'a weighted average' (or more exactly as the expected value of $p_k(n\mathbf{q})$) as follows

$$\bar{p}_k(n) = \int_0^\infty p_k(nq)\,\mathrm{d}H(q) = \int_0^\infty e^{-nq}\frac{(nq)^k}{k!}\,\mathrm{d}H(q). \qquad (2.7.2)$$

For discrete H (e.g. when it is approximated in a tabular form) this reduces using the elementary formula of conditional probabilities

$$\text{prob}\{\mathbf{k} = k\} = \sum_i p_k(nq_i)\,\text{prob}\{\mathbf{q} = q_i\}. \qquad (2.7.3)$$

Now the d.f. of $\mathbf{k}$ can be derived by the summation of (2.7.2)

$$\begin{aligned}
\bar{F}(k) &= \sum_{i=0}^{[k]} \bar{p}_i(n) = \sum_{i=0}^{[k]} \int_0^\infty p_i(nq)\,\mathrm{d}H(q) \\
&= \int_0^\infty \left[\sum_{i=0}^{[k]} p_i(nq)\right]\mathrm{d}H(q) = \int_0^\infty F(k;nq)\,\mathrm{d}H(q), \quad (2.7.4)
\end{aligned}$$

where $F(k; nq)$ denotes the Poisson d.f. with mean value nq of the number of claims. Note that the formula could also have been obtained directly using the same reasoning as applied for (2.7.2), i.e. by considering that $\bar{F}$ is, so to speak, the weighted mean of all possible Poisson functions, the weights for each value of nq being the probability of occurrences of this expected number of claims.

The claim number process **k** just introduced is called a *weighted* or *mixed Poisson process* as distinguished from the 'simple' Poisson process considered in previous sections. Naturally, types of claim number processes other than the Poisson one can be similarly weighted. The variable **q** will be designated the *structure variable* and its d.f. H the *structure distribution*.

In the following the notation $\bar{F}$ is often replaced by F if it is clear in the context that the weighted Poisson d.f. is under consideration.

(d) Illustration The mixed process can be illustrated by means of an urn or lottery model as follows. The level of the expected number of claims is first fixed for a year by drawing a lot. The lottery is arranged so that the probability of getting a value $q < \mathbf{q} \leqslant q + dq$ is $dH(q)$. Then **q** is fixed to be equal to q for the whole year. For the next year a new value is drawn for **q**, and so on.

(e) Discussion on environment It may be noted that the assumption regarding the random fluctuations of the basic probabilities is true, for example, in cases where all the probabilities of claims of each risk unit are changed simultaneously owing to meteorological conditions, changes in economic conditions, etc. Simultaneity is not, however, necessary and it is equally proper to allow for the sections j of the portfolio to have their own variations and distributions $H_j(q)$. Then the total fluctuation is to be calculated by convolution, as will be shown in Section 3.7. How the physical phenomena behind the probabilities are brought about and what kinds of phenomena exist are, of course, quite immaterial from the point of view of risk theory. It is only necessary to assume the existence of some function H which relates to the number of claims. In fact the urn model is only a simple way to illustrate how (2.7.1) can be obtained. There are, however, other ways to introduce the same formula. An example is the Polya process considered in

Section 2.9, where the process allows for changes of $\mathbf{q}$ to be considered as due to contamination.

2.8 Formulae concerning the mixed Poisson distribution

(a) The basic characteristics It will be assumed in this chapter that the portfolio is considered as a whole, not partitioned in sections, and that the time span to which the number of claims is related is one calendar year. These restrictions will be relaxed in Chapter 6.

The moments about zero of the mixed Poisson distribution $\bar{F}$ are obtained by a straightforward application of (1.5.7) and (2.7.2)

$$
\begin{aligned}
\bar{\alpha}_j &= \sum_{k=0}^{\infty} k^j \bar{p}_k(n) \\
&= \sum_{k=0}^{\infty} k^j \int_0^{\infty} p_k(nq)\,\mathrm{d}H(q) = \int_0^{\infty} \left[\sum_{k=0}^{\infty} k^j p_k(nq) \right] \mathrm{d}H(q) \\
&= \int_0^{\infty} \alpha_j(nq)\,\mathrm{d}H(q).
\end{aligned}
\tag{2.8.1}
$$

Hence these moments are obtained from those of the simple Poisson d.f. by a similar weighting as for $\bar{p}_k$ and $\bar{F}(k)$ in the previous section. Substituting the expressions (2.4.3) where n is to be replaced by nq, it follows that

$$
\bar{\alpha}_1 = \int_0^{\infty} nq\,\mathrm{d}H(q) = n \int_0^{\infty} q\,\mathrm{d}H(q) = n
\tag{2.8.2}
$$

$$
\begin{aligned}
\bar{\alpha}_2 &= \int_0^{\infty} (nq + n^2 q^2)\,\mathrm{d}H(q) = n \int_0^{\infty} q\,\mathrm{d}H(q) + n^2 \int_0^{\infty} q^2\,\mathrm{d}H(q) \\
&= n + n^2 \alpha_2(\mathbf{q}).
\end{aligned}
\tag{2.8.3}
$$

Similarly

$$
\begin{aligned}
\bar{\alpha}_3 &= n + 3n^2 \alpha_2(\mathbf{q}) + n^3 \alpha_3(\mathbf{q}) \\
\bar{\alpha}_4 &= n + 7n^2 \alpha_2(\mathbf{q}) + 6n^3 \alpha_3(\mathbf{q}) + n^4 \alpha_4(\mathbf{q}),
\end{aligned}
\tag{2.8.4}
$$

where $\mathbf{q}$ indicates that these are the moments about zero of the structure d.f. H in question.

In addition to the moments, the standard deviation, skewness and kurtosis of the distributions are often needed and will be given now. First denote

$$\sigma_{\mathbf{q}}^3 = \alpha_2(\mathbf{q}) - 1; \gamma_{\mathbf{q}} = \mu_3(\mathbf{q})/\sigma_{\mathbf{q}}^3; \gamma_2(\mathbf{q}) = \mu_4(\mathbf{q})/\sigma_{\mathbf{q}}^4 - 3. \quad (2.8.5)$$

(See item 1.5(g) for notation.) Then, expressing the central moments by means of the moments about zero (see (1.5.6)) and making use of the formulae (2.4.3) and (2.4.4) the mean, variance, skewness and kurtosis of the mixed Poisson distribution $\bar{F}$ are obtained

$$
\begin{aligned}
\bar{m} &= n \\
\bar{\sigma}^2 &= n + n^2 \sigma_{\mathbf{q}}^2 \\
\bar{\gamma} &= (n + 3n^2 \sigma_{\mathbf{q}}^2 + n^3 \sigma_{\mathbf{q}}^3 \gamma_{\mathbf{q}})/\bar{\sigma}^3 \\
\bar{\gamma}_2 &= [n + 7n^2 \sigma_{\mathbf{q}}^2 + 6n^3 \gamma_{\mathbf{q}} \sigma_{\mathbf{q}}^3 + n^4 \gamma_2(\mathbf{q})\sigma_{\mathbf{q}}^4]/\bar{\sigma}^4.
\end{aligned}
\quad (2.8.6)
$$

As might well have been expected, the mean is identical with the Poisson case, but the standard deviation and skewness are greater, thus increasing the chance of excessive claim numbers.

Because it is convenient to give the basic characteristics of the structure distribution in terms of $\sigma_{\mathbf{q}}$ and $\gamma_{\mathbf{q}}$ (seldom $\gamma_2(\mathbf{q})$), formulae in (2.8.6) include these characteristics instead of moments $\mu_j(\mathbf{q})$ which would make the equations slightly simpler.

(b) The moment generating function can be derived by weighting in the same way as for the moments

$$\bar{M}(S) = \int_0^\infty e^{nq(e^s - 1)} \, dH(q). \quad (2.8.7)$$

(c) For computation of the mixed Poisson distribution function $\bar{F}$, three alternative approaches are generally used.

(i) The structure function H will be expressed (approximated) in an *analytic form*. This is exemplified in Section 2.9.
(ii) The standard deviation and skewness (or some other characteristics) of $\mathbf{q}$ are first estimated and used in approximation formulae which will be developed for the computation of $\bar{F}$ fitting the moments. Hence *no particular assumption of the strict form of* H *is needed*. This will be the standard method applied in the following chapters.
(iii) The basic data, from which the estimate for H is to be derived,

may be given or estimated *in tabular form* such as in Table 2.8.1, where the relevant range of q is divided in intervals i and the frequencies $h_i = n_i/\Sigma n_i$ are calculated from the numbers n_i of the cases where $\mathbf{q}$ falls in the interval i. Then the mixed d.f. can be computed (see (2.7.2) and (2.7.3)) from

$$\bar{F}(k) = \sum_i F(k; nq_i) \cdot h_i, \qquad (2.8.8)$$

which is often convenient for numerical computations.

The advantage of this method is that tabular values like those in Table 2.8.1 can often fit the empirical data more closely than any analytical estimate of H, and no further idealizations are needed.

Table 2.8.2 gives examples of simple and mixed Poisson values. The mixed function $\bar{F}$ was computed using the numbers of Table 2.8.1. As seen in the table, the probabilities differ significantly, even when the H-distribution is symmetric. In many applications the structure distribution is skew, having a longer tail for large q-values. In such cases the deviations from the simple Poisson probabilities are even greater.

Exercise 2.8.1 Prove (2.8.1) and (2.8.7) directly by applying the general formula

$$E(\mathbf{X}) = E(E(\mathbf{X}|\mathbf{Y})) = \int_{-\infty}^{+\infty} E(\mathbf{X}|\mathbf{Y}=Y)\,\mathrm{d}H(Y),$$

where H is the d.f. of the variable $\mathbf{Y}$.

Table 2.8.1   *Example of the function H given in a tabular form.*

$(1-q_i)$	+0.25	+0.20	+0.15	+0.10	+0.05	0	−0.05	−0.10	−0.15	−0.20	−0.25
h_i	0.10	0.05	0.05	0.10	0.12	0.16	0.12	0.10	0.05	0.05	0.10

Table 2.8.2   *Examples of simple and mixed Poisson probabilities for $n = 100$ and for the H function are given in Table 2.8.1*

k	110	120	130	140
$1 - F(k)$	0.147	0.023	0.0017	0.0001
$1 - \bar{F}(k)$	0.279	0.132	0.0470	0.0110

2.9   The Polya process

(a) **Gamma as structure function** For analysis and for practical purposes it is often advantageous for the structure function to have a closed analytical form as mentioned in item 2.8 (c)(i) as one of the alternative approaches. The *incomplete gamma function*

$$\Gamma(x;h) = \frac{1}{\Gamma(h)} \int_0^x e^{-z} z^{h-1}\, dz \qquad (x \geqslant 0,\, h > 0), \qquad (2.9.1)$$

is often used, where h is a freely available parameter and $\Gamma(h) = \int_0^\infty e^{-z} z^{h-1}\, dz$ denotes the well-known complete Γ function satisfying $\Gamma(i+1) = i!$ for each non-negative integer i. Its special benefit is the possibility of getting many useful formulae calculated in a closed form, and it can represent a wide variety of distributional shapes. On the other hand, the existence of only one parameter limits the free adjustment of the ratio of the breadth and skewness of the distribution.

The formula suggested is

$$H(q) = \Gamma(hq;h) = \frac{1}{\Gamma(h)} \int_0^{hq} e^{-z} z^{h-1}\, dz, \qquad (2.9.2)$$

where the upper limit is chosen to give the mean value $E(\mathbf{q}) = 1$, after which one parameter h is still open to choice.

(b) **The moments and other characteristics** are easily obtained by integration and by observing that $\Gamma(x) = (x-1)\Gamma(x-1)$ (for $x \geqslant 1$).

$$
\begin{aligned}
E(\mathbf{q}) &= 1 \\
\sigma_{\mathbf{q}}^2 &= 1/h & \sigma_{\mathbf{q}} &= 1/\sqrt{h} \\
\mu_3(\mathbf{q}) &= 2/h^2 & \gamma_{\mathbf{q}} &= 2/\sqrt{h} \\
\mu_4(\mathbf{q}) &= 6/h^3 + 3/h^2 & \gamma_2(\mathbf{q}) &= 6/h.
\end{aligned}
\qquad (2.9.3)
$$

(c) **The shape of the Γ-distribution** is shown in Fig. 2.9.1 for various values of the parameter h. Values can be found in Pearson (1954) or they can be computed using expansions which will be given in Section 3.12.

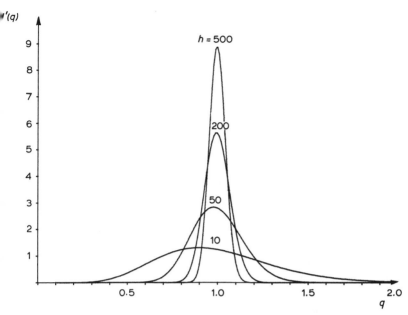

Figure 2.9.1   *The incomplete gamma function* (2.9.2).

(d) The m.g.f. and convolution For further applications presented
later we give the m.g.f. of the incomplete gamma function $\Gamma(x;h)$
(see exercise 2.9.2)

$$M_\Gamma(s) = (1 - s)^{-h} \qquad \text{(for } s < 1). \tag{2.9.4}$$

If $M_1(s)$ and $M_2(s)$ are the m.g.f.s of $\Gamma(x;h_1)$ and $\Gamma(x;h_2)$, then

$$M_1(s)M_2(s) = (1 - s)^{-h_1}(1 - s)^{-h_2} = (1 - s)^{-(h_1 + h_2)}. \tag{2.9.5}$$

Hence, according to item 1.6(b) the convolution of two incomplete
gamma functions is again an incomplete gamma function having
$h = h_1 + h_2$ as a parameter

$$\Gamma(x; h_1 + h_2) = \Gamma(\cdot\,; h_1) * \Gamma(\cdot\,; h_2)(x), \tag{2.9.6}$$

where the right-hand side is to be understood as the convolution of
the distributions evaluated at the point x. Because $\Gamma(cx;h) =
1 - e^{-cx}$, it follows that for positive integer values of h the $\Gamma(cx;h)$
is a convolution of h exponential distributions denoted by

$$\Gamma(cx; h) = G^{h*}(cx) \quad \text{for } G(x) = \Gamma(x; 1) = 1 - e^{-x}, \tag{2.9.7}$$

where everywhere $x \geqslant 0$.

(e) The probability function (2.7.2) is now transformed as follows

$$\bar{p}_k(n) = \int_0^\infty e^{-nq} \frac{(nq)^k}{k!} \frac{1}{\Gamma(h)} e^{-hq} (hq)^{h-1} h \, dq$$

$$= \frac{n^k h^h}{\Gamma(h)k!} \int_0^\infty e^{-(n+h)q} q^{h+k-1} \, dq \qquad (2.9.8)$$

$$= \frac{n^k h^h}{\Gamma(h)k!} \frac{\Gamma(h+k)}{(n+h)^{h+k}}$$

$$= \frac{\Gamma(h+k)}{\Gamma(h)k!} \left(\frac{h}{n}\right)^h \left(\frac{n+h}{n}\right)^{-(h+k)}.$$

If the meaning of the binomial coefficient $\binom{i}{j}$ is extended by use of the Γ function to cover the cases where the quantities i, j may be non-integer, this may be written

$$\bar{p}_k(n) = \binom{h+k-1}{k} \left(\frac{h}{n+h}\right)^h \left(\frac{n}{n+h}\right)^k. \qquad (2.9.9)$$

This probability formula is well known as the *negative binomial*. It can be easily verified that it reduces to the Poisson formula when $h \to \infty$ (exercise 2.9.4).

From (2.8.6) and (2.9.3), the mean, variance, skewness and kurtosis are obtained (see exercise 2.9.1)

$$\begin{aligned}
\bar{\alpha}_1 &= n \\
\bar{\sigma}^2 &= n + n^2/h \\
\bar{\gamma} &= (n + 3n^2/h + 2n^3/h^2)/\bar{\sigma}^3 \\
\bar{\gamma}_2 &= (n + 7n^2/h + 12n^3/h^2 + 6n^4/h^3)/\bar{\sigma}^4.
\end{aligned} \qquad (2.9.10)$$

(f) The moment generating function can be obtained from (2.8.7) by integration (see exercise 2.9.3):

$$\bar{M}(s) = (1 - n(e^s - 1)/h)^{-h}, \qquad (2.9.11)$$

which is valid for $s < \ln(1 + h/n)$.

If $h \to \infty$, (2.6.1) is obtained by making use of the well-known formula $\lim_{n \to \infty} (1 + a/n)^n = e^a$.

(g) The numerical calculation of $\bar{p}_k$ and $\bar{F}$ can conveniently be made by applying the recursion technique used in Section 2.5 (see (2.5.1) and (2.5.2)). Thus

$$\bar{p}_0 = (h/(n+h))^h, \tag{2.9.12}$$

and

$$\bar{p}_k(n) = (a + b/k)\bar{p}_{k-1}(n), \tag{2.9.13}$$

where

$$a = n/(n+h)$$
$$b = n(h-1)/(n+h).$$

It may be noted that integer-valued distributions having a recursion rule of the form (2.9.13), where a and b are constants not depending on k, constitute an important class of distributions. The Poisson distribution ($a = 0, b = n$) is a member of this family (see 2.5.2)). Generalizing a result of Panjer (1981), Jewell and Sundt (1981) have recently shown that the compound Poisson function is also computable by a recursion formula in certain conditions. This is discussed in Section 3.8.

A few numerical values are provided in Table 2.9.1 and give some idea of the flexibility of (2.9.9) compared with the simple Poisson d.f.

Table 2.9.1 *Examples of* $1 - \bar{F}$ *per thousand.*

n	$h =$ k	∞	100	20	10	5
10	12	208	217	243	262	281
	14	83	93	126	154	188
	16	27	34	58	84	121
50	60	72	115	205	250	285
	70	3	13	71	122	177
	80	0	1	19	53	105
100	110	147	224	312	340	356
	120	23	78	194	246	285
	130	2	20	112	172	225
	140	0	4	60	116	175

(h) Discussion The Polya process is fairly convenient for applications and leads to many important formulae, which are easy, or at least possible, for computational use. On the other hand, it requires a smoothing procedure and some idealization of the process and it does not seem easy to estimate the error due to this smoothing. Because there is only one free parameter, h, available, the Polya d.f. is not always flexible to fit various structure distributions, especially if they are rather skew, as will be seen in Section 2.10.

(i) Contamination model It is interesting to note that there is also another way to derive the negative binomial distribution, originally formulated by Eggenberger and Polya (1923). This may be done by means of an urn model as follows. Assume that N_1 red balls and N_2 white balls (reds representing accidents, diseases, fires or other casualties) are placed in an urn. A ball is drawn at random repeatedly s times. After each draw the ball is returned to the urn together with C balls having the same colour. Hence before the sth draw the number of balls in the urn is $N + (s - 1)C$, which provides the denominator for the sth probability. Here $N = N_1 + N_2$. By combinatorial reasoning it can be shown that the probability of getting exactly k red balls is

$$\text{prob}\{\mathbf{k} = k\} = \binom{s}{k} \frac{\prod_{u=0}^{k-1} (N_1 + uC) \prod_{v=0}^{s-k-1} (N_2 + vC)}{\prod_{w=0}^{s-1} (N + wC)} .$$

$$(2.9.14)$$

The purpose of this model is to introduce *contamination* into the model. Each event gives rise to an increased probability of the same kind of events in future because balls of the same colour were put into the urn.

Defining

$$1/h = C/N_1 = \text{degree of contamination}, \qquad (2.9.15)$$

and then performing the sequence of passages

$$N \to \infty \,; s \to \infty \,; sN_1/N \to n, \qquad (2.9.16)$$

it follows that the contamination, which was originally assumed to occur at discrete times, will occur continuously (i.e. in infinitely short time intervals) so that the expected number of events during a fixed observation period, say in one year, will be kept constant and equal to n. It can be proved that the passage leads to the negative binomial formula (2.9.9). Hence the negative binomial can be derived by assuming contamination between the risk units, e.g. epidemic diseases or the spreading of fire. For this reason the negative binomial distribution is often called a *Polya distribution* and the corresponding mixed process is called a *Polya process*.

Exercise 2.9.1 Prove that the moments about zero of $\Gamma(x; h)$ are

$$\alpha_i = \Gamma(h + i)/\Gamma(h), \tag{2.9.17}$$

and calculate the characteristics (2.9.3) and (2.9.10).

Exercise 2.9.2 Prove (2.9.4).

Exercise 2.9.3 Derive the moment generating function (2.9.11).

Exercise 2.9.4 Prove that the negative binomial probability function (2.9.9) is reduced to the Poisson probability as $h \to \infty$.

Exercise 2.9.5 Calculate and plot in the same diagram the Poisson function p_k and the corresponding Polya $\bar{p}_k$ for $n = 5$ and $h = 10$.

Exercise 2.9.6 The aggregate claim numbers of two stochastically independent portfolios are Polya distributed. Prove that, if the portfolios are merged, the joint distribution is again of Polya type providing that the parameters n and h are the same for both the original portfolios.

Exercise 2.9.7 Prove that the d.f. $F_n(k)$ of the Poisson variable can be expressed in terms of the gamma d.f.

$$1 - F(k; n) = \Gamma(n, k + 1).$$

Exercise 2.9.8 For which value of k does $\bar{p}_k(n)$ as given by (2.9.9) achieve its maximum?

2.10 Risk exposure variation inside the portfolio

(a) Individual risk proneness The mixed Poisson distributions also have applications in environments other than those just described.

An example is the situation when the risk proneness of the individual risk units of the insured portfolio is considered, e.g. the problem may be to find the d.f. of the number of claims arising from a single motor-car policy. The physical process may justify the assumption of a Poisson law for the accidents, but the risk parameter n, the expected number of claims per car, can be expected to vary for different cars depending on the type, use, exposure time (mileage), etc., of the car and the skill of the driver. It can be assumed that each risk unit i, a car in this example, is involved with a proneness parameter $n_i = nq_i$ which is the expected number of claims pertinent to this unit. Here n is an average value and q_i a coefficient indicating the deviation per unit from n. Let H be the d.f. which describes the variation of the q_i values (such a d.f. can be assumed to exist even though it often may be unknown or only partially estimated in practice). This function characterizes the distribution of risk inside the portfolio (or inside some particular part of the portfolio under consideration, e.g. some class of motor-car).

The distribution of the claim number variable $\mathbf{k}$ of the individual unit which is selected at random from the portfolio can be obtained by first taking the probability that the risk parameter $\mathbf{q}$ is in the interval $q_i, q_i + \mathrm{d}q$ and then assuming the Poisson law for the parameter value nq_i. The construction of the probability expression is exactly analogous to that applied in the derivation of formula (2.7.2). Only the physical environments are different – in (2.7.2) it was the variation of the Poisson parameter n from one time unit to the next, in the present case it is the variableness of it from one risk unit to the next. Hence (2.7.2) is readily applicable

$$\bar{p}_k = \mathrm{prob}\{\mathbf{k} = k\} = \int_0^\infty p_k(nq)\,\mathrm{d}H(q), \qquad (2.10.1)$$

where p_k is the standard Poisson probability (2.4.2). Also in this connection $H(q)$ is generally called a *structure function* (see Ammeter, 1948; Bühlmann, 1970). This is an important concept in many applications, including credibility theory (Section 4.10) in particular and in rate-making in general.

(b) Example For illustration consider the example given in Table 2.10.1. The statistics are taken from a study by Johnson and Hey and relate to claims under UK comprehensive motor policies in 1968. The 421 240 policies were classified according to the number of

Table 2.10.1   *Comprehensive motor policies according to the number of claims in 1968.*

k	N_k	Poisson	Neg. binomial	Two Poissons
0	370 412	369 246	370 460	370 460
1	46 545	48 644	46 411	46 418
2	3 935	3 204	4 045	4 036
3	317	141	301	306
4	28	5	21	20
5	3	—	1	1

claims in the year 1968, the average number of claims per policy being 0.131 74 and the variance 0.138 52. The column headed 'Poisson' sets out the distribution that would result if the occurrence of claims had followed the Poisson law with $n = 0.131$ 74, i.e. the expected number of claims per policy in one year. As will be apparent the Poisson distribution is theoretically shorter than the data, an observation confirmed by the chi-squared test. In other words, the hypothesis that the risk proneness is different for different policies is confirmed.

The insufficiency of the Poisson law could also be anticipated from the fact that the variance is greater than the mean, whereas they should be equal if the Poisson law were valid, as will be seen from (2.4.3).

The column headed 'Negative binomial' sets out the distribution according to this law with parameters $n = 0.$ 13 174 and $h = 2.555$, the latter being found by the method of maximum likelihood. The value of chi-square is 6.9 which gives a probability of 0.14 for 4 degrees of freedom, so that the representation is acceptable. There is a slight indication that the negative binomial may be under-representing the tail and for some applications it might be desirable to elaborate the model, but for applications which have no significantly large skewness the model may be safely used.

(c) Discrete structure function Another approach is to approximate the structure function $H(q)$ by a discrete d.f. assuming values q_1, $q_2, \ldots, q_r$ with probabilities $h_1, h_2, \ldots, h_r$. This means, in fact, that the d.f. is composed of r Poisson terms. The greater the number of free parameters, the better the possibility of achieving a reasonable fit even for heterogeneous portfolios.

In the present case a two-term distribution already gives a quite satisfactory result. The parameter values $q_1 = 0.653\,41$ and $q_2 = 2.1293$, with probabilities $0.765\,19$ and $0.234\,81$, can be found from the equation

$$hp_k(n_1) + (1 - h)p_k(n_2) = \bar{p}_k(n),$$

and equating moments with respect to k. In principle the problem is related to Gaussian quadrature and a simple treatment with a number of tables of relevant numerical values will be found in Beard (1947).

There is a substantial literature about structure functions. The problem of finding the parameters q_i and h_i for the discrete approximation was dealt with by D'Hooge and Goovaerts (1976). Gossiaux and Lemaire (1981) studied the fit of the above methods and applied them to motor-car accident statistics. Loimaranta *et al.* (1980) have presented a cluster analysis approach as a solution of the same problem.

(d) Terminology For the purposes of this book the inner variation in the collective is not relevant. The collective will be treated as a whole and the heterogeneity taken care of by the expected number of claims n. Thus in what follows $H(q)$ and the term 'structure function' *will represent only short-term variations in* n, i.e. the random fluctuation from one accounting period to another. Longer-term variations are dealt with later in Chapter 6.

The reader will appreciate that this terminology deviates from the practice sometimes assumed in the literature where a structure function may refer mainly to the internal heterogeneity of collectives.

CHAPTER 3

Compound Poisson process

3.1 The distribution of claim size

(a) Definitions Consideration is now extended from the claim number processes to processes which operate the claim *amounts*, concerning both the individual claims and their sums, the aggregate claims. A primary building block is the randomly varying size **Z** of an individual claim, i.e. the sum to be paid by the insurer at occurrence of fire, accident or any other event insured against. It is assumed that the claim sizes **Z** arising from different claim causing events are mutually independent and equally distributed, having a d.f.

$$S(Z) = \text{prob}\{\mathbf{Z} \leqslant Z\}. \tag{3.1.1}$$

Following the collective approach outlined in item 2.1(b) no regard is paid to the risk unit (policy) from which the claim has arisen. The d.f. S describes the variability of sizes of the continual flow of claims. The aspects discussed in Section 2.3 suggest that payments due to one and the same event should be united as one claim irrespective of whether or not they formally concern different policies (e.g. different owners of a property in a damaged building complex or in a vehicle). Furthermore, if two or more claims are coming from the same risk units they are considered as different claims if they are caused by different events.

The approaches, which will be dealt with in Chapters 3–7, will be formulated so as to be generally applicable, as far as possible, to all kind of insurance. In the case of life insurance the claim size Z should be defined as the difference of the sum S paid by the insurer and the policy reserve V released thereby, i.e. $Z = S - V$. Special features concerning life insurance will be discussed in Chapter 8.

The claim size variable introduces to the processes concerned a new layer of stochasticity in addition to the claim number variation.

The processes constituted by the stochastic variation of both claim number and claim sizes are called *compound processes*.

The existence of a function S is in conformity with general experience, at least as regards periods of moderate length and provided the effect of changes in monetary values is eliminated, for example by methods which will be presented later. The actual claims can be recorded and numerical estimates obtained for S. At the outset it will only be assumed that the function exists and that it is known. Subsequently the details of its practical computation will be considered and a few more common distributions will be recorded in Section 3.5.

As mentioned in Section 1.3, only distributions with positive risk sums, i.e. $Z \geqslant 0$, are dealt with in this book.

(b) Three different types of S-function occur in the applications and are shown in Fig. 3.1.1 with the corresponding densities or frequencies s.

In Fig. 3.1.1(a) $S(Z)$ is *continuous*; this form of $S(Z)$ is very common, because a large portfolio of insurance policies will consist of a wide variety of different insured amounts, and consequently the claims will be of all amounts from zero to very large. In non-life business the continuity becomes more apparent because of partial damages; this also has the effect of substantially increasing the relative incidence of the smaller claims.

The *discrete* function of Fig. 3.1.1(b) could arise from a friendly society granting fixed funeral expense benefits or from a company which has standardized the benefits under its policies, such as travel accident insurance (often sold through airport automats) where the face sums are fixed optional sums.

A *mixed type* of function is shown in Fig. 3.1.1(c); this can arise from a basic distribution of type (a), subject to re-insurance arrangements, which has the effect of cutting off the top layer of the basic risks. Similar steps can arise from legal or contractual upper limits of indemnity. If the arrangement involves different net retentions or limits for different classes of risks, several steps may be shown in the S-function.

For practical application it is sufficient to assume that the S-function is one of the types mentioned above. Furthermore, it is assumed that the derivative $S'(Z)$ exists for types (a) and (c) and is continuous except at a finite number of points.

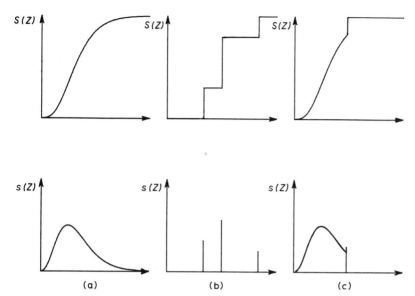

Figure 3.1.1(a)   *A continuous function;* (b) *a discrete function;* (c) *mixed type.*

(c) Outstanding claims To keep the risk-theoretical models within reasonable dimensions, it is usually assumed that the *claims are paid out immediately they are incurred.* In practice, there is inevitably some time lag between the occurrence of the event giving rise to a claim and its settlement, whether from the minor aspect of administrative procedures or from legal problems such as the determination of liability or the assessment of amount or from delays in notifying the insurer of claims which are due the so-called IBNR problem, (an abbreviation for incurred but not reported). Thus, in addition to the problems of assessing the probable amount of claims which have been notified, some allowance has to be made for the expected late-notified cases.

In principle, any errors in estimates of outstanding claims will ultimately be corrected when the claims are finally settled, but they can give rise to a shift of profits or losses between years and in that way affect also the risk fluctuation; however, they will probably be of much smaller magnitude than the 'ordinary fluctuations'. It should be noted that the assumption concerning the immediate payment of claims does not result in the elimination of the estimation errors of the outstanding claims from the model. Like any other inaccuracy of the basic assumption, it gives rise to extra fluctuations in underwriting results, probably in a periodic manner as assumed in item 1.1(f) and as will be further discussed in Section 6.2. When the model parameters are calibrated on the basis of *observed* actual fluctuations, the effect of these inaccuracies will be automatically taken into account. Furthermore, there is no essential obstacle to the introduction of the outstanding claims or rather their estimation error as a particular entry to the model. A brief indication of such an approach will be presented in item 10.2(e).

On the other hand, systematic under- or overestimation can give rise to considerable bias in the balance sheet and thus in evaluation of the actual solvency margins (risk reserves). The consideration of these as well as many kinds of 'non-stochastic' aspects, e.g. incalculable risks jeopardizing the existence of insurers such as major failures in investments or risk evaluation, misfeasance or malfeasance of management, etc., are essential parts of the general solvency control of insurance industry, but they fall outside the scope of this book (see Pentikäinen, 1982; Section 2.9).

Analysis of the development of claims estimates is a normal part of business routine and will indicate the need for some extra provisions; it might be thought, for example, that a margin is needed to deal with inflationary changes with respect to both the average level of inflation as well as the need for emergency measures in cases when the rate of inflation may occasionally be soaring. Even though inflation will be incorporated into the model assumptions, its special effects on the claims reserve will not be further discussed. Such adjustments might be needed in assessing the parameters of the overall model and will have to be dealt with in individual circumstances.

3.2 Compound distribution of the aggregate claim

(a) **Derivation of the d.f.** An insurance portfolio is again considered and it is desired to find the probability distribution of the total amount of claims **X**, or briefly the aggregate claim, which occurs during a time interval (e.g. 1 year). The probability p_k that the number of claims equals k, and the distribution function S of one claim, are assumed to be known.

The required distribution $F(X)$ gives the probability of the event $\mathbf{X} \leqslant X$. This event can occur in the following alternative ways:

(i) In the time interval no claim occurs.
(ii) The number of claims $= 1$ and the amount of the claim is $\leqslant X$.
(iii) The number of claims $= 2$ and the sum of the amounts of these is $\leqslant X$.
(iv) The number of claims $= 3$ and the sum of the amounts of these is $\leqslant X$.

etc.

The conditional probability that, if the number of claims is exactly k, the sum of these k claims is $\leqslant X$ is denoted by $S_k(X)$. Using the combined addition and multiplication rules of probability, it follows that

$$F(X) = \sum_{k=0}^{\infty} p_k S_k(X). \tag{3.2.1}$$

If it is assumed that the amounts of the claims are mutually independent, the function $S_k(X)$ is well known from probability calculus as the kth convolution of the distribution function $S(X)$, which can be calculated from the recurrence formula.

$$S_k(X) = \int_0^X S_{k-1}(X - Z) \, dS(Z) = S^{(k-1)*} * S(X) = S^{k*}(X) \tag{3.2.2}$$

and the following important formula is obtained for the d.f. of the aggregate claims

$$F(X) = \sum_{k=0}^{\infty} p_k S^{k*}(X). \tag{3.2.3}$$

(b) Terminology The distribution function (3.2.3) is called *compound*, referring to the compound process behind it. If the claim number process related to $\mathbf{X}$ is a (mixed) Poisson process then $\mathbf{X}$ is called a (mixed) *compound Poisson process* and the function (3.2.3) as (mixed) *compound Poisson d.f.* In this case, which is mostly assumed in the following, p_k is either the simple Poisson probability (2.4.2) or the mixed version (2.7.2). The prefix 'mixed' is often omitted for brevity.

The case where p_k is defined as the simple Poisson probability is often called the *Poisson case*; where p_k is the negative binomial probability (2.9.9) this is known as the *Polya case*.

For the sake of simplicity the notation $\bar{p}_k$ will be replaced by p_k provided that the meaning is clear in the particular context.

(c) On applicability The d.f. (3.2.3) is, unfortunately, directly useful for numerical computations only by making special assumptions concerning S or if n is very small. The formulae are mainly applicable when X is given and $F(X)$ is sought, and not easily in the reverse direction from $F(X)$ to X. Finding workable approximation methods is a major problem and several are given later, but first some general features of F are considered.

3.3 Basic characteristics of F

(a) Basic moments The characteristics of the (mixed) compound (Poisson) distribution can be expressed in terms of the moments of the claim number process, which were given in Section 2.8, and of the moments about zero of the S function

$$a_j = \int_0^\infty Z^j \, dS(Z), \qquad (3.3.1)$$

of the claim size d.f. S. It is convenient to choose for the lowest moment, which indicates the mean claim size, the special notation

$$m = a_1. \qquad (3.3.2)$$

(b) The moments β_j about zero of compound distributions, can be derived from the following *general* formula

$$\begin{aligned}
\beta_j &= \int_0^\infty X^j \, dF(X) \\
&= \int_0^\infty X^j \sum_{k=0}^\infty p_k \, dS^{k*}(X) \\
&= \sum_{k=0}^\infty p_k \int_0^\infty X^j \, dS^{k*}(X) \\
&= \sum_{k=0}^\infty p_k a_j^{(k)},
\end{aligned} \qquad (3.3.3)$$

where $a_j^{(k)}$ is the jth moment about zero of the sum of k individual claims

$$\mathbf{Z}_1 + \mathbf{Z}_2 + \cdots + \mathbf{Z}_k.$$

The terms of this sum are mutually independent according to assumptions made in Section 3.1 and have the same d.f. S. Hence the first moment

$$a_1^{(k)} = E(\mathbf{Z}_1 + \cdots + \mathbf{Z}_k) = kE(\mathbf{Z}_1) = km, \qquad (3.3.4)$$

and the second and third central moments of the sum of claims can be summed from its components:

$$\mu_j^{(k)} = \mu_j(\mathbf{Z}_1) + \cdots + \mu_j(\mathbf{Z}_k) \qquad (j = 2 \text{ or } 3).$$

Then the second moment about zero, needed for (3.3.3), can be calculated as follows

$$
\begin{aligned}
a_2^{(k)} &= \mu_2^{(k)} + (a_1^{(k)})^2 \\
&= k\mu_2(\mathbf{Z}_1) + k^2 m^2 \\
&= k(a_2 - m^2) + k^2 m^2 \\
&= ka_2 + k(k-1)m^2.
\end{aligned}
\qquad (3.3.5)
$$

(c) **Characteristics of compound Poisson distribution** These results are valid for compound distributions in general, i.e. for distributions which are composed of a (claim) number process and of a (claim) size process. Next the claim number process of a compound Poisson type is assumed. Substituting these expressions in (3.3.3) and making use of the earlier results (2.8.2) and (2.8.3), the moments of the aggregate claim are obtained:

$$
\begin{aligned}
\beta_1 &= \sum_{k=0}^{\infty} p_k km = m \sum_{k=0}^{\infty} kp_k = mn, \\
\beta_2 &= \sum_{k=0}^{\infty} p_k[ka_2 + k(k-1)m^2] \\
&= (a_2 - m^2) \sum_{k=0}^{\infty} kp_k + m^2 \sum_{k=0}^{\infty} k^2 p_k \\
&= (a_2 - m^2)n + m^2(n + n^2 a_2(\mathbf{q})) \\
&= na_2 + n^2 m^2 a_2(\mathbf{q}).
\end{aligned}
\qquad (3.3.6)
$$

In a similar way the higher moments can also be obtained. A more convenient method for their calculation is, however, the use of the m.g.f., as will be seen in the next section.

The central moments of the aggregate claim distribution are now readily calculated by means of (1.5.6), and by some further algebra (see exercise 3.3.5) the following important expressions can be obtained

mean $\qquad \mu_{\mathbf{X}} = E(\mathbf{X}) = nm = P,$

variance $\qquad \sigma_{\mathbf{X}}^2 = \mathrm{var}(\mathbf{X}) = na_2 + n^2m^2\sigma_{\mathbf{q}}^2.$

$\qquad\qquad\quad = (r_2/n + \sigma_{\mathbf{q}}^2)P^2,$

skewness $\qquad \gamma_{\mathbf{X}} = \mu_3(\mathbf{X})/\sigma_{\mathbf{X}}^3 = (na_3 + 3n^2ma_2\sigma_{\mathbf{q}}^2 + n^3m^3\gamma_{\mathbf{q}}\sigma_{\mathbf{q}}^3)/\sigma_{\mathbf{X}}^3$

$\qquad\qquad\quad = (r_3/n^2 + 3r_2\sigma_{\mathbf{q}}^2/n + \gamma_{\mathbf{q}}\sigma_{\mathbf{q}}^3)/(r_2/n + \sigma_{\mathbf{q}}^2)^{3/2}$

kurtosis $\qquad \gamma_2(\mathbf{X}) = \mu_4(\mathbf{X})/\sigma_{\mathbf{X}}^4 - 3$

$\qquad\qquad\quad = (na_4 + 4n^2ma_3\sigma_{\mathbf{q}}^2 + 3n^2a_2^2\sigma_{\mathbf{q}}^2 +$

$\qquad\qquad\qquad + 6n^3m^2a_2\gamma_{\mathbf{q}}\sigma_{\mathbf{q}}^3 + n^4m^4\gamma_2(\mathbf{q})\sigma_{\mathbf{q}}^4)/\sigma_{\mathbf{X}}^4, \qquad (3.3.7)$

where $\mathbf{q}$ is the structure variable. Because just the basic characteristic γ and γ_2 will be used as standard input parameters they are written into the above expressions, despite the fact that replacement of $\gamma_{\mathbf{q}}\sigma_{\mathbf{q}}^3$ by $\mu_3(\mathbf{q})$ and $\gamma_2(\mathbf{q})\sigma_{\mathbf{q}}^4$ by $\mu_4(\mathbf{q}) - 3\sigma_{\mathbf{q}}^4$ would have somewhat simplified the formulae. $P = nm$ is the *risk premium* income covering the claim expenditure due to $\mathbf{X}$, as will be defined in Section 4.1.

The relations a_2/m^2 and a_3/m^3 are needed so frequently that it is convenient to introduce special notation for them:

$$r_2 = a_2/m^2 = \text{risk index}$$
$$r_3 = a_3/m^3. \qquad (3.3.8)$$

A merit of these indexes is that, as a first approximation, they are not affected by inflation because the numerator and denominator increase in the same ratio in case of a change of the value of money.

(d) In the Poisson case i.e. when the structure variable $\mathbf{q}$ is constant $(=1)$, (3.3.7) is reduced as follows

$$\mu_{\mathbf{X}} = nm$$
$$\sigma_{\mathbf{X}}^2 = na_2$$
$$\gamma_{\mathbf{X}} = \frac{a_3}{a_2^{3/2}\sqrt{n}} = \frac{r_3}{r_2^{3/2}\sqrt{n}} \qquad (3.3.9)$$
$$\gamma_2(\mathbf{X}) = \frac{a_4}{na_2^2}.$$

(e) For the Polya case i.e. when the structure function is of gamma type, the corresponding expressions are derived by using (2.9.10)

$$
\begin{aligned}
\mu_{\mathbf{X}} &= nm \\
\sigma_{\mathbf{X}}^2 &= na_2 + n^2 m^2/h \\
\gamma_{\mathbf{X}} &= (na_3 + 3n^2 ma_2/h + 2n^3 m^3/h^2)/\sigma_{\mathbf{X}}^3 \\
\gamma_2(\mathbf{X}) &= [na_4 + 3n^2 a_2^2/h + 4n^2 ma_3/h + 12n^3 m^2 a_2/h^2 \\
&\quad + 6n^4 m^4/k^3]/\sigma_{\mathbf{X}}^4.
\end{aligned}
\tag{3.3.10}
$$

(f) Analysis of the background effects The above formulae separate the effects of the components of stochasticity introduced in item 3.1(a).

The variance $\sigma_{\mathbf{X}}^2$ is composed of two terms. The first represents the variance, if the basic parameter n were constant. The second term is the increment arising from the fluctuation in n according to the d.f. H (see (2.7.1)).

As an illustration, Table 3.3.1 sets out some examples of the relative share of the structure component in $\sigma_{\mathbf{X}}$ and the 'pure Poisson' component in

$$
\rho = (\sigma_{\mathbf{X}} - \sigma_0)/\sigma_{\mathbf{X}},
\tag{3.3.11}
$$

where σ_0 is the standard deviation obtained from equations (3.3.9) for the pure Poisson case. The model parameters for the examples where $r_2 = 44$ and $\sigma_{\mathbf{q}} = 0.038$ which will be chosen as standard values for examples in item 4.2(b). Furthermore, two Polya cases are calculated having $r_2 = 44$ and $h = 100$ or 1000.

It can be seen how the ordinary random fluctuation of the number and the size of claims is predominant for small companies, whereas for large companies the position is reversed.

Table 3.3.1   *The share ρ of the standard deviation due to the structure variation.*

n	$100\sigma_{\mathbf{X}}/P$ Standard	100ρ Standard	Polya $h = 100$	Polya $h = 1000$
10	209.8	0.0	0.1	0.0
100	66.4	0.2	1.1	0.1
1 000	21.3	1.6	9.7	1.1
10 000	7.6	13.2	44.7	9.7
100 000	4.3	51.7	79.5	44.7
1 000 000	3.9	82.8	93.4	79.5

Table 3.3.2   *The components (3.3.12) as a percentage of the total variance σ_X^2.*

n	$100\sigma_X/P$	var $(\mathbf{k})$	var $(\mathbf{Z})$	var $(\mathbf{q})$
10	209.8	2.3	97.7	0.0
100	66.4	2.3	97.4	0.3
1 000	21.3	2.2	94.6	3.2
10 000	7.6	1.7	73.6	24.7
100 000	4.3	0.5	22.8	76.6
1 000 000	3.9	0.1	2.9	97.0

A further decomposition is of interest

$$\text{var}(\mathbf{X}) = \sigma_X^2 = nm^2 + n(a_2 - m^2) + n^2 m^2 \sigma_q^2.$$
$$= m^2 \, \text{var}(\mathbf{k}) + n \, \text{var}(\mathbf{Z}) + n^2 m^2 \, \text{var}(\mathbf{q}), \qquad (3.3.12)$$

where the first term represents the variance if the claim number only where stochastic, var $(\mathbf{k}) = n$ being the Poisson variance of claim number variable $\mathbf{k}$. The second term arises when the claim size $\mathbf{Z}$ is also made stochastic. The third term represents the increment when the structure variable $\mathbf{q}$ is introduced to the model.

In Table 3.3.2 an example is shown of the magnitude of the three components which control the stability of an insurance collective, employing the same standards as above.

It is evident that the component due to the simple Poisson variation of the claim number is slight. For small collectives the variation of the claim size is predominant and for the large collectives the variation caused by the structure variable $\mathbf{q}$ is predominant. Of course, the conclusion concerns only this example and may be different for other kinds of portfolios.

(g) Limit distributions From (3.3.7) it is also possible to draw some conclusions regarding the behaviour of the process when the portfolio grows large, i.e. when n tends to infinity. This can be seen by considering the relative claim amount variable

$$\mathbf{x} = \mathbf{X}/E(\mathbf{X}) = \mathbf{X}/nm, \qquad (3.3.13)$$

which has standard deviation

$$\sigma_x = \frac{\sigma_X}{nm} = \frac{\sqrt{(na_2 + n^2 m^2 \sigma_q^2)}}{nm} = \sqrt{(r_2/n + \sigma_q^2)}. \qquad (3.3.14)$$

It is immediately apparent that σ_x tends to σ_q when $n \to \infty$. Similarly, $\gamma_x \to \gamma_q$ and $\gamma_2(\mathbf{X}) \to \gamma_2(\mathbf{q})$. These observations suggest that the limit d.f. of $\mathbf{x}$ is H, the d.f. of the structure variable $\mathbf{q}$. This is in fact the case, as was proved by O. Lundberg (1964) (see exercise 3.3.6).

In the 'Poisson case', i.e. when the structure variable degenerates to one point 1 ($\sigma_q = 0$), the standard deviation σ_x tends to zero (and only in this case). Then the law of large numbers is applicable, as can be easily seen by dividing the time interval into equal subintervals and considering $\mathbf{X}$ as a sum of independent and equally distributed variables, since $\sigma_q = 0$. In this case the central limit theorem gives the asymptotic relation

$$F(X) \approx N((X - nm)/\sigma_X) \qquad \text{for } n \to \infty, \sigma_q = 0. \tag{3.3.15}$$

In the general case when $\sigma_q > 0$, F is *not* asymptotically normal but instead has the shape of the structure d.f. H, which means that

$$F(X) \approx H(X/nm) \qquad \text{for } n \to \infty, \sigma_q > 0. \tag{3.3.16}$$

It obviously depends on the properties of both the claim size d.f. S and the structure d.f. H how rapidly the approximation (3.3.16) provides a reasonably accurate approximation for F, i.e. whether it can be used whilst n is not very large. Table 3.3.2 suggests that quite large n values are required before the structure component turns predominant.

In practical application the passage $n \to \infty$ often means that the considerations concern a comparison of the behaviour of the risk-theoretical quantities of small and large companies or perhaps an individual company versus the joint business of several companies. A passage from a small company to a large company can, in fact, mean that the latter has several classes and subclasses of business and it may well happen that these are mutually independent even if each of them can obey the model introduced in this section. Then the sum, the total amount of claims, may tend to the normal distribution in accordance with the central limit theorem. In other words, if $n \to \infty$ so that new independent groups are incorporated into the collective, then F can be approximated by the normal distribution. In practice different mixed cases can occur, e.g. the changes in general economic conditions may have simultaneous parallel effects on many classes of the portfolio whereas some other fluctuations may have effects limited to one class only. Hence care is needed in deciding which assumptions are applicable to each actual case. The problems related to the division of the portfolio into sections will be dealt with in Section 6.4. Philipson (1968) has treated these kinds of passages.

(h) **Direct calculation of F** Formulae (2.7.4) and (2.8.8) can easily be extended to the compound variable $\mathbf{X}$ (see exercise 3.3.3)

$$\bar{F}(X) = \int_0^\infty F_{nq}(X)\, dH(q), \qquad (3.3.17)$$

of if H is discrete or approximated by a discrete d.f.

$$\bar{F}(X) = \sum_i F_{nq_i}(X)h_i, \qquad (3.3.18)$$

where F_{nq} is the simple compound Poisson d.f. ($\sigma_q = 0$) having the expected number of claims nq. The merit of (3.3.18) is that it is not necessary to try to find any analytical presentation for H in cases where it is evaluated, for example from empirical data.

Exercise 3.3.1 A friendly society grants funeral expense benefits which may be £100 or £200 according to the choice of each member. The sum £100 is chosen by two-thirds of the members, the remainder choosing £200. The number of members is 100 and it is assumed that the mean death rate for each member is 0.01. Compute the distribution function $F(X)$ of the annual amount of the claims. Observe the step character of F.

Exercise 3.3.2 Compute $E(\mathbf{X})$ and, $\sigma_\mathbf{X}$ for the society mentioned in the previous exercise.

Exercise 3.3.3 Prove (3.3.17).

Exercise 3.3.4 Show that if $\mathbf{Z}_1, \ldots, \mathbf{Z}_k$ are mutually independent random variables, then the third central moments satisfy the equation

$$\mu_3\left(\sum_{j=1}^k \mathbf{Z}_j\right) = \sum_{j=1}^k \mu_3(\mathbf{Z}_j),$$

provided the moments exist.

Exercise 3.3.5 Derive $\sigma_\mathbf{X}$ and $\gamma_\mathbf{X}$ (see (3.3.7)).

Exercise 3.3.6 Let $\bar{G}_n$ be the d.f. of $\mathbf{x} = \mathbf{X}/P$ (see (3.3.13)). Show that $\bar{G}_n \to H$ as $n \to \infty$, where H is the structure d.f. It is assumed that H is *discrete*.

**3.4 The moment generating function

(a) The m.g.f. of the (mixed) compound Poisson distribution can be obtained by a straightforward application of definition (1.6.1) as follows

$$M(s) = M_X(s) = \int_0^\infty e^{Xs} \, dF(X)$$

$$= \int_0^\infty e^{Xs} \, d_X \left[\sum_{k=0}^\infty p_k(n) S^{k*}(X) \right]$$

$$= \sum_{k=0}^\infty p_k(n) \int_0^\infty e^{Xs} \, dS^{k*}(X).$$

This last integral is the m.g.f. of the variable $\mathbf{Z}_1 + \cdots + \mathbf{Z}_k$. Owing to the independence of the individual claim sizes and the fact that they have a joint d.f. S, it can be expressed (see property (iv) of item 1.6(b)) as the kth power of

$$M_Z(s) = \int_0^\infty e^{Zs} \, dS(Z). \tag{3.4.1}$$

Furthermore, replacing $p_k(n)$ by (2.7.2) gives

$$M(s) = \sum_{k=0}^\infty \left[\int_0^\infty e^{-nq} \frac{(nq)^k}{k!} \, dH(q) \right] M_Z(s)^k$$

$$= \int_0^\infty e^{-nq} \sum_{k=0}^\infty \frac{(nq M_Z(s))^k}{k!} \, dH(q) \tag{3.4.2}$$

$$= \int_0^\infty e^{nq(M_Z(s) - 1)} \, dH(q).$$

The moments about zero and the basic characteristics (3.3.7) of the mixed compound Poisson distribution can be derived making use of the m.g.f. (see exercise 3.4.1).

(b) In the Poisson case when $H(q) = \varepsilon(q - 1)$ (see (1.5.3)) the following formula is obtained as a special case of (3.4.2)

$$M(s) = e^{n(M_Z(s) - 1)}. \tag{3.4.3}$$

(c) In the Polya case the m.g.f. is (see exercise 3.4.3)

$$M(s) = \left[1 - \frac{n}{h}(M_z(s) - 1) \right]^{-h}. \tag{3.4.4}$$

$M(s)$ does not necessarily exist if the expression in brackets is negative. It is, however, positive near the origin if $S(Z)$ is continuous at the origin. Otherwise its existence must be checked for each application.

Exercise 3.4.1 Calculate the moments about zero β_i (see (3.3.6)) for $i = 1, 2, 3, 4$ and the characteristics (3.3.7) making use of the m.g.f.

Exercise 3.4.2 Check that the m.g.f (2.8.7) is obtained from (3.4.2) by substituting $S(Z) = \varepsilon(Z - 1)$.

Exercise 3.4.3 Prove (3.4.4).

3.5   Estimation of S

3.5.1   INDIVIDUAL METHOD

(a) General aspects In most applications of the theory of risk it is necessary to know the claim size distribution function S more or less accurately. It should be so fitted that the representation corresponds as closely as possible to the true distribution of the amount of one claim in the portfolio. The fit should align itself to the data which are, in general, empirical. Insurers always have data files containing detailed information of both the policies and the claims, and many kinds of statistics are produced for counting, rate-making and other purposes. Construction of the claim size distributions and other data needed for risk-theoretical analyses can be obtained directly or by some modifications as side products from these data processes.

Some methods of estimating the S function from the data available are now presented in this and subsequent sections.

(b) Policy files as basis First a method is given for computing the S function starting from the individual policies of an insurance portfolio. This approach is convenient for practical calculations only in special cases. It is presented mainly because it describes in an illustrative way the connection of the claim size d.f. and the portfolio structure, which is conventionally recorded as files containing information on the existing policies.

The risk units (policies) are numbered $i = 1, 2, 3, \ldots, N$ and the corresponding frequency rates* are assumed to be known and are denoted by $q_1, q_2, \ldots, q_N$. It is further assumed that only one claim size Z_i is possible for each unit, i.e. no partial claims can occur. For insurance classes where partial claims are possible the method is less convenient, but it can be modified also for that case when no other method is applicable, as will be shown in Section 3.5.3.

The distribution function of a claim arising from the whole portfolio can be found if the risk system is interpreted as an urn experiment. The different risks are visualized as different urns and a selection is made of an urn. The probability that the one selected is the ith is

$$q_i/n,$$

where $n = \Sigma q_i$, the sum being extended over the whole portfolio.

Since $S(Z)$ is the conditional probability that the claim is $\leqslant Z$ the addition and multiplication rules of probability give immediately

$$S(Z) = \frac{1}{n} \sum_{Z_i \leqslant Z} q_i. \tag{3.5.1}$$

Exercise 3.5.1 A company grants insurance for accidental death, the sums payable at death being standardized at £100, £250, or £500. The number of polices in these classes are 5000, 1000, and 2000, respectively. It is known that the rate of death in the two lower classes can be expected to be equal, but that, owing to

---

* The term 'probability of claim' is often used in this connection, but q_i must, in fact, be regarded as a frequency or, what is the same, the expected number of events (which might even be $\geqslant 1$). If the number of claims is distributed in a Poisson form during a certain interval, and the parameter q is very small, the probability of occurrence of at least one event is clearly $p = 1 - e^{-q} \approx q$. In this sense, reference is sometimes made in a rather loose way to the probability of an event, when, in fact, the expected number of events during this interval is meant.

anti-selection, the rate in the £500 class is estimated to be double that in the other classes. What is the S function for this business?

3.5.2 STATISTICAL METHOD

(a) Claim statistics In this method the actual claims of the portfolio in question are collected in a table according to the amounts of the claims, as in Table 3.5.1 which sets out claims arising from a combined experience of Finnish insurance portfolios comprising industrial fire risks.

Table 3.5.1 *Compilation of the claims statistics.*

1	2		3	4
i	$Z \times 10^{-3} £$	n_i	$\Delta S = \dfrac{n_i}{n}$	$S = \sum \Delta S$
1	0.010	283	0.033 953	0.033 953
2	0.016	280	0.037 664	0.071 617
3	0.025	157	0.045 479	0.117 096
4	0.040	464	0.055 413	0.172 509
5	0.063	710	0.063 707	0.236 216
6	0.100	781	0.068 234	0.304 450
7	0.158	530	0.070 466	0.374 915
8	0.251	446	0.070 370	0.445 285
9	0.398	491	0.071 745	0.517 030
10	0.631	673	0.074 009	0.591 039
11	1.000	779	0.075 761	0.666 800
12	1.585	741	0.073 025	0.739 825
13	2.512	520	0.064 899	0.804 724
14	3.981	425	0.052 757	0.857 481
15	6.310	323	0.040 152	0.897 633
16	10.000	179	0.029 698	0.927 331
17	15.849	173	0.021 660	0.948 990
18	25.119	112	0.015 765	0.964 755
19	39.811	94	0.011 310	0.976 065
20	63.096	57	0.008 222	0.984 287
21	100.000	39	0.005 599	0.989 886
22	158.489	22	0.003 767	0.993 653
23	251.189	17	0.002 424	0.996 077
24	398.107	12	0.001 582	0.997 659
25	630 957	5	0.001 022	0.998 680

Table 3.5.1 (*contd.*)

1 i	2 $Z \times 10^{-3}$£	n_i	3 $\Delta S = \dfrac{n_i}{n}$	4 $S = \sum \Delta S$
26	1 000.000	5	0.000 600	0.999 280
27	1 584.890	3	0.000 330	0.999 610
28	2 511.890	1	0.000 179	0.999 789
29	3 981.070	0	0.000 097	0.999 886
30	6 309.570	2	0.000 052	0.999 938
31	10 000.000	0	0.000 028	0.999 967
32	15 848.900	0	0.000 015	0.999 982
33	25 118.900	0	0.000 008	0.999 991
34	39 810.700	0	0.000 005	0.999 995
35	63 095.700	0	0.000 002	0.999 997
36	100 000.000	0	0.000 001	0.999 999
37	158 489.000	0	0.000 001	0.999 999
38	251 189.000	0	0.000 000	1.000 000
39	398 108.000	0	0.000 000	1.000 000
40	630 958.000	0	0.000 000	1.000 000
41	1 000 000.000	0	0.000 000	1.000 000

Monetary unit £1000. $Z_i = 10^{-2.2 + i/5}$. $n = \Sigma n_i = 8324$. n_i = number of claims in class $Z_{i-1} < Z \leqslant Z_i$. Finnish industrial fire insurance. The tail ($i \geqslant 27$) fitted with Pareto d.f. $1 - S(Z) = 7.162\ 88 \times Z^{-1.332585}$. The data were provided by Harri Lonka and Jarmo Jacobsson, Statistical Centre of the Finnish Non-Life Insurers.

(b) Tabular or analytic form A claim size table can be used as a basis for analytical curve fitting, as will be discussed in Section 3.5.4, or it can be used for straightforward numerical calculations. For example the moment integrals, which are frequently needed for applications, can be replaced by a discrete sum as follows

$$a_k = \int_0^\infty Z^k \, dS(Z) \approx \sum_i Z_i^k \, \Delta S_i, \qquad (3.5.2)$$

in which Z_i and ΔS_i are to be taken directly from Table 3.5.1. This method is often convenient and it avoids rounding-off inaccuracies which arise when the empirical distribution is replaced by some analytical curve. In other words, the empirical values as such may describe better than any analytical function the actual but always unknown distribution which is behind the observed data. On the other hand, the statistical data are only a sample from the actual distribution and care is needed to take into account the sampling errors.

(c) Piecewise construction The statistical method provides that the data base of the statistics is sufficiently large that the inaccuracy can be expected to be slight. This rarely holds for the upper tail of the distribution in cases where very large claims are possible. In such cases it may be advisable to divide the range of the relevant values of Z into two or more pieces and apply to each of them the appropriate functions for the environment in question. For example, claim sizes up to some limit Z_0 can be employed in a tabular form and the tail $Z \geqslant Z_0$ approximated by some analytic function which by experience can be expected to give a good fit. In fact this was done in Table 3.5.1 for the large Z-values, for which the shape of the empirical distribution according to Fig. 3.5.1 was already clearly irregular.

(d) Smoothing The empirical data of Table 3.5.1 and Fig. 3.5.1 were mechanically smoothed by replacing each of them by a *moving*

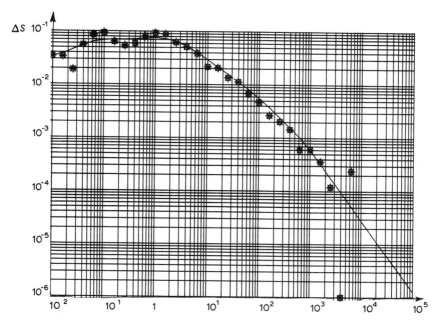

Figure 3.5.1   *Claim size densities of Finnish industrial fire insurance. The data of Table 3.5.1 are plotted on a double logarithmic graph. The points indicate observed data. Unit for Z is £1000.*

average of five values. This kind of smoothing is motivated if the sample errors are noticeable. On the other hand, some seemingly irregular bends in the curve may reflect significant special features in portfolio structure, e.g. clusters of policies of a special type, in which case their 'smoothing away' is not appropriate. A further analysis proved that this was the case in Fig. 3.5.1. Therefore the bends for small Z-values were preserved.

(e) Selection of the class interval is a problem associated with the statistical method. In Table 3.5.1, a geometrical interval is used for the claim amounts, a method found convenient in many cases. A few trials with different class intervals on numerical data will soon show that a rough partitioning is sufficient for many purposes. In fact, as will be shown later, the risk process is not very sensitive for changes of the S function except as regards the tail arising from large claims.

(f) Reinsurance A normal practice is to protect the portfolio against excessive risk fluctuations by ceding the top risks to re-insurers, as will be dealt with in Section 3.6. If only that part of the business which is retained on the insurer's own account is analysed then the estimation and curve fitting problems concerning the tail become insignificant.

(g) Effect of inflation If the claims are collected over a period during which monetary values change, it is necessary to rectify the values by means of a suitably chosen price or other index.

Because the structure of the portfolio and many other circumstances are always changing, even if slowly, the observation period should not be very long. On the other hand, very short observation periods do not include sufficient large claims to be representative. The task of the actuary is to weigh these different aspects and to try and find for each case the most appropriate method of proceeding. The problems arising from large claims can often be dealt with as described in the next section.

3.5.3 PROBLEMS ARISING FROM LARGE CLAIMS

(a) Prolonged observations period In many practical problems, where the top risks are not cut away by reinsurance, the larger

values of Z in $S(Z)$ are of critical importance and the derivation
of the distribution function in the region of these larger values is
difficult to determine with confidence from observed data. Paradoxically the least-known part of S has in these cases the greatest
effect on the numerical results. One possibility is to determine
values of $S(Z)$ for small values of Z (thus based on the greatest
number of claims) from experience extending over a short period
only. Since such experience will, in general, not include many large
claims, a further study of large claims over a longer period is needed.
Thus one year's statistics might suffice for claims say $\leqslant £100\,000$,
whilst for claims $>£100\,000$ data for perhaps 20 years may be
necessary. In this case the higher claims should be adjusted by
weights consistent with the relative amount of business. How far
this method can be used depends on how much time elapses before
the data are so changed in structure that they cannot be regarded
as reliable. The truncated distribution of small claims may be
useful as a control in testing the significance of such a structural
alteration.

(b) Individual evaluation Sometimes satistics relating to the larger
claims are unsatisfactory because of relatively rapid changes in
the risk structure of the portfolio or simply because they are not
available. In such cases the following rough method may be of use,
making use of (3.5.1). The largest risks of the portfolio are dealt
with individually and the net premium for each is determined;
next the expected average extent of damage is estimated for each
policy and the results are tabulated as in Table 3.5.2.

The placing of the estimated frequencies of partial damages in
the different damage classes would be done by an appropriately
experienced claims specialist. The method is clearly quite subjective,

Table 3.5.2   *Individual evaluation.*

Policy no.	Sum insured (£1000)	Risk premiums per thousand	Damage class in £1000		
			100–500	500–1000	1000–2000
001	400	1	0.2		
002	1000	2	0.4	0.3	
003	800	1.5	0.3	0.2	
etc.					

but in the absence of other methods it does provide some basis for further calculation. For life insurance the method is easier to use, because of the absence of partial damages. The method involves a rough idealization, since for example the risk premium is used as a measure of individual risk, whereas in practice the basis of a risk premium involves an equalization over some groups of policies.

If the portfolio is large, so that there are many cases over the limit (in the above example £100 000), suitably selected samples for the various risk sums may be taken and only the largest cases treated individually.

(c) Shadow claims If some information is available relating to large claims it is sometimes possible to introduce one or more hypothetical *shadow claims*, which, having regard to the actual portfolio, can be considered realistic although very seldom occurring. The frequency of the shadow claim can be assumed, for example, to be one claim in 10, 20, 30, or 40 years in the whole portfolio.

(d) Decomposition of the Z-range The approach presented in item 3.5.2(c) can be followed. It is often effective to use a tabular form for $S(Z)$ under some limit $Z \leqslant Z_0$ as in Table 3.5.1 and an analytic form for the tail $Z > Z_0$. This method will be further discussed in Section 3.7, but first the analytic method is treated in the following sections.

3.5.4 ANALYTICAL METHODS

It is often desirable to try and find an explicit analytical representation for a claim curve. This is the case especially if the data base is narrow for the use of the statistical method presented in Section 3.5.2 or if there is good reason to expect that the claim size d.f. is of some particular form. This approach also has the advantage that an analytic S function may be convenient to handle in many calculations; if use can be made of some well-known elementary functions for S, such as exponential, log-normal, Pareto, etc., the known properties of the function can be used to gain some insight into the characteristic features of the claim distribution. In some cases S may be of such a form that the convolutions S^{k*} can be carried out in a closed form; then an explicit expression for the d.f. F of the aggregate claim can sometimes be found, and thus the approximations avoided. Furthermore, an analytical expression for S can, of course, be of considerable value to the actuary in other connections, e.g. tariff calculations, statistical analysis, etc.

On the other hand, it must be accepted that replacing the actual data by an analytical expression always implies smoothing. The goodness of fit of S can be estimated by various well-known methods, but it is often of much greater importance to study the error introduced in the function F. This is a drawback of the analytical method. To ascertain the magnitude of the error caused by this phenomenon, different functions S can be experimented with so that they approximate the available data. In practice these fluctuations and the influence of the smoothing are, however, often ignored and the answer as to how good the results are may remain open. Fortunately, experience shows that F is not very sensitive to changes in S in those cases where the tail is truncated by means of reinsurance, as it normally is in practice.

In the following sections, consideration is given to some frequently used analytical models, some adopted because of their convenience in the calculation of (3.2.3) and some for other reasons.

3.5.5 EXPONENTIAL DISTRIBUTION

(a) Definitions In general, claims distributions show the highest frequency for the small claims, the frequency declining with increasing claim size. Thus the exponential function may provide at least a first approximation for claim size distribution

$$S(Z) = 1 - e^{-cZ} \qquad \text{(for } Z \geqslant 0\text{)}. \qquad (3.5.3)$$

The constant $c\,(>0)$ can be fixed for each application to obtain the best possible fit. This expression has the advantage that an explicit expression for the compound Poisson function F can be found by direct calculation, thanks to the fact that the convolution (3.2.2) can be obtained in closed form (see exercise 3.5.2) for $X > 0$

$$S^{k*}(X) = 1 - e^{-cX}\left[1 + cX + \frac{1}{2!}(cX)^2 + \cdots + \frac{1}{(k-1)!}(cX)^{k-1} \right]$$
$$= S^{(k-1)*}(X) - e^{-cX}(cX)^{k-1}/(k-1)! \qquad (3.5.4)$$

Note that according to (2.9.7) this formula could be written also in the form $S^{k*}(X) = \Gamma(cX, k)$. By programming the claim number probability $p_k(n)$ and S^{k*} in the form of a recursion formula, $F(X)$ can be computed at least in the Poisson and Polya cases (see recursion rule (2.5.2) or (2.9.13)).

(b) Applicability The use of an exponential function as a model for S can clearly only be occasionally useful since this simple function can only be a crude approximation to the truth and is hardly ever applicable if reinsurance cuts off the top risks. Experience has proved that often the exponential $S(Z)$ converges too fast for large Z values.

(c) Exponential polynomials The area of the applicability of the exponential distribution can be extended if S is constructed as a sum of exponentials having different parameters c

$$S(Z) = \sum_{i=1}^{r} p_i(1 - e^{-c_i Z}), \tag{3.5.5}$$

where $\sum p_i = 1$.

Exercise 3.5.2 Verify (3.5.4) and calculate μ_X and σ_X assuming the exponential claim size d.f. (3.5.3). Compute $F(2)$ for $c = 1$, $n = 1$ and $H(q) = \varepsilon(q - 1)$.

3.5.6 GAMMA DISTRIBUTION

(a) The three-parameter gamma function A way to provide more flexibility than that provided by the exponential d.f. is to use the incomplete gamma function (see (2.9.1)) in the form

$$\Gamma(aZ + b, \alpha) = \frac{1}{\Gamma(\alpha)} \int_0^{aZ + b} e^{-u} u^{\alpha - 1} \, du \qquad (Z \geqslant 0, aZ + b \geqslant 0), \tag{3.5.6}$$

as an estimate for the claim size d.f. S. There are three parameters available for fitting the curve according to the actual d.f. which can be determined so that the distribution will have the given mean (μ), standard deviation (σ) and skewness (γ). First it is useful to standardize the variable Z

$$z = (Z - \mu)/\sigma, \tag{3.5.7}$$

to have mean 0 and standard deviation 1. This transformation does
not change the skewness, as may easily be verified. Hence z also
has skewness γ. The coefficients a, b and α can then be determined
from the conditions that the function (3.5.6) should have the same
characteristics (exercise 3.5.3)

$$\bar{S}(z) = S(Z) = \Gamma(\alpha + z\sqrt{\alpha}, \alpha) \qquad (z \geqslant -\sqrt{\alpha})$$

$$= \frac{1}{\Gamma(\alpha)} \int_0^{\alpha + z\sqrt{\alpha}} e^{-u} u^{\alpha-1}\, du, \tag{3.5.8}$$

where

$$\alpha = 4/\gamma^2. \tag{3.5.9}$$

(b) For numerical evaluation of the gamma function the easily
programmable expansion

$$S(Z) = \frac{w^\alpha}{e^w \Gamma(\alpha+1)}\left[1 + \frac{w}{\alpha+1} + \frac{w}{\alpha+1}\cdot\frac{w}{\alpha+2} + \cdots\right], \tag{3.5.10}$$

is convenient, where

$$w = \alpha + z\sqrt{\alpha}. \tag{3.5.11}$$

A good approximation for the complete gamma function is obtained
from the formula

$$\Gamma(\alpha) = 1 + b_1(\alpha - 1) + b_2(\alpha - 1)^2 + \cdots + b_8(\alpha - 1)^8, \tag{3.5.12}$$

where

$$
\begin{array}{ll}
b_1 = -0.577\ 191\ 652 & b_5 = -0.756\ 704\ 078 \\
b_2 = 0.988\ 205\ 891 & b_6 = 0.482\ 199\ 394 \\
b_3 = -0.897\ 056\ 937 & b_7 = -0.193\ 527\ 818 \\
b_4 = 0.918\ 206\ 857 & b_8 = 0.035\ 868\ 343.
\end{array}
$$

This formula requires that the parameter α is $1 \leqslant \alpha \leqslant 2$. This can be
achieved by making use of the recursive formula

$$\Gamma(\alpha) = (\alpha - 1)\Gamma(\alpha - 1). \tag{3.5.13}$$

The formulae given above are useful if the skewness is not too
small. Troubles arise if this condition is not valid, because α and w
grow to such an extent that the formulae are no longer easily workable and a special technique is needed. For example, the following

Wilson–Hilferty formula (Johnson and Kotz, 1970; Section 17.5)

$$S(Z) \approx N[c_1 + c_2 \times (z + c_3)^{1/3}], \qquad (3.5.14)$$

where

$$c_1 = \gamma/6 - 6/\gamma; c_2 = 3 \times (2/\gamma)^{2/3}; c_3 = 2/\gamma,$$

is applicable particularly when α is large or (which is the same) when the skewness γ is small, i.e. precisely in the area where the expansion (3.5.10) becomes impractical. Another approach is to integrate (3.5.6) numerically (see exercise 3.5.4).

Examples of gamma densities are plotted in Fig. 3.5.2. A handicap of the gamma d.f. is that when it is used for approximation of rather skew compound Poisson distributions it is not defined (or $\bar{S}(z) = 0$) for the values

$$z < -2/\gamma. \qquad (3.5.15)$$

This may seriously worsen the fit for the short tail of the distribution.

It will be seen in Section 3.12 that the gamma d.f. is useful also for approximation of the d.f. of the *aggregate* claims, i.e. instead of S the 'target' function F itself.

Exercise 3.5.3 Prove (3.5.8) (Hint: note (2.9.17)).

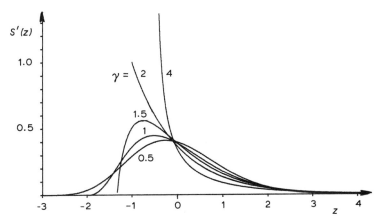

Figure 3.5.2 *Examples of gamma densities having mean* $= 0$, *standard deviation* $= 1$ *and varying skewness* γ.

Exercise 3.5.4 Assuming α to be large, integrate (3.5.6) by making use of the Simpson formula. (Hint: remove the factor $e^{-\alpha} \alpha^{\alpha - 1}$ from the integral.)

3.5.7 LOGARITHMIC-NORMAL DISTRIBUTION

(a) Definitions A frequently used claim size distribution is the *logarithmic-normal* or briefly *log-normal*. It is derived by introducing a variable $Z > a \geqslant 0$ so that

$$Y = \ln(Z - a), \tag{3.5.16}$$

is normally distributed with parameters μ and σ. Then the density of the distribution is (see exercise 3.5.5)

$$S'(Z) = \frac{1}{\sigma(Z - a)\sqrt{(2\pi)}} \exp\left[-\frac{1}{2\sigma^2}(\ln(Z - a) - \mu)^2 \right] \tag{3.5.17}$$

The parameters a, μ and σ are determined to fit the lowest moments with those of the observed or assumed distribution (Cramer 1945, p. 258). Note that μ and σ are the mean and variance of Y, not of Z. The parameter μ may well be negative. For the solution, the real root of the following equation is first determined

$$\eta^3 + 3\eta - \gamma = 0. \tag{3.5.18}$$

Then (see exercise 3.5.6)

$$\begin{aligned} a &= a_1 - \frac{1}{\eta}\sqrt{m_2} \\ \sigma^2 &= \ln(1 + \eta^2) \\ \mu &= \ln(a_1 - a) - \tfrac{1}{2}\sigma^2, \end{aligned} \tag{3.5.19}$$

where a_1, m_2 and γ are respectively the mean, variance and the skewness of the claim size distribution to be approximated. It is assumed that they are known, e.g. they are estimated from an actual claims statistics.

(b) The shapes of the log-normal density curves can be seen in Fig. 3.5.3. In order to demonstrate the scale selection, the same functions are plotted both in linear and double logarithmic scales.

(c) Two-parameter version The derivation in item (a) relates to the three-parameter form of the log-normal d.f. as compared with

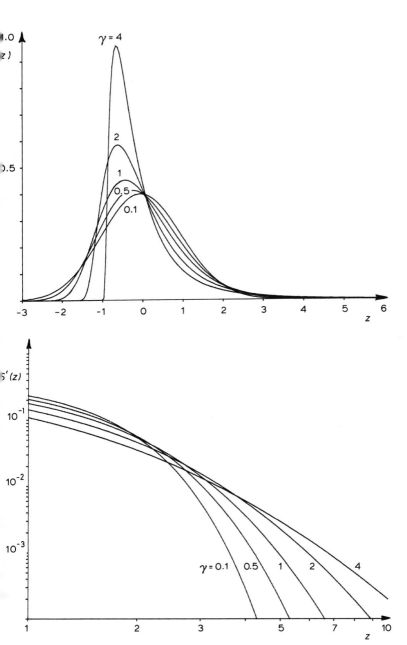

Figure 3.5.3   *A family of log-normal densities having the joint moments* $a_1 = 0$ *and* $m_2 = 1$ *but varying skewness* γ. *The whole curve is plotted on a linear scale (upper figure) and the tail on a double logarithmic scale (lower figure).*

the more common two-parameter form in which the parameter a is equal to zero. The difference between the two forms is solely a shifting of the curve along the z-axis; this is often useful for representing data where the proportion of small claims recorded has been reduced by the operation of policy conditions, such as the imposition of small excesses or no-claim discount schemes. As compared with the analytic formulae previously mentioned, the availability of three parameters provides scope for an improved fit, at least in the early and middle parts of the distribution. Further information can be found in Benckert (1962).

Exercise 3.5.5 Prove that the density of the log-normal distribution is given by (3.5.17).

**Exercise* 3.5.6 (i) The m.g.f. of a normally distributed variable $N(\mu, \sigma^2)$ is

$$M(s) = e^{\mu s}\, e^{\frac{1}{2}s^2\sigma^2}$$

Make use of this function and calculate the moments a_k of the log-normally distributed variable $\mathbf{Z}$ in the case $a = 0$.

(ii) Show that if $\mathbf{Z}$ is log-normally distributed with parameters a, μ, γ, then

$$a_1 = E(\mathbf{Z}) = e^{\mu} e^{\frac{1}{2}\sigma^2} + a$$
$$m_2 = \mathrm{var}(\mathbf{Z}) = e^{2\mu} e^{\sigma^2}(e^{\sigma^2} - 1)$$
$$\gamma = \gamma_{\mathbf{Z}} = (e^{\sigma^2} + 2)\sqrt{(e^{\sigma^2} - 1)}.$$

(iii) Prove that if S is a log-normal distribution with mean a_1, variance m_2 and skewness $\gamma\ (> 0)$, then the parameters a, μ and σ have the expressions as shown in (3.5.19).

3.5.8   THE PARETO DISTRIBUTION

(a) **Definition** Many of the actual distributions of claims that arise in insurance applications can be reasonably well approximated by the *Pareto distribution*

$$S(Z) = 1 - \left(\frac{Z}{Z_0}\right)^{-\alpha} \qquad (Z_0 \leqslant Z; \alpha > 1). \qquad (3.5.20)$$

It should be noted that the moments a_j of this d.f. only exist if

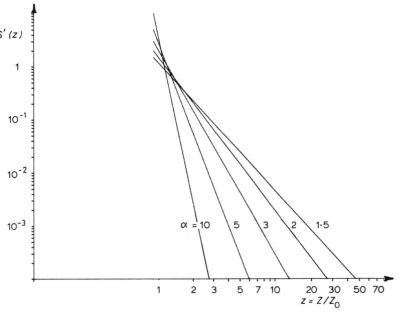

Figure 3.5.4 *A family of Pareto densities* $S'(Z) = \alpha Z_0^{\alpha}/Z^{\alpha+1}$ *(double logarithmic scale).*

$j < \alpha$ (see exercise 3.5.7). In fact the Pareto formula represents 'dangerous' distributions, where very large claims are possible.

Unfortunately, the mathematical properties of the Pareto distribution do not lead to simple expressions for convolutions, and therefore numerical integration methods have to be used.

Figure 3.5.4 shows a family of Pareto densities.

(b) Large claims Experience has shown that the Pareto distribution is often appropriate for representing the tail of distributions where large claims may occur. As was demonstrated in Section 3.5.2, the Pareto d.f. can be combined with other types of distributions; that is, $S(Z)$ can be piecewise composed of several functions, each of them being valid in disjoint intervals of the Z-axis.

(c) Danger index The parameter α can be used as an *index* of the distribution, or at least of its tail. If $\alpha < 2$ it indicates a 'very dangerous' distribution. Note that only moments of order $< \alpha$ exist (exercise 3.5.7). For example, the first and second moments exist for $\alpha > 2$ only.

Seal (1980) has collected empirical α values.

(d) Modifications If there is evidence that the occurrence of very large claims is excluded, then the Pareto d.f. is often *censored* by letting $S(Z)$ be equal to 1 from some large enough value Z_1 upwards, and (3.5.20) is replaced by

$$S_c(Z) = S(Z)/S(Z_1) \qquad \text{for } Z \leqslant Z_1. \tag{3.5.21}$$

Another modification is *truncation*, i.e. moving the 'probability mass' of the interval $Z_1 \leqslant Z$ into Z_1

$$S_{tr}(Z) = \begin{cases} 1 & \text{for } Z \geqslant Z_1 \\ S(Z) & \text{for } Z < Z_1 \end{cases}. \tag{3.5.22}$$

This modification comes up, for instance, when the risk tops are cut off by an excess of loss reinsurance treaty, as will be considered in Section 3.6.2.

Exercise 3.5.7 Calculate the moment a_j for the Pareto d.f.

3.5.9 THE TWO-PARAMETRIC PARETO AND THE QUASI-LOG-NORMAL DISTRIBUTIONS

(a) Comparisons Figure 3.5.5 demonstrates the behaviour of the exponential, log-normal and Pareto densities for large Z values. The curves are fitted to go through a point P and to have the same value of the derivatives at this point. The exponential curve converges fastest and the Pareto slowest. In other words, when the upper tail is considered, the Pareto distribution is the 'most cautious'. The log-normal distribution underestimates the risk of excessive claims as compared with the Pareto distribution and the exponential curve gives practically vanishing probabilities for them. These features, illustrated by Fig. 3.5.5, are valid in general.

(b) Experience has shown that the behaviour of the tail in practice is often between that of the Pareto and log-normal types. Therefore there is an obvious need to find distribution functions which have greater flexibility. Two such distributions are presented in this section and others will be considered in subsequent sections.

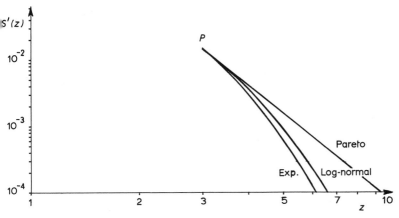

Figure 3.5.5 *Comparison of the exponential, log-normal and Pareto densities (double logarithmic scale).*

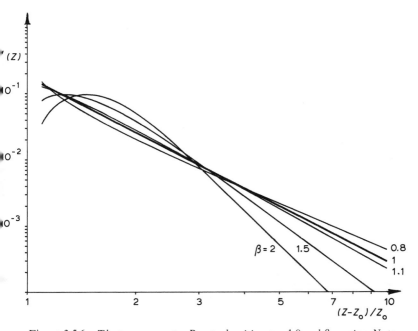

Figure 3.5.6 *The two-parameter Pareto densities, $\alpha = 1.8$ and β varying. Note that for $\beta = 1$ the one-parameter Pareto is obtained (double logarithmic scale).*

(c) The two-parameter Pareto d.f. can be defined as follows

$$S(Z) = 1 - b\left[1 + \left(\frac{Z - Z_0}{Z_0}\right)^{\beta}\right]^{-\alpha} \qquad (Z \geqslant Z_0), \qquad (3.5.23)$$

where α and β are positive parameters, Z_0 is the limit for the tail for which the formula is fitted, and b indicates the weight of the probability mass, which is situated in the tail area $Z \geqslant Z_0$, i.e. $b = 1 - S(Z_0)$.

Shapes of the distribution are shown in Fig. 3.5.6 for selected parameter values. As can be seen, the desired flow between the Pareto case ($\beta = 1$) and the log-normal type can be achieved by varying the parameter β (> 1). Some actuaries, e.g. Gary Patric (Prudential, New Jersey, unpublished letter) have reported successful results concerning the fit of (3.5.23) to actual distributions.

(d) The quasi-log-normal d.f. is another approach to obtaining curves that vary between the extreme cases presented in Fig. 3.5.5.

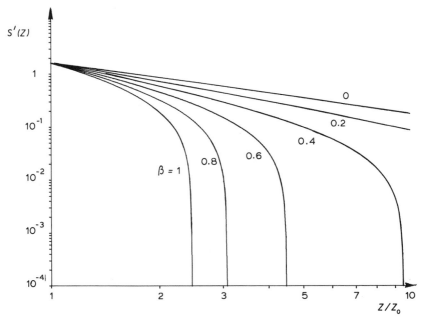

Figure 3.5.7 *Quasi-log-normal densities,* $\alpha = 1.8$ *and* β *varying (double logarithmic scale).*

It is defined by formula

$$S(Z) = 1 - b\left(\frac{Z}{Z_0}\right)^{-\alpha - \beta \ln(Z/Z_0)}, \qquad (3.5.24)$$

where the meaning of the parameters is in principle the same as in (3.5.23).

Examples of the distributions are plotted in Fig. 3.5.7. For $\beta = 0$ the Pareto case is obtained. Analysis of this d.f. can be found in Shpilberg (1977). The name 'quasi-log-normal' reflects the fact that the curves closely approximate the log-normal ones for positive β values (Dumouchel and Olsten, 1974).

3.5.10 THE FAMILY OF BENKTANDER DISTRIBUTIONS

(a) **The idea** of finding more flexibility for curve fitting can be extended. For this purpose Benktander (1970), following the earlier work of Benktander and Segerdahl (1960), suggested a family of distributions which contains as special members both the Pareto and exponential and also approximately the log-normal distributions. By suitable adjustment of parameters a better fit with actual data can be obtained; general experience of the type of the portfolio in question and the crucial choice of the distribution type, as mentioned above, are not so significant and may be replaced by parameter estimation.

The analysis is again focused on the tail $Z \geqslant Z_0$ of claim size distribution above some suitably chosen limit Z_0. For values $Z < Z_0$ some other expression or directly observed frequencies in tabular form can be used.

(b) **Extinction rate** Suppose that the claim size d.f. $S(Z)$ is known or assumed for $Z \geqslant Z_0$ and that the necessary integrals and derivatives exist; an auxiliary function $m(Z)$ will be introduced as follows

$$\begin{aligned} m(Z) &= E\{\mathbf{Z} - Z \mid \mathbf{Z} \geqslant Z\} \\ &= \frac{1}{1 - S(Z)} \int_Z^\infty (V - Z) \, dS(V) \qquad (3.5.25) \\ &= \frac{1}{1 - S(Z)} \int_Z^\infty (1 - S(V)) \, dV. \end{aligned}$$

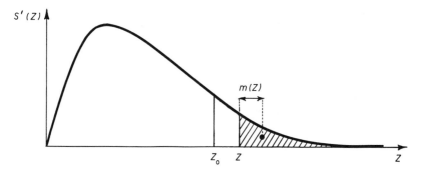

Figure 3.5.8   *The function m(Z).*

The function $m(Z)$ can be interpreted as the mean value of the claims excesses over Z or as the distance of the centre of gravity of the shaded area in Fig. 3.5.8 from the Z vertical. The latter form is obtained from the former by partial integration.

If (3.5.25) is differentiated, a differential equation

$$\frac{S'(Z)}{1 - S(Z)} = \frac{1 + m'(Z)}{m(Z)} \equiv r(Z), \qquad (3.5.26)$$

is obtained which determines the interdependence of the auxiliary function $m(Z)$ and the claim size distribution $S(Z)$.

The function $r(Z)$ is a straightforward analogy to the rate of mortality applied in life insurance mathematics. It gives the rate at which the risk of large claims is decreasing when Z grows. Benktander calls it the 'mortality of claims' and Shpilberg (1977) describes it as a 'failure rate' and refers to the terms 'hazard rate', 'force of mortality' and 'intensity function' found in the literature of reliability theory. This kind of concept has already been dealt with by Witney (1909). In this connection it could be called the *'extinction rate'*. Shpilberg has shown that this function has a direct connection with the physical progress of fire in fire insurance. Most fires are stopped at the very beginning and the amount of the claim remains slight. However, if the early extinction fails, then the chance of stopping the fire soon decreases, which in the case of large risk units results in large claims and in long tails of the functions $r(Z)$ and $S'(Z)$.

If the function S is given, then the extinction rate r is determined according to (3.5.26). The reverse relation also holds. If $r(Z)$ is given, the claim size d.f. is obtained by solving this differential equation

$$1 - S(Z) = [1 - S(Z_0)] \exp\left[- \int_{Z_0}^{Z} r(V)\, dV \right], \qquad (3.5.27)$$

which expresses S in terms of r (or m).

(c) Examples It is easily verified that for the exponential d.f. (3.5.3)

$$m(Z) = 1/c, \qquad (3.5.28)$$

and for the Pareto d.f. (3.5.20)

$$m(Z) = Z/(\alpha - 1) \qquad (3.5.29)$$

Benktander and Segerdahl have investigated a number of actual distributions containing large claims. Their results (see Benktander and Segerdahl, 1960) have the same general behaviour as that depicted in Fig. 3.5.9.

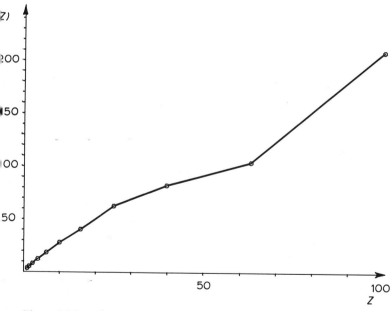

Figure 3.5.9 *The function m calculated for the unsmoothed claims frequencies given in Fig. 3.5.1. Unit is £1 000 000.*

(d) The Benktander family Observations on $m(Z)$, due to Benktander and Segerdahl (1960) and Benktander (1970), suggested an analytic formula for $m(Z)$, either

$$m(Z) = \frac{Z}{a + 2b \ln Z} \qquad a > 0, b > 0 \text{ (Type I).} \qquad (3.5.30a)$$

or

$$m(Z) = \frac{Z^{1-b}}{a} \qquad 0 \leqslant b \leqslant 1 \text{ (Type II)} \qquad (3.5.30b)$$

where

$$Z \geqslant Z_0 \qquad (3.5.31)$$

and a and b are parameters which can be chosen within the limits given so that the best possible fit with actual experience can be achieved. As is seen immediately, the exponential and Pareto cases are members of these function families. Type I gives a smaller deviation from the Pareto straight line than type II.

Substituting the functions (3.5.30) into (3.5.27), the following claim size distributions are obtained

$$1 - S_{\mathrm{I}}(Z) = cZ^{-a-1} Z^{-b \ln Z}(a + 2b \ln Z), \qquad (3.5.32a)$$

and

$$1 - S_{\mathrm{II}}(Z) = ca Z^{-(1-b)} \exp(-aZ^b/b) \qquad (3.5.32b)$$

The constant c is chosen so that continuous linking with the function chosen for $Z < Z_0$ can be achieved.

Examples of the distribution of type I are given in Fig. 3.5.10. It is appropriate to use Z_0 as a unit on the Z-axis.

Benktander (1970) has proved that the log-normal distribution, which falls (depending, of course, on the parameter choice) between the exponential and Pareto extreme cases, can be quite closely approximated by the functions (3.5.32). As is seen from Fig. 3.5.10, the Pareto distribution ($b = 0$) is the 'most dangerous' one in that it gives the greatest probability of occurrence for very large claims. Benktander has also derived this conclusion analytically.

Exercise 3.5.8 Prove (3.5.28) and (3.5.29).

Exercise 3.5.9 Prove (3.5.32a) and (3.5.32b).

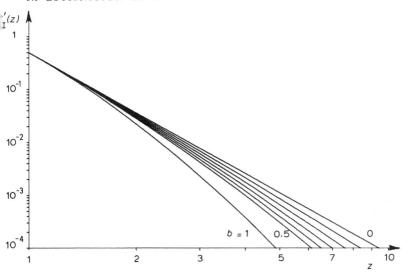

Figure 3.5.10 *A bunch of Benktander type I densities;* $a = 1.8$, $c = 0.1$ *and* $b = 0, 0.1, 0.2, 0.3, 0.4, 0.5$ *and* 1; $Z_0 = 1$.

**3.5.11 OTHER TYPES OF DISTRIBUTION

(a) General aspects In addition to the distributions dealt with in the previous sections, there are also various other forms of continuous functions used to describe claim amount distributions. In general they have proved inconvenient both in calculations and in analytical studies. However with the general availability of microcomputers the calculations may no longer be a major consideration. Furthermore the facility of recursive calculation raises the question of using *discrete distributions* and is dealt with in Section 3.8.

(b) The Pearson system is one of the major families of distribution which has proved applicable to a variety of problems. It has been found that many of the distributions are, in practice, close to type VI i.e.

$$S'(Z) = kZ^{q_1}(Z - C)^{q_2} \tag{3.5.33}$$

and lie between type V and type III. This region also includes the Pareto and log-normal distributions, although these are not members of the Pearson system. For further details consult, for example, Kendall and Stuart (1977), Section 6.2, or Johnson and Kotz (1970), Section 12.4.1.

(c) The Weibull d.f. is also often a suitable alternative and it may be written (see Johnson and Kotz, Vol. 2, 1970, Chapter 20) as

$$S(Z) = 1 - \exp\{ - [(Z - Z_0)/a]^b \} . \qquad (3.5.34)$$

(d) The inverse normal for which the density function is (see Johnson and Kotz, 1970, Chapter 15)

$$S'(Z) = (\lambda/2\pi Z^3)^{\frac{1}{2}} \exp[- \lambda(Z - \mu)^2/2\mu^2 Z], \qquad (3.5.35)$$

is also sometimes suggested for claims size d.f. It is, in fact, a modified Bessel function.

(e) Distributions related to the extreme values can still be referred to, type I being (see Johnson & Kotz 1970, Chapter 21)

$$S(Z) = \exp(- \alpha e^{-\beta Z}). \qquad (3.5.36)$$

3.6 The dependence of the S function on reinsurance

3.6.1 GENERAL ASPECTS

(a) Total and retained claim amounts It should be noted that if the problem concerns the net retained liability, the amount Z of the claim is, of course, only that part of the total claim Z_{tot} which is retained, i.e. the total claim reduced by the share Z_{re} taken by the reinsurer

$$Z = Z_{tot} - Z_{re}. \qquad (3.6.1)$$

In this formula the reinsurance arrangement is such that each claim is separately divided between cedent and reinsurer, which is the case in quota share, surplus or excess of loss reinsurance but not in stop loss reinsurance, these types being treated in subsequent sections.

If necessary the d.f. of the retained claim size Z is distinguished from the global d.f. S of Z_{tot}, denoting it, for example, by S_M if the reinsurance treaty is of such a type that it contains a retention limit

M, which is then a freely disposable parameter or variable of the system concerned.

(b) Decomposition approach In practice different net retentions are often used for different classes and for different types of risk. A distribution function S_M can then be constructed for each of these groups, and a joint distribution function for the whole portfolio – perhaps also having several steps corresponding to different retentions – is obtained as will be shown in Section 3.7.

3.6.2 EXCESS OF LOSS REINSURANCE

According to the excess of loss treaty the reinsurer pays that part of each claim $\mathbf{Z}_{tot}$ which exceeds an agreed limit M, and hence the cedent's share is $\mathbf{Z} = \min(\mathbf{Z}_{tot}, M)$. Then the d.f. S_M of the amount of one claim so far as the cedent is concerned can be expressed in terms of d.f. S of the total claim $\mathbf{Z}_{tot}$ as follows

$$S_M(Z) = \begin{cases} S(Z) & \text{for } Z < M \\ 1 & \text{for } Z \geqslant M. \end{cases} \tag{3.6.2}$$

From (3.3.1) the moments of S_M are given by

$$a_h = a_h(M) = \int_0^M Z^h \, dS(Z) + M^h(1 - S(M)). \tag{3.6.3}$$

It is convenient in practice to calculate the lowest moments (3.6.3) and the related indexes r_2 and r_3 (see (3.3.8)) in a tabular form, because they are frequently needed for various applications. Table 3.6.1 gives an example.

3.6.3 QUOTA SHARE REINSURANCE

In *quota share* reinsurance any claim, irrespective of its size, is divided between the cedent and reinsurer in one and same, prefixed ratio, 'quota', r

$$\mathbf{Z} = r\mathbf{Z}_{tot} \qquad (0 < r < 1). \tag{3.6.4}$$

Hence

$$S_r(Z) = S(Z/r). \tag{3.6.5}$$

Table 3.6.1 *Moments of the claim size d.f. on the cedent's net retention. Excess of loss treaty. The global S(Z) is the same as in Table 3.5.1. The moment $a_i(M)$ is according to (3.6.3).*

1 i	2 Z or M	3 $\Delta S(Z)$	4 $S(Z)$	5 $a_1(M)$	6 $a_2(M)$	7 $a_3(M)$	8 $r_2(M)$	9 $r_3(M)$
1	1.000E − 02	0.033 953	0.033 953	1.000E − 02	1.000E − 04	1.000E − 06	1.000E + 00	1.000E + 00
2	1.585E − 02	0.037 664	0.071 617	1.565E − 02	2.461E − 04	3.880E − 06	1.005E + 00	1.012E + 00
3	2.512E − 02	0.045 479	0.117 096	2.426E − 02	5.986E − 04	1.490E − 05	1.017E + 00	1.044E + 00
4	3.981E − 02	0.055 413	0.172 509	3.723E − 02	1.441E − 03	5.661E − 05	1.040E + 00	1.097E + 00
5	6.310E − 02	0.063 707	0.236 216	5.650E − 02	3.424E − 03	2.123E − 04	1.073E + 00	1.177E + 00
6	1.000E − 01	0.068 234	0.304 450	8.468E − 02	8.021E − 03	7.842E − 04	1.118E + 00	1.291E + 00
7	1.585E − 01	0.070 466	0.374 915	1.254E − 01	1.854E − 02	2.858E − 03	1.179E + 00	1.450E + 00
8	2.512E − 01	0.070 370	0.445 285	1.833E − 01	4.228E − 02	1.028E − 02	1.258E + 00	1.668E + 00
9	3.981E − 01	0.071 745	0.517 030	2.648E − 01	9.519E − 02	3.648E − 02	1.357E + 00	1.965E + 00
10	6.310E − 01	0.074 009	0.591 039	3.773E − 01	2.109E − 01	1.273E − 01	1.482E + 00	2.371E + 00
11	1.000E + 00	0.075 761	0.666 800	5.282E − 01	4.571E − 01	4.336E − 01	1.638E + 00	2.942E + 00
12	1.585E + 00	0.073 025	0.739 825	7.231E − 01	9.608E − 01	1.427E + 00	1.838E + 00	3.774E + 00
13	2.512E + 00	0.064 899	0.804 724	9.643E − 01	1.949E + 00	4.515E + 00	2.096E + 00	5.035E + 00
14	3.981E + 00	0.052 757	0.857 481	1.251E + 00	3.812E + 00	1.374E + 01	2.435E + 00	7.016E + 00
15	6.310E + 00	0.040 152	0.897 633	1.583E + 00	7.227E + 00	4.055E + 01	2.884E + 00	1.022E + 01
16	1.000E + 01	0.029 698	0.927 331	1.961E + 00	1.339E + 01	1.172E + 02	3.482E + 00	1.555E + 01
17	1.585E + 01	0.021 660	0.948 990	2.386E + 00	2.437E + 01	3.338E + 02	4.282E + 00	2.458E + 01
18	2.512E + 01	0.015 765	0.964 755	2.859E + 00	4.375E + 01	9.392E + 02	5.353E + 00	4.020E + 01
19	3.981E + 01	0.011 310	0.976 065	3.377E + 00	7.737E + 01	2.604E + 03	6.786E + 00	6.766E + 01
20	6.310E + 01	0.008 222	0.984 287	3.934E + 00	1.347E + 02	7.106E + 03	8.706E + 00	1.167E + 02

21	1.000E + 02	0.005 599	0.989 886	4.514E + 00	2.293E + 02	1.887E + 04	1.125E + 01	2.052E + 02
22	1.585E + 02	0.003 767	0.993 653	5.105E + 00	3.822E + 02	4.902E + 04	1.466E + 01	3.684E + 02
23	2.512E + 02	0.002 424	0.996 077	5.694E + 00	6.232E + 02	1.243E + 05	1.923E + 01	6.737E + 02
24	3.981E + 02	0.001 582	0.997 659	6.270E + 00	9.975E + 02	3.097E + 05	2.537E + 01	1.256E + 03
25	6.310E + 02	0.001 022	0.998 680	6.815E + 00	1.559E + 03	7.501E + 05	3.356E + 01	2.370E + 03
26	1.000E + 03	0.000 600	0.999 280	7.302E + 00	2.353E + 03	1.738E + 06	4.413E + 01	4.465E + 03
27	1.585E + 03	0.000 330	0.999 610	7.723E + 00	3.441E + 03	3.884E + 06	5.769E + 01	8.432E + 03
28	2.512E + 03	0.000 179	0.999 789	8.085E + 00	4.921E + 03	8.509E + 06	7.529E + 01	1.610E + 04
29	3.981E + 03	0.000 097	0.999 886	8.394E + 00	6.933E + 03	1.847E + 07	9.838E + 01	3.123E + 04
30	6.310E + 03	0.000 052	0.999 938	8.660E + 00	9.666E + 03	3.993E + 07	1.289E + 02	6.148E + 04
31	1.000E + 04	0.000 028	0.999 967	8.888E + 00	1.338E + 04	8.613E + 07	1.694E + 02	1.227E + 05
32	1.585E + 04	0.000 015	0.999 982	9.083E + 00	1.842E + 04	1.855E + 08	2.233E + 02	2.475E + 05
33	2.512E + 04	0.000 008	0.999 991	9.249E + 00	2.523E + 04	3.984E + 08	2.949E + 02	5.035E + 05
34	3.981E + 04	0.000 005	0.999 995	9.391E + 00	3.444E + 04	8.546E + 08	3.906E + 02	1.032E + 06
35	6.310E + 04	0.000 002	0.999 997	9.510E + 00	4.672E + 04	1.819E + 09	5.166E + 02	2.115E + 06
36	1.000E + 05	0.000 001	0.999 999	9.609E + 00	6.287E + 04	3.827E + 09	6.809E + 02	4.314E + 06
37	1.585E + 05	0.000 001	0.999 999	9.689E + 00	8.359E + 04	7.914E + 09	8.904E + 02	8.700E + 06
38	2.512E + 05	0.000 000	1.000 000	9.750E + 00	1.085E + 05	1.570E + 10	1.141E + 03	1.693E + 07
39	3.981E + 05	0.000 000	1.000 000	9.794E + 00	1.369E + 05	2.978E + 10	1.427E + 03	3.170E + 07
40	6.310E + 05	0.000 000	1.000 000	9.808E + 00	1.512E + 05	4.099E + 10	1.572E + 03	4.345E + 07
41	1.000E + 06	0.000 000	1.000 000	9.808E + 00	1.512E + 05	4.099E + 10	1.572E + 03	4.345E + 07

Monetary unit is £1000. Notations: $xE \pm n = x \times 10^{\pm n}$ $r_2 = a_2/a_1^2$; $r_3 = a_3/a_1^3$.

Exercise 3.6.1. An insurer having the distribution function S for the total size of claims, has a combination of two reinsurance treaties in force: (i) a quota share treaty, under which the reinsurer pays a proportion r of each claim, and (ii) an excess of loss treaty covering the retained business with a maximum net retention M. What is the distribution function of the size of one claim for the insurer's net retention?

3.6.4 SURPLUS REINSURANCE

(a) Definition The surplus treaty is applicable to the kind of insurance class where the sum insured, denoted by Q, is defined for each risk unit (policy or policies related to a property or other insured object as in fire insurance for example). The original idea behind this type of treaty was to divide not just the claims (as in excess of loss treaty) but the whole policy between the cedent and the reinsurer. More precisely if a claim of size $\mathbf{Z}_{\text{tot}}$ occurs and if the insured sum of the corresponding risk unit is $\mathbf{Q}$, then the cedent retains the whole claim $\mathbf{Z}_{\text{tot}}$ in the case where $\mathbf{Q}$ does not exceed a fixed limit M. If this is not the case, then the retained amount is proportional to the ratio $M/\mathbf{Q}$. To summarize, the cedent's share is

$$\mathbf{Z} = \frac{M}{\mathbf{Q}}\mathbf{Z}_{\text{tot}} \qquad (\text{for } \mathbf{Q} > M)$$

$$= \mathbf{Z}_{\text{tot}} \qquad (\text{for } \mathbf{Q} \leqslant M). \qquad (3.6.6)$$

Note that where the total loss $\mathbf{Z}_{\text{tot}} = \mathbf{Q}$ the outcome is the same as in excess of loss treaty, i.e. $\mathbf{Z} = M$ or $= \mathbf{Z}_{\text{tot}}$ if $\mathbf{Q} \leqslant M$. In the case of a partial loss, i.e. when $\mathbf{Z}_{\text{tot}} < \mathbf{Q}$, the cedent's share is proportional to the degree of loss $\mathbf{Z}_{\text{tot}}/\mathbf{Q}$. Hence for risk units having $Q > M$ the reinsurer participates in small claims as well, contrary to the excess of loss arrangement.

(b) The d.f. $S_M(Z)$ Now the cedent's share $\mathbf{Z}$ is determined by $\mathbf{Z}_{\text{tot}}$ and $\mathbf{Q}$ which are both random. In other words, the cedent's share $\mathbf{Z}$ of a claim depends on the distribution of the random vector $(\mathbf{Z}_{\text{tot}}, \mathbf{Q})$. An expression for S_M is derived on this basis in Section 3.6.5.

In practice this distribution can be more conveniently constructed directly from claims statistics. To this end the sum Q must be known in addition to the total claim size Z_{tot} for each claim. A number, N_Z, relating to the claims which fulfil conditions (3.6.6) must then be determined; thus all the claims for which $Q \leqslant M$ and $Z_{tot} \leqslant Z$ must be accounted for, followed by those for which $Q > M$ and $Z_{tot} \leqslant ZQ/M$. If the total number of claims in the statistics in question is N, then (see Fig. 3.6.1)

$$S_M(Z) = N_Z/N. \tag{3.6.7}$$

The claim size d.f. is a function of two variables M and Z. It can be tabulated in a two-dimensional table with columns for selected M values. Each column corresponds to column 4 in Table 3.5.1. The moments for each M are obtained from the appropriate column

$$a_h(M) = \int_0^\infty Z^h \, dS_M(Z) \approx \sum_{i=1}^{i_m} Z_i^h \cdot (S_M(i) - S_M(i-1)), \tag{3.6.8}$$

where i_m is the highest value of the row index taken into the table (see Table 3.5.1 where $i_m = 41$).

(c) **Modifications** The presentation in item (b) was simplified so that a single retention limit M was assumed to be applied for the whole portfolio or for that section of the portfolio under consideration. Practice is more complicated, however, and modifications to this rule are needed.

In fire insurance it is usual to evaluate a so-called estimated maximum loss (EML) for each risk unit. This sum Q_{EML} may be less than the insured value Q of the property. This is the case if the risk unit is large, or if it is of a type such that it is highly improbable that it will be completely lost in one fire. Then Q_{EML} is the sum which is estimated to be the loss in the worst case. The idea of rule (3.6.6) was to adjust the net retention so that the retained claim Z will be within the range $0 < Z \leqslant M$. This can now be achieved by applying retention $M' = MQ/Q_{EML}$. Substituting in (3.6.6) a modified rule is obtained (for $Q_{EML} > M$)

$$Z = \frac{M'}{Q} Z_{tot} = \frac{M}{Q_{EML}} Z_{tot}. \tag{3.6.9}$$

Hence, the outcome is the same as if the original formula (3.6.6) were applied replacing Q by Q_{EML}. This rule can be taken as guidance for construction of S_M. It ensures that the EML sums Q_{EML} are recorded properly in the policy files.

Furthermore, especially in facultative treaties, the cedent can, on the basis of a case by case adjustment, choose the retention M separately for each risk unit. For example, the retentions may be larger than the average level for risks having the best profitability and vice versa (see the case of several maxima, Section 4.6). It is difficult to give a rule for the construction of the S function which would be applicable in all environments. It will depend on the practice and working conditions of each insurer. An approach could be to divide the risk units into subgroups according to the applied retention M, and then first to derive the S function for each subgroup and second to apply the composition technique which will be presented in Section 3.7. The work need not be overwhelmingly cumbersome if the files, which anyway are necessary for normal services and reinsurance practice, are planned in a way that also allows access to the data needed for the present purpose without renewed manual policy-by-policy handling.

(d) Robustness related to the selection of rules Some tests have proved that fortunately the risk-theoretical behaviour of the claims process is fairly robust for variations in the claim size function S in so far as the top risks are cut off by reinsurance. It seems even to be possible to get an idea of the order of magnitude of the fluctuations of the aggregate claims on the insurer's net retention simply by applying the excess of loss technique presented in Section 3.6.2. Then for M is to be taken the highest level of M applied in practice (see Pentikäinen (1982), Heiskanen (1982)). These results indicate that the considerations are tolerant of fairly rough approximations if these are necessary in some special environments.

*3.6.5 TECHNIQUE USING THE CONCEPT OF DEGREE
OF LOSS

(a) Two-dimensional S Another way of handling surplus reinsurance (and also some problems in rate-making) is to recognize that the claim share $\mathbf{Z}$ on the insurer's net retention is in fact dependent on both the sum insured $\mathbf{Q}$ and the amount of the total size $\mathbf{Z}_{tot}$. The idea is first to build a *two-dimensional* d.f. of the random vector $(\mathbf{Q}, \mathbf{Z}_{tot})$

$$S(Z_{tot}, Q) = \text{prob}\{\mathbf{Z}_{tot} \leqslant Z_{tot} ; \mathbf{Q} \leqslant Q\}. \qquad (3.6.10)$$

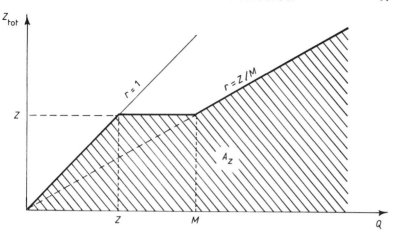

Figure 3.6.1 *Surplus reinsurance. The shaded area indicates that part of the range of the two-dimensional total claim size distribution where $\mathbf{Z} \leqslant Z$.*

Then

$$S_M(Z) = \text{prob}\{\mathbf{Z} \leqslant Z\} = \iint_{A_Z} dS(Z_{\text{tot}}, Q) = \text{prob}\{(\mathbf{Z}_{\text{tot}}, \mathbf{Q}) \in A_Z\}.$$

$$(3.6.11)$$

The double integral is to be taken over the shaded area A_Z of Fig. 3.6.1.

(b) Degree of loss denoted by $\mathbf{r}$, is now introduced

$$\mathbf{r} = \mathbf{Z}_{\text{tot}}/\mathbf{Q}. \qquad (3.6.12)$$

It follows from the definition that $0 < \mathbf{r} \leqslant 1$. The conditional d.f. G of $\mathbf{r}$ as well as the (marginal) d.f. W of $\mathbf{Q}$ can be obtained from $S(Z_{\text{tot}}, Q)$ (or rather they may be derived directly, e.g. from empiric data if available) as follows

$$G(r|Q) = \text{prob}\{\mathbf{r} \leqslant r|\mathbf{Q} = Q\} = \text{prob}\{\mathbf{Z}_{\text{tot}} \leqslant rQ|\mathbf{Q} = Q\}$$

$$= \int_0^{rQ} d_{Z_{\text{tot}}} S(Z_{\text{tot}}, Q) \bigg/ \int_0^Q d_{Z_{\text{tot}}} S(Z_{\text{tot}}, Q), \qquad (3.6.13)$$

and

$$W(Q) = \text{prob}\{\mathbf{Q} \leqslant Q\} = S(Q, Q). \qquad (3.6.14)$$

Note that $W(Q)$ is *not* the same d.f. as could be obtained by directly recording the sums insured of the portfolio files of the policies in force. The policy sums Q in (3.6.14) are weighted according to the risk proneness, which causes the differences.

(c) The moments of S_M can now be calculated

$$a_h(M) = E(\mathbf{Z}^h)$$

$$= \int_0^\infty E(\mathbf{Z}^h | \mathbf{Q} = Q) \, dW(Q)$$

$$= \int_0^M E(\mathbf{Z}_{tot}^h | \mathbf{Q} = Q) \, dW(Q)$$

$$+ \int_M^\infty E(\mathbf{Z}^h | \mathbf{Q} = Q) \, dW(Q), \qquad (3.6.15)$$

and given that $\mathbf{Z}_{tot} = \mathbf{r}Q$ and for $\mathbf{Q} > M$ $\mathbf{Z} = \mathbf{r}M$

$$a_h(M) = \int_0^M Q^h E(\mathbf{r}^h | \mathbf{Q} = Q) dW(Q) + M^h \int_M^\infty E(\mathbf{r}^h | \mathbf{Q} = Q) dW(Q)$$

$$= \int_0^M Q^h b_h(Q) \, dW(Q) + M^h \int_M^\infty b_h(Q) \, dW(Q),$$

where

$$b_h(Q) = \int_0^1 r^h \, dG(r | Q), \qquad (3.6.16)$$

which are to be interpreted as conditional moments of the loss degree $\mathbf{r}$. Note the close formal analogy with the excess of loss formula (3.6.3).

These expressions can be simplified if the distribution of the loss degree is independent of the sum Q, i.e. $G(r)$ is (at least approximately) the same for small and large insured objects:

$$b_h(Q) = b_h. \qquad (3.6.17)$$

Then

$$a_h(M) = b_h \left[\int_0^M Q^h \, dW(Q) + M^h(1 - W(M)) \right], \qquad (3.6.18)$$

(see Straub, 1978 and Venezian and Gaydos, 1980; the last consideration follows Heiskanen, 1982).

(d) Some experimental data concerning the degree of loss Unfortunately condition (3.6.17), i.e. independence of the loss degree of the sum Q, may not in general be well satisfied, as is seen in Figs 3.6.2 and 3.6.3 which exhibit the moment b_1 and the density of r for some Q values.

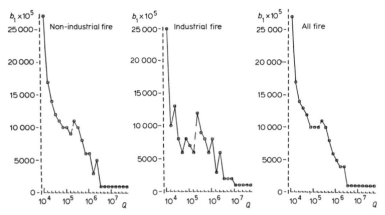

Figure 3.6.2   *The expected loss degree $b_1(Q)$ as a function of the sum Q. Finnish industrial and non-industrial fire insurance by Heiskanen (1982). Monetary unit FIM ($\approx$ £0.1).*

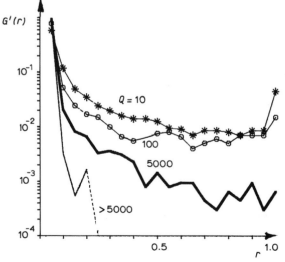

Figure 3.6.3   *Density of loss degree for some insured sums Q (in units of 1000 FIM as plotted at curves). Industrial fire insurance in Finland 1973–78. Compiled by Harri Lonka (unpublished material).*

The total losses ($r = 1$) are more frequent for small objects (Q small) than for large ones. Hence application of (3.6.18) needs critical examination of condition (3.6.17).

Another feature of interest is the rise of the curves when r increases towards 1. It corresponds to real fire experience. Once a fire has progressed beyond a certain point in a small risk unit it can seldom be stopped, and the destruction is total. (This feature has already been observed by Whitney (1909), who operated the concept loss ratio and found analogies between claim size distribution and life insurance formulae such as the force of mortality, similar to that referred to in item 3.5.10(b).)

3.7 Decomposition of the portfolio into sections

(a) Decomposition Basic data and basic distributions are often conveniently available for different sections of the portfolio, e.g. for different classes and subclasses. For the present purpose it is necessary to find techniques for deriving the distributions and characteristics concerning the whole portfolio if the corresponding distributions and characteristics are known for the separate sections. This decomposition into sections is also advantageous for the reason that the total business may be rather heterogeneous. It is thus often easier first to construct the distributions for the sections and then to combine the partial distributions.

Note that the sum process of the independent mixed compound Poisson section processes is, in general, no longer a compound Poisson process because its claim size variable depends on the randomly varying relative values of the structure variables of the sections. However, if the structure variable **q** is the same for all sections, i.e. the variation of the Poisson parameters n_j, j referring to the section, is fully synchronized, then the sum process is again of mixed compound Poisson type as will be seen in item (f). The Poisson case, where **q** degenerates to the constant 1 (see item 3.2(b)), is an example (item (e)). However in the general case, where this kind of synchronism does not exist, the main characteristics of the sum variable can be expressed in terms of the section characteristics, which is often sufficient for applications. This will be carried out such that the composed formulae are formally similar to those derived for the undivided portfolio. A benefit of this procedure is that many of the further considerations, as presented in later parts of the book, are the same irrespective of whether or not the portfolio is assumed to be divided in sections.

Hence, assume that the portfolio is divided in sections $j = 1$, $2, \ldots, J$, each section being represented by a (mixed) compound Poisson process. Let X_j denote the aggregate claim amount of section j in the time interval of unit length (e.g. one year) considered. Then the aggregate claim amount of the whole portfolio is the sum of the section amounts

$$X = \sum_{j=1}^{J} X_j . \tag{3.7.1}$$

Let

$$n = \sum_j n_j, \tag{3.7.2}$$

be again the expected number of claims, which is the sum of the corresponding section numbers. Further, let

$$v_j = \frac{n_j}{n}, \tag{3.7.3}$$

be a set of coefficients. They can be called 'distribution parameters'.

Then the notation

$$a_i = \sum_j v_j a_{ij} , \tag{3.7.4}$$

can be introduced where

$$a_{ij} = \int_0^\infty Z^i \, dS_j(Z) . \tag{3.7.5}$$

S_j is the d.f. of claim size assumed for the section j. As in the foregoing, for convenience of notation the first moments a_{1j} of the sections will be denoted by m_j and a_1 by m.

The quantity a_i can be interpreted as 'a weighted moment about zero' of the compound portfolio. This concept proves to be useful, as will be seen in what follows.

(b) Mean value Now the *expected amount* of the aggregate claims can be expressed (see (3.3.7)) as follows

$$\mu_{\mathbf{X}} = \sum_j \mu_{\mathbf{X}_j} = \sum_j n_j m_j = n \sum_j v_j m_j = nm = P, \qquad (3.7.6)$$

where $P = mn$ is (see (3.3.7)) the risk premium income.

(c) **Variance** In order to avoid covariance terms in the following formulae it is now assumed that the section variables $\mathbf{X}_j$ in (3.7.1) are *mutually independent*. The second and third central moments are then simple sums of the section moments (see exercise 3.3.4)

$$\mu_i(\mathbf{X}) = E\{(\mathbf{X} - E(\mathbf{X}))^i\} = \sum_j \mu_i(\mathbf{X}_j) \qquad \text{for } i = 2, 3. \quad (3.7.7)$$

In addition to the v_js, yet another set of distribution parameters is needed

$$\pi_j = \frac{E(\mathbf{X}_j)}{E(\mathbf{X})} = \frac{m_j n_j}{mn} = \frac{P_j}{P} = \frac{m_j}{m} v_j. \qquad (3.7.8)$$

Hence, π_j parameters are weights based on the section premium volume whereas v_j parameters are based on the claim number volume.

The variance can now be expressed as a sum of the section variances by using the notation (3.7.4) as follows (see (3.3.7))

$$\begin{aligned}
\sigma_{\mathbf{X}}^2 = \sum_j \sigma_{\mathbf{X}_j}^2 &= \sum_j (n_j a_{2j} + n_j^2 m_j^2 \sigma_{\mathbf{q}j}^2) \\
&= na_2 + n^2 m^2 \sigma_q^2 \\
&= (r_2/n + \sigma_q^2)P^2,
\end{aligned} \qquad (3.7.9)$$

where (see (2.8.5)) the notation

$$\sigma_q^2 = \sum_j \pi_j^2 \sigma_{\mathbf{q}j}^2, \qquad (3.7.10)$$

and

$$r_2 = a_2/m^2, \qquad (3.7.11)$$

are introduced. The former expression is the extension of the structure variance concept and the latter of the risk index (3.3.8).

Note that q here does not refer to any real structure variable $\mathbf{q}$; σ_q^2 simply conveys the composite effect of the section variables $\mathbf{q}_j$ on the portfolio variance. Furthermore, note the complete formal similarity of the composite expression (3.7.9) with (3.3.7).

(d) Skewness First, the third central moment of $\mathbf{X}$ can be derived in a similar way as the second (see (3.3.7))

$$\mu_3(\mathbf{X}) = \sum_j \mu_3(\mathbf{X}_j)$$

$$= \sum_j n_j a_{3j} + 3 \sum_j n_j^2 m_j a_{2j} \sigma_{qj}^2 + \sum_j n_j^3 m_j^3 \mu_3(\mathbf{q}_j) \tag{3.7.12}$$

$$= n \sum_j v_j a_{3j} + 3n^2 m^2 \sum_j \frac{a_{2j}}{m_j} \left(\frac{m_j n_j}{nm} \right)^2 \sigma_{qj}^2 + n^3 m^3 \sum_j \left(\frac{n_j m_j}{nm} \right)^3 \mu_3(\mathbf{q}_j)$$

By convention (see (3.3.8))

$$r_3 = a_3/m^3, \tag{3.7.13}$$

and by using $\gamma \sigma^3$ instead of μ_3 as suggested in item 3.3(e) the following expression is obtained for the skewness in terms of the given notation

$$\gamma_{\mathbf{X}} = \frac{\mu_3(\mathbf{X})}{\sigma_{\mathbf{X}}^3} = \left(\frac{r_3}{n^2} + \frac{3}{nm} \sum_j \pi_j^2 \frac{a_{2j}\sigma_{qj}^2}{m_j} + \sum_j \pi_j^3 \gamma_{qj} \sigma_{qj}^3 \right) \Big/ \left(\frac{r_2}{n} + \sigma_q^2 \right)^{3/2}. \tag{3.7.14}$$

This formula as well as the expression in parentheses in the final formulation of (3.7.9) are of dimension zero in respect of the monetary unit, which makes them 'immune' to the direct effect of inflation. This simplifies matters when (as later) periods longer than one year are studied.

(e) In the Poisson case the S function for the whole portfolio exists and can be composed of the section functions S_j making use of the m.g.f.s as follows (see (3.4.3)). The m.g.f. of Section j is

$$M_j(s) = \exp\left[n_j \left(\int_0^\infty e^{sZ} \, dS_j(Z) - 1 \right) \right], \tag{3.7.15}$$

and the m.g.f. of the whole portfolio is obtained by multiplication (see item 1.6(b), property (iv))

$$M(s) = \prod_j M_j(s)$$

$$= \exp\left[\sum_j n_j \left(\int_0^\infty e^{sZ} \, dS_j(Z) - 1 \right) \right] \tag{3.7.16}$$

$$= \exp\left[n \int_0^\infty e^{sZ} \, d\left(\sum_j \frac{n_j}{n} S_j(Z) \right) - n \right].$$

But this is again the m.g.f. of a Poisson d.f. for which (see (3.4.3), (3.4.1))

$$S(Z) = \sum_j v_j S_j(Z). \tag{3.7.17}$$

Hence, according to the unique correspondence of the m.g.f. and the d.f., it can be concluded that the claims size distribution of the whole portfolio can be obtained as the weighted sum (3.7.17) of the section functions where the section distributions are of the simple Poisson type.

Note that the weight parameters v_j in (3.7.17) vary randomly in the general case where a time-dependent structure variation is assumed and is not synchronized within the portfolio, e.g. if the variation of the sections is mutually independent. Then there exists no global claim size function that will be the same from year to year.

(f) Synchronized structure variation It follows from (3.4.2) that the results of the previous item hold also in the special case of varying basic probabilities when the time variation of the n_j parameters is the *synchronized* $\mathbf{n}_j = n_j \mathbf{q}$, where $\mathbf{q}$ is the same for all sections. This case can be handled by calculating first the moments (3.7.4) and substituting them as well as the joint $\sigma_{\mathbf{q}}$, $\gamma_{\mathbf{q}}$ and $\gamma_2(\mathbf{q})$ into (3.3.7) (see exercise 3.7.1).

(g) Further applications The result arrived at by means of m.g.f. in the Poisson case is, however, in one sense more general. Whilst S must, of course, be a distribution function of the size of one claim in insurance applications, there is no reason to restrict consideration to distribution functions in so far as component functions S_j are concerned. On the contrary, in order to facilitate computations it may sometimes be advisable to consider S as made up of components which cannot be interpreted as distribution functions of one claim of any actual part of the portfolio. In this wider case the functions F_j, formally defined as F in Section 3.2, are not necessarily distribution functions, but this feature does not have any essential influence on the calculations, i.e. the distribution function F of the portfolio can simply be obtained from the functions F_j by convolution

$$F = F_1 * F_2 * \cdots * F_J. \tag{3.7.18}$$

For example, suppose there are difficulties in calculating a mixed compound Poisson d.f. F directly from (3.2.1) but, from earlier computations, the distribution functions F_j of different parts of a portfolio may be known, or it may be easy to compute them separately for each of these parts, or it is possible to select a set of J functions S_j for which the corresponding F_j can be calculated in practice, and these functions satisfy (3.7.16). In these circumstances the distribution function of the whole portfolio can be obtained via these components according to (3.7.18). Then, to get F, it is necessary only to calculate $J - 1$ convolutions, an essentially easier course than the calculation of a nearly unlimited number of convolutions which is the case when (3.2.1) is used directly. For example, the expression (3.7.16) could be taken as the first J terms of the expansion of S in a series of some auxiliary functions S_j, this series having convergence properties so that the remainder may be neglected. The index j in this connection does not, of course, refer to any actual section of the portfolio.

As an example, let us suppose that the claim size distribution is (or can be approximated to be; see Section 3.8) of discrete type, i.e. only the claim sizes $Z_1, Z_2, \ldots, Z_J$ are possible, and by probabilities $q_1, q_2, \ldots, q_J$ and the claims number process is a simple Poisson one. Then the m.g.f. (3.4.3) is reduced to the form

$$M(s) = \exp\left[n\left(\sum_j \frac{n_j}{n} e^{sZ_j} - 1 \right) \right]$$
$$= \prod_j \exp(n_j e^{sZ_j} - n_j), \qquad (3.7.19)$$

where $n_j = nq_j$. But this is a product of simple Poisson m.g.f.s. That means that the d.f. of the whole portfolio can be obtained by convolution of J simple Poisson variables, each having *only one claim size* Z_j. This result can be interpreted so that the portfolio is divided in hypothetical sections $j = 1, 2, \ldots, J$. Only one claim size Z_j is possible in each section and the Poisson parameter n, the expected number of claims, is n_j. The sum of the section aggregate claims $\mathbf{X}_j$ has the same d.f. as the original portfolio under consideration.

(h) **Link to individual risk theory** As briefly referred to in item 2.1(b), risk theory can be built also taking the individual risk units (policies) as primary building blocks ('atoms') of the risk process. This was, in fact, the issue in the early history of risk theory. The foregoing important decomposition rules also lend themselves to consideration of this approach. The 'sections' j is defined to be just the risk units, and hence J is the number of policies in the portfolio. Then $\mathbf{X}_j$ in (3.7.1) is the sum of the claims arisen from the jth unit. Note that $\mathbf{X}_j$ may assume also the value 0 and that, of course, any unit may produce more than one claim. If the distributions, or at least some of characteristics related to the individual risk units, are known then the aggregate claim process can be employed using the methods derived earlier. An example is given in exercise 3.7.1.

Exercise 3.7.1 Consider a block of $N = 10\,000$ risk units j, each having a distribution of claims of mixed compound Poisson type with the same expected number $n_j = 0.1$ of claims. The standard deviation of the structure variation $\mathbf{q}_j$ of each risk unit j is $\sigma_{\mathbf{q}j} = 0.2$. Furthermore, the joint claim size d.f. of the units is approximated by a discrete d.f. as given in terms of some suitable monetary units (e.g. £1000) in the following table, where s_i is the probability that the size of a claim is Z_i.

i	1	2	3	4	5
Z_i	1	2	4	8	16
s_i	0.8	0.1	0.05	0.02	0.03

Calculate $\mu_{\mathbf{X}}$ and $\sigma_{\mathbf{X}}$ for the whole block in the following cases

(i) Assume first that structure variables $\mathbf{q}_j = \mathbf{q}$ are the same for all risk units.

(ii) Assume that the structure variables $\mathbf{q}_j$ are mutually independent.

3.8   Recursion formula for F

(a) **Derivation of the formula** A case where the compound Poisson d.f. F can be found by direct numerical calculation is that where the claim size d.f. S is a *discrete equidistant* (often called 'lattice') distribution according to which only the values

$$Z_i = iZ_1 \qquad (i = 1, 2, 3, \ldots). \tag{3.8.1}$$

can occur as the claim size. For brevity Z_1 will be taken as the monetary unit: hence $z_i = Z_i/Z_1 = i$. Let the corresponding frequencies be

$$q_i = \text{prob}\{\mathbf{z} = i\}. \tag{3.8.2}$$

Of course, any distribution can be approximated by a d.f. of this kind. In principle it is not necessary to limit the number of z_i values, but unfortunately the numerical computations very soon become laborious if the number of the points grows large. Hence the index is generally limited to some rather small range $1, \ldots, s$ so that

$$q_s > 0 \quad \text{and} \quad q_i = 0 \quad \text{for } i > s. \tag{3.8.3}$$

One or more of the probabilities for $1 \leqslant i < s$ may be zero.

It is convenient to operate with probability frequencies instead of the (cumulative) d.f. Then the basic formula (3.2.3) of the compound Poisson distribution is transformed as follows

$$f(x) = \sum_{k=0}^{\infty} p_k q_x^{k*} \quad \text{for } x = 0, 1, 2, \ldots, \tag{3.8.4}$$

where the total amount of claims is denoted by a positive integer x, and

$$q_x^{k*} = \text{prob}\{\mathbf{z}_1 + \mathbf{z}_2 + \cdots + \mathbf{z}_k = x\}, \tag{3.8.5}$$

the variables $\mathbf{z}_j$ being mutually independent and equally distributed according to (3.8.2). The recursion rule for the convolution is now

$$q_x^{k*} = \sum_{i=1}^{x} q_i q_{x-i}^{(k-1)*}. \tag{3.8.6}$$

By convention $q_0^{0*} = 1$, $q_x^{0*} = 0$ for $x \geqslant 1$. An auxiliary equation is needed as an intermediate stage for further development. It is obtained by analysing the expression

$$E_k = \sum_{i=1}^{x} i q_i q_{x-i}^{(k-1)*}/q_x^{k*}. \tag{3.8.7}$$

The quotient $q_i q_{x-i}^{(k-i)*}/q_x^{k*}$ is the conditional probability that $\mathbf{z}_k = i$ for $\mathbf{z}_1, + \cdots + \mathbf{z}_k = x$; hence E_k is the expected value of $\mathbf{z}_k$

$$E_k = E\left\{ \mathbf{z}_k \,\middle|\, \sum_{i=1}^{k} \mathbf{z}_i = x \right\}.$$

Owing to the symmetry this conditional expected value has the same value E_k for all z_i ($i = 1, 2, \ldots, k$) and the sum of all these expected values is x. Hence $kE_k = x$ or $E_k = x/k$. Substituting in (3.8.7), the equation

$$q_x^{k*} = \frac{k}{x} \sum_{i=1}^{x} iq_i q_{x-i}^{(k-1)*}, \qquad (3.8.8)$$

follows. Note that by (3.8.6) this also holds when $q_x^{k*} = 0$.

It is still assumed that the *claims number process* belongs to the *family* which obeys the *recursive formula* (see equation (2.9.13))

$$p_k = (a + b/k)p_{k-1}. \qquad (3.8.9)$$

This formula was introduced in item 2.9 (g) and it was stated that the Poisson and negative binomial distributions belong to it. Then the frequency $f(x)$ for $x > 0$ can be manipulated into a form where it is expressed by the f values calculated for $x - 1, x - 2, \ldots$.

To obtain this expression it must first be noted that according to (3.8.9)

$$f(x) = \sum_{k=1}^{\infty} (a + b/k)p_{k-1} q_x^{k*}$$

$$= \sum_{k=1}^{\infty} ap_{k-1} q_x^{k*} + \sum_{k=1}^{\infty} \frac{b}{k} p_{k-1} q_x^{k*}.$$

The convolution can be lowered one step making use of (3.8.6) and (3.8.8) and by denoting $m = \min(x, s)$

$$f(x) = \sum_{k=1}^{\infty} ap_{k-1} \sum_{i=1}^{m} q_i q_{x-i}^{(k-1)*} + \sum_{k=1}^{\infty} \frac{b}{k} p_{k-1} \frac{k}{x} \sum_{i=1}^{m} iq_i q_{x-i}^{(k-1)*}$$

$$= \sum_{i=1}^{m} aq_i \sum_{k=1}^{\infty} p_{k-1} q_{x-i}^{(k-1)*} + \sum_{i=1}^{m} \frac{b}{x} iq_i \sum_{k=1}^{\infty} p_{k-1} q_{x-i}^{(k-1)*}.$$

The inner sums are equal to $f(x - i)$ as seen from (3.8.4). So the recursion formula is obtained

$$f(x) = \sum_{i=1}^{\min(x, s)} (a + ib/x)q_i f(x - i). \qquad (3.8.10)$$

Starting from the value

$$f(0) = p_0, \qquad (3.8.11)$$

$f(x)$ can be calculated step by step for $x = 1, 2, \ldots$.

If the range s of the S distribution is not very long and if n is not very large, the recursion formula is quite convenient for computations of $f(x)$ and, of course, the d.f. is immediately obtained by summation

$$F(X) = F(xZ_1) = \sum_{v=0}^{[x]} f(v), \qquad (3.8.12)$$

where X is the aggregate claim as x multiple of the unit Z_1.

The remarks given in item 2.5(a) concerning programming are applicable also for this formula.

(b) References Panjer (1981), Bertram (1981) and Jewell and Sundt (1981) have proved the recursion rule to be valid for more general assumptions than above. Jewell and Sundt also present an exhaustive study of the family satisfying (3.8.9) and extend the consideration to some more general distributions. The recursion formula (3.8.12) for the Poisson case was presented by Adelson (1966).

(c) Example The recursion formula (3.8.10) is exact. However, if as a first step of the calculation the original claim size d.f., which may be of continuous type, is first discretized, an inaccuracy will arise due to rounding off and for other reasons. To test the sensitivity of the results to this discretization procedure a truncated Pareto d.f.

$$S(Z) = \begin{cases} 0 & (Z < 1) \\ 1 - Z^{-2} & (1 \leqslant Z < 21) \\ 1 & (Z \geqslant 21), \end{cases} \qquad (3.8.13)$$

was replaced by a discrete equidistant d.f., the probability mass being concentrated in $r + 1$ points

$$Z = 1, 1 + \Delta, 1 + 2\Delta, \ldots, 1 + r\Delta = 21$$

where $\Delta = 20/r$. In order to test the effect of the length of the interval the alternative values 20, 5, 2 and 1 were assumed for r. The probabilities assigned to these points were

$$q_{1+i\Delta} = S(1 + (i + \tfrac{1}{2})\Delta) - S(1 + (i - \tfrac{1}{2})\Delta) \qquad i = 1, 2, \ldots, r - 1,$$

and at the end points of the interval $[1, 21]$

$$q_1 = S(1 + \tfrac{1}{2}\Delta); q_{1+r\Delta} = q_{21} = 1 - S(1 + (r - \tfrac{1}{2})\Delta).$$

The examples in Table 3.8.1 demonstrate the sensitivity of the result

Table 3.8.1   *Examples of F(x) for x < 0 and 1 − F for x > 0 per thousand. Pareto claim size d.f. (3.8.13), Poisson claim number d.f., n = 50, x = (X − m_x)/σ_x the normed variable.*

| | Number of intervals r | | | | |
x	20	10	5	2	1
3	5.2	5.2	5.8	7.9	0.2
2	34.7	35.1	35.1	38.1	129.5
1	151.5	153.4	155.2	156.5	155.1
−1	152.8	158.9	156.3	160.5	47.5
−2	9.0	8.7	7.4	1.8	10.5

to the density of the interval number r. Obviously the method tolerates a fairly coarse interval net.

Gerber (1982) has suggested methods according to which the inaccuracy due to the discretization rounding can be evaluated.

Exercise 3.8.1   Calculate Polya $F(X)$ for the parameter combination $n = 2$, $h = 10$. $S(Z)$ is a two-point discrete function $Z_1 = 1$, $Z_2 = 2$, $S(1) = 0.2$ and $X = 0, 1, 2, 3, \ldots, 6$.

3.9   The normal approximation

(a) Need for approximation methods It will be apparent from the foregoing chapters that the compound Poisson function F which gives the distribution of the aggregate claims is, unfortunately, complicated as regards computation particularly in practical applications. Direct methods of attack on the numerical treatment of F often lead to very cumbersome expressions so that it is, in general, not easy to deal with problems concerned with, for example, different methods of reinsurance, net retentions, and safety loadings. The recursion formula presented in the previous section may be useful for applications only in small collectives and in problems where X is given and F is requested. Furthermore, it is extremely difficult to obtain a broad survey of the problems. Even if the nature of the problems justifies more detailed computations, simple working approximations are necessary; it follows that one of the problems of applied risk theory is the finding of proper approximations.

(b) The central limit theorem of the probability calculus is a classical approximation much used in risk theory as well. For this purpose, first the variable **X** will be 'standardized' or 'normalized', transferring it in the form

$$\mathbf{x} = (\mathbf{X} - \mu_X)/\sigma_X, \qquad (3.9.1)$$

where (see (3.3.9)), limiting the consideration to the Poisson case,

$$\begin{cases} \mu_{\mathbf{x}} = nm \\ \sigma_{\mathbf{x}} = \sqrt{(na_2)} \end{cases}. \qquad (3.9.2)$$

The normed variable $\mathbf{x}$ has mean 0 and standard deviation 1. The central limit theorem says that the d.f. $\bar{F}$ of $\mathbf{x}$ tends to the normal d.f.

$$N(x) = \frac{1}{\sqrt{(2\pi)}} \int_{-\infty}^{x} e^{-\frac{1}{2}u^2} \, du, \qquad (3.9.3)$$

when n tends to infinity, i.e.

$$F(X) = \bar{F}(x) \approx N(x). \qquad (3.9.4)$$

(c) Discussion of the area of applicability In Chapter 4 and later it will be shown that the normal approximation essentially simplifies the calculations, and makes it possible to provide a broad survey of problems involving many variables and basic functions in a way which is not otherwise possible or can only be done with considerable difficulties. Unfortunately, however, the accuracy of this approximation is not satisfactory if the skewness of the distribution is large, as is demonstrated in Fig. 3.9.1, where normally distributed values are compared with the so-called NP values calculated by a method which will be presented in the next item. Provided that the accuracy of the NP values is satisfactory, the deviations from them indicate the degree of inaccuracy of the normal approximation.

Figure 3.9.1 suggests that if the skewness γ is small – as it is for portfolios which are protected by normal reinsurance and which are not very small – the normal approximation gives quite a good fit. However, if γ exceeds 0.1 the deviations grow rapidly, especially at the tails of the distribution. The normal d.f. then generally underestimates the risk of excessive claims and should not be used if safe evaluations are requested.

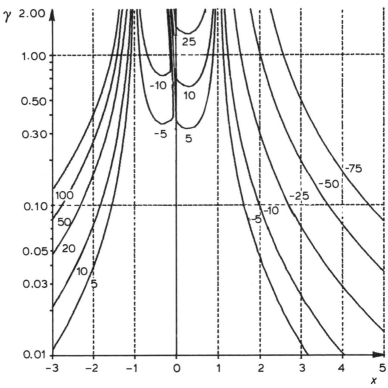

Figure 3.9.1 *Comparison of the normal d.f. (N) and the NP d.f. (N_γ) as a function of x and γ. The relative deviation $100\,(N - N_\gamma)/N_\gamma$ for $x < 0$ and $100[(1 - N) - (1 - N_\gamma)]/(1 - N_\gamma)$ for $x > 0$ is computed and then the value pairs x, γ are sought and plotted for which these deviations are equal to $-75, -50, \ldots, 50, 100$ so constituting 'a map' to give the altitudes of the deviations. For example, for $x = 2$ and skewness $\gamma = 0.1$ one can read that the relative deviation is about -11%, i.e. the normal approximation gives a value for $1 - F$ which is 11% less than the one obtained by the NP method. The discontinuities at $x = 0$ are due to the presentation of F and $1 - F$ at either side of this line, due to the fact that $F(0) \neq 1 - F(0)$ for $\gamma > 0$.*

(d) Numerical values of the normal d.f. can be obtained from standard textbooks or can be programmed making use of the following expansion (Abramowitz and Stegun, 1970).

First calculate

$$R = \frac{1}{\sqrt{(2\pi)}}\, e^{-\frac{1}{2}x^2}(b_1 t + b_2 t^2 + b_3 t^3 + b_4 t^4 + b_5 t^5), \qquad (3.9.5a)$$

where

$$t = 1/(1 + 0.231\ 641\ 9|x|),$$

and the values of b_i, $i = 1, 2, \ldots, 5$ are respectively

$$0.319\ 381\ 530,\ -0.356\ 563\ 782,\ 1.781\ 477\ 937,$$
$$-1.821\ 255\ 978,\ 1.330\ 274\ 429.$$

Then

$$N(x) = \begin{cases} R & \text{for } x \leqslant 0 \\ 1 - R & \text{for } x > 0. \end{cases} \tag{3.9.5b}$$

When the value $N = N(x)$ of the function is given and the matching argument value x is requested, first calculate

$$t = \begin{cases} \sqrt{(-2 \ln N)} & \text{for } 0 < N \leqslant 0.5 \\ \sqrt{(-2 \ln(1 - N))} & \text{for } 0.5 < N < 1, \end{cases} \tag{3.9.6a}$$

and

$$y = t - \frac{c_0 + c_1 t + c_2 t^2}{1 + d_1 t + d_2 t^2 + d_3 t^3}, \tag{3.9.6b}$$

where

$$c_0 = 2.515\ 517,\quad c_1 = 0.802\ 853,\quad c_2 = 0.010\ 328$$
$$d_1 = 1.432\ 788,\quad d_2 = 0.189\ 269,\quad d_3 = 0.001\ 308.$$

Then

$$x = \begin{cases} -y & \text{for } 0 < N \leqslant 0.5 \\ y & \text{for } 0.5 < N < 1. \end{cases} \tag{3.9.6c}$$

The absolute amount of the error is estimated to be $< 7.5 \times 10^{-8}$ for (3.9.5b) and $< 4.5 \times 10^{-4}$ for (3.9.6c).

3.10 Edgeworth series

The normal approximation (3.9.4) is in fact only a special case of a more general formula, known as an Edgeworth expansion

$$F(X) \approx G(x) = N(x) - \tfrac{1}{6}\gamma N^{(3)}(x) + \tfrac{1}{24}\gamma_2 N^{(4)}(x) + \tfrac{1}{72}\gamma^2 N^{(6)}(x) + R(x), \tag{3.10.1}$$

where N is again the normal d.f. (3.9.3), x is the normed variable (3.9.1) and γ and γ_2 are the skewness and kurtosis (3.3.7) of $\mathbf{X}$. The remainder term contains $1/n$ at least in power $3/2$ in the Poisson case.

The Edgeworth expansion is most simply obtained by means of the characteristic function of F, expanding the exponential in a MacLaurin series and reverting back to the distribution functions after integration, making use of the correspondence of the characteristic function and the distribution function. Details of the derivation of the formula are given in Appendix B.

Reference to (3.10.1) shows that the normal approximation is merely the form given by the Edgeworth expansion when the first term only is retained, i.e. by ignoring terms of $O(1/\sqrt{n})$. If the explicit expressions of higher derivatives of the normal function N are introduced into (3.10.1), it can be shown that the error of the Edgeworth expansion tends to infinity as the number of terms increases without limit. The Edgeworth expansion is not a convergent but a divergent series. However by taking a suitable number of terms it gives acceptable results in the neighbourhood of the mean value. It can be generally expected that the result is good up to a distance of twice the standard deviation from the mean, but for points outside this interval the result soon deteriorates. From the point of view of risk theory this is unfortunate since in most problems the main interest arises from points at a distance of two to three times the standard deviation to the right of the mean. For this reason some improvement on this series is needed, and this is given in the following sections.

3.11   Normal power approximation

(a) Background   The normal power approximation was originally found by Kauppi and Ojantakanen (1969). They computed, in a parallel manner, normal approximated values and actual values of the compound Poisson F in cases where these are computable exactly or the accuracy is within well-controlled limits. It was found that, in general, the differences obeyed a certain simple pattern. This observation suggested a correction of the standardized (see (3.9.1)) argument **x** in a way which transformed it into another, approximately normally distributed, variable **y**. Also a theoretical derivation was soon found for the formula and eventually it proved to be a special case of a similar transformation originally due to Cornish and Fisher (1937). A good account of the idea can be found in Kendall and Stuart (1977, paragraphs 6.25–27).

Generally speaking the situation in the present case, as also in many other occasions in mathematical statistics, is that a variable **x** tends towards normality when the population to which it is related becomes large. In our application, this means that the volume variable, the expected number of claims n, should be large, making the skewness small; according to item 3.9(c), this is an indication for the acceptability of the normal approximation for the standardized compound Poisson variable **x**. However, if the background collective is small or a skew structure function is assumed, significant deviation from normality appears. The idea is to find a transformation

$$\mathbf{x} = v(\mathbf{y}), \tag{3.11.1}$$

which converts a normally $N(0, 1)$ distributed variable **y** into another variable **x**, which can be better fitted to actual distributions. It is convenient to try to find a function v which includes some free parameters. The latter will be chosen, for example by equating lowest moments, to give a maximal fit with the compound d.f. employed. Then we have $F(X) = \bar{F}(x) \approx N(v^{-1}(x))$ where $\bar{F}$ is the d.f. of the standardized compound Poisson variable (3.9.1) and v^{-1} is the inverse of the function v.

(b) Derivation of the *NP* formula It can be proved that a suitable transformation v in a polynomial form can be obtained by inverting the Edgeworth expansion G (see (3.10.1)).

First denote $y + \Delta y = x$. Then the required relationship (i.e. $x = v(y) = y + \Delta y$) between x and y can be obtained from the equation

$$N(y) = G(y + \Delta y) \approx \bar{F}(x), \tag{3.11.2}$$

which determines y so that $N(y)$ gives (approximately) the same value as the Edgeworth expansion. This equation can be written in the compound Poisson case (structure variation omitting)

$$N(y) - N(y + \Delta y) + \tfrac{1}{6}\gamma N^{(3)}(y + \Delta y) - \tfrac{1}{24}\gamma_2 N^{(4)}(y + \Delta y)$$
$$- \tfrac{1}{72}\gamma^2 N^{(6)}(y + \Delta y) + O(n^{-3/2}) = 0. \tag{3.11.3}$$

It is now solved by means of Newton's method, according to which the solution of an equation $f(u) = 0$ can be found if some approximate solution $\bar{u}$ is known as the expansion

$$u = \bar{u} - \frac{f(\bar{u})}{f'(\bar{u})} - \frac{1}{2}\frac{f''(\bar{u})}{f'(\bar{u})}\left[\frac{f(\bar{u})}{f'(\bar{u})}\right]^2 - \cdots$$

Now f is the l.h.s. of (3.11.3), $\bar{u} = y$ and $u = y + \Delta y$. Further, the derivatives of the normal d.f. N are needed in form

$$N''(y) = -yN'(y); \quad N^{(3)}(y) = (y^2 - 1)N'(y); \quad N^{(4)}(y) = (y^3 - 3y)N'(y); \ldots$$
(3.11.4)

which are readily obtained by differentiating (3.9.3). Similarly the higher derivatives of $N(y)$ can be expressed as polynomials in y multiplied by the first derivative $N'(y)$ (so-called Chebyshev–Hermite polynomials, see Kendall and Stuart, 1977, par. 6.14). Substituting in (3.11.3) and after some straightforward calculations the method gives

$$\Delta y = \frac{\frac{1}{6}\gamma(y^2 - 1) + \frac{1}{24}\gamma_2(y^3 - 3y) + \frac{1}{72}\gamma^2(y^5 - 10y^3 + 15y)}{1 + \frac{1}{6}\gamma(y^3 - 3y) + O(n^{-1})}$$

$$+ \frac{1}{2}\frac{y + O(n^{-1/2})}{1 + O(n^{-1/2})}\left[\frac{\frac{1}{6}\gamma(y^2 - 1) + O(n^{-1})}{1 + O(n^{-1/2})}\right]^2 + O(n^{-3/2})$$

$$= \frac{1}{6}\gamma(y^2 - 1) + \frac{1}{24}\gamma_2(y^3 - 3y) - \frac{1}{36}\gamma^2(2y^3 - 5y) + O(n^{-3/2}),$$

from which the sought transformation $v(y)$ is obtained

$$x = v(y) = y + \Delta y = y + \frac{1}{6}\gamma(y^2 - 1) + \frac{1}{24}\gamma_2(y^3 - 3y)$$
$$- \frac{1}{36}\gamma^2(2y^3 - 5y) + O(n^{-3/2}). \tag{3.11.5}$$

If only the first correcting term is taken into account, then the following approach to find an approximated value for the compound Poisson function $F(X)$ is obtained. First solve y from

$$x = (X - \mu_{\mathbf{X}})/\sigma_{\mathbf{X}} = y + \frac{1}{6}\gamma_{\mathbf{X}}(y^2 - 1). \tag{3.11.6}$$

Then

$$F(X) = \bar{F}(x) \approx N(y), \tag{3.11.7}$$

or, substituting y into $N(y)$

$$F(X) \approx N\left[-\frac{3}{\gamma_{\mathbf{X}}} + \sqrt{\left(\frac{9}{\gamma_{\mathbf{X}}^2} + 1 + \frac{6}{\gamma}\frac{X - \mu_{\mathbf{X}}}{\sigma_{\mathbf{X}}}\right)}\right]. \tag{3.11.8}$$

If the next two terms in (3.11.5) are taken into account and $\gamma_{\mathbf{X}}$ and $\gamma_2(\mathbf{X})$ are again denoted briefly by γ and γ_2, the extended version is obtained

$$x = y + \frac{1}{6}\gamma(y^2 - 1) + \frac{1}{24}\gamma_2(y^3 - 3y) - \frac{1}{36}\gamma^2(2y^3 - 5y). \tag{3.11.9}$$

The root y of this equation can be found by direct solution or other methods and substituted into (3.11.7).

These formulae are called *NP approximations* (normal power approximations). They are properly applicable only for $x > 1$. For the remaining range some modifications are given later, but first some special features and the question of accuracy will be discussed.

(c) Discussion The foregoing results can be interpreted in two formally different ways. It can be said that the compound Poisson variable is developed as a semi-convergent series (3.11.5) and a suitable number of terms will be accepted to give numerical approximative values for the relationship between x and y.

Another interpretation is obtained when the number of accepted terms is fixed. The relationships $x \rightarrow y$ and $y \rightarrow x$ are then uniquely defined for all real values of these variables as will be seen in the sequel, and an explicit transformation $v(y)$ is found as required in item (a). Ultimately a new d.f., $N(v^{-1}(x))$, is constituted. If, as will be the case in what follows, the short version (3.11.6) is assumed, then $v(y)$ includes one parameter, only, the skewness γ, and can be suitably denoted by $v_\gamma(y)$. Furthermore, it is convenient to introduce the notations

$$N_\gamma(x) = N(v_\gamma^{-1}(x)). \qquad (3.11.10)$$

The mean, the standard deviation and the skewness of this distribution are approximately 0, 1 and γ (= free parameter) respectively if the short version (3.11.6) is used. It is convenient to say that $\mathbf{x}$ is *NP*-distributed, denoted $NP(0, 1, \gamma)$. The variable $\mathbf{X} = \mu_\mathbf{X} + \mathbf{x}\sigma_\mathbf{X}$ (see (3.9.1)) is then also *NP* distributed having $m_\mathbf{X}$, $\sigma_\mathbf{X}$, $\gamma = \gamma_\mathbf{X}$ approximately as mean, standard deviation and skewness. Note that a linear transformation does not change the skewness, i.e. $\mathbf{x}$ and $\mathbf{X}$ have the same skewness. In brief it can be said that $\mathbf{X}$ is $NP(\mu_\mathbf{X}, \sigma_\mathbf{X}, \gamma_\mathbf{X})$ distributed having the d.f. $N_\gamma[(X - m_\mathbf{X})/\sigma_\mathbf{X}]$.

As the compound Poisson distribution was approximated by the normal d.f. $N(\mu_\mathbf{X}, \sigma_\mathbf{X}^2)$ in Section 3.9, so it will now be approximated by the $NP(\mu_\mathbf{X}, \sigma_\mathbf{X}, \gamma_\mathbf{X})$ distribution. The crucial benefit of this approach is, of course, that now three parameters are available instead of only two. In fact, the normal d.f. is extended to a family of functions having an extra parameter γ available. For $\gamma = 0$ the NP function reduces to the N function.

Since the proof is based on the assumption that F can be represented by a finite number of the leading terms of the Edgeworth expansion, the result would not be expected to be better than that obtained by the direct use of (3.10.1). This argument however proves, quite surprisingly, to be wrong. Experience of the application of (3.11.8) has shown, as will be presented in subsequent items, that if γ is not great it gives fairly good results, whereas the Edgeworth expansion is usually unsatisfactory for deviations some distance from the mean. At first sight this seems to be unsound, because it would not be expected that an inaccurate formula would be improved by making further approximations when inverting it. But it is not necessarily so. The Edgeworth expansion is not a convergent but a divergent series and its fitness depends, among other things, on how many of its terms are accepted for the approximation. The same argument holds true for the inverted expansion, and it is no miracle if the leading terms of one expansion give more accurate approximations than those of another expansion. This is in fact a well-known feature for semi-convergent series.

(d) *NP* function structure It is worth noting that the *NP* function (3.11.8) includes as parameters only the mean value μ_X, standard deviation σ_X and skewness γ_X of the distribution of the aggregate claim **X**. The background distributions of the claim numbers and claim sizes are not directly needed; they have an effect only via the moments which determine the above characteristics (see (3.3.9) or (3.3.7)). Hence for computations only these characteristics are needed. This is an important observation, because often just the moments can be directly derived from the empirical data (see (3.5.2), (3.6.3), (3.6.8) and Section 3.7 and an analytic formulation of the claim number and claim size distributions is not needed. On the contrary, an attempt to force these distributions into the form of some standard analytic function may give rise to rounding-off errors which are difficult to control and which are, in fact, rather unnecessary.

(e) Extension of the area of applicability The above formulae were originally derived only for the simple compound Poisson distribution for which they are, as the normal approximation too, asymptotically correct. They can be formally applied *to any distribution* by substituting the respective characteristics of the distribution into (3.11.8). For example, the *mixed* compound Poisson d.f. can be approximated by calculating the characteristics using (3.3.7). The tests referred to in the following item prove that accuracy is still about as good as in the Poisson case, in so far as the criteria presented in the following are satisfied. This is understandable since $N_\gamma(X/nm)$ tends to $NP(1, \sigma_q, \gamma_q)$ as $n \to \infty$. In other words, it approximates the structure function as a limit distribution. But this is precisely the function towards which the mixed compound Poisson d.f. F tends according to equation (3.3.16).

(f) Accuracy The usefulness of the NP method has been tested by comparing it with other methods, which give exact or at least controlled values for the compound function F; the works of Kauppi and Ojantakanen (1969), Pesonen (1967a, 1969), Berger (1972) and Pentikäinen (1977) may be referred to. Typical results are given in Fig. 3.11.1 and in Table 3.11.1. The *accuracy becomes critical when*

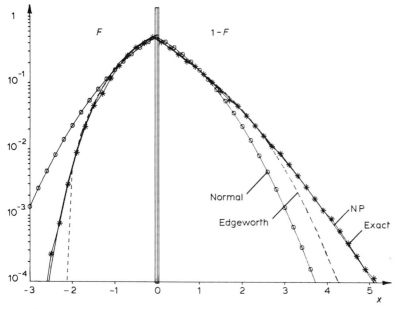

Figure 3.11.1 *Example of the Normal, Edgeworth and NP approximated values. Polya d.f. F with h = 100, n = 25, claim size d.f. Pareto with α = 2 truncated and discretized in points Z = 1, 2, ..., 21 (see Table 3.11.2). The slight irregular bends are due to the calculation of this strictly discrete function at equidistant points which did not coincide with the steps of F, and with irregular rounding off small errors resulted.*

Table 3.11.1 *Compound Poisson values computed by the recursive formula (3.8.12) and NP formula. Truncated Pareto claim size d.f. $\alpha = 3, 1 \leqslant z \leqslant 11$ discretized in 11 points, $\gamma = 0.18, n = 100$.*

	x	$\bar{F}$	N_γ	$(N_\gamma - F)/\bar{F}\%$	$N_\gamma - \bar{F}$
$\bar{F}$	−3.0	0.0004	0.0004	−3.16	−0.0000
	−2.5	0.0039	0.0034	−13.58	−0.0005
	−2.0	0.0184	0.0174	−5.12	−0.0009
	−1.5	0.0617	0.0616	−0.19	−0.0001
	−1.0	0.1560	0.1594	2.12	0.0033
	−0.5	0.3092	0.3178	2.78	0.0086
$1 - \bar{F}$	0.0	0.4762	0.4877	2.41	0.0115
	0.5	0.2946	0.3004	1.97	0.0058
	1.0	0.1571	0.1587	0.99	0.0016
	1.5	0.0721	0.0715	−0.86	−0.0006
	2.0	0.0286	0.0276	−3.55	−0.0010
	2.5	0.0099	0.0092	−7.07	−0.0007
	3.0	0.0025	0.0026	3.86	0.0001
	3.5	0.0007	0.0007	−0.52	−0.0000
	4.0	0.0002	0.0001	−5.81	−0.0000

for positive x-values the skewness is increasing up to, say 1.5 *or* 2, *first at the periphery of the* x *values and then over the whole range.* For negative values of the argument x the deterioration of the relative deviations for larger x values begins to appear from skewness values rather less than 1, even if the absolute differences are still quite small. Table 3.11.2 is intended to illustrate the critical area. For this purpose, rather heterogeneous distributions were taken as examples and in addition the parameter n, the expected number of claims as an indicator of the size of the portfolio, is very small. Hence another critical condition is that n *should not be very small* (< 25).

Fig. 3.11.1 illustrates typical behaviour of the different formulae. The normal d.f. is symmetric and therefore incapable of approximating skewed distributions. The Edgeworth expansion is clearly better, but nowhere near so effective as the *NP* formula, which gives, even for as small n as 25, a quite good approximation over the whole relevant range.

In practice the size of the portfolio in insurance companies usually makes the skewness parameter small because the volume parameter n is in the denominator of its expression (see (3.3.7)). It is mostly of order of magnitude of 0.1–0.4, and often less. The examples given

Table 3.11.2   *Polya distributed values, h and n as given in the table. Truncated Pareto claim size d.f. ($\alpha = 2$, $1 \leqslant Z \leqslant 21$, discretized in 21 points. In the upper block $\bar{F}$ for $x < 0$ or $1 - \bar{F}$ for $x \geqslant 0$, and in the lower block the relative deviations of NP values from the corresponding $\bar{F}$ or $1 - \bar{F}$ values.*

		∞	100	100	10	10	100	5	100
	h								
	n	100	100	25	25	10	10	5	5
	γ	0.3281	0.3316	0.6453	0.6749	0.7743	1.0280	1.1426	1.4599
	-2 $\bar{F}$	0.0131	0.0130	0.0063	0.0031	0.0019	0.0004	0.0456	0.0277
	-1	0.1605	0.1605	0.1593	0.1518	0.1558	0.1445	0.1644	0.1195
	0	0.4793	0.4789	0.4465	0.4558	0.4479	0.4497	0.4175	0.4076
x	1 $1-\bar{F}$	0.1534	0.1547	0.1500	0.1550	0.1554	0.1449	0.1530	0.1320
	2	0.0308	0.0309	0.0361	0.0373	0.0395	0.0468	0.0441	0.0450
	3	0.0040	0.0040	0.0067	0.0071	0.0080	0.0112	0.0115	0.0160
	4	0.0003	0.0003	0.0010	0.0011	0.0013	0.0024	0.0026	0.0046

$$[(N_\gamma - \bar{F})/\bar{F}] \times 100$$

	-2	1.2	1.3	-9.4	63.8	92.5	167.2	-98.6	-99.7
	-1	0.2	0.2	4.9	10.7	9.8	25.2	13.4	71.9
	0	-0.2	-0.2	2.4	-0.1	0.2	-3.9	1.7	-0.9
x	1	3.4	2.6	5.8	2.3	2.1	9.5	3.7	20.2
	2	1.2	0.8	6.3	4.5	3.9	-1.7	9.1	19.0
	3	-4.2	-3.0	3.6	3.2	5.3	0.9	10.1	2.2
	4	-3.4	1.2	-1.4	4.2	6.7	3.6	13.6	0.8

The slight irregularities in relative deviations are partially due to the same rounding off effects as mentioned at Fig. 3.11.1.

here as well as the experience referred to earlier, or otherwise gained in connection with applications, suggest that the *NP* approximation can be safely used in such circumstances. Obviously Table 3.11.1 and Table 3.11.2 for $n \geqslant 25$ and $h \geqslant 100$ may give a typical picture of the accuracy, whereas Table 3.11.2 for small n and h illustrates mainly borderline conditions.

Note that the different approaches for calculation of the compound Poisson d.f. complement each other. The normal approximation is preferable for large and only slightly skewed distributions as Fig. 3.9.1 suggests. The *NP* formula is applicable also for medium-size collectives having a considerable skewness. For quite small collectives, where the *NP* approximation also often fails, exact methods like the recursive calculation dealt with in Section 3.8 are appropriate, as is the straightforward simulation which will be presented in Section 6.8.2. On the other hand, these accurate methods are not suitable for numerical calculations if the collective, i.e. n, is large and the claim size d.f. is not forced into some simplified form.

(g) The long version (3.11.9) often improves the approximation (Pesonen, 1969; Pentikäinen, 1977). However, as y increases, i.e. at the tails of the distributions, the suitability of this version may worsen in an irregular way and its utility is not well mapped as yet. Mainly for this reason, the short version only will be used in the following.

(h) Extension to negative x values The compound Poisson function F is a basic building block in the more complicated types of problems dealt with in the following chapters. Often it is needed for the whole range of the variable $\mathbf{X}$, i.e. also for negative values of the standardized variable $\mathbf{x}$ in (3.9.1). In some problems the value of the function F is given and the matching variable value X is to be calculated. For integrations and simulations fast formulae are needed for F, its inverse F^{-1} and derivative F'. The original form of the NP approximation is not suitable for all these purposes and it will now be manipulated accordingly.

For brevity let

$$g = \gamma/6 \quad \text{and} \quad h = \gamma_2/24.$$

To derive a workable formula for the 'short tail' $(x < 1)$ in the extended version (3.11.9), y is expressed as a power series of g and h

$$y = a_{00} + a_{10}g + a_{20}g^2 + a_{01}h + \cdots,$$

where the coefficients a_{ij} are unknown and have to be found. Only terms including second and lower powers of $1/\sqrt{n}$ are taken into the expansion. Substituting in (3.11.9) and equating to zero the coefficients of each power of g and h, the expansion

$$y = x - g \times (x^2 - 1) + g^2 \times (4x^3 - 7x) - h \times (x^3 - 3x) + \cdots$$

$$(3.11.11)$$

is obtained after some algebraic reductions.

In the middle of the distribution the first two terms are sufficient, but for the tail the third term is still needed. To avoid discontinuity it is appropriate to incorporate the third term at the point

$$x_0 = -\sqrt{(7/4)} \qquad (3.11.12)$$

as it is zero at this point. Hence

$$y = x - g \times (x^2 - 1) + g^2 \times (4x^3 - 7x) \times \varepsilon(x_0 - x), \quad (3.11.13)$$

where ε is the step function (1.5.3).

(i) **Summary** For convenience the original formula (3.11.8) and the modified formulae are summarized as follows

(i) *X given, F(X) to be found*

$$x = (X - \mu_X)/\sigma_X \quad \text{(for } \mu, \sigma \text{ and } \gamma \text{ see (3.3.7))}$$

$$g = \gamma/6; \; x_0 = -\sqrt{(7/4)}$$

$$y = \sqrt{\left(1 + \frac{1}{4g^2} + \frac{x}{g}\right)} - \frac{1}{2g} \qquad \text{for } x \geq 1$$

$$= x - g(x^2 - 1) + g^2(4x^3 - 7x)\varepsilon(x_0 - x) \qquad \text{for } x < 1$$

$$F(X) \approx N(y). \tag{3.11.14}$$

By using the notation of (3.11.10) the above relations can be written briefly

$$F(X) \approx N_y(x) = N[v_y^{-1}(x)], \tag{3.11.14a}$$

where $v_y^{-1}(x)$ is the transformation $x \to y$ defined by the third and fourth lines of (3.11.14) and depicted in Fig. 3.11.2.

(ii) *F(X) given, X to be found*
Four auxiliary constants are first calculated

$$y_0 = -\sqrt{\left(\tfrac{7}{4}\right)} - \tfrac{3}{4}g$$

$$P = \frac{11}{144}\frac{1}{g^2} - \frac{7}{12}$$

$$Q = \frac{17}{1728}\frac{1}{g^3} + \frac{5}{96}\frac{1}{g} - \frac{1}{8}\frac{y}{g^2} \tag{3.11.15}$$

$$D = \sqrt{(P^3 + Q^2)},$$

where y is the root of $F(X) = N(y)$, i.e. $y = N^{-1}(F(X))$. Then

$$x = y + g(y^2 - 1) \qquad\qquad \text{for } y \geq 1$$

$$= \frac{1}{2g} - \sqrt{\left(\frac{1}{4g^2} + 1 - \frac{y}{g}\right)} \qquad \text{for } y_0 \leq y < 1 \quad (3.11.16)$$

$$= \sqrt[3]{(D - Q)} - \sqrt[3]{(D + Q)} + \frac{1}{12g} \quad \text{for } y < y_0,$$

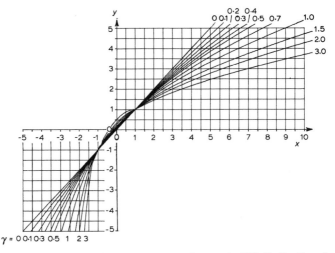

Figure 3.11.2 *NP transformation* $x \to y$, *where* y *is* $N(0, 1)$ *distributed and* $x = v_\gamma(y)$ *is* $NP(0, 1, \gamma)$ *distributed.*

and finally

$$X = \mu_X + x\sigma_X. \qquad (3.11.17)$$

The last part of formula (3.11.16) is found from (3.11.14) by means of Cardan's solution.

By using the notations of (3.11.10) the above relations can be written briefly

$$X = \mu_X + \sigma_X \cdot v_\gamma[N^{-1}(F(X))], \qquad (3.11.17a)$$

where $v_\gamma(y)$ is now defined by (3.11.16).

Fig. 3.11.2 gives a view of the variable transformation $x \to y$ according to (3.11.14). It can also be used as a nomogram which gives y approximately when x is given or vice versa.

(j) The density function f of F is required for applications where convolutions and other integrals are to be computed. It can be derived from the equations given by differentiation

$$f(X) = \bar{F}'(x)\frac{dx}{dX} = \bar{f}(x)\frac{1}{\sigma_X},$$

$$\bar{f}(x) = \frac{1}{\sqrt{(2\pi)}} e^{-\frac{1}{2}y^2}\frac{dy}{dx} \qquad\qquad (3.11.18)$$

$$\frac{dy}{dx} = \frac{1}{1 + 2gy}, \qquad\qquad \text{for } x \geqslant 1$$

$$= 1 - 2gx + g^2(12x^2 - 7)\varepsilon(x_0 - x) \quad \text{for } x < 1.$$

where, as above, $g = \gamma/6$.

When X is given, the corresponding y is to be calculated from (3.11.14) and is then to be placed in (3.11.18).

Convenient approximations exist for programming of the normal function N or its inverse (see (3.9.5) and (3.9.6)).

(k) **Asymptotic behaviour** It was stated in item 3.3(g) that the relative compound Poisson variable $\mathbf{x} = X/mn$ has for $n \to \infty$ the limits $\sigma_\mathbf{x} = \sigma_\mathbf{q}$ and $\gamma_\mathbf{x} = \gamma_\mathbf{q}$ and that its d.f. tends to the structure d.f. H. Then $NP(1, \sigma_\mathbf{x}, \gamma_\mathbf{x})$ tends to $NP(1, \sigma_\mathbf{q}, \gamma_\mathbf{q})$, hence approximating the structure function $H(X/mn)$ (see (3.3.16)). How good a fit the NP function can give for $\bar{F}(x)$ for large values of the volume parameter n depends, obviously, on how well the NP function can approximate the structure d.f. H. This depends on the shape of H. However, in practical applications this problem often has only academic value, because the strict form of H is seldom known. Usually only its standard deviation $\sigma_\mathbf{q}$ can be evaluated and, perhaps, also the skewness $\gamma_\mathbf{q}$ to some degree. Then obviously the NP function with the same parameters can represent it as well as any other d.f., unless perhaps some particular reason justifies other conclusions.

Note that in the Polya case where the structure distribution is *assumed* to be a gamma function, the limit distribution is also a gamma function. Then the gamma approximation presented in Section 3.12 may seem to be a natural approach. However, as will be seen, the NP and gamma functions having the same mean value, standard deviation and skewness give the same numerical values to a very close degree.

(l) Discussion A drawback of the above approach is that the derivative (3.11.18) has discontinuities at points 1 and x_0. They can be removed by applying the so-called spline technique for example, but this would lead to more complicated expressions and increase the computation time. Moreover, it would not generally give a much better result than the direct application of (3.11.18), because these formulae are needed mainly for the calculation of integrals of type $\int A(x)\mathrm{d}F(x)$ where A is some function depending on the application in question. The errors on either side of the discontinuity points have opposite signs and hence are likely to offset each other in integration.

The poor fit for negative values of the standardized variable x has already been mentioned in item (f). If the parameter n is small, this can result in a just significant probability that X has a negative value (whilst X was assumed overall non-negative, see Section 1.3). This is demonstrated in exercise 3.11.2, giving a simple test for the applicability of the formula in circumstances where the negative tail of the distribution is required.

Even if the formulae (3.11.14) to (3.11.18) are not so simple in form as one could wish – mainly due to the necessity to split the range of the variable x into sections having different expressions – they are easily programmable and convenient for fast computation. A major benefit is that they can be operated in either direction, $X \to F(X)$ and $F(X) \to X$.

(m) The Wilson–Hilferty formula (3.5.14) is another example of 'normalizing' transformation (3.11.1). Applied now to the direct calculation of $\bar{F}(x)$ it gives values very close to those given by the NP formula when the skewness γ is not very large ($\leqslant 2$ for positive x and $\leqslant 1$ for negative x values).

Exercise 3.11.1 Let the moments about zero of the claim size d.f. be $a_1 = £10^3$, $a_2 = £^2\,10^8$ and $a_3 = £^3\,10^{14}$ and let the standard deviation and the skewness of the structure distribution be 0.1 and 0.5 and the expected number of claims $n = 10\,000$. Calculate the probability that the total amount of claims exceeds $14 \times £10^6$ by using (a) the Normal approximation, (b) the NP formula and (c) the Wilson–Hilferty formula.

Exercise 3.11.2 Show that when a compound Poisson variable is approximated by the NP formula, a condition for probability of negative values to be $< \varepsilon$ is that

$$n > r_2 x_\varepsilon^2 / (1 - x_\varepsilon^2 \sigma_q^2), \qquad (3.11.19)$$

where x_ε is the root of $\varepsilon = N_\gamma(x)$. Calculate the lower boundary (3.11.19) of n for $\varepsilon = 10^{-4}$, $r_2 = 10$, $r_3 = 200$, $\sigma_q = 0.05$ and $\gamma_q = 0.5$.

3.12 Gamma approximation

(a) Three-parameter gamma function The mixed compound Poisson function F can be approximated also by the incomplete gamma function $\Gamma(ax + b, \alpha)$, where again x is the normed variable (3.9.1) and the parameters a, b and c are determined from the condition that the mean, standard deviation and skewness should be equal to those of F. As was seen in Section 3.5.6, these conditions result in

$$F(X) \approx \Gamma(\alpha + x\sqrt{\alpha}, \alpha) \qquad x \geqslant -\sqrt{\alpha}, \qquad (3.12.1)$$

where

$$\alpha = 4/\gamma^2.$$

Now γ is the skewness of the aggregate claim distribution (instead of claim size d.f. in (3.5.9)).

References for calculation technique were given already in Section 3.5.6 (see also Bohman and Esscher, 1964; Pentikäinen, 1977 and Seal 1977).

(b) Applicability The NP approximation and gamma approximation are compared in Fig. 3.12.1. In the area which is mostly needed for applications both approximations give about the same values. Only when the skewness increases to the level of 2 do the values diverge for the positive x values and for the negative x values already before it. But these are variable areas where both approximations are unreliable. The gamma distribution is not defined for values less than $-2/\gamma$ (or is defined to be 0).

Experience of the application of these formulae suggests that their ability to give a satisfactory fit is roughly equal. The choice of the formula should depend on the convenience for the user in the context of each application. A handicap is that the gamma approximation

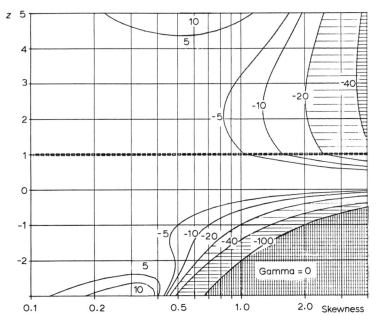

Figure 3.12.1 *Comparison of the gamma and NP functions. The niveau curves of the relative deviation* $(\Gamma - N_\gamma)/N_\gamma \times 100$ *for* $x \leqslant 0$ *and* $[(1 - \Gamma) - (1 - N_\gamma)]/(1 - N_\gamma) \times 100$ *for* $x > 0$ *as functions of the normed variable x and the skewness γ are plotted in a semi-logarithmic scale. In the area bordered by the niveau curves $+5$ and -5 the absolute value of the deviation is less than 5%. In the right hand side lower corner $\Gamma = 0$.*

is not easy to handle in problems where the function value $F(X)$ is given and the matching argument X is required.

Exercise 3.12.1 Instead of the three-parameter version just applied, a two-parameter version $\Gamma(ax, \alpha)$ can also be used. Calculate a and α from the condition that the approximating function should have as mean and standard deviation μ_X and σ_X. What is its skewness?

Exercise 3.12.2 Develop the Wilson–Hilferty argument $y =$ the expression in brackets in (3.5.14) as series and verify that the lowest terms coincide with the *NP* expansion for $z > 1$. (Hint: Manipulate the expression in a form where the quantity $\gamma z/2$ can be used as the argument of the series development.)

**3.13 Approximations by means of functions belonging to the Pearson family

(a) The Pearson system The idea of both the NP approximation and the gamma approximation was to find an analytic d.f. which has a shape known by experience to be generally of close fit to distributions functions of aggregate claims, and then to equate the lowest moments. Besides these two functions there are also a number of others which are suggested for similar use. An approach to solving the problem is to assume that the approximating function belongs to the Pearson system of curves (see item 3.5.11(b)). Use of two moments gives the normal approximation described earlier. The use of three moments implies that the assumed distribution of F is the Pearson type III (gamma distribution) and the use of four moments implies a distribution of type I (beta distribution). The available tabulations of the various Pearson distributions can be used when the parameters have been found.

For some applications the table of values of standardized deviates at various probability levels for given values of the model parameters γ_1 and γ_2 (Johnson *et al.*, 1963) may be sufficient for practical purposes, and may afford a rapid method of approximation since the effect of the factors γ_1 and γ_2 can be easily assessed.

(b) The beta density function

$$f(x; p, q) = \frac{x^{p-1}(1-x)^{q-1}}{B(p, q)} \quad \text{for } 0 < x < 1$$
$$= 0 \qquad\qquad \text{for } x \leqslant 0 \text{ or } x \geqslant 1 \qquad (3.13.1)$$

with

$$B(p, q) = \int_0^1 u^{p-1}(1-u)^{q-1} \, du,$$

was used by Campagne when the rules for the EEC convention for solvency margins were under consideration. Here x is the claims ratio defined as the claims paid for the insurer's own account divided by the premiums including also loading for expenses. p and q are parameters, the mean of $\mathbf{x}$ being

$$\mu_{\mathbf{x}} = p/(p + q)$$

and variance

$$\sigma_x^2 = \frac{pq}{(p+q)^2(p+q+1)}.$$

A description of the method and some follow-up investigations can can be found in De Wit and Kastelijn, 1980. The mean m_x for ten Dutch companies was found to be 0.43, σ_x 0.089 and $p = 12.9$, $q = 16.9$. The probability $x > 0.78 = m_x + 3.9\sigma_x$ is, according to these values, 0.0003.

**3.14 Inversion of the characteristic function

According to a general theorem of Fourier transforms the transform (1.6.8) $F \to \varphi$, which couples any d.f. to its characteristic function, has an inverse transform, which gives F uniquely at continuity points

$$F(X) = \frac{1}{2\pi} \lim_{T \to \infty} \int_{-T}^{+T} \frac{1 - e^{-isX}}{is} \varphi(s) \, ds + \tfrac{1}{2}F(0). \tag{3.14.1}$$

Thus, in case F is a compound Poisson d.f. and if n, H and S are known, the characteristic function can be calculated (see Section 3.4) and thereafter F according to (3.14.1). Though apparently simple, this method leads to the problem of quadrature of complex functions, which may oscillate widely, and numerical methods have to be used with care. Successful applications have been made by Bohman (1964) and Seal (1971) and more recently by the use of fast Fourier transforms backed up by a computer facility (Brigham, 1974; Bertram, 1981).

3.15 Mixed methods

(a) **The decomposition of S** can be achieved in various ways and a convenient method may be used for each component. One possibility is to divide S into components according to the size class of claim (see item 3.7(g)).

If the largest class consisting of claims ($\geqslant Z_1$) is taken as one component, it can be expected that for the remaining part the normal or the NP approximation will suffice as soon as the number of claims is sufficiently large, say a few thousand (Fig. 3.15.1) since the

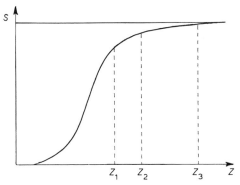

Figure 3.15.1   *Decomposition of S function.*

failure of these approximations in practice largely arises from the long tail of the S distribution.

The tail left outside the large class of ordinary claims can then be divided into one or more components. Since each class derived in this way generally includes only a small number of claims, one possible method is to use a Monte Carlo method (Section (6.8) for each component, or the recursion formula (Section 3.8).

(b) An example of the mixed method in handling of *catastrophic risk* is given in item 6.8.4(f) and it is dealt with by Rantala (1982), who also treats the 'multichannel problem' brought about by the fact that a major catastrophe may affect simultaneously, through quite numerous treaties, insurers who have accepted risks via the world-wide reinsurance network.

CHAPTER 4

Applications related to one-year time-span

4.1 The basic equation

(a) One year as time-span The various formulae developed in the previous sections provide the means to solve problems of central interest in the area of applications of risk theory. In this chapter consideration is restricted to a one-year time-span only, such as when evaluating the limits in which the underwriting result will fluctuate and how it depends on background factors like the size of the portfolio, the distribution of the claim size, reinsurance, the level of the safety loadings, etc. Limitation of the study to one year makes it possible to express many of the interdependences of the variables involved in a form which is easy to handle when analysing the structure of the risk process. Of course, a one-year time-span is not sufficient for consideration of many important problems concerning e.g. solvency, long-range planning, etc. and this restriction will be relaxed in later chapters. However, results concerning a short period are of interest in many connections, e.g. it may be useful to know the range of fluctuation of the annual underwriting gain or loss. Features unveiled for the one-year case are then easily extended for longer periods in an analogous way.

(b) Risk premium In previous chapters the claims process only was examined and now a new variable will be introduced, namely the risk premium income

$$P = E(\mathbf{X}) = \mu_{\mathbf{X}} = mn. \tag{4.1.1}$$

This, by definition, is the expected value of claims, all the variables now being related to a one-year period (see (3.3.7)).

(c) Safety loading It is further assumed that the risk premium is increased by a safety loading. This can be done in a number of different ways, e.g. by relating it to the risk premium, to the standard deviation of the assumed risk or to the variance, or by using some combination of these components as follows

$$L_i = \lambda' P_i + \lambda'' \sigma_{\mathbf{X}i} + \lambda''' \sigma_{\mathbf{X}i}^2. \tag{4.1.2}$$

Here the lambdas are coefficients, the determination of which is one of the central problems in premium rating. The subscript i refers to individual policies or group of policies. Of course the lambdas may be different for different types or groups of insurance. From the point of view of most considerations in risk theory the question of how the individual policies are loaded is not relevant. The important quantity is the *total income* arising from these loadings, i.e. ΣL_i. Then a weighted safety loading coefficient will be defined by

$$\lambda = \Sigma L_i / \Sigma P_i. \tag{4.1.3}$$

It can first be calculated separately for different sections of the portfolio, after which the coefficient λ for the whole business is obtained from the (average) section loadings applying (4.1.3) to section data

$$\lambda = \frac{1}{P} \Sigma L_j = \Sigma \frac{P_j}{P} \lambda_j = \Sigma \pi_j \lambda_j, \tag{4.1.4}$$

where j refers to section. The weighting factors are the same as defined already by (3.7.8).

In order to incorporate the safety loading in the model, the loaded premium $(1 + \lambda)P$ will mostly be used instead of the risk premium P. Even if the safety loading is formally written in linear form, it means a weighted average as defined by (4.1.3) and (4.1.4), and the type of rating formula e.g. (4.1.2) or any other is irrelevant. The coefficient depends, of course, on the structure and also, for non-linear loading formulae, on the size of the portfolio, because $\lambda_i = L_i / P_i$ may be different for different risk units i. However, the structure of the portfolio is normally changing only slowly, so that λ is a fairly stable quantity and can be used as one of the characteristics of the portfolio.

(d) Underwriting process It is now assumed that the premium

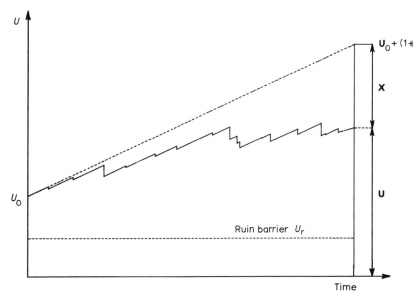

Figure 4.1.1   *The risk process as a difference of incoming premiums and out-going claims.*

income is accumulated to a *risk reserve* **U** and the claims are paid out from it as demonstrated in Fig. 4.1.1.

A basic problem to which many other considerations are related to is to examine the distribution of the risk reserve **U** at the end of the accounting period. In fact **U** − U_0 means underwriting gain (or loss, if negative). Then the range of variation of this quantity is sought. This problem can also be formulated to concern the so-called one-year *ruin probability* ε, the probability that **U** could drop under some ruin barrier U_r which will be defined for the problem under consideration. It can be, for example, the statutory minimum solvency margin. Recall that the ruin probability can be defined in a continuous or discrete way (see item 1.4(a)), i.e. according to whether **U** will be less than U_r at any time during the observation period or only at its end. For reasons discussed in Section 1.4 the latter possibility, the 'year-end ruin probability', will be used in the following. The answer to the ruin question is immediately provided by means of the d.f. F of $\mathbf{X}$ as follows

$$1 - \varepsilon = \text{prob}\{\mathbf{U} \geqslant U_r\} = \text{prob}\{\mathbf{X} \leqslant U_0 - U_r + (1 + \lambda)P\}$$
$$= F(U_0 - U_r + (1 + \lambda)P). \tag{4.1.5}$$

$1 - \varepsilon$ is often called the 'survival probability'.

(e) **Basic equation** To get the equation in a form which gives the interdependence of the involved variables explicitly, it is assumed that the NP approximation is applicable.

For brevity $\mathbf{U}$ is here and later often scaled by putting $U_r = 0$, and U_0 will be denoted by U if the clarity in the context concerned does not necessitate the subscript. Furthermore, let y_ε be the value of the standardized variable which corresponds to the ruin probability ε according to the equation

$$\varepsilon = N(-y_\varepsilon) = 1 - N(y_\varepsilon). \tag{4.1.6}$$

For example, $y_{0.01} = 2.326$ and $y_{0.001} = 3.090$. The shorter form y will sometimes be used in place of y_ε.

Making use of the above notation and the NP formula (3.11.16) (for $y \geqslant 1$) and (3.11.17) the relation (4.1.5) can be written in the form of the following basic equation

$$U = y_\varepsilon \sigma_{\mathbf{X}} - \lambda P + \tfrac{1}{6}\gamma_{\mathbf{X}}(y_\varepsilon^2 - 1)\sigma_{\mathbf{X}}. \tag{4.1.7a}$$

Assuming $\mathbf{X}$ as a compound Poisson variable and substituting the expressions of the standard deviation and the skewness from (3.3.7) this equation can be written

$$U = y_\varepsilon P\sqrt{(r_2/n + \sigma_{\mathbf{q}}^2)} - \lambda P$$
$$+ \tfrac{1}{6}P(y_\varepsilon^2 - 1) \times (r_3/n^2 + 3r_2\sigma_{\mathbf{q}}^2/n + \gamma_{\mathbf{q}}\sigma_{\mathbf{q}}^3)/(r_2/n + \sigma_{\mathbf{q}}^2). \tag{4.1.7b}$$

In the particular case where the normal approximation is applicable the above equations are reduced to the shorter form

$$U = y_\varepsilon \sigma_{\mathbf{X}} - \lambda P = y_\varepsilon P\sqrt{(r_2/n + \sigma_{\mathbf{q}}^2)} - \lambda P. \tag{4.1.8}$$

These equations contain either explicitly or implicitly the quantities

$$\varepsilon, \lambda, M, U, \sigma_{\mathbf{q}}, \gamma_{\mathbf{q}} \text{ and } n \text{ or } P. \tag{4.1.9}$$

Furthermore, the coefficients r_2 and r_3 and the risk premium income P depend on the claim size d.f. S or rather on its lowest moments a_1,

a_2 and a_3. The maximum net retention M is included in the list (4.1.9) because these moments depend on it, M being one of the 'primary control variables' (see Section 3.6). As a primary volume variable either n or P will be used. When one of them is given as well as the other variables (4.1.9) and the claim size d.f. S then the basic equation is determined.

The portfolio under consideration may mostly be divided into sections and the basic variables (4.1.9) are derived from the section variables and data as presented in Section 3.7. This phase of the calculations will be assumed to be ready made and will be no longer referred to. Then it is sufficient to treat the portfolio as if it were undivided.

The main problems of concern in this chapter are of the type where the claim size function S is given together with six of the quantities (4.1.9), the seventh being the object of study.

A more general family of problems is introduced by treating more than one of the quantities (4.1.9) as unknown. In this case the basic equation does not give a definite solution, but auxiliary conditions can be added, for example, maximizing the expected value of profit. To do this it is necessary to obtain the expression for the mean value of the profit, according to the actual circumstances, and to derive a solution of the bound extremal problem which satisfies (4.1.7) or (4.1.8) and at the same time gives a maximum to the profit function. Another case arises where the company wishes to use different net retentions M for different lines of business, in which event there are several unknown, retention limits M instead of a single value. This again leads to a bound extremal problem in several unknown variables; an example of this type will be considered in Section 4.6.

4.2   Evaluation of the fluctuation range of the annual underwriting profits and losses

(a) **Problem setting** An important application of risk theory is the determination of the range in which the annual profit or loss resulting from the underwriting operation may fluctuate. Thus the lowest point U_1 of the risk reserve may be sought, below which the risk reserve **U** will not fall for a given probability $1 - \varepsilon$ (Fig. 4.2.1(a)). Another way of formulating the problem is to ask what must be the

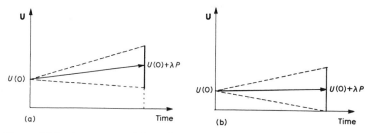

Figure 4.2.1 *Two ways of formulating the problem of reserve fluctuation: by seeking (a) the lowest point U_t and (b) the initial reserve $U = U(0)$.*

initial amount $U = U(0)$ such that the reserve will not be exhausted at the end of the accounting period (Fig. 4.2.1(b)). The latter approach will be assumed in this chapter but the former problem setting will prove important in subsequent chapters.

(b) Standard data A solution can be obtained directly by applying (4.1.5) or, if the NP approximation is applicable – as it usually is – the NP formula (4.1.7) or the normal approximation (4.1.8). Examples showing how U can be examined as a function of the other six variables (4.1.9) are set out in Figs. 4.2.2–4.2.6. In order to make the sequence of the applications mutually comparable, and also comparable with the applications presented in Chapter 7 for longer time spans, the same standard data will be used, unless otherwise mentioned, for the variables (4.1.7) and for the basic distributions as follows:

$$\varepsilon = 0.001$$
$$\lambda = 0.04$$
$$n = 10\,000 \tag{4.2.1}$$
$$M = £10^6$$
$$\sigma_q = 0.038$$
$$\gamma_q = 0.25$$
$$S_M(Z) \text{ according to Table 3.6.1.}$$

The value of U which satisfies (4.1.7), when the above data are substituted in it, is $U = 15.72 \ £10^6$. The risk premium income corresponding to the data is $P = 73.0 \ £10^6$.

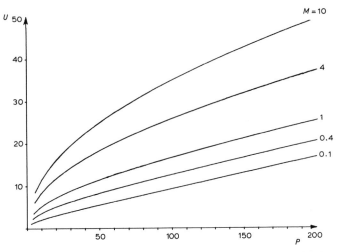

Figure 4.2.2 U as a function of net premiums P and net retention M. Unit is £10^6. Standard data (4.2.1).

(c) Risk reserve $U = U(P, M)$ The initial minimum risk reserve U as a function of the risk premiums P and the retention limit M is depicted in Fig. 4.2.2. As understandable, U is an increasing function of both P and M. The structure of both dependencies will be discussed more fully later. Note that both U and $P = n \times m(M)$ depend on M.

(d) Solvency ratio $U/P = f(P, \lambda)$ In some situations a more appropriate approach is to formulate the problem in terms of the relative amount for the risk reserve rather than the absolute amount U. In the following this will be called the *solvency ratio* and will be denoted by u. This is done in Fig. 4.2.3 where minimum initial solvency ratio u is calculated as a function of P and λ. It quite obviously tends asymptotically to some horizontal level, a feature which will be analytically explained subsequently. If λ is high and the business volume large, then no initial capital U at all is necessary, i.e. the safety loading alone is sufficient to cover the adverse fluctuations. In the special case where the structure variation has degenerated ($\sigma_q = 0$) u tends to $-\lambda$ when $n \to \infty$.

Even though a larger insurer needs more initial capital U than a smaller one, according to Fig. 4.2.2 the *relative* need, i.e. the smallest

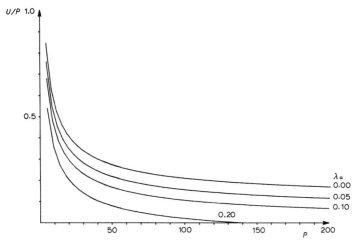

Figure 4.2.3   *The solvency ratio* $u = U/P$ *as a function of* P *and* λ. *Standard data* (4.2.1).

still safe solvency ratio, is a *decreasing* function of the company size.

(e) Net retention $M = f(n, U)$ Next the net retention limit M is examined as a function of U and n in Fig. 4.2.4. In this example M affects significantly the risk coefficients r_2 and r_3 (see (3.3.8)) as seen in Table 3.6.1. In the double logarithmic scale the curves are approximately linear. Of course, for claim size distributions containing only small risks the structure of the figure is another type – the curves have a vertical asymptote when M increases beyond the values of the maximum claim sizes.

Retention problems are discussed further in Section 4.5.

(f) Ruin probability $\varepsilon = f(n, U)$ Figure 4.2.5 sets out the ruin probability $\varepsilon = 1 - F$ as a function of n and U.

In order to demonstrate the influence of the structure function its variance was removed in two cases ($\sigma_q = 0$) dotted in the figure. As seen, the change for large collectives (n large) is quite crucial. This means that the structure variation is the main cause of the fluctuations of large portfolios, whereas the 'pure Poisson' fluctuation is dominant for small portfolios. This very same feature was already anticipated by Table 3.3.2.

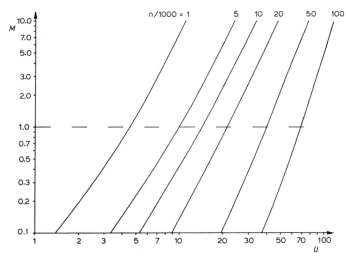

Figure 4.2.4 *The net retention M as a function of U and n. Monetary unit is* £10⁶ *(double logarithmic scale).*

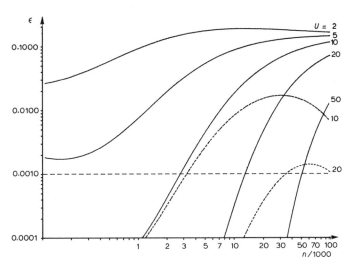

Figure 4.2.5 *The ruin probability ε as a function of n and U. Two Poisson cases ($\sigma_q = 0$) are plotted by dotted lines.*

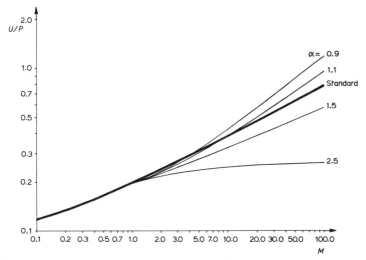

Figure 4.2.6 $u = U/P$ as function of M for different Pareto-distributed tails.
Unit for M is $£10^6$.

If λ is positive the ruin probability as a function of the size variable
n has, in general, a maximum even though its location may be,
owing to the structure component ($\sigma_q > 0$, $\gamma_q > 0$), quite remote.
In the Poisson cases the maximum is clearly seen.

(g) The effect of the claim size d.f. To show the effect of the choice
of claim size function S, calculations based on some Pareto distributions are set out in Fig. 4.2.6 together with values for our standard
distribution.

It was assumed that $S(Z)$ is in all cases the same and equal to
the standard up to the value $Z_0 = £10^6$, and the tail is upwards
Pareto distributed (see (3.5.20)). Even though only 0.072% (see
Table 3.6.1, line 26) of the probability mass of the $S(Z)$ distribution
is located in the area $Z > Z_0$ its influence on the behaviour of the
tail of the function $u = U/P = u(M)$ is quite significant. This means,
among other things, that if a portfolio gross of reinsurance is
considered, its solvency properties may depend quite crucially on
the assumptions concerning the upper tail of the claim size distribution. As already expected (see item 3.5.8(c) and Table 3.5.1) the
standard distribution is to be classified as 'dangerous'.

(h) Effect of the risk of catastrophic claims The estimation of the chance of occurrence of very great claims is one of the major practical difficulties in risk theory, owing to the fact that the experience basis is nearly always limited and unexpected events may give rise to losses of unforeseen dimensions. It was suggested in item 3.5.3(c) that in uncertainty hypothetical 'shadow' claims should be incorporated into the claims statistics when the claim size d.f. is derived. Another way to investigate the sensitivity of the outcomes for large claims is to assume that, in addition to the 'normal' claims expenditure X, a large single claim X_c will still occur with some estimated frequency q. Because q is expected to be very small, the occurrence of two extra large claims in one year can be omitted. Then the d.f. $F(X)$ of the aggregate claim is changed to the form

$$\bar{F}(X) = (1 - q)F(X) + qF(X - X_c), \qquad (4.2.2)$$

which is the straightforward convolution of the original distribution and the distribution consisting of the single claim X_c, the latter being binomial with fixed sum X_c.

An example of the application of equation (4.2.2) can be found in exercise 4.2.5.

(i) Profile figure Because it is not easy to get an adequate view of the interdependence of the variables involved by merely constructing figures like Figs 4.2.2–4.2.6, an attempt to give a synthesis is made in the profile Fig. 4.2.7. The idea is first to calculate U for average circumstances (basic alternative). Then the different variables are changed individually so that the sensitivity of U to the background factors can be examined and a mental picture obtained of the risk structure.

Exercise 4.2.1 It is assumed that the risk properties of an insurance portfolio are so improved that the frequency of claim decreases equally for each risk unit by 10%. How much could the reserve fund U be decreased if the ruin probability ε is maintained at the original level and the premiums remain unchanged. Equation (4.1.8) can be used, in millions of £, with data $U = 20, n = 10\,000$, $m = 0.01, r_2 = 30, \sigma_q = 0$ and $\lambda = 0.05$.

Exercise 4.2.2 A friendly society grants funeral expense benefits and each member of the society can choose a benefit of either £100

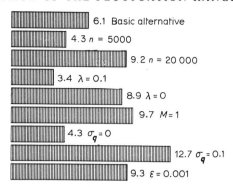

Figure 4.2.7 *Dependence of the risk reserve U according to the basic equation (4.1.7). U is calculated first to the basic combination $n = 10\,000$, $M = 0.4$, $\lambda = 0.05$, $\sigma_q = 0.04$, $\gamma_q = 0.25$, $P = 54.6$, $\varepsilon = 0.01$, having unit = £10^6. Then the variables changed as given in the figure and the value of U is plotted individually at each bar.*

or £200. It is assumed that $\lambda = 0.5$, $n = 20$, $\sigma_q = 0$ and $\varepsilon = 0.01$. How large should the reserve fund U be according to (4.1.8) if it is not known in advance how many members will choose the option 100 and how many the option 200 and, consequently, what mix of these options is to be assumed so as to maximize the risk?

Exercise 4.2.3 Assume that the distribution function of one claim can be represented by the exponential function $S'(z) = e^{-z}(z \geqslant 0)$ (taking the average size of claims as the monetary unit). The expected number of claims n is 1000 and $\sigma_q = 0.04$. How large should the safety loading λ be according to (4.1.8) if there is no reinsurance and no reserve fund, and if ε is fixed at 0.01?

Exercise 4.2.4 Let the claim size d.f. be of Pareto type, equal to $1 - z^{-\alpha}$ for $z \geqslant 1$ expressed in suitable monetary units; excess of loss reinsurance is arranged with maximum net retention M. Calculate M by one decimal from (4.1.7) when $\alpha = 2.5$, $U = 20$, $n = 100$, $\lambda = 0.1$, $\sigma_q = 0$ and $y_\varepsilon = 2.33$. Hint: Derive an expression for U as a function of M and then find (by trial and error) the requested numerical value of M.

Exercise 4.2.5 Let the portfolio be the standard one defined by the data of (4.2.1). How is the ruin probability ε changed if the chance of an extra claim X_c according to item 4.2(h) is assumed? Experimental values are $X_c = £5$, 10 and 20 million respectively. The extra claim X_c is expected to occur once in 20 years. F can be approximated by the NP function.

4.3   Some approximate formulae

(a) Asymptotic behaviour Although the procedure presented in the previous section is not very troublesome in practice, it still does not provide a clear insight into the interdependence of the basic quantities (4.1.9). To obtain a comprehensive survey it is more useful to derive explicit even if approximate expressions.

First manipulate (4.1.7) into the form

$$U/P = (y + \gamma_X(y^2 - 1)/6)\sqrt{(r_2/n + \sigma_q^2)} - \lambda. \qquad (4.3.1)$$

When $n \to \infty$ it follows that

$$\frac{U}{P} \to \left(y + \frac{y^2 - 1}{6}\gamma_q\right)\sigma_q - \lambda, \qquad (4.3.2)$$

since according to (3.3.7) the skewness $\gamma_X \to \gamma_q$. Hence only the terms related to the variation of the basic probabilities are left. This is again the result mentioned in item 3.3(g), i.e. the mixed compound Poisson distribution asymptotically tends to the structure distribution H.

It is seen from (4.3.2) that in the general case $(\sigma_q > 0)$ the limiting value of U/P is positive or negative depending on the size of λ. The character of the process is essentially different in the Poisson case where $\sigma_q = 0$, i.e. when variation of the basic probabilities vanishes. Then $U/P \to -\lambda$ and the standard deviation $\sigma_X \to 0$. As was seen in item 3.3(g) in fact the variation of the basic probabilities constitutes the fluctuation in large collectives. This same feature is seen in Fig. 4.2.5. The horizontal asymptote, which was anticipated already from Fig. 4.2.3, can be explained by (4.3.2).

(b) Distribution-free approximations Situations often occur in which general ideas of the magnitude of M or U are needed, when the function S is not known or when for other reasons it is not possible to make use of it in calculations involving (4.1.7). In these circumstances it is possible to find a distribution-free estimate for U.

The structure variation affects the expected number of claims $\mathbf{n} = n\mathbf{q}$ via the variable $\mathbf{q}$ making $\mathbf{n}$ larger or smaller than n. While the premium P is assumed to the fixed $P = (1 + \lambda) \times E(\mathbf{X})$, the effect is equivalent with the fact that the safety loading $\lambda E(\mathbf{X}) = P - E(\mathbf{X}|\mathbf{n}(t))$ varies from year to year. Furthermore, the structure variation affects the width of the variation range as seen by equation (4.1.7b). These observations make it possible to find upper limits for the various fluctuation ranges replacing the effect of the structure variations by a conservative deterministic choice of λ and n. This approach is the more appropriate when the long-term cycles are also to be taken into account (see Section 7.4).

Assuming that the portfolio is reinsured so that the individual claim sizes are limited to $\leqslant M$, the inequality

$$a_i = \int_0^M Z^i \, dS_M(Z) \leqslant M \int_0^M Z^{i-1} \, dS_M(Z) = Ma_{i-1}, \quad (4.3.3)$$

can be utilized. The equality is valid only if the size of one claim is constant and equal to M. Putting this limit in (4.3.1) and using the convention $P = mn$, a distribution-free upper limit for U is obtained

$$U \leqslant y\sqrt{(PM)} - \lambda P + \tfrac{1}{6}(y^2 - 1)M. \quad (4.3.4)$$

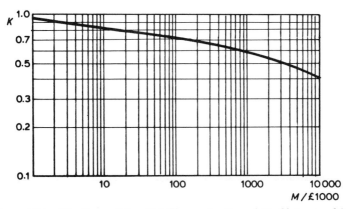

Figure 4.3.1   *The factor K (see (4.3.5)) as a function of M. Claim size d.f. as given in Table 3.6.1.*

To get an idea of how rough the approximation (4.3.4) may be, its main 'error factor', the ratio

$$K = P\sqrt{(r_2/n)}/\sqrt{(PM)} = \sqrt{(a_2/Mm)} \qquad (4.3.5)$$

of the main terms in (4.1.8) and (4.3.4) is plotted in Fig. 4.3.1 for the standard d.f. (Table 3.6.1). This figure as well as numerous other examples suggests that for the commonly used values of M the factor K lies in the interval 0.5 to 0.8 and that the value $K \approx 0.6$ can be used as an estimate. K is (possibly with some rare local exceptions) a decreasing function of M and it tends to zero when $M \to \infty$.

It follows that the approximation (4.3.4) can safely be improved into the form

$$U \approx Ky\sqrt{(PM)} - \lambda P + \tfrac{1}{6}(y^2 - 1)M, \qquad (4.3.6)$$

where K is to be fixed according to the application in question.

Assigning to K the value 0.6 further simplification is obtained

$$U \approx 1.4\sqrt{(PM)} - \lambda P \qquad (\varepsilon = 0.01) \qquad (4.3.7a)$$

$$\approx 1.9\sqrt{(PM)} - \lambda P \qquad (\varepsilon = 0.001). \qquad (4.3.7b)$$

The last term in (4.3.6) is omitted because it is significant only for large values of M and, should M be large, the first term on the right-hand side is an overestimation, as seen from Fig. 4.3.1 and thus compensates for the omission.

Some curves representing the approximation (4.3.7b) are shown in Fig. 4.3.2 and, for comparison, a curve calculated directly by means of the basic equation (4.1.7) omitting the structure variation (i.e. $\sigma_q = 0$). The closeness of the approximation is due to the fact that, for the distribution used in the figure, K does not deviate very much from its assumed value of 0.6.

(c) **The most dangerous distribution** The formula (4.3.4) has a nice interpretation. It corresponds exactly to a hypothetical portfolio where all claims are equal to M and where the expected number of claims $n = P/M$. For this particular claim size distribution the moments a_i are $= M^i$ and the equality in (4.3.3) and (4.3.4) is valid. Hence this portfolio is the *most dangerous* among all having the

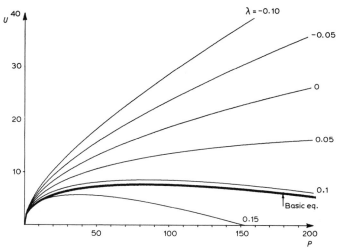

Figure 4.3.2 *U values, assuming* $M = £10^6$, *computed by approximation* (4.3.7b) *and for* $\lambda = 0.1$ *also by the basic equation* (4.1.7).

same P and the claims being limited in the interval $0 \leqslant Z \leqslant M$, i.e. it needs the largest initial reserve U.

(d) Some general properties of the solvency structure can be seen from (4.3.7) and from Fig. 4.3.2. The magnitude of the lowest, still safe, risk reserve U as a function of the volume of the portfolio, measured by P, is a parabola. If λ is non-positive then U *increases* at least *proportionately to the square root of the premium income P*. If, however, λ is positive, the curve of U has a maximum given by:

$$U_1 = \frac{K^2 y^2}{4\lambda} M \qquad \text{for } P_1 = \frac{K^2 y^2}{4\lambda^2} M = U_1/\lambda. \qquad (4.3.8)$$

Even if (4.3.7) is only approximate, the general shape of the results is correct, however, the true values of U for large values of M being, in fact, smaller.

The formula (4.3.8) gives a distribution-free upper limit for the relationship of M to U or to P respectively, which will be further discussed in Section 4.5. It should be recalled, however, that the derivation of the above results was made assuming that the omission of the structure variation can be compensated for by a conservative selection of the values to be assigned to the parameters λ and n (or P).

4.4 Reserve funds

(a) Two types of objectives Insurance legislation generally contains provisions which are intended to give guarantees of the solvency of insurers so that 'insurance consumers' can, as far as possible, be safeguarded from the serious consequences which could result if an insurer were incapable of meeting pending claims or fulfil other commitments. For this purpose, among other measures, minimum amounts for solvency margins are prescribed.

The dichotomy of the objectives of solvency politics must be appreciated. The public interest, as presented in legislation, is restricted to safeguarding the insurance consumers. For this purpose it is sufficient to prescribe for the solvency margin a legal minimum which is high enough to make it very unlikely that it could be exhausted in *one* accounting year. If the actual solvency margin drops below the legal minimum, then the insurance company is to be wound up unless immediate remedial measures are successfully carried out in order to get the solvency margin back to the adequate level. This minimum amount of the solvency margin is often called the *wind-up barrier* or *ruin barrier*. The problem of defining it is in principle the same as that discussed above and described in Fig. 4.2.1(b). The problem was, however, simplified in so far as only the fluctuations of the claims business are taken into account. In practice, of course, losses and fluctuations in investments and other non-insurance risks are, in addition, to be considered (see Benjamin (1977); Pentikäinen (1952, 1982); Pesonen (1964, 1967(b)). On the other hand, it is a matter of fact that the solvency condition is not satisfactory from the point of view of the insurers. An objective must be a safe survival for a period longer than one year. For this purpose the time span must be extended from one year to longer periods. This will be done in Chapter 6.

(b) Statutory minimum solvency margins are considered in this section. The foregoing results offer a ready formula for that part of them required for underwriting operations. Owing to the general nature of the problem, just the distribution-free approximation formulae are appropriate for the purpose. Because the objective of

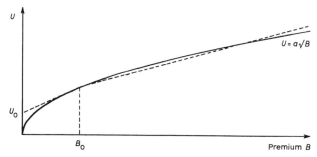

Figure 4.4.1   *A model for statutory solvency margins.*

legislation is above all to ensure that the values of reserve funds are adequate also when applied to the weakest cases, it is reasonable to assume that the safety loading λ is not positive. Then, according to (4.3.7) and Fig. 4.3.2, U obviously must be an increasing function of the volume of the company, i.e. an increasing function of the premium income P. Hence it is of the type which is plotted by solid line in Fig. 4.4.1, being a parabola for $\lambda = 0$. According to practice, instead of the risk premiums the gross premiums B, including also loading for expenses, are used as a basis for the rule.

The parabolic curve can be approximated by a broken line as presented in the figure. Expressed as a formula it is

$$U = U_0 + aB - b(B - B_0)^+. \qquad (4.4.1)$$

Solvency margin rules of just this type are applied, for example, in the decrees of the EEC (European Economic Community) in 1973. According to the EEC rule, $a = 0.18$, $b = 0.02$ and B_0 is 10 million monetary units. Alternatively the basis is defined as aggregate claims instead of the gross premiums and then the constants are $a = 0.26$, $b = 0.03$ and $B_0 = 7$ million units. The constant U_0 is 0, but instead a certain minimum amount for U is defined (for details see Kimball and Pfennigstorf, 1981).

In Great Britain up to 1978 a similar rule was applied with $a = 0.2$, $b = 0.1$ and $B_0 = £2\,500\,000$. In Finland, where this type of formula had already been introduced in 1953, $U_0 = 0.2$ millions of FIM, $a = 0.2$, $b = 0.1$ and $B_0 = 4$ millions of FIM.

(c) A merger of portfolios That the need for reserve funds is dependent on the size of the company can also be illustrated by means of the following example. Let C_1 and C_2 be two insurance companies. The respective minimum reserve funds U_1 and U_2 are computed by means of (4.1.7). The question can now be asked: how is the need for reserve funds changed, if these two companies are incorporated by a merger into one company C?

Assuming independence of the portfolios, the following expression for the minimum reserve U of the merged company C is obtained (see exercise 3.3.4) by means of (4.1.7)

$$U = y_\varepsilon \sqrt{\sigma^2} - \lambda P + \tfrac{1}{6}(y_\varepsilon^2 - 1)\frac{\mu_3}{\sigma^3}\sigma$$

$$= y_\varepsilon \sqrt{\sigma_1^2 + \sigma_2^2} - \frac{\lambda_1 P_1 + \lambda_2 P_2}{P_1 + P_2}P + \tfrac{1}{6}(y_\varepsilon^2 - 1)\frac{\mu_{3,1} + \mu_{3,2}}{\sigma_1^2 + \sigma_2^2}$$

$$= y_\varepsilon \sqrt{\sigma_1^2 + \sigma_2^2} - \lambda_1 P_1 - \lambda_2 P_2 + \frac{(y_\varepsilon^2 - 1)}{6} \times \frac{\mu_{3,1} + \mu_{3,2}}{\sigma_1^2 + \sigma_2^2},$$

where the (second) subscripts refer to the original companies.

$$U_1 + U_2 - U = y_\varepsilon [\sqrt{\sigma_1^2} + \sqrt{\sigma_2^2} - \sqrt{\sigma_1^2 + \sigma_2^2}]$$

$$+ \frac{y_\varepsilon^2 - 1}{6}\left(\frac{\mu_{3,1}}{\sigma_1^2} + \frac{\mu_{3,2}}{\sigma_2^2} - \frac{\mu_{3,1} + \mu_{3,2}}{\sigma_1^2 + \sigma_2^2}\right) > 0. \qquad (4.4.2)$$

The inequality follows on the inequalities $\sqrt{a} + \sqrt{b} > \sqrt{(a + b)}$ and $\dfrac{a}{b} + \dfrac{c}{d} > \dfrac{a + c}{b + d}$ which are valid for every positive a, b, c, d.

The inequality (4.4.2) proves that the reserves needed by the merged company are always less than that of the separate component companies together, if the security level $1 - \varepsilon$ is unchanged.

The rule can be readily extended to deal with the incorporation of more than two companies and cases where the structure variations of the companies are not independent.

The result is of general interest; it proves that the larger the company, the smaller a solvency ratio needed. The same fact can also be seen directly from (4.3.1), which shows that the relative minimum reserve U/P is a decreasing function of the volume variable $n = P/m$.

One can say that a merger helps to use the existing reserves in the most effective way, or what amounts to the same thing, a merger releases 'idle reserves' if the security level is not changed. In practice a fiscal merger of the companies is, of course, not necessary.

The same advantages can also be reached by exchange of reinsurance on a reciprocal basis. This problem will be further considered in Sections 5.1 and 5.2.

Exercise 4.4.1 The following characteristics are computed from the statistics of an insurance company C_1 : $m_1 = £1000$, $r_{2,1} = 40$, $r_{3,1} = 400$, $\sigma_{q,1} = 0.05$, $\gamma_{q,1} = 0.1$ and $n_1 = 1000$. The company has a reserve fund $U_1 = £500\,000$ and safety loading $\lambda_1 = 0.1$.

Another insurance company C_2 with the following characteristics: $m_2 = £500$, $r_{2,2} = 50$, $r_{3,2} = 500$, $\sigma_{q,2} = 0.1$, $\gamma_{q,2} = 0.5$, $n_2 = 200$ and $\lambda_2 = 0.05$ is merged with company C_1.

If the ruin probability ε according to (4.1.7) of the former company is not allowed to increase following the merger, how large should the reserve fund U be for the merged company?

4.5 Rules for the greatest retention

(a) Definition of problem The compound Poisson function or the basic equation (4.1.7) can also be used for calculating the proper dimensions for the net retention according to the reinsurance philosophy of the cedent. The problem can be defined as follows. The cedent has an amount U available to meet adverse fluctuations of the risk business. In general this amount would not be the same as, for example, the total solvency margin or the reserve funds, but would be taken as the amount of resources which could be lost without too much inconvenience. U may include the company's so-called hidden reserves, i.e. margins in technical reserves, in valuations and other balancing technical items in addition to the specific reserves. A conservative approach is to include in U, if possible, merely hidden items. Furthermore, owing to the risk of several consecutive adverse annual results, it may be advisable to take as U some part only of the resources. This problem can be treated more appropriately when the time span is extended from one year to longer periods (Chapter 6). However, it may often be useful also to know the range of the annual fluctuation as a function of the chosen level of net retention. Therefore consideration limited to one year only is also of interest and will be given in this chapter. By this means the results can be derived more easily and provide a better qualitative general view of the structures.

Hence the problem is formulated as what should be the maximum net retention M such that, by probability $1 - \varepsilon$, the fluctuating result of risk business does not consume a given initial reserve U in one year.

Broader views of the problem are considered by Beard (1959) and in numerous subsequent text books on reinsurance.

(b) The effect of the level M of the net retention has already been studied in Figs 4.2.2, 4.2.4 and 4.2.6 for excess of loss treaty applying the data given in Table 3.6.1. Similar figures can be obtained also for other types of reinsurance by virtue of the technique considered in Section 3.6.

Owing to the fact that the solvency properties are fairly robust for the d.f. of the claim size as long as the net retention limit M is not very high (see Pentikäinen, 1982, Section 4.2.3), the values obtained for excess of loss type of reinsurance may be used as an approximate guide for surplus treaties as well. This is useful owing to the fact that the latter type of treaties is rather inconvenient to handle as discussed in Section 3.6.4. This conclusion was confirmed by Heiskanen (1982) who calculated various cases by both excess of loss and surplus rules.

(c) A straightforward solution can be obtained by plotting U as a function of M as shown in Fig. 4.5.1, which was calculated applying the basic equation (4.1.7).

When the value of U is given, then the matching M can be read from the graph. For example, if $U = 5$ then $M = 0.087$. An alternative method is, of course, to solve the equation for M directly by numerical methods; however, this may be somewhat laborious, because M is buried in the claim size function S (see Section 3.6). By a suitable computer technique it is, however, fairly tractable. An example can be found in Fig. 4.2.4 and in Fig. 4.5.2.

(d) The contradiction between profitability and solvency The   risk premium income $P = nm(M)$ calculated net of reinsurance is an increasing function of M. The increase is fairly rapid for small M values, slow for large values and is stopped when M is equal to the largest risks of the portfolio. This is illustrated in Fig. 4.5.1 by a P curve. Because the ceded reinsurance premiums can be expected to include safety and expense margins (the interest should be regarded,

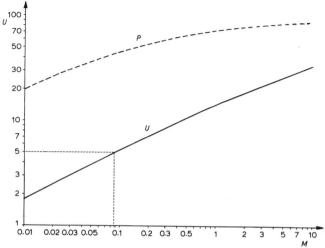

Figure 4.5.1   *Risk reserve U as a function of the net retention M. Unit is £10⁶. Standard data according to item 4.2(b).*

among other factors; see item 10.2(b)), it would pay, in expectation of profit, to have as high a maximum net retention M as possible. On the other hand the range of fluctuations also increases with M and the maintenance of solvency puts an upper limit on M as presented above. This suggests as an optimal policy of having as high a maximum M as the above basic equation allows within the limits of the resources U which are available for covering of adverse fluctuations.

One should appreciate, however, that the real life situation may be more complicated than that just assumed. For example, the cedent may have the opportunity of obtaining satisfactory reciprocity against the ceded business and in this way balance the profitability. The risk exchange between insurers will be discussed in Section 5.2.

The problem of the optimal level of net retentions is considered by Rantala (1982, Chapter 6) and is exemplified in exercise 4.5.5.

The reinsurance cost is further discussed in Section 7.3 and item 10.2(b), and the problem of balancing contradictory business objectives such as profitability and solvency in Section 10.4.

(e) The effect of the background factors (see (4.1.9)) can be examined

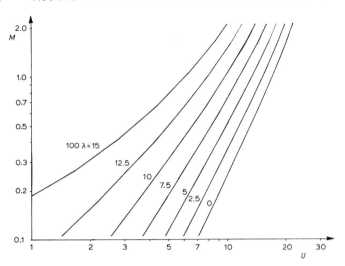

Figure 4.5.2   *M as a function of U and λ.*

as in Fig. 4.5.2, where the dependence of M on U and the safety loading λ is investigated.

(f) A distribution-free rule   As was presented for the case of reserve funds in Section 4.3, in considering the net retention M it is sometimes useful to have a rapid rule for evaluation of the order of magnitude of this quantity. Such a rule is readily obtained by applying the approximation (4.3.5) for (4.3.2), omitting the correction term including $\gamma_{\mathbf{x}}$

$$U = y\sqrt{(K^2 MP + \sigma_{\mathbf{q}}^2 P^2)} - \lambda P,$$

and solving

$$M = [(\lambda^2 - y^2 \sigma_{\mathbf{q}}^2)P^2 + 2\lambda UP + U^2]/K^2 y^2 P. \qquad (4.5.1)$$

This equation could be handled like (4.3.6) or (4.3.7) and a figure like Fig. 4.3.2 could be given. However, a slightly different technique will be applied, which is sometimes useful when the number of variables involved is large. Instead of absolute variables P, U and M their ratios

$$w = M/U \quad \text{and} \quad u = U/P \qquad (4.5.2)$$

will be employed. Then (4.5.1) can be written in the form

$$w = \frac{1}{K^2 y^2}\left(\frac{\beta}{u} + u + 2\lambda\right),\tag{4.5.3}$$

where

$$\beta = \lambda^2 - y^2\sigma_q^2.\tag{4.5.4}$$

The ratio w is a hyperbolic function of the solvency ratio u as plotted in Fig. 4.5.3.

If the coefficient β is positive, then the curve has a minimum

$$u_1 = \sqrt{\beta}$$
$$w_1 = \frac{2(\lambda + \sqrt{\beta})}{K^2 y^2}.\tag{4.5.5}$$

If β is negative, then the curve is increasing for $u > 0$ and w is negative for

$$u < -\lambda + y\sigma_q.\tag{4.5.6}$$

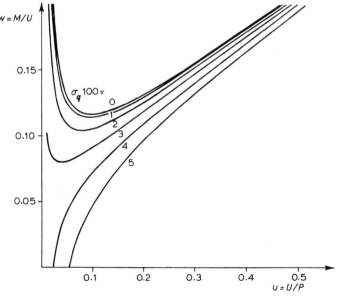

Figure 4.5.3   *The relative amount of net retention $w = M/U$ as a function of the solvency ratio u according to equation (4.5.3).*

This means that owing to the structure variation, introduced into the equations by means of σ_q, no reinsurance arrangement can stabilize the business unless the solvency ratio u exceeds the limit provided in (4.5.6).

(g) Rules of thumb are sometimes presented, according to which the retention M is supposed to be some particular ('empirical' or traditional) quota of the premium income P or of the reserves U, e.g. $M = q'P$ or $M = q''U$. One rule of this type is readily obtained from (4.5.5) written as follows

$$M \geqslant \frac{2(\lambda + \sqrt{(\lambda^2 - y^2\sigma_q^2)})}{K^2 y^2} U. \tag{4.5.7a}$$

In the special case, when no variation of the basic probabilities exists (or it is omitted or included in λ), i.e. $\sigma_q = 0$, we have

$$M = \frac{4}{K^2 y^2} \lambda U \approx \lambda U \qquad \text{(for } \varepsilon = 0.001) \tag{4.5.7b}$$

This formula is, in fact, the same as (4.3.8). It leads to a rule of thumb which is often used in practice by insurers: that the net retention should be a certain percentage of the reserves U which the company is willing to lose for covering losses during a year. If λ is taken to be e.g. 5%, M is $0.05U$. This estimate is based, however, on such a weak premise that it may not be very useful except in a few special cases. Neither does it offer any noticeable simplification compared with (4.5.1).

Another rule, according to which M is related to the premium income, could be obtained from the latter part of (4.3.8).

Exercise 4.5.1 Prove that the minimum risk reserve U defined by (4.1.8) and assuming $\sigma_q = 0$ has a derivative

$$U'(M) = \left[\frac{My\sqrt{n}}{\sqrt{(a_2(M))}} - \lambda n \right] (1 - S(M)). \tag{4.5.8}$$

Exercise 4.5.2 Find conditions according to which the derivative (4.5.8) has a negative value at $M = 0$.

Exercise 4.5.3 Examine the shape of the function $U(M)$ defined in exercise 4.5.1. When does this function have a minimum for a finite M? Note that the type of the solution depends on the sign of the derivative at the origin (see exercise 4.5.2).

Exercise 4.5.4 Suppose that the standard data (other than M) and distributions given in item 4.2(b) are valid and $U = 10$ million. What should the maximum net retention M be according to the basic equation (4.1.7)? Calculate also an approximate value by means of (4.5.1) taking $P = £65$ million and $K = 0.6$.

Exercise 4.5.5 The insurer considered in exercise 4.5.4 allocates from its freely disposable profit a small increment ΔU for its current risk reserve U and increases the net retention M by an amount ΔM according to the basic equation (4.1.7). The premium income net of reinsurance P increases then by ΔP, which includes a safety loading (corresponding to the profit, solvency and expenses of the reinsurer) $\lambda_r = 0.1$. What is the rate of return i_r of the amount ΔU, i.e. the expected increment of the cedent's profit margin divided by ΔU? The formulae derived for exercise 4.5.1 may be used.

Exercise 4.5.6 Find, applying the idea presented in exercise 4.5.5, an upper limit for the risk reserve U if it is required that the rate of return i_r must be at least i_0. Evaluate a numerical value for it in the case treated in exercise 4.5.5 for $i_0 = 0.1$.

Exercise 4.5.7 A new policy is added to a life insurance portfolio. Annual rate of death for it is q and the insurer will accept amount M of it for net retention. What should M be if the ruin probability ε calculated according to (4.1.8) were not changed? The new policy has the same safety loading λ as for the average of the portfolio. Derive for M a simple rule, if q is small, the expected number of claims n large and $\sigma_q = 0$ (M is to be expressed as a function of the variables λ, n, U, P and the moments about zero of the claim size d.f. S).

Exercise 4.5.8 Let the claim size d.f. be, in suitable monetary units,

$$S(Z) = \begin{cases} 0.8Z & \text{for } 0 \leqslant Z \leqslant 1 \\ 1 - 0.2Z^{-2} & \text{for } Z > 1. \end{cases}$$

What should the maximum net retention M be, when excess of loss treaty is applied and $n = 100$, $U = 20$, $\lambda = 0.05$ and $\varepsilon = 0.01$? Use the short version (4.1.8) of the basic equation.

4.6   The case of several Ms

(a) The problem The basic equation in its short form (4.1.8) will now be utilized to deal with the case when the portfolio is subdivided into independent sections indexed by $j = 1, 2, \ldots, r$, each of which has its own claim size d.f. S_j, safety loading $\lambda_j > 0$, expected number of claims n_j, net retention M_j and structure variable $\mathbf{q}_j$. First the moments a_k about zero are defined separately for each section. They depend on the retentions M_j (see (3.6.3) and (3.6.8)) and can be denoted by $a_{kj}(M_j)$. For brevity, let $m_j = m_j(M_j) = a_{1j}(M_j)$.

The problem is to determine the M_js so that:

(i) the expected amount of profit as a function of the M_js

$$f(M_1, M_2, \ldots, M_r) = \sum_j \lambda_j n_j m_j, \qquad (4.6.1)$$

is maximized; and

(ii) the basic equation (4.1.8) is satisfied for the whole portfolio:

$$Q(M_1, M_2, \ldots, M_r) = U - y\sigma_{\mathbf{X}} + \sum_j \lambda_j n_j m_j = 0, \qquad (4.6.2)$$

where (see (3.7.9))

$$\sigma_{\mathbf{X}} = \sigma_{\mathbf{X}(M_1 \cdots M_r)} = \sqrt{\left(\sum_j (n_j a_{2j}(M_j) + n_j^2 m_j(M_j)^2 \sigma_{\mathbf{q}j}^2) \right)}.$$

(b) Solution This bound extremal problem is solved by the use of the so-called Lagrange method by introducing a function

$$F = f - \rho Q,$$

where ρ is an auxiliary variable.

For a real solution some assumptions concerning the portfolio and reinsurance are needed. As an example the problem will be dealt with by assuming excess of loss reinsurance. To facilitate the calculations it is further assumed that λ_j is independent of the retention M_j. The existence of continuous derivatives S_j' can also be assumed without any essential restriction, since the possible step points of S_j can be closely approximated by a continuous differentiable segment of curve.

By using these assumptions, we have

$$a'_{kj}(M_j) = \frac{\partial}{\partial M_j}\left[\int_0^{M_j} Z^k S'_j(Z)\,dZ + (1 - S_j(M_j))M_j^k\right]$$

$$= kM_j^{k-1}(1 - S_j(M_j)),$$

and

$$\frac{\partial F}{\partial M_j} = n_j(1 - S_j(M_j))\left\{(1 - \rho)\lambda_j + \frac{\rho y}{\sigma_{\mathbf{x}}}M_j + \frac{\rho y}{\sigma_{\mathbf{x}}}n_j m_j \sigma^2_{\mathbf{q}j}\right\} = 0. \quad (4.6.3)$$

The extremal values can be found among the joint zero points of Q and of these derivatives. Putting the factors in braces equal to zero it follows that

$$M_j = \frac{\sigma_{\mathbf{x}}(\rho - 1)}{y\rho}\lambda_j - n_j m_j \sigma^2_{\mathbf{q}j}. \quad (4.6.4)$$

Solving the M_js from these equations and substituting into (4.6.2), ρ can be determined.

Equations (4.6.3) give only the necessary conditions for solution. In actual cases, where the data involved are known, it has to be investigated whether solutions exist which among other things depend on the values of U. A further step is finding a numerical solution when the distributions and data are given. This may give rise to considerable problems, because the variables M_j are buried in the moment expressions.

The problem concentrates on the search for variables which give an absolute maximum for the profit function f on the surface $Q = 0$. Note that also one or more of the factors $1 - S(M_j)$ in (4.6.3) may be 0, which means that the section in question needs no reinsurance and the consideration is to be limited to the remaining part of the portfolio.

(c) **The Poisson case** It is of interest to observe that the expression by which λ_j is multiplied in (4.6.4) does not depend on the section j, i.e. it is the same for all of them. Therefore in the particular Poisson case where $\sigma_{\mathbf{q}j} = 0$ for every j, the following theorem can be derived on the assumptions mentioned at the beginning of this section.

The limits of retention M_j have to be chosen proportional to the corresponding safety loadings λ_j.

(d) General discussion It was assumed above (when (4.1.8) was applied) that the normal approximation is justified, but it is important to note that the normal approximation has not been assumed for each component j individually. It thus follows that the theorem is certainly valid as long as the normal approximation is applicable to the whole business: in view of the central limit theorem this is a less restrictive condition than if the corresponding assumptions were made for the various subgroups.

The foregoing result is of general interest when consideration is being given to the overall reinsurance policy of a company. It is not an unexpected result in the sense that it indicates that the greater λ_j is (or, what is equivalent, the greater the expected profitability of a class of insurance or group of policies) the greater the amount that should be retained for the net account. In this context it is not necessary to have regard to such items as the cost of reinsurance in relation to the arrangements made, since it can be assumed that allowance has already been made for these in arriving at the estimates of λ_j. As a special case it follows that the proper course is to make the retentions M_j equal, if all the λ_j s are equal and the second terms in (4.6.4) due to the variation of the basic probabilities are the same order of magnitude (or can be omitted).

4.7   Excess of loss reinsurance premium

(a) The formula for the excess of loss reinsurance premium is one of the direct applications of the compound Poisson function. The treaty is mostly formulated by extending the presentation in Section 3.6.2, so that the reinsurer pays the share $Z_{re} = Z_{tot} - A$ of each claim Z_{tot} which exceeds a limit A but no more than $B - A$, as seen in Fig. 4.7.1.

Then the reinsurance net premium is, according to the general formula (4.1.1) for the risk premium,

$$P_{X/L}(A, B) = nE(\mathbf{Z}_{re}) = n\left[\int_A^B (Z - A)\,dS(Z) + (B - A)(1 - S(B)) \right],$$
$$(4.7.1a)$$

where n is the expected number of *all* claims in the whole portfolio concerned, including also claims for which $\mathbf{Z}_{re} = 0$.

In the particular case where $B = \infty$, (4.7.1) can be written in the

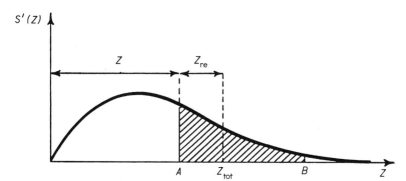

Figure 4.7.1 *Excess of loss treaty. The total amount of a claim* Z_{tot} *exceeding the limit (net retention) A is divided between the cedent and the reinsurer:* $Z_{tot} = Z + Z_{re}$.

form (see 3.6.3)

$$P_{X/L}(A, \infty) = n[a_1(\infty) - a_1(A)] \qquad (4.7.1b)$$

and hence, regarding $\mathbf{Z}_{re}(A, B) = \mathbf{Z}_{re}(A, \infty) - \mathbf{Z}_{re}(B, \infty)$

$$P_{X/L}(A, B) = n[a_1(B) - a_1(A)]. \qquad (4.7.2)$$

If the moments are available in a tabular form, such as in Table 3.6.1, then $P_{X/L}$ is readily obtained. For example, let $n = 1000$, $A = £10^6$ and $B = £10^7$; then according to the table $P_{X/L} = 1000 \times (8.888 - 7.302) \times 10^3 = £1.586 \times 10^6$.

(b) Variance It is well known in practice that the application of the simple formulae just given is rather vulnerable to the inaccuracy of the tail of the claim size distribution S, which is very often present due to the fact that the experience base is scarce. To compensate for the uncertainty (and the greater volatility), safety loadings are included in the reinsurance premium which may be quite substantial and can fundamentally affect the consideration of the appropriateness of this treaty type. For example, formulae are often suggested where net premium is loaded by a safety margin which is proportional to the standard deviation or variance of the risk involved. The variance of the claims on the reinsurer's liability can be expressed in terms of the second moments as follows (see exercise 4.7.1).

$$\sigma_{re}^2 = n[a_2(B) - a_2(A)] - 2AP_{X/L} + P_{X/L}^2\sigma_q^2. \qquad (4.7.3)$$

The premium is also very sensitive even to slight inflation, as is demonstrated in exercise 4.7.3.

In this example, and assuming $\sigma_q = 0.05$, the value

$$\sigma_{re}^2 = 1000 \times (1.338 \times 10^4 - 2.353 \times 10^3) \times 10^6$$
$$- 2 \times 10^6 \times 1.586 \times 10^6 + 1.586^2 \times 0.05^2$$
$$= £10^{12} \times 7.86;$$

$\sigma_{re} = £10^6 \times 2.80$ is obtained from Table 3.6.1.

Exercise 4.7.1 Prove (4.7.3).

Exercise 4.7.2 The upper tail of the claim size is supposed to follow the Pareto d.f.

$$S(Z) = 1 - b(Z_0/Z)^\alpha \qquad (Z > Z_0).$$

Calculate the excess of loss premium (4.7.2) for $Z_0 < A < B$.

Exercise 4.7.3 The claim size distribution $S(Z)$ can be approximated by $0.9Z$ for $0 \leqslant Z \leqslant 1$ and by the Pareto distribution $1 - 0.1Z^{-3}$ for $Z \geqslant 1$ where the unit of the monetary variables is $£10^5$. The limits of the excess of loss treaty are $A = 2$ and $B = 5$. Calculate the net premium $P_{X/L}$ as a percentage of the total premium P. Suppose that due to inflation the sizes of claims are uniformly increased by 10%, but the premium is not changed. What is the expected loss of the reinsurer?

Exercise 4.7.4 The claim size d.f. is exponential $S(Z) = 1 - e^{-cZ}$ and excess of loss reinsurance is applied with the retention limit M. What is the d.f. of the claim size on the reinsurer's liability? What is the variance of the aggregate claims of the reinsurer's share?

4.8 Application to stop loss reinsurance

(a) General formula In stop loss reinsurance the reinsurer pays that part of the *total* amount of claims X which exceeds a certain amount, say A. The reinsurer's liability is often limited to an amount $B - A$ so that the payment is no more than this if the total claim X exceeds B. Furthermore it is common for the reinsurer's liability to be limited to a certain share $(1 - c)$ of the excess $X - A$, the remaining share c being met by the cedent. The reinsurer's share of the claims may be summarized as follows

$$\mathbf{X}_{re} = \begin{cases} 0 & \text{when } \mathbf{X} \leqslant A \\ (1-c)(\mathbf{X}-A) & \text{when } A < \mathbf{X} < B \\ (1-c)(B-A) & \text{when } \mathbf{X} \geqslant B, \end{cases}$$

where $\mathbf{X}$ is the total claim.

The reinsurance risk premium $P_{SL}(A, B)$ is easily expressed as follows

$$P_{SL}(A, B)/(1-c) = \int_A^B (X-A)\, dF(X) + (B-A)\int_B^\infty dF(X), \quad (4.8.1a)$$

where F denotes again the distribution function of the aggregate claims. By integrating by parts the above expression can be written as

$$(B-A)F(B) - \int_A^B F(X)\, dX + (B-A) - (B-A)F(B),$$

so that the net premium becomes

$$P_{SL}(A, B) = (1-c)\int_A^B (1 - F(X))\, dX. \quad (4.8.1b)$$

(b) Discussion Like the excess of loss premium, the stop loss premium is sensitive to uncertainties of the tail of the claim size distribution as well as to inflation. In addition it is sensitive to inaccuracies and to the structure variations of the number of claims **n**. Table 4.8.1 demonstrates how the stop loss premium depends on the variation of the basic probabilities indicated by σ_q and γ_q (see Section 2.7) as well as on other environmental aspects.

It is important to notice that not only the short-term oscillation of the basic probabilities (assumed when the mixed compound Poisson process was defined in item 2.7(c)) but also the long-term cycles and trends mentioned in item 2.7(b) (consideration of which is left until Section 6.1) very strongly affect the stop loss premium. It can be assumed that allowance will be made for trends and that the parameters, especially n, will be adjusted accordingly. Even if the long-term cycles, e.g. when ruin probabilities are evaluated, are in general intricate to handle, they can be considered in connection with the rating problem as a random fluctuation of the same character as the short-term oscillation. Obviously a convenient method is to choose the characteristics σ_q and γ_q so large as to include the cycles in their range. Clearly this implies, however, that the reinsurance treaty extends over a reasonably long time. Without special precautions the premium calculated in this way may be insufficient during that half of the cycle during which the claim frequencies are high, but this can be expected to be compensated during the other half of the wave if the contract is not discontinued before.

(c) NP formula   If the compound function F can be approximated by the NP formula, the stop loss premium (4.8.1) can be expressed in terms of the normal d.f. N and its first derivative N'. In the simple case, when the reinsurer pays the whole excess $X - A$, the following expression is obtained

$$P_{SL}(A) = P_{SL}(A, \infty) = (P - A)(1 - N(y_A)) + \sigma_X(1 + \gamma_X y_A/6)N'(y_A), \tag{4.8.2}$$

where the total risk premium P is defined by (4.1.1), σ_X and γ_X by (3.3.7) and y_A is related to A via the NP transformation, i.e. (see (3.11.14) and (3.11.14a))

$$y_A = v_\gamma^{-1}\left(\frac{A - P}{\sigma_X}\right).$$

(see exercise 4.8.1).

Then the premium in the general case is

$$P_{SL}(A, B) = (1 - c)[P_{SL}(A) - P_{SL}(B)], \tag{4.8.3}$$

Table 4.8.1 exhibits some examples of the stop loss risk premiums.

The first group in the table demonstrates the effect of the limits A and B. The other arguments are fixed.

The second group illustrates how the heterogeneity of the individual risk sums affects the stop loss rate. The risk indexes r_2 and r_3 are chosen from Table 3.6.1, assuming that the portfolio is first protected by an excess of loss treaty having $M = 1$, 10 and 100 in £ millions respectively and the retained business is then subject to the stop loss cover exemplified in the table.

The third group of examples shows how the rates depend on the size of the portfolio, letting n vary and keeping the other arguments fixed. As expected, the rates (calculated as percentages) needed to

Table 4.8.1 *Examples of stop loss risk premiums according to (4.8.2).*

n	$\dfrac{m}{£1000}$	r_2	$\dfrac{r_3}{1000}$	σ_q	γ_q	$\dfrac{A}{P}$	$\dfrac{B}{P}$	$\dfrac{P(A)}{P}$	$\dfrac{P(B)}{P}$	$\dfrac{P(A,B)}{P}$
1000	6.00	20.0	0.7	0.04	0.30	1.00	1.40	0.0587	0.0004	0.0583
1000	6.00	20.0	0.7	0.04	0.30	1.10	1.50	0.0231	0.0001	0.0230
1000	6.00	20.0	0.7	0.04	0.30	1.20	1.60	0.0072	0.0000	0.0072
5000	7.30	44.0	4.5	0.04	0.30	1.25	1.75	0.0005	0.0000	0.0005
5000	8.90	169.0	122.7	0.04	0.30	1.25	1.75	0.0134	0.0001	0.0133
5000	9.60	681.0	4314.0	0.04	0.30	1.25	1.75	0.1014	0.0390	0.0624
100	7.30	44.0	4.5	0.04	0.30	1.25	1.75	0.1868	0.0836	0.1032
300	7.30	44.0	4.5	0.04	0.30	1.25	1.75	0.0721	0.0118	0.0603
1000	7.30	44.0	4.5	0.04	0.30	1.25	1.75	0.0168	0.0002	0.0166
3000	7.30	44.0	4.5	0.04	0.30	1.25	1.75	0.0020	0.0000	0.0020
3000	7.30	44.0	4.5	0.00	0.00	1.25	1.75	0.0015	0.0000	0.0015
3000	7.30	44.0	4.5	0.05	0.50	1.25	1.75	0.0023	0.0000	0.0023
3000	7.30	44.0	4.5	0.10	1.00	1.25	1.75	0.0062	0.0000	0.0062
3000	7.30	44.0	4.5	0.20	1.50	1.25	1.75	0.0275	0.0014	0.0261

cover the risk of a small collective are substantially higher than those necessary for a large collective.

In the last group of examples the structure parameters σ_q and γ_q vary. It is seen also that the structure function fundamentally affects the rates.

Ammeter (1953) and Bohman and Esscher (1964) have developed extensions in the case of a Polya process for the stop loss premium (with $B = \infty$).

Exercise 4.8.1 Prove (4.8.2).

4.9 An application to insurance statistics

(a) The problem It is by no means necessary to limit the application of the theory of risk to the whole portfolio of an insurance company. On the contrary, it is applicable to any insurance collective. A common example is in the collection of insurance statistics, where the collective in question can be a group of policies for similar risks, and for which a premium tariff is being calculated separately taking claim frequencies as risk premiums. In this connection the problem of the accuracy of the claims frequency derived from the statistics often arises; or, in other words, how large must the group in question be so as to give an adequate statistical basis for rate-making.

As an example, consider a certain group of similar policies which have been observed during a certain period – in general, several years. Suppose that the total amount of the claims during this period has been £800 000. The total amount of the insurance in force in this group is £700 000 000, this amount being the sum of the average sums of each year. The so-called burning cost is now obtained as $f = 800\,000/700\,000\,000 = 1.14$ per thousand and the problem is to estimate the accuracy of this quantity.

(b) Confidence limits Assuming the mixed Poisson process the solution is a direct application of the NP formula (4.1.7). The expected total amount of claims can be interpreted as a risk premium P, and $X - P$, the deviation of the observed claim amount X from its expectation, as the error due to random fluctuation. Then the relative error is $\Delta f/f = (X - P)/P$. Hence with probability $1 - \varepsilon$

$$\frac{X_1 - P}{P} \leqslant \frac{\Delta f}{f} \leqslant \frac{X_2 - P}{P} \, ,$$

where

$$F(X_2) = 1 - \varepsilon/2 \, ,$$
$$F(X_1) = \varepsilon/2 \, .$$

The true value of P is, of course, unknown and therefore estimates are to be used, derived from past experience or simply by using the observed amount X as P.

First let $\varepsilon/2 = N(y_1)$ and $1 - \varepsilon/2 = N(y_2)$, where N is the normal d.f. and $y_1 = -y_2$. Further, let x_1 and x_2 be the corresponding NP corrected variables $x = v_\gamma(y)$ according to (3.11.16). Then

$$X_i = P + x_i \sigma_{\mathbf{X}} \qquad (i = 1, 2),$$

and

$$x_1 \frac{\sigma_{\mathbf{X}}}{P} \leqslant \frac{\Delta f}{f} \leqslant x_2 \frac{\sigma_{\mathbf{X}}}{P} \, . \tag{4.9.1}$$

Here (see (3.3.7))

$$\sigma_{\mathbf{X}}/P = \sqrt{(r_2/n + \sigma_{\mathbf{q}}^2)}, \tag{4.9.2}$$

and for the formulae (3.11.16) the skewness is the same as given in (3.3.7) (note that a linear transformation, here $X \to X/P$, does not affect the skewness).

The computation of the indices r_2 and r_3 and the evaluation for σ_q and γ_q can be computed from the statistics in question, or (if they are not known and an advance estimation of the error is needed) they may be obtained from the general experience of the insurance class in question.

As an example let $n = 100$, $r_2 = 10$, $r_3 = 200$, $\sigma_{\mathbf{q}} = 0.1$ and $\gamma_{\mathbf{q}} = 0$. Then

$$\sigma_{\mathbf{X}}/P = \sqrt{(10/100 + 0.1^2)} = 0.33,$$

and

$$\gamma_X = (200/100^2 + 3 \times 10 \times 0.1^2/100 + 0)/(0.33)^3 = 0.64,$$

and for $\varepsilon = 0.05$, $y = \pm 1.96$ according to the nomogram of Fig. 3.11.2 $x_1 = -1.7$ and $x_2 = 2.3$. Hence

$$-1.7 \times 0.33 \leqslant \Delta f/f \leqslant 2.3 \times 0.33,$$

or

$$-0.6 \leqslant \Delta f/f \leqslant 0.8.$$

(c) **The normal approximation** can replace the NP formula if only the order of magnitude is needed, or when the data base is large. Then

$$|\Delta f/f| \leqslant y_\varepsilon \sqrt{(r_2/n + \sigma_{\mathbf{q}}^2)}. \tag{4.9.3}$$

In this example $|\Delta f/f| \leqslant 0.7$. As usual the normal approximation has underestimated the risk of large positive deviations. Because the risk groups in statistical considerations are often rather limited, the applicability of the normal approximation and even the NP formula may be uncertain. However, these approximations give fairly reliable values particularly if the frequency is not very small. ε need not be as small as it customarily is in risk theory, which also adds to the usefulness of the formulae. Often it is necessary to know only the order of magnitude of the relative error.

Note that if the statistical material under consideration is derived from several years' data, then the structure variation of consecutive years can be expected to offset each other and σ_q can be assumed to be approximately 0. On the other hand, serious bias can be expected to arise due to trends and cycles (see item 2.7(b)), which should be estimated in one way or another (see McGuinness, 1970).

(d) A straightforward estimation It may be further noted that, e.g. for rapid checking of the order of magnitude the same estimation problem can easily be solved by dividing the observation period into sub-periods, preferably years, and by calculating the quotient f_v separately for each year v. Then the estimation

$$\left|\frac{\Delta f}{f}\right| \leqslant \frac{y_\varepsilon}{\bar{f}} \sqrt{\left(\frac{\Sigma(f_v - \bar{f})^2}{N(N-1)}\right)}, \qquad (4.9.4)$$

holds, where $\bar{f} = \Sigma f_v/N$, N is the number of sub-periods and ε the confidence level. The details of this method will not be developed because they lie outside the scope of the theory of risk. In practice the risk-theoretical formula (4.9.2) is perhaps most useful in cases where the claim statistics are being forecast in advance, and some estimation of the error is needed at this stage when a statistical basis for (4.9.4) does not exist. Equation (4.9.2) can be useful in some cases in defining an appropriate classification of risks or in deciding how many years of statistics are needed to obtain a satisfactory reliability.

Exercise 4.9.1 It is known that for certain fire risks $f \approx 0.1\%$ and the number of claims per annum is about 1000. How many years of statistics are needed to estimate f with an accuracy of 20% on 10% confidence level? The risk index r_2 is estimated to be 100 and $\sigma_q = 0$. The normal approximation can be used.

4.10 Experience rating, credibility theory

(a) Profit return Bonus systems are applied in connection with some insurance classes. For example the no-claim bonus of motor-car insurance is well known in many countries. Another bonus system is sometimes attached to reinsurance treaties and also to direct insurance contracts. If the original safety loaded risk premium is $(1 + \lambda)P$ and the actual amount of claims related to this particular collective (treaty or policy) in a year is $\mathbf{X}$, a bonus or 'profit return' can be agreed, e.g. according to the formula

$$\mathbf{G} = k[(1 + \lambda)P - \mathbf{X}]^+. \qquad (4.10.1)$$

Assuming that on average the safety loading $\lambda P = \lambda E(\mathbf{X})$ should cover the profit return and denoting $X_0 = (1 + \lambda)E(\mathbf{X})$

$$E(\mathbf{G}) = k(1 + \lambda)E(\mathbf{X})F(X_0) - k \int_0^{X_0} X \, dF(X) \leqslant \lambda E(\mathbf{X}).$$

Partial integration gives

$$k \int_0^{X_0} F(X) \, dX \leqslant \lambda E(\mathbf{X}). \tag{4.10.2}$$

This equation defines the constant k. Ammeter (1963) has studied systems where the variance of $\mathbf{G}$ is minimized or where the net premium $P - \mathbf{G}$ is as correct as possible even if the original rating of P is erroneous.

(b) **Example** If F can be approximated by the NP d.f. N_γ (3.11.14a), the formula (4.10.2) can be written in the form

$$k \int_0^{(1 + \lambda)P} N_\gamma \left(\frac{X - P}{\sigma_\mathbf{X}} \right) dX \leqslant \lambda P,$$

which gives, after some simplifications

$$k \leqslant x_0 \bigg/ \int_{-\infty}^{x_0} N_\gamma(x) \, dx,$$

where $x = (X - P)/\sigma_\mathbf{X}$ and $x_0 = \lambda P/\sigma_\mathbf{X} = \lambda/\sqrt{(r_2/n + \sigma_\mathbf{q}^2)}$ (see (3.3.7)).

If, for example, $\lambda = 0.1$, $r_2 = 25$, $r_3 = 1000$, $\sigma_\mathbf{q} = 0.2$, $\gamma_\mathbf{q} = 0.5$ and $n = 100$, then $k \leqslant 0.85$. This means that the insurer can return at most 85% of the profit. The remainder of the profit is needed to cover the risk of excessive losses $\mathbf{X} > P$.

If instead of the NP function the normal approximation had been used, the k value would be 92% in the above example.

(c) **Discussion** The structure of the contract between the policy-holder and the insurer is, in essence, the same as the conventional stop loss reinsurance. The policyholder bears the small fluctuations of claims partially on his own account, whereas the risk of large losses is insured as has been presented in Section 4.8.

It should be noted that it is unusual in practice for $E(\mathbf{X})$ and hence also λ to be known in advance for *each* risk collective under consideration. In fact the situation is precisely the same as described in Section 2.10, where the concept 'risk exposure variation inside the portfolio' was introduced. Hence the standard deviation σ_q and the skewness γ_q should now be interpreted as related to the *risk variation inside* that group of risks from which the particular unit concerned is selected. The initial premium P is the average premium derived for the whole group and the profit return **G** is designed to compensate for the deviations of the exposure rates of the individual units from this joint average level.

(d) Experience rating The whole philosophy of experience rating has not yet been discussed. In general, the main reason for the practical application of experience rating is to try to reach reasonable premiums by starting from a hypothetical value P_0 and subsequently correcting it by using the actual claims experience by means of some agreed rule, for example similar to that given in (4.10.3). When defining what are considered to be 'reasonable premiums', attention is to be paid partly to the requirement that, at least over several years, the mean premium should not be too far from the actual expected value of claims, and partly to the requirement that the premium should not show too much random fluctuation. An example of this kind of arrangement is set out in the following system of 'sliding premiums', which has been extensively studied in the USA under the title 'credibility theory'.

Consider a risk or a group of risks which have the same initial premium P_0. This group can be, as mentioned at the beginning of this section, a collective of persons or objects subject to some group contract. The same method can, however, also be applied for the adjustment of the general tariffs, in which case it is applied separately to the different tariff groups, e.g. brick houses in some defined area, etc.

Suppose further that it is agreed that the premium for the next year is calculated according to the formula

$$\mathbf{P}_1 = Z\mathbf{X}_0 + (1 - Z)P_0, \tag{4.10.3}$$

where $\mathbf{X}_0$ is the total amount of claims in this collective in the preceding year. The 'breaking constant' Z, called '*credibility*', is chosen from the interval:

$$0 < Z \leqslant 1,$$

and will be fixed small enough to eliminate excessively large random fluctuations. More precisely it is subject to the condition that pure random fluctuations will not, with probability $1 - \varepsilon$, result in a change in the premium P in excess of $100p\%$ calculated from $E(\mathbf{X})$. Expressed in symbols this is the case if the constant Z satisfies the condition

$$Z\Delta X \leqslant pE(\mathbf{X}), \tag{4.10.4}$$

where ΔX is obtained from

$$F(E(\mathbf{X}) + \Delta X) - F(E(\mathbf{X}) - \Delta X) = 1 - \varepsilon, \tag{4.10.5}$$

which assumes that the d.f. F of $\mathbf{X}$ is known or presumed. Then the absolute value of the deviation $\Delta\mathbf{X} = \mathbf{X} - E(\mathbf{X})$ can be larger than ΔX only with probability ε.

If it can be assumed that the NP approximation gives a satisfactory approximation for F, then item 4.9(b) is applicable because $\Delta f/f$ is in fact $\Delta\mathbf{X}/E(\mathbf{X})$ and, confining the analysis to the upwards jumps of $\mathbf{X}$,

$$Zx_\varepsilon\sqrt{(r_2/n + \sigma_{\mathbf{q}}^2)} = p,$$

where according to (3.11.6)

$$x_\varepsilon = y_\varepsilon + \tfrac{1}{6}\gamma_{\mathbf{X}}(y_\varepsilon^2 - 1),$$

and y_ε is the root of $1 - \varepsilon = N(y_\varepsilon)$ and r_2 is again the risk index (3.3.8). Hence we have

$$Z = \frac{p}{x_\varepsilon\sqrt{(r_2/n + \sigma_{\mathbf{q}}^2)}}. \tag{4.10.6a}$$

Because for minor risk collectives, for which the experience rating is usually applied, the variation of the basic probabilities may be less significant than the other fluctuation (see Table 3.3.2), the formula can be simplified by putting $\sigma_{\mathbf{q}} = 0$. Then

$$Z = \frac{p}{x_\varepsilon}\sqrt{\frac{n}{r_2}}. \tag{4.10.6b}$$

The expected number of claims n which makes $Z = 1$ i.e.

$$n_0 = \frac{x_\varepsilon^2}{p^2}r_2, \tag{4.10.7}$$

is of special interest.

Table 4.10.1   *Values of n_0 for full credibility (constant claim size).*

		ε	
p	10%	5%	1%
0.01	27 057	38 416	66 347
0.05	1 082	1 537	2 654
0.1	271	384	663
0.2	68	96	166

Following the terminology of the American credibility theory it is said that if $Z = 1$, there is *full credibility*.

In the special case where the risk sums are all equal or, what is equivalent, if only the number of claims is recorded for calculating the frequency of the claims, then $r_2 = 1$ and the values of n_0 which are large enough for full credibility are immediately obtained by means of tables of the normal distribution, which is used instead of NP formula, as in Table 4.10.1.

In most practical cases the risk sums are not equal and hence r_2 is not 1. The variation in the value of this quantity depends significantly on the degree of heterogeneity of the risk sums and consequently the limit of full credibility can be considerably larger than is given in Table 4.10.1. The values of r_2 may often be of the order of 5 to 10, but in cases where large risk sums can occur the values can be much larger, as is seen for example in Table 3.6.1.

If the expected number of claims n is smaller than the value obtained from (4.10.7) then the constant Z has values smaller than 1 and the term *partial credibility* is used. From (4.10.6b) and (4.10.7), one of the well-known formulae of credibility theory can be immediately obtained by eliminating the coefficient of $\sqrt{n}$ in (4.10.6b)

$$Z = \sqrt{(n/n_0)} \qquad (4.10.8)$$

In the foregoing it was assumed that the NP approximation could be used. However, owing to the small size of the risk collective which often arises in cases subject to experience rating or to credibility theory, the NP formula can be doubtful, even if very small values of ε are not needed for which the accuracy of the formula is most unsatisfactory. The uncertainty can of course be avoided by calculating the quantity x_ε by using some other method of computation. A drawback is, however, that x_ε may depend on n. The experience of American actuaries suggests nevertheless that even the normal approximation gives values which are satisfactory in practical work.

(e) Limit value Applying (4.10.3) for a sequence of t years and developing the algorithm into a series it follows that

$$\mathbf{P}_t = Z\mathbf{X}_{t-1} + (1 - Z)\mathbf{P}_{t-1}$$

$$= Z \sum_{i=1}^{t} (1 - Z)^{i-1} \mathbf{X}_{t-i} + (1 - Z)^t P_0. \tag{4.10.9}$$

If the expected value $\mu = E(\mathbf{X}_i)$ is assumed to be equal for all i values, then

$$E(\mathbf{P}_t) = Z \sum_{i=1}^{t} (1 - Z)^{i-1} \mu + (1 - Z)^t P_0$$

$$= [1 - (1 - Z)^t]\mu + (1 - Z)^t P_0, \tag{4.10.10}$$

which tends to μ as $t \to \infty$. Thus, in the long run $\mathbf{P}_t$ is expected to tend to the theoretically correct unknown mean value μ. Hence the formula fulfils the requirement of fairness. The coefficient Z regulates the fluctuation of the sliding premium rate.

Owing to the fact that $\mathbf{P}_t$ depends on the claims amounts $\mathbf{X}_{t-i}$ of the preceding years by means of weights having the elapsed time i in exponents, the algorithm (4.10.9) and the formula (4.10.3) are sometimes called *exponential*.

(f) The Bayesian approach Another way to build up experience rating theory is to make use of the theory of variation of risk inside the portfolio as discussed in Section 2.10. It is assumed that the risk variation variable $\mathbf{q}$ has d.f. H inside some particular risk collective, e.g. in a group of a certain type of industrial plants (see item 2.10(a)). Note that $\mathbf{q}$ is now not the time-dependent structure variable that is employed in most parts of this book, but instead a variable describing the heterogeneity of the risk intensities in the collective from which the risk unit under consideration is randomly drawn. It is supposed that the function H is known, but the value of the risk parameter q for any individual risk unit is unknown. Then the d.f. $F(X;q)$ and its density $f(X;q)$ are both functions of the parameter q, as illustrated in Fig. 4.10.1.

The correct premium for any risk unit depends on unknown

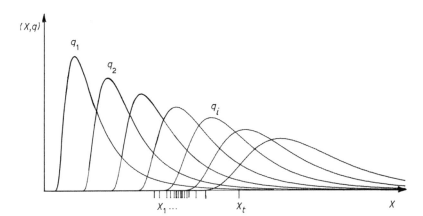

Figure 4.10.1   *A sample of $f(X;q)$ for different parameter values q and a cluster of observed X values.*

q as follows

$$P(q) = \int_0^\infty X f(X;q)\,\mathrm{d}X. \tag{4.10.11}$$

On the other hand the average premium of the whole collective is

$$P = \int_0^\infty \int_0^\infty X f(X;q)\,\mathrm{d}X\,\mathrm{d}H(q) = \int_0^\infty P(q)\,\mathrm{d}H(q). \tag{4.10.12}$$

Now let us assume that for the risk unit concerned a sequence of total claims $X_1, \ldots, X_t$ for t years is observed as illustrated in Fig. 4.10.1. It can be expected that they are clustered in a more or less narrow area on the X-axis. Heuristically it is easily conceived that this kind of accrued experience makes it possible to conclude what is the order of magnitude of the unknown parameter q. Obviously those values are most probable which correspond to the curves having their modes in just that area where the X values are clustered. The well-known Bayesian rule enables us to find an expression for the probability density of the unknown parameter q by the condition that $\mathbf{X}$ has the observed sequence of values. Then an obvious idea is to amend the premium formula (4.10.12) by weighting $P(q)$ by these conditional probabilities as follows

$$P_{t+1} = E(\mathbf{X}_{t+1} | X_1, \ldots X_t) = \int_0^\infty P(q) \left[\frac{\prod\limits_{i=1}^t f(X_i, q) \, dH(q)}{\int_0^\infty \prod\limits_{i=1}^t f(X_i, q) \, dH(q)} \right].$$

(4.10.13)

The expression in brackets is just the conditional Bayesian probability density.

If the density function f is known, as assumed, then in principle this expression gives an estimate for the premium for the next year.

The expression (4.10.13) has been widely examined and it is proved *inter alia* that in the Polya case where H is the incomplete gamma function and F the mixed Poisson (and, as Jewell (1976) has shown, also for some other function mixtures) the formula can be reduced to the very simple form

$$P_{t+1} = (1 - Z_t)P + Z_t \bar{X}_t ,$$

(4.10.14)

where

$$\bar{X}_t = \frac{1}{t} \sum_{i=1}^t X_i,$$

(4.10.15)

is the mean value of the observed data and

$$Z_t = \frac{t}{t + A} .$$

(4.10.16)

Here A is a constant which is independent of t but dependent on the size of the collective from which the X values are drawn. This is formally similar to the exponential formula (4.10.3), but now the credibility factor Z depends on time t. When t increases, Z tends to 1, which means that more and more emphasis is given to the mean value of the observed data $\bar{X}$.

There is an important difference between the formula (4.10.3) and the credibility rule (4.10.14). In the former the effect of each X_i gradually vanishes, whereas in the latter all Xs have an effect with same weights.

It is of interest to know that a formula of just the type of (4.10.14) was found, largely by a trial and error method, in the USA some 60 years ago and has been in use since then. The theoretical derivation was found much later (Bailey, 1945, and Mayerson, 1965). The presentation given above follows Jewell (1976).

(g) The least squares approach A third way of building credibility theory has been developed by Bühlmann (1967) and others. The idea is to construct from the observed data X_i some predicting function $g(X_1, \ldots, X_t)$ which, as well as possible, can give a forecast for the amount of claims X_{t+1} of the next year. The simplest approach is to choose g linear

$$\mathbf{g}_{t+1} = a_0 + \sum_{i=1}^{t} a_i \mathbf{X}_i, \qquad (4.10.17)$$

where the coefficients $a_0, a_1, \ldots$ are to be determined by means of the least-squares principle, i.e. minimizing the expression

$$E\{(\mathbf{X}_{t+1} - \mathbf{g}_{t+1})^2\}, \qquad (4.10.18)$$

It can be proved that, subject to some fairly general conditions, a formula can be found which is of just the same shape as (4.10.14) and (4.10.16) even if the constant A is different.

A good survey of credibility theory can be found, for example, in Jewell (1980).

Exercise 4.10.1 Calculate the variance σ_p^2 of the sliding premium $\mathbf{P}_t$ defined by (4.10.9) assuming that the variables $\mathbf{X}_t$ are mutually independent and have an equal variance σ^2. Furthermore, prove that σ_p is finite when $t \to \infty$ even in the case where the individual variances are different but have a finite upper limit.

Exercise 4.10.2 Let the safety loaded risk premium B of a risk unit be $> E(\mathbf{X})$. A bonus $\mathbf{G} = k(B - \mathbf{X})^+$ will be given. What is the largest value of k which does not render a systematic loss for the insurer? Express this limit value in terms of B and $F(X)$ and prove that it is $\leqslant 1$.

Exercise 4.10.3 A commercial firm has insured 1000 lorries by a collective treaty. The premium without loadings is £300 per vehicle and will be adjusted in accordance with the credibility formula (4.10.3). The total sum of claims in the first year is £180 000 and the number of claims 200. What should the premium be for the next year if the credibility coefficient Z is determined by using values $r_2 = 10$, $\sigma_q = 0$, $p = 0.1$ and $x_\varepsilon = 2$?

CHAPTER 5

Variance as a measure of stability

5.1 Optimum form of reinsurance

(a) Problem setting In Chapter 4, the ruin probability was the main criterion used for the solvency of insurers. The implementation was based on the calculation of the variation range of the aggregate claims, which mostly lead to use of the normal, the NP or another approximation. Another way is to use directly the variance

$$\text{var}(\mathbf{X}) \equiv V(\mathbf{X}) \equiv \sigma_{\mathbf{X}}^2 = \int_0^\infty (X - E(\mathbf{X}))^2 \, dF(X), \qquad (5.1.1)$$

of the aggregate claims as a measure of stability. In the case where the normal approximation is applicable, the minimum initial risk reserve is by a given safety level $1 - \varepsilon$ proportional to the standard deviation $\sigma_{\mathbf{X}}$, as can be seen from (4.1.8). Hence the smaller the variance is the safer is the position, assuming that the other quantities involved are not changed, at least not enough to offset the effect. If several policy options are available, for example different reinsurance arrangements, the best of them is, from the point of view of solvency, that which gives the smallest variance (providing, of course, that it is not realizable too much at the expense of some other aspects, e.g. weakened safety loading or decreased business volume). It is natural to expect that this conclusion will also be valid more generally than merely for the normal approximation. That is the issue in this chapter. The problem of finding an optimal reinsurance arrangement is transformed to the problem of minimization of the variance $V(\mathbf{X})$.

The variance has been explicitly calculated in Section 3.3 for the compound Poisson variable. However, in the present approach it is not necessary to make the assumptions that the compound

Poisson or normal properties apply, and the way is open to some general risk-theoretical questions of a rather broad nature.

(b) The optimality of stop loss reinsurance Consider the following problem. A company wants to find a reinsurance policy which gives the smallest variance for the retained business provided the reinsurance risk premium P (without any safety loadings) is fixed. The total amount of claims resulting from the claims process during a time period (e.g. one year) under consideration is assumed to be given by the random variable $\mathbf{X}_{tot}$. Furthermore, it is assumed that reinsurance is arranged in a way which defines a uniquely determined claims amount $\mathbf{X}$

$$0 \leqslant \mathbf{X} \leqslant \mathbf{X}_{tot} \quad \text{and} \quad E(\mathbf{X}) = P, \tag{5.1.2}$$

on the cedent's net retention for each claim process realization. It is not necessary to specify further the type or details of the reinsurance treaty; for example any of the standard forms dealt with in Sections 3.6, 3.7 and 3.8 or their mixes are acceptable. The problem is now to find that reinsurance arrangement which has the smallest variance $V(\mathbf{X})$ subject to conditions (5.1.2).

It is suggested that the required solution is the stop loss treaty (see Section 4.8) defined by

$$\mathbf{X}^* = \min(\mathbf{X}_{tot}, M), \tag{5.1.3}$$

where the retention limit M is a constant determined by condition

$$E(\mathbf{X}^*) = P.$$

The problem setting is illustrated in Fig. 5.1.1.

For the proof of the assertion it is first noted that, since $0 \leqslant \mathbf{X} \leqslant \mathbf{X}_{tot}$, it follows from (5.1.3) that the following sets of realizations are identical

$$\{\mathbf{X} + \mathbf{X}^* > 2M\} = \{\mathbf{X} > M\} = \{\mathbf{X} - \mathbf{X}^* > 0\}. \tag{5.1.4}$$

All such realizations satisfy

$$\mathbf{X}^2 - \mathbf{X}^{*2} = (\mathbf{X} + \mathbf{X}^*)(\mathbf{X} - \mathbf{X}^*) \geqslant 2M(\mathbf{X} - \mathbf{X}^*). \tag{5.1.5}$$

But this inequality is valid also for the rest of the realizations, because by (5.1.4) these satisfy the inequalities $0 \leqslant \mathbf{X} + \mathbf{X}^* \leqslant 2M$ and $\mathbf{X} - \mathbf{X}^* \leqslant 0$, or together $(\mathbf{X} + \mathbf{X}^*)(\mathbf{X} - \mathbf{X}^*) \geqslant 2M(\mathbf{X} - \mathbf{X}^*)$. By taking

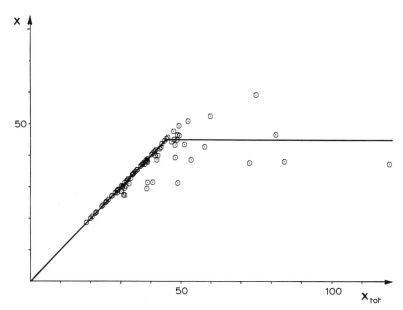

Figure 5.1.1 *The stop loss treaty* (**X***) *and excess of loss treaty* (**X**). *The realizations (amounts retained on the cedent's own account) of* **X*** *are on the straight lines plotted solidly and the realizations of* **X**, *shown by circles, are distributed in the half axis angle* $0 \leqslant \mathbf{X} \leqslant \mathbf{X}_{\text{tot}}$. *Compound Poisson aggregate claim d.f.* $n = 20$, *claim sizes Pareto-distributed,* $\alpha = 2$, $Z_0 = 1$ (*see* (3.5.20)), *net retention for the excess of loss arrangement* $M = 5$.

expected values in (5.1.5), and recalling the assumption $E(\mathbf{X}) = E(\mathbf{X}^*)$, it is obtained conclusively

$$\begin{aligned} V(\mathbf{X}) - V(\mathbf{X}^*) &= E(\mathbf{X}^2) - E(\mathbf{X}^{*2}) \\ &= E(\mathbf{X}^2 - \mathbf{X}^{*2}) \geqslant 2M\,E(\mathbf{X} - \mathbf{X}^*) = 0. \end{aligned} \quad (5.1.6)$$

Hence the variance is minimized by the stop loss reinsurance. Obviously there is equality in (5.1.6) only if $\mathbf{X} = \mathbf{X}^*$ (with probability 1).

This result shows that the stop loss reinsurance (5.1.3) is the optimal solution among all reinsurance formulae in the sense that it gives for a fixed reinsurance risk premium the smallest variance for the company's net retention. In other words, if the level V of the variance of the retained business is fixed, the stop loss reinsurance leaves the maximum premium income to the ceding company and thus minimizes the reinsurance risk premium.

The above proof is due to Martti Pesonen (1983).

(c) Loaded reinsurance premium In practice, however, there can be heavy safety and expense loadings in stop loss premiums, because this form of reinsurance gives a large relative variance to the reinsurer. The problem is therefore modified accordingly. Again let $\mathbf{X}_{tot}$ be the total amount of claims, $\mathbf{X}$ the retained part thereof, and $\mathbf{X}_{tot} - \mathbf{X} = \mathbf{X}_{re}$ the reinsurer's share. Suppose that the reinsurance premium is defined as

$$P_{re} = E(\mathbf{X}_{re}) + f(V(\mathbf{X}_{re})), \tag{5.1.7}$$

where f is a given 'loading' function. It is necessary to assume only that f is non-decreasing. The net reinsurance cost is evidently $f(V(\mathbf{X}_{re}))$ on average. Suppose further that the cedent wishes to retain a variance of fixed size, say $V(\mathbf{X}) = V$. The problem is to determine how the *form of reinsurance* should be chosen, if reinsurance costs are to be as low as possible; in other words, which insurance arrangement minimizes $V(\mathbf{X}_{re})$ if $V(\mathbf{X})$ is fixed. Now

$$V(\mathbf{X}_{re}) = V(\mathbf{X}_{tot}) + V(\mathbf{X}) - 2(E(\mathbf{X}_{tot}\mathbf{X}) - E(\mathbf{X}_{tot})E(\mathbf{X})).$$

From this expression it can be concluded, since $V(\mathbf{X}_{tot})$ and $V(\mathbf{X})$ are constants, that the reinsurance cost attains its minimum on average if the correlation coefficient

$$\frac{E(\mathbf{X}_{tot}\mathbf{X}) - E(\mathbf{X}_{tot})E(\mathbf{X})}{\sqrt{[V(\mathbf{X}_{tot})V]}}$$

of the variables $\mathbf{X}$ and $\mathbf{X}_{tot}$ reaches its maximum value $+1$. As is well known from probability calculus, this is the case if $\mathbf{X} = a\mathbf{X}_{tot}$, where the positive constant a is defined from $V = V(\mathbf{X})$ giving

$$\mathbf{X} = \sqrt{\left(\frac{V}{V(\mathbf{X}_{tot})}\right)}\mathbf{X}_{tot}. \tag{5.1.8}$$

Thus a reinsurance of quota share form (see Section 3.6.3) gives the desired result.

Hence a quite general theorem is proved that if the reinsurance premium increases with the reinsurer's variance, and is thus of the form (5.1.7), the most inexpensive way to reach a given variance is to use the reinsurance form (5.1.8).

Exercise 5.1.1 Let $\mathbf{X}_{tot}$ be the aggregate claim without reinsurance and $\mathbf{X}$ and $\mathbf{X}_{re} = \mathbf{X}_{tot} - \mathbf{X}$ the shares of the cedent and the reinsurer(s) when some reinsurance treaty is applied $(0 \leqslant \mathbf{X} \leqslant \mathbf{X}_{tot})$. In many reinsurance arrangements, for example in excess of loss and in surplus treaty, the value of the aggregate claim $\mathbf{X}_{tot}$ does not determine the values of $\mathbf{X}$ and $\mathbf{X}_{re}$, these variables depending on how $\mathbf{X}_{tot}$ is composed as a sum of individual claims. Prove that there is, however, always a function R such that $\mathbf{R} = R(\mathbf{X}_{tot})$ satisfies the conditions

(i) $0 \leqslant \mathbf{R} \leqslant \mathbf{X}_{tot}$
(ii) $E(\mathbf{R}) = E(\mathbf{X})$
(iii) $V(\mathbf{R}) \leqslant V(\mathbf{X})$
(iv) $V(\mathbf{R}_{re}) \leqslant V(\mathbf{X}_{re})$,
where $\mathbf{R}_{re} = \mathbf{X}_{tot} - \mathbf{R}$.

Hint: choose $\mathbf{R} = E(\mathbf{X}|\mathbf{X}_{tot})$, i.e. for every X let $R(X) = E(\mathbf{X}|\mathbf{X}_{tot} = X)$ = mean value of the different outcomes which all result in a joint total aggregate claim.

Note that by replacing $\mathbf{X}$ by $\mathbf{R}$ one can improve the variance of *both* the cedent *and* the reinsurer without any extra cost to any of the parties compared with the original rule (E. Pesonen, 1967a).

In this respect, more important results for general application have been obtained by Martti Pesonen (1983).

5.2 Reciprocity of two companies

(a) The problem to be considered arises when two companies C_1 and C_2, whose total amounts of claims $\mathbf{X}_1$ and $\mathbf{X}_2$ are supposed to be independent, wish to exchange reinsurance on a reciprocal basis and desire to find an optimum method which satisfies the two conditions:

(i) The expected profit on the exchange must be zero.
(ii) The variance of the net retained business after the exchange must be minimized as far as possible for the two companies.

(b) The type of risk exchange In order to fulfil requirement (i) it is simply assumed that the reinsurance premiums are unloaded risk premiums, i.e. of form (5.1.7) with $f = 0$. If then condition (ii) is the only remaining decision criterion, it is easily seen that the exchange should be of quota share type, i.e. the final total amounts should be

$$
\begin{array}{ll}
\text{for } C_1 & c_1 \mathbf{X}_1 + (1 - c_2)\mathbf{X}_2 \\
\text{for } C_2 & (1 - c_1)\mathbf{X}_1 + c_2 \mathbf{X}_2.
\end{array}
\tag{5.2.1}
$$

To prove this suppose that the final arrangement has given the variance V_1^R to company C_1. This can be written $V_{11} + V_{21}$, where V_{11} eminates from C_1's remaining original business and V_{21} from accepted reinsurance, since the amounts $\mathbf{X}_1$ and $\mathbf{X}_2$ were assumed to be independent of each other. Analogously the final variance of C_2 can be written in the form $V_{12} + V_{22}$. Suppose now that the reinsurance $C_1 \rightarrow C_2$ was not of the quota share form. Then without changing the other variances the variance V_{12} of C_2 could be reduced by means of reinsurance (5.1.8). Similarly without changing other variances the optimal variance V_{21} is reached by using a reinsurance of form (5.1.8), i.e. of the quota share form (5.2.1) as asserted. Then

$$
\begin{array}{l}
V_1^R = c_1^2 V_1 + (1 - c_2)^2 V_2 \\
V_2^R = (1 - c_1)^2 V_1 + c_2^2 V_2.
\end{array}
\tag{5.2.2}
$$

(c) Pareto optimal The remaining question is to determine how the constants c_1 and c_2 should be chosen.

First observe that V_1^R is, in the c_1, c_2 plane, constant on the periphery of an ellipse having midpoint 0, 1 and principal axes $\sqrt{(V_1^R/V_1)}$ and $\sqrt{(V_1^R/V_2)}$. For different values of V_1^R a family E_1 of concentric ellipses is obtained. Similarly the condition for V_2^R determines another family E_2 of concentric ellipses having midpoint $(1, 0)$ and principal axes $\sqrt{(V_2^R/V_1)}$ and $\sqrt{(V_2^R/V_2)}$.

Evidently a necessary condition for agreement is that $V_1^R \leqslant V_1$ and $V_2^R \leqslant V_2$. Geometrically this means that the point (c_1, c_2) should be located in the common area of the two ellipses E_1' and E_2' corresponding to the values $V_1^R = V_1$ and $V_2^R = V_2$ (shaded in Fig. 5.2.1). Through any point P goes one and only one ellipse $E_1(V_1^R)$ of the family E_1 and another ellipse of the family E_2. Now let the point P move along $E_1(V_1^R)$. Then V_1^R is preserved unchanged but V_2^R is changing all the time according to which of the ellipses E_2 is intercepted until a point is reached in which $E_1(V_1^R)$ is tangential to one of the E_2 ellipses. Then V_2^R has reached its minimum. So a point

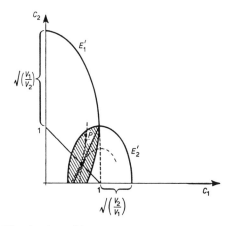

Figure 5.2.1   *The families of level ellipses. E'_1 and E'_2 plotted by solid lines: the cases $V_1^R = V_1$ and $V_2^R = V_2$.*

is reached from which it is no longer possible to move to any direction without worsening the benefit (variance) of C_1 or C_2. This reasoning shows that this is the situation always and only in those points where one of the ellipses of each family is tangential to an ellipse of the other family inside the shaded area. It is easily seen that this set of points is the segment of the straight line $c_1 + c_2 = 1$ which goes through the midpoints of E_1 and E_2 (see exercise 5.2.3). This kind of point set is called a *Pareto optimal*, a concept which in a similar way is important in the theory of games and economic behaviour.

(d) Reciprocity condition We have now concluded that it is reasonable to choose c_1 and c_2 from

$$c_1 + c_2 = 1. \tag{5.2.3}$$

But there is still a conflicting situation. Company C_1 prefers to go as near the midpoint $(0, 1)$ as possible; the other company prefers points near the midpoint $(1, 0)$. A compromise has to be found somewhere in that part of this straight line which lies inside both ellipses.

Suppose now that the companies have agreed to meet, in addition to the conditions (i) and (ii), a third one:

(iii) The volume of exchange must be balanced.

That is to say, the reinsurance premium from $C_1 \to C_2$ must be equal to the reinsurance premium from $C_2 \to C_1$, i.e.

$$(1 - c_1)P_1 = (1 - c_2)P_2. \tag{5.2.4}$$

Then the constants c_1 and c_2 become uniquely determined from the equations, the solution being

$$c_1 = P_1/(P_1 + P_2)$$
$$c_2 = P_2/(P_1 + P_2).$$

(e) Multi-unit risk exchange The above consideration can obviously be extended to the cases where more than two, say n, insurers are involved. Instead of level ellipses, ellipsoids in n-dimensional space are then operated and the optimal points are sought inside their joint space segments by methods of the theory of multiplayer games. This topic is illustrated in the following section, where formally a different type of problem will be treated, but the idea of minimization of variances is the same as in the risk exchange problem.

Exercise 5.2.1 There are r insurance companies having the same distribution function of the total amount of claims X_i, the claims of each company being independent of those of the others. The companies want to find a reciprocal exchange of business so that each company i pays the amount $R(X_j)$ of the claims of each other company j, and the standard deviation of the claims on each company's own retention (including the amounts of the other companies' claims received) must be minimized. Prove that the function $R(X) = X/r$ is the required solution. Note that the equality of distributions implies the equality of business volumes and other parameters.

Exercise 5.2.2 A major concept in the classical theory of risk was the so-called *relative mean risk* ρ, which was defined as

$$\rho = \sigma_X/P$$

σ_X and P being the standard deviation and risk premium income respectively. ρ was used as a measure of the stability of the insurance collective concerned.

(i) What is $\rho = \rho_0$ for a collective having equal risk sums and mixed Poisson claim number process?

(ii) Prove that ρ_0 is the minimum for all collectives having the same P, n and structure function H, if the mixed compound Poisson distribution is assumed.

(iii) Rewrite the basic equation (4.1.8) making use of ρ.

Exercise 5.2.3 Prove that the Pareto optimal derived in item 5.2(c) is on the straight line (5.2.3).

5.3 Equitability of safety loadings: a link to theory of multiplayer games

(a) **Safety loading problem** Yet another example may be given of how variances or equivalently standard deviations may be used as a yardstick in solvency treatments. Even if the details of premium rating are beyond the scope of this book, a special aspect related to safety loading will be dealt with in order to illustrate the variance approach. As has just been stated, and as will be demonstrated later, when long-term survival conditions are examined, premiums must necessarily be loaded by safety margins. It was stated in item 4.1(c) that regarding solvency conditions it is relevant that the *total* yield accrued from the whole portfolio is large enough. The solvency aspects do not determine how the loading is to be distributed among the individual policies or groups of the insured. This is to be decided on the basis of rules and principles, which are in the realm rather of general non-life insurance mathematics or business philosophy than risk theory, and there are numerous partially contradictory suggestions for the purpose. We pick up only one of them, which follows ideas orginally presented by Borch (1962).

The issue is the minimum solvency margin U which is needed to protect a supposed portfolio. As reasoned above it should be dimensioned according to the range of fluctuations arising in the risk business concerned. The first term of the basic equation (4.1.7) gives an approximation for it, i.e. U must be proportional to the standard deviation of the aggregate claims amount **X**

$$U = y\sigma_{\mathbf{X}} = yP\sqrt{(r_2/n + \sigma_q^2)}, \qquad (5.3.1)$$

where y is again a safety factor, say 3. In the case of proprietary companies it is expected that the portfolio pays interest to this safety capital. In the case of a mutual company, U will perhaps have to be created by self-financing and maintained from the safety loadings, a point which may be crucial especially in inflatory environments. These aspects suggest safety loading λ, which gives a *total* yield λP proportional to U, or what is approximately the same, to the standard deviation σ_X of the aggregate claims.

Another way to reason the same outcome is to suppose a hypothetical situation where a certain group of policy-holders are going to establish an insurance company and U is the minimum initial capital to be got by levying it from them in one way or other.

(b) Multiplayer approach We are now going to discuss what kind of consequences may result if the safety loading is defined proportional to the minimum initial capital (5.3.1), i.e. $\lambda P = kU$ where k is a proportionality factor. Let us take a simplified example assuming that the portfolio is composed of three groups of the insureds, which are each of different types but all internally homogeneous. Group 1 is comprised of small risks, like motor cars, family property etc. Group 2 contains large risks like industrial fire, marine, aviation etc. Group 3 risks are characterized by exceptionally great short-term variation of the basic probabilities, such as for forests or in other insurance against natural forces. The basic characteristics are given in Table 5.3.1.

The quantities U_j are the risk reserves according to (5.3.1) if *each group separately* built an insurance collective. Furthermore, applying the composition rules (3.7.9) the risk reverse $U_{123} = 27.8$ of the whole united portfolio is obtained. It is considerably less than the sum of the components (column 7 in Table 5.3.1). Without loss of generality the proportionality factor k, relating U to λ, can be

Table 5.3.1 *Example of an internal composition of a portfolio and minimum solvency margins* (5.3.1) *of the groups* $j = 1, 2, 3$ *and combined groups ij. Monetary unit is* £10^6, r_{2j} *is the risk index* (3.3.8), σ_{qj} *is the standard deviation of the structure variation,* m_j *is the mean claim size and* $P_j = n_j m_j$.

1	2	3	4	5	6	7	8	9	10	11	12	13
j	n_j	r_{2j}	σ_{qj}	m_j	P_j	U_j	ij	U_{ij}	G_{ij}	G_i	G_i^σ	G_i^V
1	10 000	5	0.05	0.0028	28.0	4.6	12	26.8	4.2	2	1.2	0.3
2	5 000	150	0.10	0.0088	44.0	26.4	13	8.1	3.2	5.1	7.1	9.2
3	1 000	5	0.80	0.0028	2.8	6.7	23	27.2	5.9	3	1.8	0.6
$\sum$	16 000	—	—	—	74.8	37.7				10.1	10.1	10.1

taken to be 1. Then the difference can be called 'the gain G' obtained when the groups are united as one collective:

$$G_{123} = U_1 + U_2 + U_3 - U_{123} = 10.1.$$

Now the problem is how to divide reasonably this gain among the groups, i.e. to find amounts G_i satisfying the condition

$$\sum_{i=1}^{3} G_i = G_{123}. \tag{5.3.2}$$

A natural aspect is to expect that the shares G_i should be at least equal to what can be gained if any two of the groups establish together a collective (excluding the third). For example, if groups 1 and 2 join, their reserve would be, by again using (5.3.1), $U_{12} = 26.8$ and the gain $G_{12} = U_1 + U_2 - U_{12} = 4.2$. In a similar way the two other combinations can be evaluated as given in columns 9 and 10 of Table 5.3.1. An obvious condition for the co-operation of all the three groups is now

$$G_i + G_j > G_{ij} \qquad (i \neq j, i, j = 1, 2, 3), \tag{5.3.3}$$

i.e. the gain of each group should be better than what can be achieved if any two of them joined leaving the third outside. As shown in column 11 by means of an example there exist shares which satisfy conditions (5.3.2) and (5.3.3). On the other hand the solution is not unique; it is still open for further conditions. The situation is analogous to that found in the previous section in the form of the Pareto optimal (5.2.9).

The example given above is a typical n players co-operative game (Borch, 1962). The set of solutions satisfying the above conditions is called the *core* of the game and the consideration can be extended to an arbitrary number of insurers participating in the risk exchange.

(c) Equitability aspects An approach sometimes suggested is to load policies or policy groups by safety loadings proportional to standard deviation (or variance) of the risk. If the solvency margin (and safety loading yield proportional to it) were divided according to the group standard deviations, which by (5.3.1) are proportional to the risk reserves given in column 7, the gains G_i^{σ} given in column 12 would result. It is interesting to observe that these shares do not satisfy conditions (5.3.3). The groups of small risks were overloaded in benefit of the big risks (group 2).

The situation would be still more blatant if the variance principle were applied, i.e. the loadings were defined proportional to variances. This is shown in column 13 of the table.

The above examples were intended, among other things, to warn of the fact that too straightforward an application of conventional rating principles can violate the equitable treatment of different types of policies; in particular, the great mass of small risks may easily be paying for the risk equalization of big risks.

(d) Company size Another interesting observation is that the safety loading $\lambda = kU/P$, according to (5.3.1), is smaller the greater is the portfolio. This means that in theory a large insurer can apply a lower safety loading than a small insurer, if the other conditions are equal.

(e) Utility approach The variance or the standard deviation of the collective concerned was used as a measure of stability, the optimization of which was the objective of the reinsurance arrangements. One should appreciate that instead of these quantities other optimization target functions can also be used. The *utilities*, which will be discussed in Section 10.4, are often suggested for the purpose, and rules for Pareto optimals can be obtained (Borch, 1960, 1961). Bühlmann and Jewell (1979) have proved that the risk exchange between insurers can be presented in well-defined forms if it is assumed that all insurers accept an exponential utility function for the guidance of their procedure. Martti Pesonen (1983) has extended the considerations to quite general cases.

CHAPTER 6

Risk processes with a time-span of several years

6.1 Claims

(a) Finite time horizon In the preceding chapters the time-span used was generally limited to one year. This restriction is now relaxed. In what follows the argument will be extended to an arbitrary finite – and in Chapter 9 for infinite – time T.

The financial status of insurers is usually stated at the end of each calendar (accounting) year, and possibly also at other times, e.g. at the end of each quarter. Accordingly a *discrete* treatment of risk and other business processes is assumed, i.e. the state of the process is observed and calculated at equidistant time points $t = 1, 2, \ldots, T$ (Fig. 6.1.1). For brevity of presentation a year is used as the accounting and time unit. This does not restrict the theory because any other accounting period can be treated as a basic unit (see the discussion about the continuous and discrete approaches in item 1.4(b)).

The aggregate claims of year t will be denoted $\mathbf{X}(t)$. The accumulated amount $\mathbf{X}(t_1, t_2)$ in years $t_1, \ldots, t_2$ is then

$$\mathbf{X}(t_1, t_2) = \sum_{t=t_1}^{t_2} \mathbf{X}(t) = \mathbf{X}(1, t_2) - \mathbf{X}(1, t_1 - 1). \qquad (6.1.1)$$

As was specified in item 3.1(c), $\mathbf{X}(t)$ includes both the *paid* and *outstanding* claims.

(b) Extension of the basic assumptions It was stated in Section 2.7, and shown e.g. in Fig. 2.7.3, that the basic parameters of the claim process are continually subject to alterations which are partially revealed as trends and partially as more or less regular, often cyclical, changes. The effect of these phenomena is so significant that they

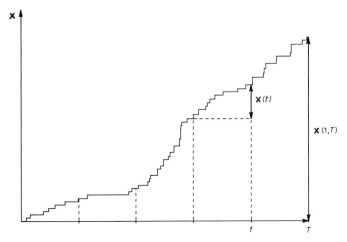

Figure 6.1.1 *A realization of a claims process extended over T years.*

cannot be omitted in long-term considerations. The assumptions concerning the mixed compound Poisson process are now extended accordingly; first, in this section, the parameter n (the expected number of claims) is discussed, and then, in subsequent sections, some other bases are also taken up.

(c) The trends in the parameter n are partially due to the gradual change of the size of portfolio and are partially affected also by alterations in the risk exposure inside the portfolio. They can be taken into account by assuming that the model parameter n is time dependent. This can be done conveniently by means of a growth factor $r_g(t) = n(t)/n(t - 1)$, or equivalently

$$n(t) = n \prod_{\tau = 1}^{t} r_g(\tau), \qquad (6.1.2a)$$

where briefly $n = n(0)$. The corresponding rate $r_g - 1$ is denoted by i_g (see item 1.5(f)).

The growth rate need not be the same from year to year. However, if consideration is limited to relatively short periods, its constancy can be assumed. The formulae can be considerably simplified in this way. Hence, in most connections in the following, trends are introduced into the model by simply assuming them exponential and by putting

$$n(t) = n r_g^t. \tag{6.1.2b}$$

Another approach would be to use linear formula

$$n(t) = n + r_g' t. \tag{6.1.2c}$$

(d) The cycles Besides the trends there are the periodic variations in claims frequencies; these are considered next. Even though the variations concerned are often in practice rather irregular, they are by convention called 'cycles'. They are distinguished from the short-term 'oscillation' already introduced in Section 2.7; these are composed of only variations appearing as waves which extend over two or more years, whereas the 'structure variations' of consecutive years are mutually independent. The simplest way is to find some suitable deterministic formula to indicate the relative deviations, denoted by $z(t) = \Delta n(t)/n(t)$ of $n(t)$ from its trend flow (6.1.2b). A deterministic sinusoidal form

$$z(t) = z_m \sin(\omega t + v), \tag{6.1.3}$$

is assumed as an example (Fig. 6.1.2), where z_m is the amplitude,

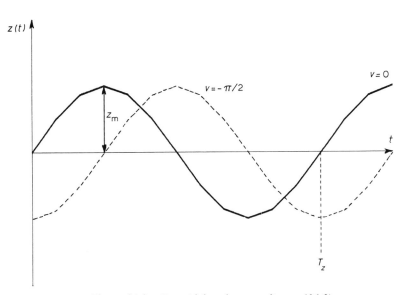

Figure 6.1.2 *Sinusoidal cycles according to (6.1.3).*

v the phase and ω is the frequency coefficient

$$\omega = 2\pi/T_z, \tag{6.1.4}$$

T_z being the length of wave. The observations, which were referred to in Section 2.7, suggest this shape, at least as a first approximation in solvency considerations (but not necessarily when the model is designed for forecasting; see items (g) and (h)).

(e) Autocorrelative time series A more sophisticated way to handle the 'cycles' is to make use of the well-developed theories of time series.

Fig. 6.1.3 exhibits a couple of typical economic time series. The 'cycle' variable $z = \Delta n/\bar{n}$ periodically soars and then swings down for another period until another upswing occurs.

A simple approach in modelling z is to assume that its value $z(t)$ depends on the state of the process in previous times $t - 1, t - 2, \ldots$. If z is high at these times, $z(t)$ is also likely to be high, but several years continued growth can be a portent of stagnation to come. In addition z is subject to more or less strong irregularities which can be assumed to be purely random fluctuations. These features provide a basis for building

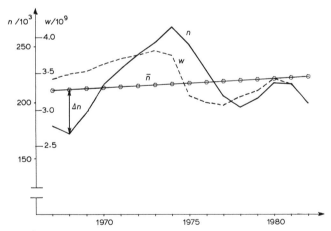

Figure 6.1.3 *Employment accidents n and working man-hours w in industry 1960–81 (Federation of Accident Insurance Institutions in Finland). n̄ depicts the trend of n.*

mathematical models to describe the process of the type

$$\mathbf{z}(t) = f(\mathbf{z}(t-1), \mathbf{z}(t-2), \ldots) + \varepsilon(t) + b_1 \varepsilon(t-1) + b_2 \varepsilon(t-2) + \cdots,$$

$$(6.1.5a)$$

where the 'descriptor' or 'predictor' function f conveys the feedback of the past experience to the future. The terms $\varepsilon(t)$, the so-called 'noise', represent the random effect, which is often assumed to be normally ($N(0, \sigma^2)$ distributed.

Linear functions are often satisfactory approximations for (6.1.5a)

$$\mathbf{z}(t) = a_1 \mathbf{z}(t-1) + a_2 \mathbf{z}(t-2) + a_3 \mathbf{z}(t-3) + \cdots$$
$$+ \varepsilon(t) + b_1 \varepsilon(t-1) + b_2 \varepsilon(t-2) \ldots, \qquad (6.1.5b)$$

which are known as ARMA processes (autoregressive moving average, see Chatfield, 1978). The cycles can be generated by suitable choice of coefficients as can be shown analytically (see item 6.2(e)). In terms of the theory there exists a strong *autocorrelation* between the consecutive variable values.

If $b_1 = b_2 = \ldots = 0$ then (6.1.5a) is reduced to a so-called auto-regressive, briefly AR process. A benefit of the ARMA approach is that a stationary time series may often be described by a model involving fewer parameters than a pure AR process (Chatfield 1975, paragraph 3.4.5).

According to Wold's decomposition theorem (see Chatfield, 1978, Section 3.5) any discrete stationary process can be expressed as the sum of two uncorrelated processes, one purely deterministic and one purely indeterministic. The best-known examples of purely deterministic processes are those whose realizations are simply of the sinusoidal form (6.1.3).

(f) Exogenous impacts Even though, as can be proved (see item 6.2(e)), the time series approach described generates processes which may be of the same type as those observed in practice, they can often be improved further by incorporating some exogenous impulses into the system. A clear indication can be found by comparing the curves of Fig. 6.1.3. The variation of the number of accidents is clearly correlated with the working activity of the industry which, furthermore, depends on the general economic climate of the national economy, on booms and recessions. This phenomenon has already been discussed in item 2.7(b). Such observations suggest an extension of the time series formulae by introducing exogenous variables $w_i(t)$, which are links with the general economy of the country; such variables might include the gross national product (GNP), traffic intensity, volume of investments, total number of man-hours worked, etc. Then (6.1.5a) is generalized as follows

$$\mathbf{z}(t) = f(\mathbf{z}(t-1), \mathbf{z}(t-2), \dots, ; \mathbf{w}_1(t), \mathbf{w}_2(t), \dots) + \varepsilon(t). \qquad (6.1.6)$$

Suggestions and analyses of this kind of dependence can be found in Helten (1977) and in the theses of Becker (1981). Similar results are reported also by e.g. McGuinness (1970), Witt and Miller (1980), Bohman (1979), Balzar and Benjamin (1980, 1982), Pentikäinen (1982) and Rantala (1982).

As an illustration of the method related to (6.1.6), an application presented by Becker (1981, p. 190) is given in Fig. 6.1.4. The formula applied is of the following linear form

$$\frac{\Delta f}{f} = 0.92 \frac{\Delta k}{k} + 0.29 \frac{\Delta N}{N} - 0.57 u_{-1}, \qquad (6.1.7)$$

where f is motor third-party claims per vehicle, k is total traffic kilometres in the relevant year, N is the sales of new saloon and estate cars, and u_{-1} is a residue term related to the preceding year. The coefficients are determined by the least squares method (Coherence–Orcutt method, see Becker, 1981, p.73). The autoregressive effect is achieved through the last term having a negative coefficient. As is seen from Fig. 6.1.4, the suggested formula gave quite a good fit in the case concerned.

(g) Forecasting If a model is constructed to give a *forecast* for the future flow of business, either on the company level or more generally e.g. for some line of all insurers, obviously a formula of type (6.1.6) is most appropriate. Exogenous variables w_i have to be found which are best fitted to the environment in question, as demonstrated in Fig. 6.1.4. For instance the GNP is often used. This and other similar variables should first be adjusted for trends by treating as in item (c). Then deviations of the actual data from the trend-adjusted flow are often useful indicators, as demonstrated in Fig. 6.1.5.

Unfortunately the possibilities of finding reliable forecasts are quite limited as regards general economic indicators. Mostly they

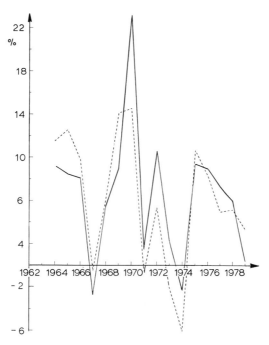

Figure 6.1.4 *Relative changes in the amount of losses per vehicle. German motor third-party insurance. The actual values (solid line) and the forecast (dashed line) are according to (6.1.7). Reproduced by permission from Becker (1981).*

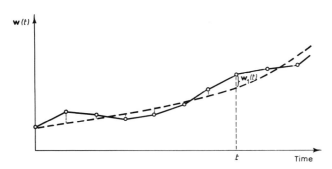

Figure 6.1.5 *Formulation of exogenous variables* **w**(t), *decomposed into an exponential trend (dashed line) and a 'cyclic variable'* $w_1(t)$. *The former is intended to be taken into account via the growth equations* (6.1.2).

have to be limited to one or two years only so that the construction of predictors for the insurance industry is a matter of some difficulty.

(h) General purpose models Fortunately in many standard risk-theoretical considerations it is not necessary to know exact times for the peaks or troughs of future cycles. This is the case for example when the general structures of the insurer's business are examined, or when the effect of the cycles and an insurer's capacity to overcome cyclically bad periods is studied. For example, in the case of solvency tests it is sufficient to appreciate that such cycles are present and to have estimates for their amplitudes and wavelengths. To obtain conservative evaluations it is often advisable to assume that the adverse half of the cycle begins immediately, which means that the phase parameter v in (6.1.3) should be put equal to 0. In this connection, in particular, the sinusoidal form of the wave is a natural assumption.

For technical reasons it is often convenient to keep the long-term waves purely deterministic, with the possible exception of the phase v, which can sometimes be assumed stochastic. The random variation, i.e. the 'noise' of the basic probabilities, will be moved to the variable $\mathbf{q}$ already introduced in Section 2.7, dimensioning its d.f. H accordingly.

(i) Summarizing the above presentation, the (mixed) compound Poisson process is now further generalized by replacing the variable $\mathbf{n} = n\mathbf{q}$ (see Section 2.8) by

$$\mathbf{n}(t) = n \prod_{\tau=1}^{t} r_g(\tau)(1 + \mathbf{z}(t))\mathbf{q}(t), \qquad (6.1.8a)$$

or for a constant growth rate

$$\mathbf{n}(t) = n \times r_g^t \times (1 + \mathbf{z}(t)) \times \mathbf{q}(t). \qquad (6.1.8b)$$

The cycle variable $\mathbf{z}(t)$ can be defined to be either deterministic, e.g. by applying formula (6.1.3), or it can be generated by means of a time series technique as drafted in the preceding items. The former approach will be mainly followed in the subsequent consideration (hence notation z is used instead of $\mathbf{z}$ even though it is not necessary to exclude the possibility of stochastic approaches in many connections).

The separation between the trend variables and the cycle variables can be supposed to be made, so that on the long run the mean value of the effect of the cycle variable z is zero. This means that systematic changes in claim number intensities should be introduced to the model via the trend variable $r_g(t)$.

For most subsequent applications the mean value of $\mathbf{n}(t)$, denoted briefly by $n(t)$, is required. Since $\mathbf{q}(t)$ was assumed independent of the growth and cycle variables having $E(\mathbf{q}) = 1$, $n(t)$ is obtained from

$$n(t) = n \times \prod_{\tau=1}^{t} r_g(\tau) \times (1 + z(t)) \qquad (6.1.9a)$$

or for a constant growth rate

$$n(t) = n \times r_g^t \times (1 + z(t)), \qquad (6.1.9b)$$

where the value of $z(t)$ is given or generated for each year t separately

(j) Inflation is another aspect which must be taken into account in long-term considerations. Even a modest inflation changes values sufficiently for the monetary variables calculated at the beginning and at the end of the period under consideration to deviate so much that the variation cannot be ignored. The models not only have to cope with modest inflation but also must be workable in environments where the inflation may be rather high, or may vary from year to year.

The effect of inflation is introduced into the model by means of an inflation rate $i_x(t)$. The subindex x refers to *claim inflation* as distinct from the premium inflation which will be introduced in Section 6.2.

In most connections it is convenient to replace the inflation rate by an 'inflation factor' (for notation see item 1.5.(f).

$$r_x(t) = 1 + i_x(t). \qquad (6.1.10a)$$

In principle $r_x(t)$ can be stochastic. However, in what follows only deterministic cases will be considered.

As a special case, e.g. when average flows for long periods are examined, the rate of inflation can be assumed to be a constant i_x. The corresponding factor will be then denoted by

$$r_x = 1 + i_x. \qquad (6.1.10b)$$

(k) Distinction of the inflation effects One of the difficulties in inflation analyses is that variables like claims, rates, etc. of different subsections of any portfolio may change by different degrees during inflation. It is generally expected that personal indemnities mainly follow salary indexes, whereas property indemnities are more related to the index of construction or to the index of wholesale prices. In order to guide the evaluation of the claim index the average sizes of the individual claims were recorded for some business classes in Fig. 6.1.6, where some general indexes are also given for comparison. A similar analysis can be found in the report of Munich Reinsurance Company (1971). The numbers show quite considerable deviations from each other and from the indexes. This is, of course, due to the fact that, besides inflation, numerous other factors affect the claim sizes – legislation defining indemnities in mandatory insurance classes, changes in policy conditions as well as trends in construction techniques, renewal of buildings, plants and vehicles, etc. Extension of the insurance contracts to cover many subsidiary perils and damages and moving to multiline policies explain the low growth of fire claim sizes in Fig. 6.1.6. It is difficult in practice to attribute the changes in claim sizes to inflation rather than other reasons. Therefore only the joint effect will be considered. The factor r_x will be termed the *inflation factor* despite the fact that

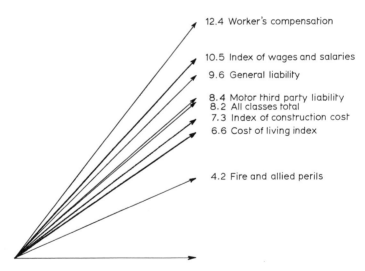

12.4 Worker's compensation

10.5 Index of wages and salaries

9.6 General liability

8.4 Motor third party liability
8.2 All classes total
7.3 Index of construction cost
6.6 Cost of living index

4.2 Fire and allied perils

Figure 6.1.6 *Claim inflation 1958–75 of Finnish non-life insurers measured by the average claim size (Pentikäinen, 1982).*

it is assumed to represent not merely inflation, but also time dependent changes of the claim sizes as a whole. Note that some of the background factors, such as changes in policy conditions, may also affect the shape of the claim size d.f. S, for example the frequencies of small claims may increase more rapidly than those of large ones. This may require special attention and necessitate frequent updating of the calculation bases, the d.f. S of claim sizes included.

The fact that the different variables follow different indexes obviously continually changes the distributions and parameters which are needed for the models. Those parts of business which are strongly affected by inflation have a tendency to be weighted more than other sections. Obviously the differentiation of the inflation effects ought to be taken into account in models which are intended to be used for more detailed analysis, especially on the company level. Decomposition formulae will be given in Section 6.4. In the following, however, a joint time-dependent rate of inflation for all monetary variables is mostly assumed in order to prevent the presentation from becoming unwieldy. If the purpose of the model is not to develop accurate forecasting models but instead to evaluate the range of fluctuations, it is unlikely that serious errors result.

(1) Aspects of the selection of the inflation premise The proper grounds for calculation of the effect of inflation depend essentially on the local conditions and are to be fitted accordingly. For example, in conventional fire and other property insurance it may be a practice that the face value is adjusted annually and then fixed for an accounting period, normally one year ahead and the so-called *pro rata* rule is applied for partial damages. It may, however, be difficult for the insurer to make a reduction in partial claims, even though the face value does not fully correspond to the current value of the property at the time of loss, if the face value was at least approximately correct at the beginning of the accounting period. Hence, despite the normal fixing of the values to be constant for each policy period, the claims may have a tendency to slide up continually. This is clearer in lines like liability, where indemnities are determined on the basis of actual costs or salaries. Note still the relevance of time lags between the claims inflation and the premium inflation which will be considered in item 6.2(a).

The practice already may be that the continuation of inflation is accepted as a normal working hypothesis, and necessary margins in premium rates and reserve calculations are provided to meet losses which cannot be covered from future premiums. Problems arise, however, when the actual inflation temporarily exceeds the assumed level, e.g. the technical reserves may need reinforcement, which causes extra expenditure in accounts. Aspects such as this should be considered when analysis of the effect of inflation is made and the bases for calculation, the factor $r_x(t)$, are chosen. The problems caused by inflation shocks will be considered in Section 7.6.

A further complication is the experience that the level of inflation as a rule is correlated with the growth cycles of the national economy. For example, a boom may *simultaneously* both increase the claim ratio, as stated in item (f), and push up inflation, and in that way worsen the claim ratio. This synchronism cannot be ignored; its consideration will be deferred to item 7.6(d).

(m) Interdependence of inflation and interest rates   Another observation of importance is the interdependence of inflation rate and interest rate. Both market forces and the government policy, and the central banks provide an increment in the interest rate to compensate for the inflation losses of money lenders and savers. This important relationship will be dealt with in Section 6.3, and it will be proved that, instead of the inflation rate, a more relevant factor for the economy and solvency of insurers is the ratio between the inflation rate and the interest rate.

(n) Inflation immune ratios   It will be assumed in the following that inflation affects the claims amounts of all sizes according to the same ratio $i_x(t)$ (see (6.1.10a)). The moments about the origin of the claim size distributions, as defined by (3.3.1), are changed as follows

$$a_k(t) = r_x(t)^k a_k(t-1). \qquad (6.1.11)$$

It is useful to notice that the ratio

$$a_k/a_1^k, \qquad (6.1.12)$$

is not changed; it is 'immune' to claims inflation. Some analytical simplifications in many considerations can be achieved by making use of this property, as will be shown later. The indexes r_2 and r_3 as defined by (3.3.8) are of just this type.

The immune assumption means that the shape of the claim size function S is not changed by inflation, i.e. only the scale of the claim size variables is to be corrected by the inflation factor. In other words, inflation hits both small and large claims equally. As far as experience shows, this may be satisfactorily true at least for short periods and when the inflation rate is not exceptionally high and does not change much from year to year. It can also be used as a working hypothesis for calculations without fear of serious bias because, as is seen, the risk-theoretical behaviour of the processes is fairly robust against changes in the shape of the S function. Of course, for actual applications it is desirable to test this assumption; and in any case, for this – and also for many other – reasons the shape of this function should be recalculated fairly frequently according to accrued experience. In particular, excessive inflation shocks may give rise to a need to check the assumptions rapidly and to take special precautions, e.g. concerning the long-tail business.

Note that the assumption about constancy of ratios (6.1.12) implies that the reinsurance policy is not changed other than that the monetary limits are changed in proportion to inflation.

(o) **Mean values** After the definition in item (n) we are now ready to calculate the main characteristics of the annual claims expenditure $X(t)$ and its accumulated amount $X(1, t)$. The mean values are obtained directly from the sum (6.1.1)

$$\mu_X(1, t) = \sum_{\tau = 1}^{t} \mu_X(\tau), \qquad (6.1.13)$$

where according to (3.3.7), (6.1.8a) and (6.1.11)

$$\mu_X(\tau) = nm(1 + z(\tau)) \prod_{u = 1}^{\tau} (r_g(u)r_x(u)). \qquad (6.1.14)$$

As before, the notation

$$n = n(0) \quad \text{and} \quad m = a_1(0), \qquad (6.1.15)$$

is used. The values of z are obtained or generated separately and substituted in this formula.

In the special case when the growth rate and inflation rate are both constant, this formula is reduced as follows

$$\mu_X(\tau) = nmr_g^\tau r_x^\tau (1 + z(\tau)). \qquad (6.1.16)$$

If the cycles introduced by means of the variable z are omitted, then the expression (6.1.13) is changed into a geometric series and can be summed to

$$\mu_{\mathbf{X}}(1, t) = nm \frac{r_{gx}^t - 1}{r_{gx} - 1} r_{gx}, \qquad (6.1.17)$$

where the coefficient (see item 1.5(f) for notation)

$$r_{gx} = r_g r_x, \qquad (6.1.18)$$

can be interpreted as the *factor of the total growth of the nominal values.*

(p) Variance In general cases the variance of the accumulated aggregate claims (6.1.1) is

$$\sigma_{\mathbf{X}}^2(t_1, t_2) = \mathrm{var}\, \mathbf{X}(t_1, t_2)$$

$$= \sum_{\tau = t_1}^{t_2} \mathrm{var}\, \mathbf{X}(\tau) + \sum_{\tau_1 \neq t_2} \mathrm{cov}(\mathbf{X}(\tau_1), \mathbf{X}(\tau_2)). \quad (6.1.19)$$

In most applications in the following the cycles will be taken into account by means of some deterministic rule, e.g. (6.1.3). The inflation factor $r_x(t)$ will also either be given in a deterministic way or it is assumed to be subject, if at all, to random fluctuation (noise) of a short-term nature. Furthermore, given that the structure variables $\mathbf{q}(t)$ of consecutive years are assumed independent, the covariance terms of the above formula vanish. Hence, we have

$$\sigma_{\mathbf{X}}^2(t_1, t_2) = \sum_{\tau = t_1}^{t_2} \sigma_{\mathbf{X}}^2(\tau), \qquad (6.1.20)$$

where (see (3.3.7)), if inflation is also deterministically defined,

$$\sigma_{\mathbf{X}}^2(\tau) = n(\tau)a_2(\tau) + \mu_{\mathbf{X}}(\tau)^2 \sigma_{\mathbf{q}}^2 = [r_2/n(\tau) + \sigma_{\mathbf{q}}^2]\mu_{\mathbf{X}}(\tau)^2. \quad (6.1.21)$$

The latter formulation makes use of the immunity aspect, which was stated in connection with (6.1.12). The effect of inflation enters into consideration only through the factor $\mu_{\mathbf{X}}(\tau)$ whereas the expression in the square brackets is not affected. The expected number of claims $n(\tau)$ is defined by (6.1.9a).

A more general treatment of (6.1.19) can be found in Rantala (1982, Section 1.5).

(q) **Skewness** For the calculation of the skewness the third central moment is needed and is obtained in a similar way to the variance (see (3.3.7))

$$\mu_3(\mathbf{X}(t_1, t_2)) = \sum_{\tau=1}^{t} [r_3/n(\tau)^2 + 3r_2\sigma_q^2/n(\tau) + \sigma_q^3\gamma_q]\mu_\mathbf{X}(\tau)^3. \quad (6.1.22)$$

Also in this formula the expression in the brackets is immune against inflation.

(r) **Distribution function F** In numerous applications the d.f.

$$F(X; 1, t) = \text{prob}\{\mathbf{X}(1, t) \leqslant X\}, \quad (6.1.23)$$

of the aggregate claims amount $\mathbf{X}(1, t)$ is needed. A rigorous formula for F could be obtained by $t - 1$ convolutions of the corresponding distribution functions related to each year of the period. However, in practice it can be obtained with satisfactory accuracy by means of the NP formula or by the gamma approximation. Of course the parameter n is to be replaced (see (6.1.9a)) by

$$n(1, t) = \sum_{\tau=1}^{t} n(\tau), \quad (6.1.24)$$

and the mean value and standard deviations are to be taken from (6.1.13) and (6.1.20). The skewness

$$\gamma = \gamma_\mathbf{X}(1, t) = \mu_3(\mathbf{X}(1, t))/\sigma_\mathbf{X}(1, t)^3, \quad (6.1.25)$$

is obtained by means of (6.1.22).
    Then

$$x = x(1, t) = (X - \mu_\mathbf{X}(1, t))/\sigma_\mathbf{X}(1, t), \quad (6.1.26)$$

is transformed into y according to (3.11.14), after which

$$F(X; 1, t) = \bar{F}(x; 1, t) \approx N_\gamma(x) = N(y). \quad (6.1.27)$$

(s) **Discussion on the assumptions** It was assumed that inflation affects the claim sizes proportionally, the shape of the d.f. S remaining unchanged. All other changes and variations were directed to affect only the expected number n of claims. This is one of the model assumptions which have not been investigated well so far. It could well be supposed that e.g. the increased claim frequency could cause a proportionately larger increase in small claims than in large. Then the claim size d.f. S would also be deformed in shape. This would possibly suggest the introduction of a claim size d.f. S, which is intercorrelated with the parameter n in one way or another. It would essentially complicate the considerations, even though it may not be quite intractable in simulation approaches, which will be dealt with later. Fortunately, as will be seen, the risk-theoretical behaviour of the solvency structures is fairly robust against changes in the shape of the function S in so far as the top risks are excluded by means of reinsurance. So it cannot be expected that the assumptions made would result in a serious bias in outcome.

6.2   Premium income $P(1, t)$

(a) **Premium inflation** As was stated already in item 6.1(j) it is necessary to distinguish the inflation effects affecting the claims and the premiums. If the inflation rate is changed in some particular year t it usually increases claims immediately, but it may be possible to amend premium rates after some time lag t_p. Some experience indicates (Revell, 1979; Pentikäinen, 1982, Section 3.3.14) that the time lag is often of the order of up to 2 years, until the changed rates can be effective. This is notoriously due to the fact that it takes some time until the situation is ascertained, decisions made, new rates calculated and changes implemented. Increased premiums can be applied for many insurance classes, not before the next period after their adoption. Market forces and regulatory authorities, if any, can still render further delays.

Premium inflation is now introduced into the model by means of rate $i_p(t)$ and the corresponding factor (for notation see item 1.5(f))

$$r_p(t) = 1 + i_p(t). \tag{6.2.1}$$

As a standard assumption, the relation between the claims inflation and the premium inflation can be expected to be

$$r_p(t) = r_x(t - t_p). \tag{6.2.2}$$

This means that the long-run level of both inflation rates is the same; they differ only by the time lag t_p, which is one of the model parameters. The equalization of the levels is not a limitation of the model, because possible deviations will be dealt with by means of the safety loading to be defined in item (c) below.

For brevity, consideration will be limited to the case where both the premium inflation and the claim inflation (item 6.1(j)) are deterministic.

The discussion in item 6.1(1) about the importance of considering the local conditions is equally relevant to time lag. If e.g. the rates are successfully linked with an index, or in any other way are based on some quantity such as salary, which automatically follows inflation, the time lag may be small and possibly relevant only if a major inflation shock occurs.

Further consideration of problems caused by inflation can be found in discussion papers of the Casualty Actuarial Society (1980).

(b) Risk premium Now a formula for the pure risk premium for year t can be given by making use of (4.1.1) and (6.1.14)

$$P(t) = nm \prod_{\tau=1}^{t} [r_g(\tau)r_p(\tau)], \tag{6.2.3}$$

The effects of the cycle variable z and of the structure variable $\mathbf{q}$ were not taken into account, because the mean value of the former was assumed to be zero for a long period (item 6.1(i)), and the mean value of the latter was equal to 1 (item 2.7(c)). In other words, it is appropriate to define the risk premium to correspond to *long-run* expected average claim expenditure so that the cycles and the structure variable can be omitted. So far as the volume increment controlled by r_g is due to the growth of the portfolio, the premium income provided by (6.2.3) is automatic. Otherwise, of course, the continuing updating of the rates is supposed.

In the case of steady inflation (see (6.1.16) and (6.1.18)) this formula can be simplified to

$$P(t) = nm(r_g r_p)^t = nmr_{gp}^t, \tag{6.2.4}$$

where (see item 1.5(f) and equation (6.2.2)) $r_{gp} = r_g r_p = r_{gx}$.

Note that in general $P(t) \neq EX(t)$ if cycles are present. However, when t grows,

$$P(1, t)/\mu_X(1, t) \to 1,$$

where $P(1, t) = P(1) + \cdots + P(t)$.

(c) Safety loading Also the safety loading λ, being defined as weighted average for the portfolio (see item 4.1(c)), should be time dependent. Hence the safety loaded premium (still without loading for expenses) is

$$P_\lambda(t) = (1 + \lambda(t))P(t), \tag{6.2.5}$$

and the accumulated premium income for period $[t_1, t_2]$ is

$$P_\lambda(t_1, t_2) = \sum_{\tau = t_1}^{t_2} P_\lambda(\tau). \tag{6.2.6}$$

The safety loading λ is one of the crucial control parameters of the model. It may have been originally aimed, as its name suggests, at maintaining the insurer's solvency and, if not considered separately, also to generate necessary underwriting profit. The definition provided above is, in fact, broader: λ indicates the deviation of the safety loaded risk premium from the level which corresponds to the long-term mean value of the claims expenditure **X**. Consequently λ is affected by quite numerous factors, as will be discussed in the following item and later. It is a general indicator of the adequacy of the premium rates.

(d) Parameter uncertainty It is a matter of fact that many of the central data of distributions needed for premium rating, reserve calculations and risk theory considerations are never known exactly; there are only estimates subject to statistical inaccuracy, and there are continual changes in portfolio and risk structures. This uncertainty eventually affects the safety loading, which is not only stipulated by the management to be at some target level, say λ_0, but is affected also by various errors in rating, by unexpected claims development, by deviations of the actual expenses from those anticipated by expense loadings, and also by the net result of investments as will be discussed later. This uncertainty is aggravated because the estimation of the trading result, and hence the actual safety margin of rates, cannot be made until after some time delay, which for the so-called long-tail insurance classes may be quite considerable.

A very instructive approach is to make the safety loading a control parameter which provides an instrument to correct biases arising from the various errors and inaccuracies in rating and in other control measures, as well as providing, as far as possible, the target safety income $\lambda_0 P$. This mechanism is best demonstrated by a simplified example in item (e), which makes use of the technique of time series theory. It makes it possible for example to simulate the behaviour of management when adverse results of underwriting are faced.

The parameter uncertainty is in no sense a feature only of risk theory. It concerns nearly all mathematical models which are intended to describe actual phenomena. Its harmful effects can be controlled by assigning conservative values to the uncertain parameters, or by making sensitivity analyses applying alternative parameter selections – optimistic, pessimistic and likely.

(e) Profitability control by means of λ will be exemplified in this item. Even though oversimplified, the example will throw light on some central features of the decision process of insurers. A more comprehensive development of control systems will be pursued in Section 7.7. Suppose that an insurer wishes to have for the safety loading λ a target level λ_0. Estimates for λ are made annually on basis of the trading results, and the value applied in the rates of the next following year is corrected for the observed deviations from target level in the two (or more) most recent years as follows

$$\bar{\lambda}(t) = \lambda_0 + a_1(\lambda(t-1) - \lambda_0) + a_2(\lambda(t-2) - \lambda_0) \quad (6.2.7a)$$

where $\bar{\lambda}(t)$ is the value of the safety loading to be applied in the calculation of rates for year t and the λs are estimated values based on the actual outcomes of the process. The coefficients a_1 and a_2 are to be chosen to give suitable control effect for the formula. For example $a_1 = a_2 = -0.5$ would mean an attempt to correct the observed deviations in two years. The safety loading 'forecast' $\bar{\lambda}$ is affected by the fluctuation of the claim expenditure $\mathbf{X}$, errors in the premiums and all the types of parameter uncertainties mentioned above, which result in inaccuracies of the estimates of λ.

The effects of the control rule provided by (6.2.7a) can be described by an AR-type process (see item 6.1(e)).

$$\lambda(t) = \lambda_0 + a_i[\lambda(t-1) - \lambda_0] + a_2[\lambda(t-2) - \lambda_0] + \varepsilon(t), \quad (6.2.7b)$$

where the ε term introduces the stochastic variation to the system. It is due, among other things, to the uncertainties involved in the estimation of $\lambda(t-1)$ and $\lambda(t-2)$ and furthermore to inflation, changes in risk exposure etc.

The properties of the solution of (6.2.7) can be suitably investigated by the Monte Carlo technique, which is presented in Section 6.8. An example is given in Fig. 6.2.1 and another in exercise 6.8.2. Analyses on AR processes can be found in Cox and Miller, 1965, p. 282, Chatfield, 1975, p. 49 and Rantala, 1982, Section 2.2.1 (see also exercises 6.2.1 and 6.8.2).

The process is useful for risk theory applications if it is stationary, which means, broadly speaking, that there is no systematic change (no trend) in the mean and no systematic change in the variance, when the strictly periodic variations have been removed (see Chatfield 1978, paragraph 2.2 and for a strict definition see paragraph 3.2). The necessary and sufficient conditions for the stationarity of the above AR process are (Chatfield, 1978, paragraph 3.4.4)

$$a_1 + a_2 < 1$$
$$a_1 - a_2 > -1$$
$$a_2 > -1.$$

The above series can be extended in a straightforward way to include more than two terms.

The process is oscillating if $a_1^2 + 4a_2 < 0$ having the wavelength

$$T = 2\pi/\varphi,$$

where $\varphi = \arctan \sqrt{(-a_1^2 - 4a_2)}/a_1$ with $0 < \varphi < \pi$ (see exercise 6.2.1).

The safety loading control will be discussed later on the basis of more flexible and realistic formulae (Section 7.7). The general features described prove to be generally valid. The parameter uncertainty and the necessary subsequent correction mechanism render oscillation in the safety loading, and through that in trading results and risk reserve.

Note that (6.2.7a) is, in essence, a modification of the experience rating (see Section 4.10).

(f) Written premiums In most risk theory considerations attention is focused on the claims and the risk process related to them. Then it is natural to use risk premium income P or safety loaded one P_λ as one of the basic variables. Often, however, it is necessary to find a link with the quantities which are employed in accounting practice and can be found in income statements and balance sheets. Therefore, in what follows, depending on the context and application

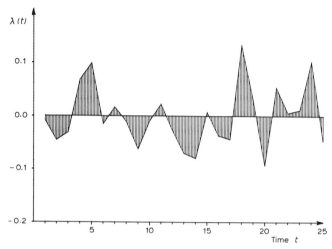

Figure 6.2.1   *A simulated solution of the difference equation (6.2.7b) for $a_1 = -0.5, a_2 = -0.5, \lambda_0 = 0$ and ε a normally distributed variable having mean 0 and standard deviation $\sigma = 0.05$. The variation range is approximately ± 0.1 and the wavelength 3.2 years.*

under consideration, risk premiums P and loaded premiums will be used in a parallel manner. The latter will be denoted by B and defined mostly as the earned premium income on the insurer's net retention. For this purpose, *loading coefficient for expenses c* is introduced. It combines the premiums as follows

$$P_\lambda = (1 - c)B. \tag{6.2.8}$$

Note that the premium incomes P_λ and B in the subsequent considerations may be either stochastic, as follows from control rules like (6.2.7), or deterministic. However, the notations P_λ and B will mostly be used instead of the stochastic symbols $\mathbf{P}_\lambda$ and $\mathbf{B}$ (see item 1.5(a)).

The safety loading is sometimes calculated on the basis of the pure risk premium income P and sometimes – which in some connections is more convenient – on the basis of the written premiums B. These loading rates will be distinguished by subscripts p and b. Hence

$$\lambda_p P = \lambda_b B, \tag{6.2.9}$$

or

$$\lambda_b = \frac{P}{B} \lambda_p, \qquad (6.2.10)$$

Then the risk premium can be expressed in terms of B as follows

$$P = (1 - c - \lambda_b)B, \qquad (6.2.11)$$

and the two safety loadings are linked to each other by the equation

$$\lambda_p = \lambda_b/(1 - c - \lambda_b). \qquad (6.2.12)$$

Note that λ_p is the same as was denoted in (6.2.5) and in previous connections by λ. The concept and the notation will be developed still further in item 6.5(g), taking into account also the effect of yield of investments.

(g) Variations in expense loading c In practice also the expense ratio c changes from year to year, which may suggest its definition as a time-dependent variable. From experience the range of variations is, however, slight. It is convenient to keep c constant and let its actual variation be reflected in the safety loading, which is a conjunction of various variations. Of course, c is also a weighted average of c values of the portfolio sections and must be as frequently updated as all other data.

(h) A simplified approach As presented, both the aggregate claims **X** and, if a control rule as (4.2.7) is assumed, the premium income **B** are stochastic and also subject to long-range 'cycles'. In fact, what is most relevant is the joint effect on the loss ratio $\mathbf{f} = \mathbf{X}/\mathbf{B}$. Unfortunately, handling of this kind of stochastic quotient is often intricate, even though it may not be an insuperable problem in simulations. Therefore, in some connections it may be useful to simplify the model by defining P and B as deterministic and letting **X** fluctuate so that the loss ratio $\mathbf{f}$ has about the same variation as if both **B** and **X** were stochastic. The effect can be expected to be about the same in both approaches. This is easily seen by denoting $\mathbf{B} = \bar{B} + \Delta\mathbf{B}$, $\mathbf{P} = \bar{P} + \Delta\mathbf{P}$ and $\mathbf{X} = \bar{X} + \Delta\mathbf{X}$ where $\bar{B}, \bar{P}$ and $\bar{X}$ are the mean values, which can be programmed to be deterministic, and $\Delta\mathbf{B}$, $\Delta\mathbf{P}$ and $\Delta\mathbf{X}$ are the stochastically fluctuating parts of these quantities. **B** and **P** and consequently $\Delta\mathbf{B}$ and $\Delta\mathbf{P}$ (see item (f) above) can be assumed to deviate only by a constant (or at least approximately constant) proportionality factor. Hence $\Delta \mathbf{B}/\bar{B} \approx \Delta \mathbf{P}/\bar{P}$. Then

$$
\frac{\mathbf{f}}{1 - \varepsilon - \lambda_b} = \frac{\bar{X} + \Delta \mathbf{X}}{\bar{P} + \Delta \mathbf{P}} = \frac{\bar{X}}{\bar{P}} \left(\frac{1 + \Delta \mathbf{X}/\bar{X}}{1 + \Delta \mathbf{P}/\bar{P}} \right) \approx \frac{\bar{X}}{\bar{P}} \left(1 + \frac{\Delta \mathbf{X}}{\bar{X}} - \frac{\Delta \mathbf{P}}{\bar{P}} \right)
$$

$$
\approx \frac{\bar{X}}{\bar{P}} \left(1 + \frac{\Delta \mathbf{X} - \Delta \mathbf{P}}{\bar{X}} \right) = \frac{\bar{X} + (\Delta \mathbf{X} - \Delta \mathbf{P})}{\bar{P}} \tag{6.2.13}
$$

providing that the relative stochastic deviations are not large and given that $\bar{X} \approx \bar{P}$. Hence, the fluctuation of $\mathbf{f}$ is about the same, whether both $\Delta \mathbf{X}$ and $\Delta \mathbf{P}$ fluctuate or whether their sum is replaced by a modified $\Delta \mathbf{X}'$ having a range of fluctuation about the same as the original sum of these variables; that is, if P is taken as deterministic and the standard deviation and skewness of the claim fluctuation are adjusted to correspond to the fluctuation of the loss ratio. This approach would be expected to be most useful in cases where the long-term variations, i.e. trends and 'cycles', are programmed to be deterministic, and consequently the values of $\Delta \mathbf{X}$ (and $\Delta \mathbf{P}$) for consecutive years are mutually independent.

Exercise 6.2.1 Solve the difference equation (6.2.7b) in the deterministic case $\varepsilon(t) \equiv 0$. When is the solution an oscillating function of t? What is the wavelength? (Hint: the solution is of the form $f(t) \equiv \lambda(t) - \lambda_0 = Ab^t$, A and b being constants; furthermore, if $f_1(t)$ and $f_2(t)$ are solutions, $C_1 f_1(t) + C_2 f_2(t)$ is as well.) Consider the special case $a_1 = a_2 = -0.5$ with initial conditions $f(-1) = 0.1$ and $f(0) = 0.05$.

The time series (6.2.7b) is further illustrated by exercise 6.8.2. Readers who are familiar with the Monte Carlo technique should study it in this connection.

6.3 Yield of investments

(a) Investment income The considerations contained in the foregoing chapters and sections were limited to premium income and claims expenditures, the difference in which constitutes the 'underwriting result' according to common terminology. However, insurers nearly always have assets in excess of what is needed for current cash transactions. These excess funds, which may be quite substantial, are invested in order to earn interest. In fact, the ordinary underwriting result, calculated without regard to the yield of investments, may be inadequate to ensure the continuation of the business; it can occasionally be even negative. Hence investment income is so substantial a component of the total business structure that it is necessary to take it into account when the insurer's business as a whole is considered, regardless of whether it should be taken into account when e.g. the premium rates are determined and the acceptability of the underwriting results are evaluated. It will now be introduced into the model. The investment income is, in addition to premiums and claims, a third source of time-dependent variation.

The interest income will be divided into two parts, one allocated to the technical reserves and the other to the risk reserve, as will be considered in detail later. The key variable will be the *interest rate*. It refers to the total *actual* rate at which the insurer earns from his investments in year t. It will be denoted by $i_i(t)$ or briefly i_i (subscript i for interest; for notation see item 1.5(f)).

The interest rate depends, of course, on the accounting practice applied for the calculation of the return gained on investments. When the actual profitability is analysed, then it is a natural approach to regard both the cash flow and changes in market values. The latter is determined by asset valuation principles, which may vary from country to country, may be different for different types of investments, and may depend on, among other things, the capital market properties of the country. The book values of assets may follow the market values or they may be different. In the latter case the difference (if positive) between the market values and the book values constitutes 'a hidden reserve'. Another method could be described as the 'actuarial' approach where the net gain from the insurance operation is assumed to be accumulated in a fund which earns some assumed interest.

It is beyond the scope of this book to discuss valuation principles in any detail. In what follows it is assumed that the interest rate $i_i(t)$ is defined in one way or another. It will be up to the user of the model to plan and decide, for example, how the asset valuations are made, and whether the hidden reserves are to be counted as a component of the solvency margin and the changes in it as 'interest income'. The model should be operable for any valuation method. The important point to be watched is the consistency between the rates derived from the accounting records and those used for model building.

Sometimes 'interest rate' refers to the *actuarial* interest rate, which is used for premium and reserve calculations. These two rates need not be equal; normally the actuarial rate is less than the actual one. The actuarial rate is intended to assign some part of the investment income to support the underwriting business. For example, for the increment of technical reserves, particularly in life insurance, the calculation principles preassume certain interest income attributable for the purpose. Then only the marginal interest income is freely available for an increase in the solvency margin, for dividends or other purposes. The technique will be developed in item 6.5(h) and later, so that it is not necessary to separately distinguish the actuarial rate. Therefore, in the subsequent considerations only the actual rates will be employed.

(b) General aspects An insurer has normally several approaches in planning an investment program, as investment objects may be e.g. bonds, equities, loans, real estate, etc. On the one hand the return should be maximized, and on the other hand the risk of losses should be minimized, or at least kept within some reasonable limits. A further aspect is to find, as far as is possible, protection against inflation. International business is usually subject to currency risks. The legislation in some countries may impose restrictions on the choice of investment objects or it can regulate the return rates.

There is a well developed 'portfolio theory' dealing with the aspects involved in investment policies, e.g. contradictory aspects of high return and risk reduction. For examples, textbooks of Christy and Clendenin (1978), Levine (1975) and Lorie and Hamilton (1973) may be referred to. The application of the theory to insurance environment has been discussed by Ferrari (1968) and subsequently by others such as Butsic (1979). Pioneering work to build a comprehensive model whereby the investment transactions are incorporated into the general framework of the economy of an insurer, in addition to the traditional treatment of underwriting and other aspects is attributed to McGuinness (1954).

A further major complication is the fact that the financial effects of the yield of investments do not depend on the nominal interest rate only but rather on its relation to the rate of inflation, i.e. the relevant factor is the *real* rate of return (which, during high inflation, may even be occasionally negative). This topic will be briefly considered in item (e) and in more detail in item 6.6(a).

Clearly 'the asset risks', i.e. the risks involved with investments, are much more diversified in different countries than are the 'liability risks' generated by the claims expenditure and rating. Therefore it seems to be quite difficult to find any proven detailed technique for their consideration which could be valid to a satisfactory degree in the very varying circumstances existing in different countries. Only some rather general aspects can be discussed in this section, and then the investment income will be incorporated into the general model as a special entry in Chapter 10, where business planning is considered.

While a more sophisticated technique for the handling of asset risks in connection with risk theoretical considerations is at present deemed to be beyond the scope of this book, pending future development of the theory, this need not occasion any serious gap in the model. As in the case of many other uncertainties, it is always possible to make deterministic or semi-deterministic assumptions about the anticipated future development of the return rates and asset risks. In fact this will be provided in Chapter 10. If, in turn, reasonably optimistic, pessimistic and likely hypotheses are used as input data, useful information about the sensitivity of the model to asset risks can be obtained. Surely such an approach, even though seemingly crude, is better than complete ignorance of the asset risks.

(c) Decomposition of the investment portfolio For advanced models it may be first necessary to evaluate investment yield separately for different kinds of investments like mortages, equities, and real estate. The distribution between the investment categories and asset structure in general, including also cash, deposits, fixed property, etc., is one of the model bases and is subject to the investment strategies of the insurer, which will be discussed later in Chapter 10 in connection with business planning. In the following sections and chapters it will be mainly assumed that the interest rate $i_i(t)$ is a *weighted average* of all sorts of investments of the insurer concerned and the decomposition problem is not dealt with.

(d) Bases for investment income One of the major problems in model building is to find proper assumptions concerning the future interest rate. For the purpose it is appropriate first to analyse experience about the different investment components mentioned, and then to construct the average expected flow or, if not deter-

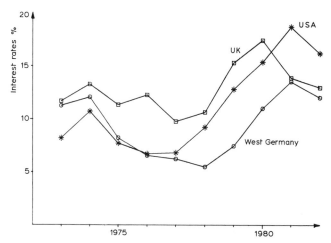

Figure 6.3.1 *Commercial bank lending rates to prime borrowers in West Germany, in the UK and in the USA. Annual averages for years 1973–81 and for half of 1982.*

ministic, distribution of the rate. Examples of the actual flow of rates are given for illustration in Figs 6.3.1 and 6.3.2.

Figure 6.3.1 exhibits lending rates in three countries. It is clearly seen that there are periods of low and high rates having a length of several years. The short-term random variations have small amplitude compared with these long waves, which are the predominant source of change. Furthermore, the flow of rates is markedly parallel in all three countries. The interest rates in major countries are necessarily highly correlated, because the central banks must keep them reasonably close in order to prevent violent outflows from low-interest countries to high-interest countries and the consequent effects on the relative values of currencies.

The difficulty of forecasting or in finding any useful distribution is the fact that the general level of interest yields in investment markets is simultaneously subject both to market forces and also to the policy of governments and central banks, which in most countries determine or strongly affect the level of interest rates. In fact, the major changes are due to political decisions, which may be related also to international trends and stresses.

A drastic increase of an obviously unforeseeable character in

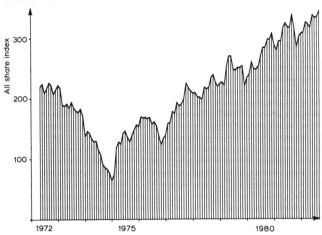

Figure 6.3.2   *Actuaries' all share index, UK 1972–82.*

the interest rate is seen in Fig. 6.3.1, in particular in the flow of the rate in the USA in the years 1979–81.

Still more volatile is the current market value of the shares. This is illustrated in Fig. 6.3.2, where the actuaries' all share index in the UK for years 1972–82 is depicted. A temporary plunge down more than 50 per cent can be seen; however, the yields on shares vary much less than the share prices. A well-planned investment policy may very much preclude the possibility of capital losses. Some shares may decline in value, but if only sound securities are bought, they will refind the original price level if given enough time.

It is highly doubtful whether modelled forecasting of interest rates is feasible for more than perhaps a few years ahead. For analysis of the general behaviour of an insurer's economy and for some particular applications, simulation of the gain rates may be useful by employing cycle generating time series (Godolphin and the Maturity Guarantees working party, 1980). The problem and application under consideration will determine which kind of prognoses and techniques for the calculation of the yield on investments can be accepted. If the solvency of an insurer is evaluated, then a cautious assumption as to rate and possibly some kind of hypothetical depreciation may be advisable. In rate-making and corporate planning alternative prognoses can be applied in order to get a feel for the sensitivity of the model outcomes to the various assumptions.

In what follows the choice of the prognoses is left open and it is assumed that the rate $i_i(t)$ is given in one way or another either as a deterministic flow or as a stochastic one or preferably as a mix of both types.

(e) Real rate of interest One should appreciate that, factually, the interest rate i_i is a less relevant factor for the insurer's financial position and solvency than is its relationship to the inflation rate and growth rate, i.e. a modified rate which can be called a 'real rate'. It will be introduced in item 6.5(g).

Hence, it is not rewarding to make great efforts to find prognoses for the nominal yield of investments, if the often equally important rate of inflation cannot be treated in a balanced way.

(f) Investment losses Besides the yield, the depreciation (or possibly appreciation) of the values of investments, especially securities, needs to be considered. If the market value slides below the book value, the depreciation of the latter must immediately be reflected as negative income. The possibility of this event should be taken into account in one way or another, at least when the factors affecting the solvency of insurer are evaluated.

A current practice in many countries is not to book the assets at market values. In particular, due to inflation, considerable *underestimations in assets* may arise, which are a cushion against unexpected losses in investments and can well be taken into account in solvency evaluations and also when the model assumptions are deliberated.

More details of the non-stochastic risks including the asset risks are discussed in Pentikäinen 1982, Section 2.9.

6.4 Portfolio divided in sections

(a) Decomposition It is often necessary to divide the portfolio in sections, as already presented in Section 3.7 in the one year case as well as in considerations extended over a horizon of several years. Then by using the following formulae the data related to the total business can be calculated from the sectional data. In order to avoid covariance terms it will be assumed that the aggregate claims $\mathbf{X}_j$ of each section are mutually independent (mixed) compound Poisson variables as defined in Section 6.1.

The total amount of claims $\mathbf{X}(t_1, t_2)$ inherited from the years $t_1, t_1 + 1, \ldots, t_2$ is a double sum of the sectional amounts of the aggregate claims of each period

$$\mathbf{X}(t_1, t_2) = \sum_{\tau = t_1}^{t_2} \sum_j \mathbf{X}_j(\tau). \tag{6.4.1}$$

(b) The mean value is the straightforward sum of the corresponding sectional mean values

$$\mu_{\mathbf{X}}(t_1, t_2) = \sum_{j, \tau} \mu_{\mathbf{X}_j}(\tau) = \sum_{\tau} \sum_j n_j(\tau) m_j(\tau)$$

$$= \sum_{\tau = t_1}^{t_2} n(\tau) m(\tau), \tag{6.4.2}$$

where, making use of the decomposition formulae of Section (3.7) and equations (6.1.9a) and (6.1.14)

$$n(\tau) = \sum_j n_j(\tau) = \sum_j n_j(1 + z_j(\tau)) \prod_{u=1}^{\tau} r_{gj}(u),$$

and

$$m(\tau) = \sum_j \frac{n_j(\tau)}{n(\tau)} m_j(\tau)$$

$$= \sum_j v_j(\tau) m_j(\tau) = \sum_j v_j(\tau) m_j \prod_{u=1}^{\tau} r_{xj}(u).$$

The coefficients v_j were defined by (3.7.4); they can now be time dependent. It is often rational first to compute the weighted sectional values for each year τ and then to sum with respect to the time τ as on the second line of (6.4.2).

(c) The variance is derived similarly as a double sum (see (3.7.9))

$$\sigma_{\mathbf{X}}^2(t_1, t_2) = \sum_{\tau, j} \sigma_{\mathbf{X}_j}^2(\tau) = \sum_{\tau = t_1}^{t_2} \sum_j [n_j(\tau) a_{2j}(\tau) + \mu_{\mathbf{X}_j}(\tau)^2 \sigma_{qj}^2]. \tag{6.4.3}$$

Here again it is preferable first to determine the sectional weighted quantities for each year τ and then to sum according to τ. It is assumed that the structure function H does not change from year to year. Hence σ_q and γ_q are independent of time.

(d) Skewness Finally the third moment, needed for the calculation of the skewness, is obtained from

$$\mu_3(\mathbf{X}(t_1, t_2)) = \sum_{\tau, j} \mu_3(\mathbf{X}_j(\tau)). \tag{6.4.4a}$$

After some manipulation the formula can be expressed in the form

$$\mu_3(\mathbf{X}(t_1, t_2)) = \sum_{\tau = t_1}^{t_2} \mu_{\mathbf{X}}(\tau)^3 [A_1(\tau)/n(\tau)^2 + A_2(\tau)/n(\tau) + A_3(\tau)] \tag{6.4.4b}$$

where (see (3.7.12) and (6.1.22))

$$A_1(\tau) = \frac{a_3}{a_1^3}$$

$$A_2(\tau) = 3 \sum_j \frac{a_{2j}}{a_{1j}^2} v_j(\tau) \pi_j(\tau)^2 \sigma_{\mathbf{q}j}^2 \tag{6.4.5}$$

$$A_3(\tau) = \sum_j \pi_j(\tau)^3 \gamma_{\mathbf{q}j} \sigma_{\mathbf{q}j}^3.$$

(e) Simplifications The formulae can be simplified if some or rather all of the variations rates are *the same for all sections*. For example, in inflation affects all sections to the same degree so that $r_{xj}(t) = r_x(t)$ for all j, then the expressions in brackets in (6.4.3) and in (6.4.4b) are not affected by inflation, because the coefficients π_j are then immune against inflation (see (6.1.12)). They may, however, depend on time as do the factors A in (6.4.5). If the distribution parameters v_j and π_j are independent of time, and the cycle variable z is the same for all sections, the quantities A_i are independent of time. The writing out of the various alternatives is left to the reader (see exercise 6.4.1).

(f) The premium income of the whole portfolio is always a straight-forward sum of the section quantities

$$B(t_1, t_2) = \sum_j B_j(t_1, t_2), \tag{6.4.6}$$

and similarly

$$P(t_1, t_2) = \sum_j P_j(t_1, t_2). \tag{6.4.7}$$

(g) Sectional or global processing When the comprehensive simulations and straightforward calculations are performed, there are two alternative approaches with regard to the section combination:

(i) The model parameters are first derived and calculated on the basis of the section parameters as weighted averages as given above, and then the computation (either simulation or direct analytical handling of the problem) is performed for the whole portfolio.

(ii) All the simulations and calculations are done separately for each section, and finally the section outcomes are summed up.

The first approach is, of course, very much more economical than the second as far as computation time and other resource requirements are concerned. It means, however, that the cycles, real growth and even inflation must be the same for all sections as mentioned in item (e). If this cannot be assumed, approach (ii) may be more rational, or a special technique is needed to calculate the weighted average parameters.

(h) Robustness concerning the claim size d.f.   Another feature to be taken into account when choosing between approaches (i) and (ii) in item (g) is the effect of the claim size d.f. S. Experience seems to indicate that the behaviour of the claims process retained after cutting the risk tops by reinsurance is fairly robust concerning the choice of this distribution, as long as the net retention M is not too high (Pentikäinen, 1982, Section 4.2.2). This is a feature anticipated already in Section 4.3. Hence for deduction of the aggregate distribution it may be possible to use a fairly coarse division of the portfolio into sections, uniting insurance classes which by experience have fairly similar risk structures.

Exercise 6.4.1 Write (6.4.3) in a simplified form providing that the parameters v_j and π_j are independent of time and that the rates of growth, cycles and inflation are constant and the same for all sections.

6.5   Trading result

(a) Basic equation   The consideration can now be extended from the one-year basic equation presented in Section 4.1 to a finite time environment. For this purpose the increment $\Delta U(t) = U(t) - U(t-1)$ of the risk reserve U for any year t will be defined as the difference of incomes and expenditures as follows

$$\Delta U = B + I - X - C - D, \tag{6.5.1}$$

where B, is the earned premium income included safety loadings and loading for expenses (see item 6.2(f)), I is the net income from investments (see Section 6.3), X are claims paid and outstanding, C are expenses, and D are dividends, bonuses, etc. For brevity, the argument t is omitted.

All amounts are to be calculated on the insurer's net retention, that is, deducting the shares of reinsurers.

The basic equation (6.5.1) constitutes an *algorithm*, by means of which the risk reserve U is obtained for year t when its value for the year $t - 1$ is known. The equation provides that all the variables involved are defined and numerical values (or analytic expressions) for them can be assigned. Many of the definitions are given already in preceding sections; the rest will be pursued in the following.

(b) Broad and narrow approaches The basic equation (6.5.1) can be treated by quite general conditions, taking into account numerous inside and outside impacts and presses and business strategies. As a rule the model gets so complicated that often only simulation can cope with it. This general study will be postponed to Chapter 7. It is useful before that to deal with the model by making some simplifying assumptions. In this way it is possible to throw light on many special problems which are of interest and which can serve as building blocks for more comprehensive approaches.

(c) The yield of interest will first be partitioned into two components

$$I = i_i W_{-1} + i_i U_{-1}, \tag{6.5.2}$$

where W is the technical reserve, i_i is the rate of interest (see item 6.3(a)) and the subscript -1 indicates time shift to the previous year. By using this formula and replacing ΔU by $U - U_{-1}$, the basic formula (6.5.1) assumes the form

$$U = (1 + i_i)U_{-1} + B + i_i W_{-1} - X - C - D. \tag{6.5.3}$$

(d) Interest period There are different practices for calculation of interest and growths. One assumes that transactions like reception of premiums, payment of claims, etc. are concentrated at the end of the counting period (year); another concentrates them at the midpoint. The latter is almost the same as supposing the money flows to be continuous. The midpoint approach seems to be more natural and better fitted to real world circumstances. Its drawback is, however, that many of the variables should be provided with factors $\sqrt{(1 + i_i)}$ for the half-year interest yield, which complicates the formulae and obscures readability. Therefore these square root factors will be omitted. This renders, of course, a slight bias in interest and growth amounts. Bias is fortunately offset well if the rate factors r_g, r_i, etc. are derived from the actual data by applying the very same calculation method. Then the differences in the final outcomes are negligible irrespective which of the above methods is applied, providing of course that the same method is always applied subsequently.

(e) Dividends **D** can be included in the expenses **C** in the consideration in this chapter. This simplification can be justified by the fact that in practice it is both usual and advisable to create a business strategy which consolidates dividends at some fixed level rather than allows them to vary from year to year. Furthermore, the expenses are assumed to be given deterministically; hence the notation **C** is replaced by C.

(f) Ratio form of the basic equation In order to avoid inconveniences caused by inflation and real volume growth in long-run considerations, it is often useful to use, instead of absolute monetary quantities, their ratios to the premiums B. These ratios have dimension zero with respect to the monetary unit, and are thus not directly affected by inflation. We therefore move on to the relative variables

$$\mathbf{u} = \mathbf{U}/B; \quad \mathbf{f} = \mathbf{X}/B; \qquad c = C/B; \quad \mathbf{w} = \mathbf{W}/B, \qquad (6.5.4)$$

dividing equation (6.5.3) by B

$$\mathbf{U}/B = (1 + i_i)\mathbf{U}_{-1}/B + 1 + i_i\mathbf{W}_{-1}/B - \mathbf{X}/B - C/B,$$

or

$$\mathbf{u} = (1 + i_i)\frac{B_{-1}}{B}\mathbf{u}_{-1} + 1 + i_i\mathbf{w}_{-1}\frac{B_{-1}}{B} - \mathbf{f} - c. \qquad (6.5.5)$$

The ratio **u** will be called the *solvency ratio*. Even though B may be stochastic in some applications by virtue of the safety loading λ (see item (6.2(e))), the 'deterministic' symbol B will be mostly used.

(g) Dynamic calculus of the yield of interest Expression (6.5.5) gives rise to the following definitions and notation. It is convenient to introduce a new rate and a new factor

$$i_{igp} = i_i B_{-1}/B \quad \text{and} \quad r_{igp} = r_i B_{-1}/B, \tag{6.5.6}$$

to replace the classical interest rate i_i and the interest factor $r_i = 1 + i_i$. It combines the interest rate with the growth of the nominal values of business volume, which is measured by the premium volume B. The growth ratio B/B_{-1}, which will be frequently needed later, is occasioned by (premium) inflation (with rate i_p) and by real growth (with rate i_g) (see items 6.2(b) and 6.2(f)).

$$B/B_{-1} = (1 + i_g)(1 + i_p) \equiv r_{gp} \equiv 1 + i_{gp}. \tag{6.5.7}$$

Hence

$$i_{igp} = i_i/r_{gp}, \tag{6.5.8a}$$

and

$$r_{igp} = r_i/r_{gp}. \tag{6.5.8b}$$

All the factors and ratios may be time dependent, although the argument t is not written out for brevity reasons. The subscripts are chosen to indicate the factors interest, growth and premium inflation involved (see notation, item 1.5(f)). This rate and factor can be interpreted as generalizations of the classical i_i (interest rate) and r_i (accumulation factor $= 1 + i_i$), operated in the 'static' interest calculus based on constant values of the money. The rate i_{igp} and the factor r_{igp} are their counterparts in 'dynamic calculus' where both the value of money and the real volume of business are changing. Note that the rule $r_i = 1 + i_i$ cannot be extended to r_{igp}, i.e. generally $r_{igp} \neq 1 + i_{igp}$.

Then (6.5.5) can be rewritten

$$\mathbf{u} = r_{igp}\mathbf{u}_{-1} + 1 - c + i_{igp}w_{-1} - \mathbf{f}. \tag{6.5.9}$$

Furthermore, $(1 - c - \lambda_b)B$ is what is left of the premiums when the loading for expenses (and dividends) and safety loading λ_b are deducted, i.e. the net premiums P (see (6.2.11))

$$(1 - c - \lambda_b)B = P.$$

On the other hand, by definition $P = E(\mathbf{X})$, i.e. the long-term expected value of the claims. Denoting the mean claims ratio

$$\bar{f} = E(\mathbf{X})/B, \tag{6.5.10a}$$

it follows that

$$1 - c = \bar{f} + \lambda_b, \tag{6.5.10b}$$

and

$$\mathbf{u} = r_{igp}\mathbf{u}_{-1} + \lambda_b + i_{igp}\mathbf{w}_{-1} + \bar{f} - \mathbf{f}. \tag{6.5.11}$$

(h) Aggregate safety loading A useful observation made in practice (Pentikäinen, 1982, pp. 3. 1–7) is that the ratio $\mathbf{w} = \mathbf{W}/\mathbf{B}$ is fairly constant from year to year (the average value $w = 1.71$ was found for the Finnish non-life companies). This makes it possible to simplify the above equations by replacing the variable $\mathbf{w}_{-1}$ by a constant parameter w. (However, $\mathbf{w}$ may be different for different classes of insurance and for different insurers). This finding suggests that the expression

$$\lambda = \lambda_b + i_{igp}w, \tag{6.5.12}$$

which after the replacement $\mathbf{w}_{-1} = w$ appears in (6.5.11) should be defined as an 'aggregate' safety loading. It will be introduced to this equation in order to put it formally in a more compact shape, allowing easier use and providing a better general view of the most essential relationships. This approach will be followed in Chapters 6 and 7 but relaxed in Chapters 8 and 10. The second part of the investment income $\mathbf{I}$, related to the solvency margin $\mathbf{U}$ according to (6.5.2), remains expressively in the basic equation.

The aggregate safety loading (6.5.12) will be denoted by λ_{tot} if it needs to be distinguished from λ_p and λ_b. In the following, λ will mostly be used for it, and it is up to the user of the model whether it is interpreted as λ_{tot} or λ_b.

In practice λ_b may often be quite low, even occasionally negative, as recent experience has proved. The introduction of the yield of interest alone makes the total safety margin sufficiently large.

One must, however, appreciate that the yield of interest is not necessarily freely disposable; this has already been stated in item 6.3(a) in reference to the actuarial rate of interest. The technical bases often provide that the premium income is supported by the yield of interest and the underwriting reserves are credited by some yield calculated according to a technical rate of interest. This is the practice in particular in life assurance. From this point of view it would be perhaps a more natural approach to allocate a corresponding part of the yield of interest directly to enforcing the reserves; or, which is an equivalent approach, to affiliate it to the premium income B, i.e. to define B as a sum of 'ordinary' premiums and the yield of interest, which is technically assigned to finance the underwriting business in the rating schedules. For the sake of simplicity, however, this is not done here.

(i) Basic equation The basic equation can now be expressed as follows

$$\mathbf{u} = r_{\text{igp}} \mathbf{u}_{-1} + \lambda + \bar{f} - \mathbf{f}, \tag{6.5.13}$$

which is convenient for the analysis of the underwriting business.

The coefficients may be time dependent and one or more of them may be stochastic, for example the safety loading, the interest rate and inflation buried in the factor r_{igp}.

The sum $\bar{f} + \lambda$ represents in a ratio form what remains of the gross premium B when the loading for expenses is set aside. It is the safety loaded risk premium related to B and will be denoted by p_λ. Regarding (6.5.10b) we have

$$p_\lambda = \bar{f} + \lambda = 1 - c - \lambda_b + \lambda. \tag{6.5.14}$$

This equation can then be written in an alternative form

$$\mathbf{u} = r_{\text{igp}} \mathbf{u}_{-1} + p_\lambda - \mathbf{f}. \tag{6.5.15}$$

The interpretation of the basic equation (6.5.13) is obvious. The relative amount of the risk reserve $\mathbf{u}$ (solvency ratio) changes from year to year for the following reasons:

(i) Yield of interest on the initial amount $\mathbf{u}_{-1}$ increases the solvency ratio, but inflation and real growth according to (6.5.8) reduce it. All these effects are included, by definition, in the factor r_{igp}.

(ii) Safety loading λ increases $\mathbf{u}$ owing to the 'ordinary' loading λ_b and owing to the yield of interest gained by the underwriting reserve according to (6.5.12).

(iii) The fluctuating deviation of the loss ratio from its mean value $(\bar{f} - \mathbf{f})$ is moved to $\mathbf{u}$.

(j) Influence channels of the background factors It must still be recalled that the important factor r_{igp} (see (6.5.8b)) conveys to the basic equation the *joint* effect of yield of investments, inflation and real growth of the business volume. No one of these three factors appears in the equation explicitly (implicit influence channels, however, exist; e.g. i_i is included in the formula (6.5.12) of λ, and r_g affects n (according to (6.1.2a–c)). This proves the assertion expressed in item 6.3(e) according to which the relationship of these three factors is more relevant than each of them separately.

Errors in the expense factor c or (what is the same) in $\bar{f}$, as well as calculation of estimates for yield of interest, inflation, growth, cycles etc., affect directly the safety loading λ, and this should be chosen accordingly. When the model is used for simulations, this effect may provoke cycles in a way which was described in item 6.2(e) and will be discussed in Section 7.7.

6.6   Distribution of the solvency ratio u

(a) Dynamic discounting In what follows, inflation-adjusted (i.e. moving rather than constant) values of money will be operated, as was reasoned in item 6.1(j). It is therefore necessary to modify the conventional concepts of interest calculation accordingly. For this purpose 'a dynamic discounting factor' will be introduced, synthesizing the rates of interest, growth and inflation (see item 6.5(g)) as follows

$$r(\tau, t) = \prod_{v=\tau+1}^{t} r_{igp}(v) = \prod_{v=\tau+1}^{t} \frac{r_i(v)}{r_g(v)r_p(v)} = \frac{B(\tau)}{B(t)} \times \prod_{v=\tau+1}^{t} r_i(v). \quad (6.6.1a)$$

In the particular case where all the factors involved are constants this is reduced to a power expression

$$r(\tau, t) = r_{\text{igp}}^{t-\tau}. \tag{6.6.1b}$$

If the growth and inflation are omitted, i.e. B is constant, it is further reduced to the well-known accumulation factor $r_i^{t-\tau} = (1 + i_i)^{t-\tau}$.

The following properties and conventions of the dynamic factor are needed

$$r(t_1, t_2)r(t_2, t_3) = r(t_1, t_3)$$
$$r(t - 1, t) = r_{\text{igp}}(t) \tag{6.6.2}$$
$$r(t, t) = 1.$$

(b) Analysis of the u algorithm Whilst the premises of the trading process are so general that interest, inflation, growth of the portfolio and safety loading are stochastic and/or follow some specially programmed dynamic or other rules, often the simulation which will be considered in Section 6.8 is the only workable technique for coping with the process numerically. It is, however, useful also to investigate the problem with simplified assumptions, as mentioned already in item 6.5(b). The results so obtained may as such be of interest, and they may reveal properties which are also characteristic for more general processes. In fact the conventional risk theory has been mainly built on these simplified bases. Hence in this section it is assumed that the future flow of interest, real growth, inflation and safety loading are all *deterministically* given but not necessarily constant from year to year. The stochastic variation is limited to claims only.

By recursive application of the **u** algorithm (6.5.15) and by using the concepts and notation introduced in item (a), the following expression is obtained

$$\mathbf{u}(t) = u(0)r(0, t) + \sum_{\tau=1}^{t} p_\lambda(\tau)r(\tau, t) - \sum_{\tau=1}^{t} \mathbf{f}(\tau)r(\tau, t). \tag{6.6.3a}$$

In the particular case where the rates of interest, growth and inflation are not time dependent this equation is modified in form

$$\mathbf{u}(t) = u(0)r_{\text{igp}}^{t} + \sum_{\tau=1}^{t} p_\lambda(\tau)r_{\text{igp}}^{t-\tau} - \sum_{\tau=1}^{t} \mathbf{f}(\tau)r_{\text{igp}}^{t-\tau}. \tag{6.6.3b}$$

It is convenient to rewrite (6.6.3a) as

$$\mathbf{u}(t) = R(t) - \mathbf{f}(1, t), \qquad (6.6.4)$$

where

$$R(t) = u(0)r(0, t) + \sum_{\tau=1}^{t} p_\lambda(\tau)r(\tau, t)$$

$$\mathbf{f}(1, t) = \sum_{\tau=1}^{t} \mathbf{f}(\tau)r(\tau, t). \qquad (6.6.5)$$

The variable $\mathbf{f}(1, t)$ is the discounted accumulated claim ratio. If the yields of interest, inflation and growth were disregarded, $\mathbf{f}(1, t)B(t)$ would be the accumulated claim amount $\mathbf{X}(1, t)$ considered in Section 6.1. The first term $R(t)$ in the decomposition (6.6.4) is the (hypothetical) limit amount which would be achieved if no claims occurred; i.e. $R(t)$ is the sum of the first two terms in the right-hand side of (6.6.3a) representing the income issues, yield of interest, and premiums of the process.

The interrelations between the variables involved can be seen in Fig. 6.6.1.

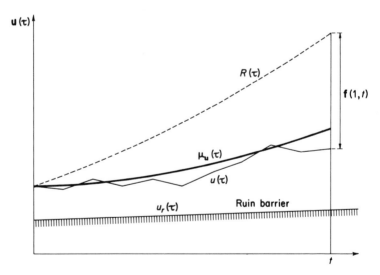

Figure 6.6.1 *The solvency ratio process* **u**.

(c) The mean value of u Some formulae related to the **u** process will be now deduced, beginning with mean values. The terms of the last sum in (6.6.3a) have the mean (see (6.1.14) and (6.2.11))

$$\mu_f(\tau) = \frac{nm \times (1 + z(\tau)) \times \prod_{v=1}^{\tau} r_g(v) r_x(v)}{nm \times \prod_{v=1}^{\tau} r_g(v) r_p(v)/(1 - \lambda_b - c)}$$

$$= (1 - c - \lambda_b) \times (1 + z(t)) \times D(\tau), \qquad (6.6.6)$$

where

$$D(\tau) = \prod_{v=1}^{\tau} r_x(v) \Big/ \prod_{v=1}^{\tau} r_p(v), \qquad (6.6.7)$$

is an auxiliary function showing the effect of the time lag between claim and premium inflations (see (6.2.2)). If the lag is zero, then $D(\tau) \equiv 1$.

The expectation of **u**(t) can now be written (see (6.5.14))

$$\mu_u(t) = u(0)r(0, t) + (1 + \lambda - \lambda_b - c) \sum_{\tau=1}^{t} r(\tau, t)$$

$$- (1 - c - \lambda_b) \sum_{\tau=1}^{t} (1 + z(\tau)) D(\tau) r(\tau, t)$$

$$= u(0)r(0, t) + \lambda \sum_{\tau=1}^{t} r(\tau, t)$$

$$+ (1 - c - \lambda_b) \sum_{\tau=1}^{t} [1 - (1 + z(\tau)) D(\tau)] r(\tau, t). \qquad (6.6.8)$$

The first two terms of the last expression give the average flow of the solvency ratio without the cyclical fluctuation, and the last term sets forth the cycles.

If $r_{igp} < 1$, as often happens in practical applications, the possible downward or upward trend declines when t grows and $\mu_u(t)$ continues oscillation around a horizontal equilibrium level. This equilibrium level can be obtained from (6.6.8) by dropping the effect of cycles, i.e. by putting $z(\tau) \equiv 0$. Then the formula is transformed to a geometric series, the sum of which is

$$\mu_u(t) = u(0)r_{igp}^t + \lambda \frac{1 - r_{igp}^t}{1 - r_{igp}}, \qquad (6.6.8a)$$

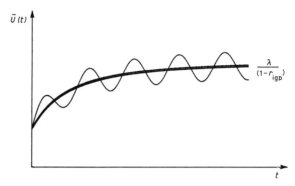

Figure 6.6.2   *The trend of the average solvency ratio and the deviation caused by the cycles according to (6.6.8) when $r_{igp} < 1$.*

having an asymptotic equilibrium level (see Fig. 6.6.2)

$$E_u = \lim_{t \to \infty} \mu_u(t) = \frac{\lambda}{1 - r_{igp}}. \qquad (6.6.9)$$

(d) Variance According to the assumptions made in item (b), the stochasticity is limited only to the last term in (6.6.3), i.e. to the accumulated claim ratio denoted by $f(1, t)$ in (6.6.5). Hence

$$\sigma_u^2(t) = \sigma^2(f(1, t)). \qquad (6.6.10)$$

By using equation (6.1.21) the variance of the solvency ratio can be written

$$\sigma_u^2(t) = \sum_{\tau=1}^{t} \sigma_x^2(\tau) r(\tau, t)^2 = \sum_{\tau=1}^{t} [r_2/n(\tau) + \sigma_q^2] \mu_f(\tau)^2 r(\tau, t)^2. \qquad (6.6.11)$$

The asymptotic value corresponding to (6.6.9) is again finite if $r_{igp} < 1$. Assuming that $r_g > 1$, it is

$$\lim_{t \to \infty} \sigma_u^2(t) = \frac{\sigma_q^2 (1 - c - \lambda_b)^2}{1 - r_{igp}^2}. \qquad (6.6.12)$$

(e) Skewness The third central moment is

$$\mu_3(u(\tau)) = - \sum_{\tau=1}^{t} [r_3/n(\tau)^2 + 3r_2 \sigma_q^2/n(\tau) + \sigma_q^3 \gamma_q] \times \mu_f(\tau)^3 \times r(\tau, t)^3,$$

and the skewness

$$\gamma_u(1, t) = -\gamma_f(1, t) = \mu_3(\mathbf{u}(t))/\sigma_u^3(t) \qquad (6.6.13)$$

Its asymptotic value is

$$\lim_{t \to \infty} \gamma_u(1, t) = -\gamma_q \frac{(1 - r_{igp}^2)^{3/2}}{1 - r_{igp}^3}, \qquad (6.6.14)$$

provided that $r_{igp} < 1$ and $r_g > 1$.

The reader should note the minus sign of γ_u and $\mu_3(\mathbf{u})$.

(f) The distribution of the solvency ratio u A strict calculation of the d.f. of $\mathbf{u}(t)$ would provide $t - 1$ convolutions as has already been stated in item 6.1(r). This approach will be considered in the next section. It is, however, impracticable for most applications and again, therefore, approximative methods are needed.

It can be expected that the approximation technique employed in Chapter 3 for the one year case (normal, NP, gamma or Wilson–Hilferty formulae) is also applicable to the variables related to several years' process, the more so because the stochastic element in (6.6.3), the term $\mathbf{f}(1, t)$, is a sum of independent one-year variables and therefore better smoothed than any one of them.

Hence, as a straightforward application of the NP approximation the variable $\mathbf{f}(1, t)$ is first standardized

$$\mathbf{x} = \mathbf{x}(1, t) = \frac{\mathbf{f}(1, t) - \mu_f(1, t)}{\sigma_f(1, t)}, \qquad (6.6.15)$$

and the NP transformation $x \to y = v_\gamma^{-1}(x)$ with skewness $\gamma = \gamma_x = \gamma_f(1, t)$ is made (see (3.11.14)). Then we have

$$\text{prob}\{\mathbf{x} \leqslant x\} \approx N_\gamma(x) = N(y). \qquad (6.6.16)$$

The required d.f. of $\mathbf{u}(t)$ can now be obtained with regard to the connection between the variables $\mathbf{f}(1, t)$ and $\mathbf{u}(t)$ as defined in (6.6.4) and shown in Fig. 6.6.1. It will be denoted by

$$G(u_0, u; t_1, t_2) = \text{prob}\{\mathbf{u}(t_2) \leqslant u \,|\, \mathbf{u}(t_1 - 1) = u_0\}. \qquad (6.6.17a)$$

In most applications $t_1 = 1$ and u_0 is a constant which need not be given in the notation. Then a short notation is more convenient, as follows

$$G_t(u) = G(u_0, u; 1, t)$$
$$= \text{prob}\{\mathbf{u}(t) \leqslant u \,|\, u(0) = u_0\}$$
$$= 1 - \text{prob}\{\mathbf{f}(1, t) \leqslant R(t) - u \,|\, u(0) = u_0\}$$
$$= 1 - \text{prob}\{\mathbf{x} \leqslant x\}$$
$$\approx 1 - N(y), \qquad\qquad (6.6.17b)$$

where, since $\mu_{\mathbf{f}}(1, t) = R(t) - \mu_{\mathbf{u}}(t)$ and $\sigma_{\mathbf{f}}(1, t) = \sigma_{\mathbf{u}}(t)$ (see Fig. 6.6.1),

$$x = (\mu_{\mathbf{u}}(t) - u)/\sigma_{\mathbf{u}}(t), \qquad\qquad (6.6.18)$$

and, as above, $y = v_y^{-1}(x)$ with $\gamma = \gamma_{\mathbf{f}}(1, t) = -\gamma_{\mathbf{u}}(t)$.

Here and in the following the case whereby the d.f. F or G is discontinuous is ignored, which could provide an auxiliary term $\text{prob}\{\mathbf{u}(t) = u\}$ (or similar) when the passage from $\mathbf{u}(t)$ to $\mathbf{f}(1, t)$ is made.

In addition, either gamma approximation, presented in Section 3.12, or the Wilson–Hilferty formula (item 3.11(m)) can be used for the calculation of $F(X; 1, t)$ and $G_t(u)$ in a similar way to the NP formula based on the same characteristics as above.

(g) The probability of the state of ruin As a special case of the above problem, one can ask what is the probability $\varphi(t)$ that a sample path is in the state of ruin at the end of the year t, i.e. that $\mathbf{u}(t) \leqslant u_r(t) = U_r(t)/B(t)$, where $U_r(t)$ is the ruin barrier (see item 4.1(d)) and $B(t)$ is again the premium income. A straightforward application of (6.6.17) gives

$$\varphi(t) = \text{prob}\{\mathbf{u}(t) < u_r(t)\}$$
$$= G_t(u_r(t)). \qquad\qquad (6.6.19)$$

This formula will prove a very useful building block for the finite time ruin probability calculations, as will be shown in Section 6.9.

For readers' convenience, the steps of the calculation of the 'ruin state probability' $\varphi(t)$ are summarized as follows:

(i) Calculate $\mu_{\mathbf{u}}(t)$ from (6.6.8).
(ii) Calculate $\sigma_{\mathbf{u}}(t) = \sigma_{\mathbf{f}}(1, t)$ from (6.6.11).
(iii) Calculate $\gamma_{\mathbf{f}}(1, t) = -\gamma_{\mathbf{u}}(t)$ from (6.6.13).
(iv) Define the ruin barrier $u_r(t) (= U_r(t)/B(t))$.

(v) Put $x = (\mu_u(t) - u_r(t))/\sigma_u(t)$.

(vi) Perform the NP transformation $x \to y = v_\gamma^{-1}(x)$ according to (3.11.14) by using the skewness $\gamma = \gamma_f(1, t) = -\gamma_u(t)$ as the skewness γ needed for the formula.

(vii) Then $\varphi(t) \approx 1 - N(y)$.

A common practice is to manipulate the scale of the solvency margin so that the ruin barrier $U_r(t)$ is chosen as the zero level. Then $u_r(t) = 0$ and $x = \mu_u(t)/\sigma_u(t)$.

6.7 Ruin probability Ψ_T (u), truncated convolution

(a) Survival probability The ruin problem related to an arbitrary number T of years can now be considered. First some quite general formulae are derived. Let the insurer's risk reserve at time points 0 (initially), 1, 2,..., be $U(0)$, $U(1)$, $U(2)$,..., respectively, each being a random variable except $U(0)$, which is known and briefly denoted by U_0.

The process consists of yield of interest earned for the risk reserve $U(t)$, incoming safety loaded premiums and outgoing claims as depicted in Fig. 6.7.1. Furthermore, a ruin barrier $U_r(t)$ is provided

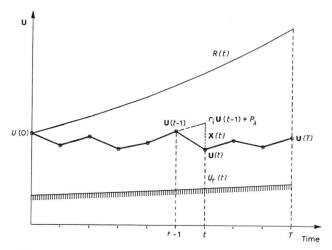

Figure 6.7.1 *A discrete risk process defined by the algorithm* $U(t) = r_i U(t-1) + P_\lambda(t) - X(t)$. *R(t) is that (hypothetical) risk reserve which would be obtained if no claims occurred.*

as a function of t. The idea is mainly to demonstrate the convolution method. The formulae achieved are not very expedient for computations compared with the approaches dealt with in subsequent sections.

As reasoned in item 1.4(b), the argument is limited to the discrete checking of the state of the solvency and the approach will be numerical rather than analytic. The continuous problem is treated by Seal (1974, 1978, 1980). Beard (1971) and Taylor (1978) have presented modifications for its numerical treatment. The trick of integrating over the tails rather than over the main part of the distributions, as will be made in item (d), follows Seal's presentation.

The probability of ruin during the first T years is

$$\Psi_T = \Psi_T(U_0) = \text{prob}\{\mathbf{U}(t) < U_r(t) \quad \text{for at least one } t = 1, \ldots, T\}.$$
$$(6.7.1)$$

Furthermore, the 'survival function'

$$W_T(U) = W_T(U_0, U) = \text{prob}\{\mathbf{U}(T) \geq U \text{ and } \mathbf{U}(t) \geq U_r(t) \text{ for } t < T\}$$
$$(6.7.2)$$

will be introduced. Then

$$W_T(U_r(T)) = 1 - \Psi_T, \qquad (6.7.3)$$

is the 'survival probability', i.e. the probability that a realization of the process survives at least T years, i.e. $U(t) \geq U_r(t)$ for every $t = 1, \ldots, T$.

(b) Visualization of the process Before proceeding to the derivation of the survival equations it may be useful to summarize the basic concepts and to attempt to find a concrete image of them. For this purpose, each realization can be visualized by a sample path random walking point by point $t = 1, 2, \ldots$ and the whole process as a bundle of these paths. The density of the bundle is high in the middle and decreases away from it, as illustrated in Fig. 6.7.2, where crosscuts of the density distribution are plotted for a sequence of discrete times. In fact, these crosscut densities are just the densities related to the distribution of $\mathbf{U}(t)$. During the process some of the sample paths fall below the ruin barrier and will be earmarked as 'ruined' the remainder having 'survived'. As time passes, sample paths are continually moving from the set of the survived to the set of the ruined.

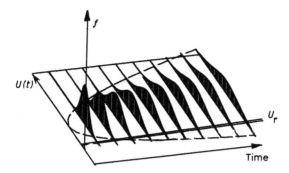

Figure 6.7.2 *A three-dimensional visualization of the random process* **U**. *The function f is the density of the 'crosscut' variable* **U**(t) *for different t-values.* U_r *is the ruin barrier. The 1 per cent confidence limits are plotted on the ground plane.*

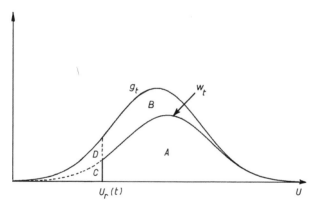

Figure 6.7.3 *A crosscut of the process, the distribution of the state of the business measured by means of the risk reserve* **U**(t) *at time t. The function* g_t *is the density of all cases and* w_t *represents the portion of such sample paths which still survived at* $t - 1$.

The paths may be terminated at the occasion of ruin in some of the applications and only the set of the sample paths still surviving is conducted forward. (See the simulated figures, like Fig. 6.8.5 below, where this visualization is performed).

One of the crosscuts of Fig. 6.7.2 is depicted in Fig. 6.7.3. The function g_t represents the distribution of all sample paths passing time t. It is (in the continuous case) the derivative of the d.f. G_t of

$U(t)$ (see 6.6.17)). The function w_t plotted in the figure is defined as the derivative of the survival function

$$w_t(U) = - W_t'(U), \tag{6.7.4}$$

or equivalently

$$W_t(U) = \int_U^\infty w_t(V)\, dV. \tag{6.7.5}$$

The function w_t can be interpreted as the *relative* density of those sample paths not being ruined before time t. In other words $w_t(U)\, dU$ gives the conditional probability that a sample path started at $t = 0$ goes through the interval $(U, U + dU]$ at time t and has not been in a state of ruin before that. This function is not a density function in the ordinary sense because its integral extended over the whole range $(-\infty, \infty)$ of U is not equal to 1 but $1 - \Psi_{t-1}$.

Now, let A, B, C and D denote the areas of the domains determined by g_t, w_t and $U_r(t)$ as shown in Fig. 6.7.3, and, as before, let $1 - \varphi(t)$ be the probability that a sample path is not in state of ruin at t. Then

$$\begin{aligned}
A + B &= 1 - \varphi(t) \\
C + D &= \varphi(t) \\
A &= W_t(U_r(t)) = 1 - \Psi_t \qquad (6.7.6)\\
A + C &= 1 - \Psi_{t-1} \\
C &= 1 - \Psi_{t-1} - A = \Psi_t - \Psi_{t-1} \equiv \Delta\Psi_t.
\end{aligned}$$

The area C represents the probability $\Delta\Psi_t$ that the process first time is ruined at time t.

(c) An algorithm for W_t   Now let the risk process be constituted by the recurrence equation

$$U(t) = r_i(t)U(t-1) + P_\lambda(t) - X(t), \tag{6.7.7}$$

for $t = 1, 2, \ldots$, where $r_i(t)$ and $P_\lambda(t)$ are assumed deterministic, and the claim amounts $X(t)$ are mutually independent.

If $F(X; t)$ denotes the d.f. of $X(t)$, then W_1 has the expression

$$\begin{aligned}
W_1(U) &= \text{prob}\{r_i(1)U_0 + P_\lambda(1) - X(1) \geqslant U\} \\
&= \text{prob}\{X(1) \leqslant r_i(1)U_0 + P_\lambda(1) - U\} \qquad (6.7.8)\\
&= F(r_i(1)U_0 + P_\lambda(1) - U; 1),
\end{aligned}$$

in terms of $F(X; 1)$. In order to get a recurrence formula for W_t let $R(t) = r_i(t) U_0(t-1) + P_\lambda(t)$ be the upper bound for $U(t)$ (see Fig. 6.7.1). Then the following sequence of so-called truncated convolutions is obtained for $t = 2, 3, \ldots$

$$W_t(U) = -\int_{U_r(t-1)}^{R(t-1)} F(r_i(t)Y + P_\lambda(t) - U; t)\, dW_{t-1}(Y).$$

(6.7.9)

The running variable Y is to be interpreted as the value of $U(t-1)$ The integrand gives the probability that a sample path at time $t-1$ is in state $Y < U(t-1) \leqslant Y + dY$ and at $t\, U(t) \geqslant U$, which provides that the claims of year t should be less or equal to the argument assigned for F in the above integrals.

For numerical results the d.f.s $F(X; t)$ of $X(t)$ are first calculated by the methods discussed in the preceding chapters. Then the function W_t can be obtained successively for $t = 2, 3, \ldots$ by some method of numerical integration. However, even if feasible especially when computers are used, this method may be laborious. If some approximation is to be used for F, e.g. the NP or Γ formula, then the accumulation of inaccuracy as well as the normal rounding-off errors under the rather long sequence of computations may be difficult to control. This is so especially because the integration is mostly to be extended over the modes of distributions, and the order of magnitude of the required $1 - \Psi_T$ may thus be too close to the rounding-off errors of the largest terms involved in the integrations.

(d) Indirect calculation of the ruin probability The calculations can be greatly facilitated if the convolutions are arranged such that, instead of almost the whole range of the running variable Y, only a tail of the distribution is needed for integration. This can be done as follows.

The set of all sample paths related to the conditional probability $W_T(U)$ can be obtained as a difference of the following two sets

(I) The set of all paths which begin at $U(0) = U_0$ and satisfy $U(T) \geqslant U$, irrespective of whether the process is in a state of ruin before the year T or not.

(II) The set of all those sample paths which are in a state of ruin, i.e. satisfy $\mathbf{U}(t) < U_r(t)$, at one or more of the intervening points $t = 1, 2, \ldots, T - 1$.

Set II can be further divided into $T - 1$ disjoint subsets according to the time when the sample path was *last* in a state of ruin. Then the survival probability can be obtained as the probability related to the set I less the sum of the probabilities of the subsets of II, i.e.

$$W_T(U) = \text{prob}\{\mathbf{U}(T) \geqslant U\}$$
$$- \sum_{t=1}^{T-1} \text{prob}\{\mathbf{U}(t) < U_r(t); \mathbf{U}(\tau) \geqslant U_r(\tau)$$
$$\text{for } \tau = t + 1, \ldots, T - 1; \mathbf{U}(T) \geqslant U\}. \tag{6.7.10}$$

The calculation of the above expressions is based on the d.f. $G(U_0, U; t_1, t_2)$ of the risk reserve $U(t)$ which was derived in Section 6.6 (see (6.6.17a)), where now $\mathbf{u}(t) = \mathbf{U}(t)/B(t)$.

Also the survival function $W_t(U)$ is needed for varying periods and therefore is denoted accordingly

$$W(Y, U; t_1, t_2) = \text{prob}\{\mathbf{U}(\tau) \geqslant U_r(\tau) \qquad \text{for } \tau = t_1, \ldots, t_2 - 1;$$
$$\mathbf{U}(t_2) \geqslant U \,|\, \mathbf{U}(t_1 - 1) = Y\}.$$

Then (6.7.10) can be written

$$W(U_0, U; T_0, T) = 1 - G(U_0, U; T_0, T)$$
$$- \sum_{t=T_0}^{T-1} \int_{-\infty}^{U_r(t)} W(Y, U; t, T) \, d_Y G(U_0, Y; T_0, t), \tag{6.7.11}$$

which makes the successive calculations possible, taking first $T_0 = T$ (for this value of T_0 the Σ term is to be dropped), then $T_0 = T - 1$ etc., and finally

$$1 - \Psi_T = W_T(U_r(T)) = W(U_0, U_r(T); 1, T). \tag{6.7.12}$$

For further calculations, the values of $W(Y, U; T_0, T)$ are needed only for the value $U = U_r(T)$ and for the range $Y \leqslant U_r(t)$ ($t = T$, $T - 1, \ldots$).

By means of numerical integrations, e.g. by Simpson's formula, the auxiliary function W can first be calculated for a set of points $Y = U_r(t) - vh$ with step h and $v = 0, 1, 2, \ldots$ until it vanishes in the range of the accuracy demanded. Hence a matrix of values can be computed

$$[W(v, t)]_{v,t} = [W(U_r(t) - vh, U_r(T);t, T)]_{v,t}$$

$$\text{for } t = T - 1, T - 2, \dots, 1; v = 0, 1, 2, \dots, \qquad (6.7.13)$$

after which Ψ_T is obtained from (6.7.12) and (6.7.11) by another series of numerical integrations.

The benefit of this method is that the intervals over which the integrals are to be taken are shorter than in the direct truncated convolution and mainly consist of the tails of the distributions. Whilst the integration is not extended over the mode of the distribution, the rounding-off errors do not cause problems.

Note that the calculation algorithm can be arranged also by defining the set II according to the time when the ruin *first* occurs, as will be shown in exercise 6.7.1. The benefit of the approach given is, however, that the matrix (6.7.13) does not depend on the initial capital U_0 and can be used unchanged when Ψ_T is computed for several values of U_0.

Exercise 6.7.1 Rearrange the calculation algorithm (6.7.11), distinguishing between the subsets of II on the basis of when the ruin *first* occurs.

6.8 Monte Carlo method

6.8.1 RANDOM NUMBERS

(a) Uniformly distributed random numbers The Monte Carlo technique makes use of so-called random numbers, which are sequences of equally distributed mutually independent random variables or samples (realizations) of such sequences.

Consider as an example a random variable **r** which is uniformly distributed over the interval (0, 1). Its distribution function is

$$R(r) = \begin{cases} 0 & \text{for } r \leqslant 0 \\ r & \text{for } 0 < r \leqslant 1 \\ 1 & \text{for } r > 1. \end{cases} \qquad (6.8.1)$$

This distribution is also called *rectangular* owing to the shape of its density function. A sequence of uniformly distributed random numbers is obtained or *generated*, taking a set of variables $\mathbf{r}_1, \mathbf{r}_2, \dots$, which all are uniformly (6.8.1) distributed and mutually independent. Such sequences are needed as basic building blocks for the Monte Carlo simulations as will be seen in the sequel. Several approximate techniques are suggested for their generation. They operate like a lottery, producing a list of winning numbers: each number in the interval $(0, 1)$ (rounded to a certain number of decimals) should have exactly the same probability of appearing in the sequence. Because the practicable methods can generate sequences which only approximately satisfy the theoretical assumptions they are often called *pseudo*random numbers.

As a rule the Monte Carlo method needs such a large number of random numbers that these have to be generated by computer. Ready-made programmes exist for the purpose and are described in item (e).

(b) Arbitrarily distributed random numbers Let $\mathbf{r}$ be uniformly distributed and let F be a given d.f., and transform $\mathbf{r}$ into a new random variable $\mathbf{X} = F^{-1}(\mathbf{r})$. F need not be strictly increasing: it can be for example a discontinuous step function. Therefore $F^{-1}(r)$ is defined to mean the smallest X satisfying the inequality $F(X) \geqslant r$ where $0 < r < 1$. (For technical reasons an open interval is often used instead of closed $0 \leqslant r \leqslant 1$, which could lead to inconveniences e.g. in formulae as (6.8.2) and (6.8.6) where logarithms appear.)

Then

$$\begin{aligned}
\text{prob}\{\mathbf{X} \leqslant X\} &= \text{prob}\{F^{-1}(\mathbf{r}) \leqslant X\} \\
&= \text{prob}\{\mathbf{r} \leqslant F(X)\} = F(X),
\end{aligned}$$

which means that F is the d.f. of $\mathbf{X}$. This observation gives (in principle) a simple procedure for generating random numbers having an arbitrary given d.f. F. They are obtained as a transformation from the uniformly distributed numbers. Figure 6.8.1 illustrates the idea.

For example, random numbers

$$\mathbf{X} = -(1/a) \ln \mathbf{r} \qquad (\mathbf{r} \text{ uniformly } (0, 1) \text{ distributed}) \qquad (6.8.2)$$

have the exponential d.f.

$$F(X) = 1 - e^{-aX} \qquad (X \geqslant 0), \qquad (6.8.3)$$

as is readily seen (see exercise 6.8.1).

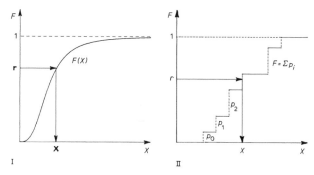

Figure 6.8.1   *Generation of random numbers* $\mathbf{X}$ *distributed according to* F; *(I) continuous case; (II) discrete case.*

(c) Monte Carlo method   To illustrate the simulation technique, known as the Monte Carlo method, the convolution of two distribution functions F_1 and F_2 is calculated. The idea is to make use of the well-known fact that the sum of two independent random variables having d.f.s F_1 and F_2 is $F_1 * F_2$ distributed. First two sequences of random numbers $(\mathbf{X}_{11}, \mathbf{X}_{12}, \ldots, \mathbf{X}_{1s})$ and $(\mathbf{X}_{21}, \mathbf{X}_{22}, \ldots, \mathbf{X}_{2s})$ are generated, the former being distributed according to F_1 and the latter according to F_2. For example the technique presented in the preceding item can be applied. Then putting $\mathbf{X}_i = \mathbf{X}_{1i} + \mathbf{X}_{2i}$ a sequence $(\mathbf{X}_1, \ldots, \mathbf{X}_s)$ is obtained. This is a sequence of random numbers distributed in accordance with the function $F = F_1 * F_2$. To obtain numerical values of this distribution function, or more precisely an estimate thereof, the values X_i of $\mathbf{X}_i$ given by the random number generator are rearranged according to their magnitudes and, denoting by $\mathbf{c}(X)$ 'the counter number' of all $X_i \leqslant X$, the estimate $F(X) \approx \mathbf{c}(X)/s$ immediately follows.

It will thus be seen that the simulation method is, in fact, exactly equivalent to a method of observing the actual values appearing in some experiment and building up the statistical estimate of the distribution function. No physical experiment is actually carried out but instead is 'played' or 'simulated' by means of random numbers. This method has been increasingly used in connection with various research projects, particularly when the direct calculation of the distribution functions is complicated. It can also be usefully applied in the field of risk theory, especially in cases where other methods are intractable owing to the complexity of the model.

(d) Evaluation of accuracy   Because the value of $\hat{p} = c(X)/s$ is obtained as a random sample it is subject to inaccuracy like any other sample. In fact it is binomially distributed, having standard deviation

$$\sigma = \sqrt{\left(\frac{p(1-p)}{s} \right)},$$

where p is the true (unknown) value of $F(X)$. Using the normal approximation, the maximum error at confidence level $1 - \varepsilon$ is

$$\Delta_s = y_\varepsilon \sigma = y_\varepsilon \sqrt{\left(\frac{p(1-p)}{s} \right)} \leqslant \frac{y_\varepsilon}{2\sqrt{s}} \qquad (6.8.4)$$

where $y_\varepsilon = N^{-1}(1 - \varepsilon/2)$. The limit Δ_s depends on the sample size s as shown in Table 6.8.1, where both the absolute and relative $(= \Delta_s/p)$ values of the limit are given for some p values.

Thus to get one more decimal place the sample size must be multiplied a hundredfold. The table suggests a rather large sample size when the tail of distribution is to be evaluated, which may make simulation costly. The textbooks suggest, however, methods to make the simulation more efficient, e.g. by means of the so-called variance reduction technique (see Rubinstein 1981, Section 4.3, and Sections 6.8.2 and 6.8.3 in the following).

Fortunately, if what is needed is mainly an idea of the shape of the distribution and of its variation range, a reasonably limited sample size may be sufficient. This is demonstrated in Fig. 6.8.2, where

Table 6.8.1   *Examples of the absolute and relative limits of the simulation errors according to (6.8.4). Confidence level $1 - \varepsilon = 0.95$; $y_\varepsilon = 1.96$.*

				p				
	0.5		0.1		0.01		0.001	
s	Δ_s	$\Delta_s/p(\%)$	Δ_s	$\Delta_s/p(\%)$	Δ_s	$\Delta_s/p(\%)$	Δ_s	$\Delta_s/p(\%)$
100	0.0980	19.6	0.0588	58.8	0.0195	195.0	0.0062	619.5
1 000	0.0310	6.2	0.0186	18.6	0.0062	61.7	0.0020	195.9
10 000	0.0098	2.0	0.0059	5.9	0.0020	19.5	0.0006	61.9
100 000	0.0031	0.6	0.0019	1.9	0.0006	6.2	0.0002	19.6
1 000 000	0.0010	0.2	0.0006	0.6	0.0002	2.0	0.0001	6.2

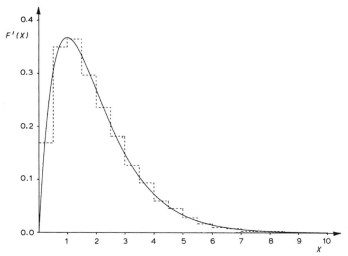

Figure 6.8.2   *Exact values of* $\Gamma'(X;2)$ (*solid line*) *and its simulated estimate* (*the heights of the dotted pillars*); *sample size* 2000.

$\Gamma(X;2)$ (see (2.9.1)) is simulated. Already a visual investigation gives a good insight about the distribution and makes it possible also to evaluate the position and magnitude of the mode and the tail.

It is still easier to view the position and the confidence boundaries of the bundles of sample paths, as will be seen in Section 6.8.4, where the sample size is often no more than 100. This is due to the fact that a visual investigation can benefit *the entire* configuration, which includes information on a very great number of simulation outcomes, whereas the registered number of 'ruins', $c(X)$, is derived from a few samples only. On the other hand, of course, a visual evaluation is to some extent subjective. This may possibly be helped by a curve-fitting technique, which supports e.g. the estimation of the ends of the distribution using all the information included in the sample and not only the extreme sample outcomes (in fact, this is the idea in visual investigation, too).

The benefits and shortcomings are discussed further in item 6.8.4(g).

(e) Generation of uniformly distributed random numbers As a primary input for simulations, uniformly distributed (pseudo)random numbers are needed. They are often available as ready-made standard commands in computers or can be readily generated as a sequence by some standard formula. One in common use is the so-called *mixed congruential* formula (see Mihram, 1972, Section 2.8.7)

$$r_k = ar_{k-1} + b \pmod{10^d} \qquad (d \text{ positive integer}). \qquad (6.8.5)$$

The kth random number r_k is obtained from the preceding number r_{k-1} taking d last digits from (6.8.5). If b is a positive integer not divisible by 2 or 5 and a is of the form $1 + 20^i$ (i any positive integer) the formula generates a sequence of 10^d different numbers until it begins to repeat the same sequence.

The initial number r_0, the so-called 'seed', can be chosen freely from the *open* interval (0, 1). For many applications it is necessary to employ generators which do not give 0 or 1 as output.

Roughly speaking, a computer takes about the same time to generate a random number as it takes for a couple of multiplications.

(f) Normally distributed random numbers In addition to uniformly distributed random numbers, normally distributed numbers are often needed as input for more sophisticated simulators. A suitable standard method makes use of the following so-called *log and trig formula* (see Hammersley and Handscomb, 1964)

$$\begin{aligned} \mathbf{x}_1 &= \sqrt{(-2\ln(\mathbf{r}_1))} \times \cos(2\pi\mathbf{r}_2) \\ \mathbf{x}_2 &= \sqrt{(-2\ln(\mathbf{r}_1))} \times \sin(2\pi\mathbf{r}_2), \end{aligned} \qquad (6.8.6)$$

where $\mathbf{r}_1, \mathbf{r}_2$ is a pair of uniformly distributed mutually independent random numbers on the interval (0, 1) and the generated pair $\mathbf{x}_1, \mathbf{x}_2$ consists of normally distributed mutually independent random numbers having mean 0 and standard deviation 1.

A simple way of generating approximately normally distributed random numbers is first to generate m uniformly distributed mutually independent random numbers. Their sum $\mathbf{x}$ is approximately normally $N(m/2, m/12)$ distributed. Often $m = 12$ is chosen. Then $\mathbf{x} - 6$ is approximately normally $N(0, 1)$ distributed. It gives, however, a bias in the periphery of the distribution range and is therefore unsuitable for many risk-theoretical applications.

Exercise 6.8.1 Construct random number generators which produce numbers distributed according to the following functions:

(a) *Poisson law* (2.4.2) distinguishing the cases where the expected number n is
   small
   large (use the Wilson–Hilferty formula (3.5.14) and ex. 2.9.7) and the generator for normally distributed random numbers, item 6.8.1(f).
(b) *Exponential* (6.8.3)
(c) *Incomplete gamma function* $\Gamma(ax, h)$ (2.9.1) where h is a positive integer (use the convolution rule (2.9.7)).
   Note: More general Γ generators can be found in Rubinstein, (1982, Section 3.6.2).
(d) *Log-normal* (3.5.17)
(e) *Pareto* (3.5.20)

Exercise 6.8.2 Study the behaviour of the time series defined by the difference equation (6.2.7b) where $\lambda(-1) = 0.1$, $\lambda(0) = 0.05$, $a_1 = 0$, $a_2 = -1$, $\lambda_0 = 0$ and the ε terms are normally distributed random variables having mean $= 0$, $\sigma = 0.03$. Plot $\lambda(t)$ for $t = 1, 2, \ldots, 25$ first putting $\sigma = 0$ and then three (or more) realizations regarding the given value of σ (readers who have no random number generator available can use numbers given in Appendix E). Verify that the wavelength is the same as that obtained by the analytic calculation presented in exercise 6.2.1.

6.8.2 DIRECT SIMULATION OF THE COMPOUND POISSON FUNCTION

(a) Straightforward simulation for calculation of the compound d.f. of the aggregate claim amount (see (3.2.3))

$$F(X) = \sum_{k=0}^{\infty} p_k S^{k*}(X), \qquad (6.8.7)$$

for a given X, or simultaneously for a given set X_j $(j = 1, 2, \ldots)$ of X values, can be carried out by repeating the following three steps s times. The distribution functions of the claim number process and the claim size are assumed given.

(i) Generate the claim number k applying the technique presented in the preceding section (see exercise 6.8.1(a)).

(ii) Generate k numbers $Z_1, Z_2, \ldots, Z_k$ each being distributed according to the given claim size d.f., and sum them

$$X_{sim} = \sum_{i=1}^{k} Z_i. \tag{6.8.8}$$

(iii) Set the counter: $c(X_j) \to c(X_j) + 1$ if $X_{sim} \leqslant X_j$ $(j = 1, 2, \ldots)$. Finally

$$F(X_j) \approx c(X_j)/s \qquad (j = 1, 2, \ldots). \tag{6.8.9}$$

(b) Variance reduction The procedure presented in item (a) can be made faster and the simulation inaccuracy can be reduced if the claim number frequency is calculated analytically and only the second phase, steps (ii) and (iii), generating the claim amount (6.8.8), are simulated. This is an example of the so-called variance reduction technique well known in the textbooks (Rubinstein, 1981, Section 4.3).

The procedure described in item (a) is modified as follows.

(i) $s_k = sp_k$ (rounded as integer) will be the sample size assigned to k $(s = \Sigma s_k$; if s deviates from the 'original' s because of the rounding-offs the 'new' s can be adapted).

(ii) Carry out steps (ii) and (iii) of item (a) s_k times for each k for which $s_k > 0$.

(iii) $F(X)$ is obtained from (6.8.9).

The variance reduction example just given demonstrates a general feature of the simulation technique. It pays to first calculate analytically as many steps of the calculations as conveniently possible and to limit the simulation to those links which are not otherwise reasonably manageable.

(c) Stratified sampling The efficiency of simulation can still be improved if the sample is concentrated in those k values for which the terms of the sum (6.8.7) are the largest, or more exactly in those which most affect the variance of the simulation outcome.

The procedure described in the preceding item will be modified so that instead of the 'natural' sample size $s_k = p_k s$ another sample of size w_k, the so-called strata size, will be assigned for each k. The strata sizes are to be determined so that optimal efficiency can be achieved. For details consult, for example, Rubinstein (1981) Chapter 4.3.

(d) Discussion The direct Monte Carlo method is at its best if n is relatively small, i.e. when small collectives are studied. It is suitable e.g. for treatments of catastrophic claims; an example will be given in item 6.8.(g). Its applications are given, for example, by Hovinen (1964), Seal (1969a), Sugars (1974), Roy (1981) and Galitz (1982).

If n is large, as it often is, computing time and costs soon grow beyond reasonable limits, especially if the portfolio is to be divided into sections each needing a separate calculation. Then some other technique is necessary, for example along the lines which will be presented in the following section.

Exercise 6.8.3 The claim numbers are assumed to be Poisson distributed with parameter $n = 2$ and the claim sizes Pareto distributed, $Z \geqslant 1$, $\alpha = 3$. Simulate $F(X)$ for integer values of X by using methods described in items (a) and (b). Readers not having a computer available can use the random numbers given in Appendix E (and set s small).

6.8.3 A RANDOM NUMBER GENERATOR FOR THE CYCLING MIXED COMPOUND POISSON VARIABLE $\mathbf{X}(t)$

(a) Recapitulation of definitions A fast method for generating random numbers which are approximately distributed according to the premise defined in Section 6.1 for the aggregate claim $\mathbf{X}(t)$ can be obtained by making use of the NP formula in cases where the collective concerned is not very small. Let us recall the definitions:

(i) The claim number process is of the mixed Poisson type with a Poisson parameter (the 'conditional' expected number of claims) $\mathbf{n}(t) = n(t)\mathbf{q}(t)$ for $t = 0, 1, 2, \ldots, T$. The structure variables $\mathbf{q}(t)$ are mutually independent and have a joint d.f. H.

(ii) The trends are given by a deterministically defined factor

$r_g(t)$ which affects the average claim numbers $n(t)$ according to (6.1.2).

(iii) The average claim number $n(t)$ may be also subject to cycles, which will be given either deterministically or randomly, as was discussed in items 6.1(d)–(g).

(iv) The claim sizes obey a d.f. S which is changed from year to year according to a deterministically given 'inflation' factor $r_x(t)$; the shape of S remains, however, unchanged as presented in item 6.1(n). This assumption implies that the risk indexes r_2 and r_3 defined by (3.3.8) are independent of time (see (6.1.12)).

In order to get a simulated realization of the cycling mixed compound Poisson variable $X(t)$ (t integer), a value for the cycle variable $z(t)$ must first be generated if it is stochastic, or calculated if it is deterministic. Next, a value q of the structure variable $q(t)$ has to be generated. Which method is appropriate for the purpose depends on the known or assumed properties of this variable, e.g. some of those considered in the previous sections. A convenient approach is to use the NP generator which is presented in item (b) below. The characteristics σ_q and γ_q are needed as input parameters. Then the value of the Poisson parameter $n(t)$ for the year t is, according to (6.1.8a)

$$n = n(0) \times \prod_{\tau=1}^{t} r_g(\tau) \times (1 + z(t))q(t). \qquad (6.8.13)$$

The d.f.

$$F_n(X) = F(X \,|\, n(t) = n). \qquad (6.8.14)$$

of $X(t)$ under the condition $n(t) = n$ reduces now to a simple compound Poisson d.f. Its mean value, standard deviation and skewness are, according to (3.3.9) and to assumption (iv) above

$$\mu(t) = n m(t), \qquad (6.8.15)$$

with

$$m(t) = m \prod_{\tau=1}^{t} r_x(\tau),$$

$$\sigma(t) = m(t)\sqrt{(nr_2)}, \qquad (6.8.16)$$

and

$$\gamma(t) = \frac{r_3}{\sqrt{(nr_2^3)}} \, . \qquad (6.8.17)$$

If n is not very small, as was assumed in item 6.8.2(d), the NP approximation can be applied for F_n.

(b) NP generator Suppose that t is fixed and the Poisson parameter n (see (6.8.13)) has been generated. The simulated value of $X(t)$ is then obtained by generating a random number distributed according to the d.f. (6.8.14). This will be done by making use of a NP generator, which generates random numbers distributed according to the standardized NP distribution N_γ. It is first introduced in this item. Having the skewness γ as an input parameter, the generator is readily obtained from the NP formulae derived in Section 3.11. as follows:

(i) Generate first a normally $(0, 1)$ distributed random number y, as was dealt with in item 6.8.1(f).
(ii) Transform it into $NP(0, 1, \gamma)$ distributed x by means of the transformation $x = v_y(y)$ defined by (3.11.16) and (3.11.17a). This transformation is the same one which is depicted in Fig. 3.11.2 but using the nomogram in the direction y to x.

The final value of $X(t)$ is obtained from

$$X_t = \mu(t) + x\sigma(t).$$

Note that for generation of another random number having the d.f. of $X(t)$ a new value for n, too, must be generated.

(c) X generator We shall now summarize the procedure for the generation of the cycling mixed compound Poisson process $X(t)$ $(t = 1, 2, 3, \dots)$. This random number generator consists of the following sequence of operations:

Deterministic initializations, needed only once: Put

$$g_0 = r_3/r_2^{3/2} \, , \qquad (6.8.18)$$

where r_2 and r_3 are the risk indexes (3.3.8).

Furthermore, calculate for $t = 1, \ldots, T$

$$\bar{n}(t) = r_g(t)\,\bar{n}(t-1); \; \bar{n}(0) = n(0)$$
$$m(t) = r_x(t)\,m(t-1); \; m(0) \text{ given.} \qquad (6.8.19)$$

Operation steps to be repeated for each sample path for $t = 1, 2, \ldots, T$.

(1) Generate the cycle variable $z = z(t)$. Either a deterministic formula such as (6.1.3) or a separately constructed time series generator such as (6.1.6) can be used. (Note that if z is deterministic, this step can be moved to (6.8.19) because it is common for all realizations.)

(2) Generate the structure variable $\mathbf{q}$ distributed according to H. If only the mean $(= 1)$, variance and skewness of H are known, then the NP generator with skewness γ_q can be used for generation of the value q of $\mathbf{q}(t)$: if x_1 is the value given by the NP generator, put $q = 1 + x_1 \sigma_q$.

(3) $n = \bar{n}(t) \times (1 + z) \times q$.

(4) $\gamma = g_0/\sqrt{n}$.

(5) Generate x using the NP generator with skewness γ.

(6) $X(t) = n \times m(t) + x \times m(t) \times \sqrt{(nr_2)}$.

A sample path for $X(t)$ is obtained by letting the time variable t run $1, 2, \ldots, T$. Of course, the variables $\mathbf{z}, \mathbf{q}$ and $\mathbf{x}$ must be generated separately for each t.

(d) Applicability As the NP formula itself, so also understandably the generator based on it is satisfactory only if the simulated collective, measured in terms of the expected number of claims n, is not very small. For small n values the direct simulation may be workable. Hence these methods complement each other; the NP generator is appropriate for large collectives and the direct simulations for small ones. The critical value of n distinguishing the 'large' and 'small collectives' can be evaluated from (3.11.19), and it seems to be usually 20–50 depending on the breadth of the claim size distribution, measured by the risk index r_2.

6.8.4 SIMULATION OF THE SOLVENCY RATIO $\mathbf{u}(t)$

(a) u process The whole risk process, i.e. the claims as well as the flow of the solvency ratio $\mathbf{u}(t)$, can now be simulated. For this purpose the sequence $\mathbf{X}(1), \mathbf{X}(2), \ldots, \mathbf{X}(T)$ or rather the corresponding ratios $\mathbf{f}(t) = \mathbf{X}(t)/B(t)$ are to be generated as presented in Section 6.8.3. Furthermore assumptions and basic data for premium calculation and for the yield of interest are now needed as described in Sections 6.2 and 6.3. The approaches may be either deterministic or stochastic and dynamic control rules can be programmed as examples in later sections demonstrate. Equation (6.5.15) then immediately gives $u(t)$ and a sample path can be generated such as that in Fig. 6.8.3 where, to begin with a simple case, safety loading and rates for interest, inflation and growth were kept constant.

(b) Stochastic bundle Following the idea of the Monte Carlo method the simulation is repeated numerous times. A bundle of sample paths is thus obtained, as shown in Fig. 6.8.4.

The mean line and the confidence boundaries are evaluated by means of equations (6.6.6) and (6.6.11) and will be discussed in Section 6.9.

A 'stochastic bundle' like that in Fig. 6.8.4 is an important tool in analysing risk behaviour of the portfolio. The shape and position of the bundle make it possible to draw conclusions about the solvency and other features of the process. If the bundle is safely

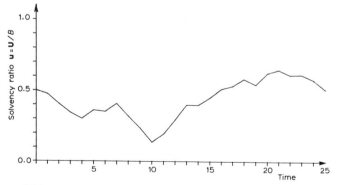

Figure 6.8.3   *A sample path of the business flow process; algorithm* (6.5.13) *has been used.*

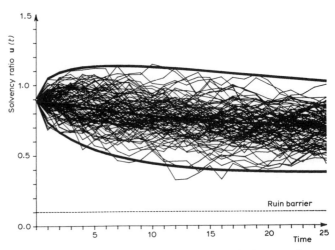

Figure 6.8.4 *A bundle of realizations of an insurer's business flow process generated by virtue of the algorithm* (6.5.15). *Data standards are as given in item* 7.1(d), *however, with no cycles and* $u(0) = 0.9$. *The confidence boundaries are determined by the condition that an average* 1% *of the sample paths at given time t may be outside them.*

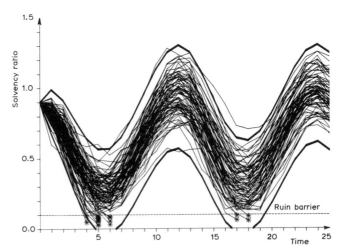

Figure 6.8.5 *Risk process subject to cyclical variation of the basic probabilities having the amplitude* $z_m = 0.1$, *and wavelength* $T_z = 12$ *years. Inflation varying as will be explained in item* 7.6(d). *Other data as in Fig.* 6.8.4. *Ruins* 18/100. *The stars indicate the ruin of the sample path.*

over the ruin barrier (e.g. the legal minimum amount of solvency margin), it indicates a solvent state.

(c) Analysis of background factors The Monte Carlo method can be used to examine the structure of the risk process and its dependence on the initial conditions and background assumptions. As an illustration, cyclic variation via (6.1.3) was introduced to the process of Fig. 6.8.4 and the process changed in a dramatic way.

The example depicted in Fig. 6.8.5 was constructed assuming that the phase of the cycles is the same all the time, i.e. $v = 0$ in (6.1.3). If this assumption is relaxed making v stochastic and uniformly distributed in interval $[1, 2\pi]$, Fig. 6.8.5 is changed as seen in Fig. 6.8.6. This example demonstrates the flexibility of the Monte Carlo method. It allows quite varying conditions and assumptions; among other things numerous variables may be made stochastic.

(d) Ruin probability The Monte Carlo method also makes it possible to evaluate the ruin probability. Each sample path which dropped below the ruin barrier was terminated by an asterisk and registered as a ruin. Then the registered number of ruins in relation

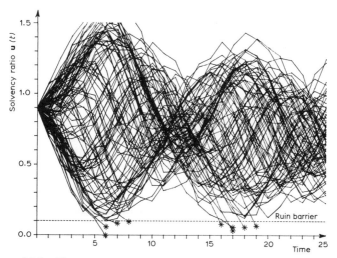

Figure 6.8.6   *The same process as in Fig. 6.8.5, but now the phase of the business cycle is randomized.*

to the whole number of the sample paths is an estimate for the ruin probability Ψ_T (in Fig. 6.8.5, 18/100).

(e) **Dynamics** The model given is still simplified and was aimed solely at demonstrating the simulation method. It will be further developed later, taking into account dynamics which may appear in actual circumstances. When an insurer approaches a critical state measures will be probably sought to improve profitability, e.g. economising in costs, reducing risks such as lowering the net retentions, acquiring additional solvency margin, etc. On the other hand if theory and practice are compared, i.e. by asking whether or not the model outcomes are in acceptable coincidence with actual experience, it must be kept in mind that insurers, being in a weak solvency situation, seldom become bankrupt. They are instead usually merged with other companies. So the actual number of observed 'ruins' is not comparable with the theoretical ruin number; rather the latter is comparable with the number of dissolved companies (mergers included) even though, of course, a merger can also arise for reasons other than the threat of an imminent ruin.

(f) **Catastrophic risks** If the expected number of claims n is very small, then the direct method presented in Section 6.8.2 may be appropriate to generate the annual claims amount $X(t)$. As an example, the risk of 'supercatastrophes', i.e. earthquakes, tornados, etc., is simulated in Fig. 6.8.7.

It is assumed that an insurer has numerous globally distributed reinsurance contracts and that the maximum estimated loss M is determined so that the amount of claims originated from one and the same occurrence, e.g. a wind storm, cannot exceed M *per contract*. It is, however, well known that in the case of a major catastrophe numerous contracts may be affected simultaneously. Hence, the insurer can be involved in the same event through several channels of the international reinsurance network, and his liability may be a major multiple of the per-contract prior estimation M, i.e. instead of M, say, kM where k is a multiplier to be evaluated. Landin (1980) has examined this 'channel problem' and estimated that the multiplier k is roughly proportional to the total amount X_{cat} of all indemnities caused to all insurers by this one occurrence. On the other hand, the d.f. of X_{cat} can be well approximated by the Pareto d.f. In this way it is possible to construct the necessary

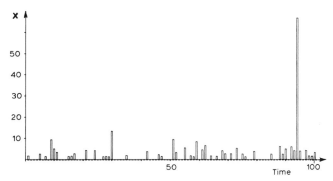

Figure 6.8.7 *Simulated supercatastrophes. Parameters derived by Rantala (1982) from data given by D. Landin. Total losses exceeding £15 million counted as catastrophes (wind storms). Average annual number of events n = 0.5, claim sizes Z according to Pareto d.f. with index 1.76. The insurer's liability calculated using the channel multiplier hypothesis.*

distributions and perform the straightforward simulation (for details see Rantala, 1982, Chapter 5). The configurations achieved seem to fit with the actual experience for example the data published by McGuinness (1966).

For evaluation of the flow of the total claims expenditure, comprised of 'normal' and catastrophic claims, it may be advisable to perform the simulation using the two approaches described in parallel. The normal claims are simulated by means of the random number generator described in Section 6.8.3, and the supercatastrophes are simulated simultaneously by the direct method considered in Section 6.8.2 and modified by the channel risk. Finally the annual simulated outcomes of both approaches are summed up. Figure 6.8.8 gives an example of how a 'normal' risk process like that given in Fig. 6.8.4 is changed when the risk of catastrophic claims is incorporated into the model.

(g) Benefits and disadvantages of simulation The Monte Carlo method is overall a very powerful tool; it can be applied to rather complicated models because of the algorithm technique which proceeds step by step from time t to time $t + 1$. The transition rules can then be chosen in flexible ways and the assumptions concerning trends, cycles, inflation, short-term oscillation, claim size d.f., reinsurance etc. can be fitted to the actual environment without

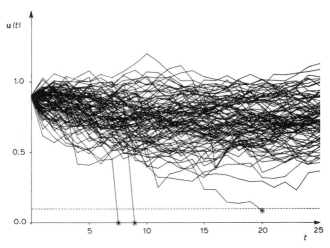

Figure 6.8.8 *Simulation of risk business exposed by the risk of supercatastrophes. Otherwise the same process as in Fig. 6.8.4.*

too urgent a need to simplify, approximate or smooth them in some analytical or other manner convenient for calculations, which is a major drawback of the most direct methods.

The main disadvantage of simulation is that it gives only samples as outcome, and is thus always involved with sample inaccuracy which may make it necessary to increase the sample size so much that the method becomes costly or even intractable. However, it can provide a satisfactory insight into the stochastic bundle and thus quite a good impression of the structure of the process with moderate sample sizes, as was discussed in item 6.8.1(d).

Anyway, if direct analytic treatment is applicable it generally is more expedient, and the role of simulation is above all to deal with cases where other techniques are impracticable.

6.9 Limits for the finite time ruin probability Ψ_T

(a) Heuristic observations as guidance The simulation pictures of the previous section, e.g. Figs 6.8.4 and 6.8.5, assume that the ruin probability related to the process depends on how far the stochastic bundle is located from the ruin barrier. To make the shape of the bundle clearer its confidence boundaries were plotted. The upper and lower limits were both determined so that on average at each time only 1/100 of the sample paths fell outside the confined area. The *NP* formula was used with the mean values, standard deviations and skewness derived in Section 6.6. If the bundle intersects the ruin barrier, it is clearly an indication of significant risk of ruin and the risk is the greater the longer and deeper the lower limit runs in the risky area. This heuristic observation can be used as guidance for finding exactly defined upper and lower limits for the ruin probability.

(b) Simple limits The ruin state probabilities

$$\varphi(t) = \text{prob}\{U(t) < U_r(t)\}, \tag{6.9.1}$$

considered in item 6.6(g) are now utilized. In this and in the next item no restrictive assumptions such as those made in Section 6.6 are needed. Hence also elements other than claims can be stochastic and the values related to the consecutive years need not be independent.

Now let A_t be the set of all the sample paths of the process under consideration which are in state of ruin at t. Then

$$\text{prob}(A_t) \leq \text{prob}\left(\bigcup_{t=1}^{T} A_t\right) \leq \sum_{t=1}^{T} \text{prob}(A_t). \tag{6.9.2}$$

The middle term, the union of the sets A_t, is the set of all the sample paths which are at one or more times in a state of ruin. Since it is just the finite time ruin probability required, the limit inequalities

$$\max_{1 \leq t \leq T} \varphi(t) \leq \Psi_T \leq \sum_{t=1}^{T} \varphi(t), \tag{6.9.3}$$

are obtained.

The upper limit deduced can be illustrated by means of Fig. 6.7.3, writing

$$\Psi_T = \sum_{t=1}^{T} \Delta\Psi_T. \tag{6.9.4}$$

The area C in the figure is equal to $\Delta\Psi_t = \Psi_t - \Psi_{t-1}$, which is always a part of the area $C + D = \varphi(t)$; from this (6.9.3) follows.

(c) Improved limits The above limits can be still further improved in a simple way. For this purpose, note that the sample paths which are in a state of ruin in more than one year are counted several times in the upper limit. An exact value for ruin probability could be found if each sample path, being ruined one or more times, could be counted only once. This is, however, difficult to achieve without unreasonable complications, but it is fairly easy to remove from each term $\varphi(t)$ the counting of those paths which were in state of ruin already at the previous time $t - 1$. To show this we will introduce an auxiliary quantity, the probability $\varphi(t - 1, t)$ that a sample path is in state of ruin at both $t - 1$ and t. Its evaluation will be dealt with in item (e). Providing it is obtainable, a corrected probability

$$\varphi_c(t) = \varphi(t) - \varphi(t - 1, t) \qquad (\varphi_c(1) = \varphi(1)) \qquad (6.9.5)$$

can be introduced, giving the probability that the sample path is in a state of ruin at time t but was not at $t - 1$.

By similar reasoning, the inequalities (6.9.3) can now be replaced by the following inequalities

$$\max_{2 \leqslant t \leqslant T} \left[\varphi(t - 1) + \varphi_c(t) \right] \leqslant \Psi_T \leqslant \sum_{t = 1}^{T} \varphi_c(t). \qquad (6.9.6)$$

These inequalities have proved to be very useful owing to the experience that the upper limit and the lower limit are generally quite close to each other; this makes it possible to use the upper limit as a safe approximation for the finite time ruin probability Ψ_T, as will be discussed in item (f) and as is illustrated in the next chapter.

**(d) A further improvement The limit (6.9.6) is still somewhat rough since the sample paths which indicate ruin before time $t - 1$ but subsequent recovery are unnecessarily counted for $\varphi_c(t)$. This bias can be somewhat reduced if auxiliary assumptions are made on the process concerned. They can be of the type which make sure that $\text{prob}\{U(t) < U_r(t) \,|\, U(t_1) = U_1\}$, where $t_1 < t$, should be a non-increasing function of U_1. This means that the better the state of a sample path is at time t_1 the better is the chance that it is not in a state of ruin at any later time t. Intuitively, it seems natural to assume that risk processes in practical applications are normally of this type. Instead of attempting to construct a strict theory, the idea is described heuristically by making use of Fig. 6.7.3.

The aim is to replace $\varphi_c(t)$ by

$$\varphi_{cc}(t) = \frac{1 - \Psi_{t-1}}{1 - \varphi(t-1)} \times \varphi_c(t). \qquad (6.9.7)$$

in the upper limit of (6.9.6). As seen from (6.9.4) $\varphi_c(t)$ is, in fact, aimed to approximate $\Delta \Psi_t$ and it should be replaced by another expression which is more closely related to $\Delta \Psi_t$. Now $\Delta \Psi_t$ represents all those sample paths which are first time ruined at t. Hence they emanate from the set of paths which are not ruined during the first $t - 1$ years. They are presented by the area $A_{t-1} = 1 - \Psi_{t-1}$ (Fig. 6.7.3 applied for the year $t - 1$). The paths which were counted above for $\varphi_c(t)$ emanate from the whole set of sample paths which are not in a state of ruin at $t - 1$, the corresponding probability being $1 - \varphi(t-1) = $ area $A_{t-1} + B_{t-1}$. Evidently $\Delta \Psi_t / \varphi_c(t)$ is smaller than the ratio of the probabilities of the parent sets $(1 - \Psi_{t-1})/(1 - \varphi(t-1)) = A_{t-1}/(A_{t-1} + B_{t-1})$. This follows from the fact that those paths which are already ruined before $t - 1$ are, according to our auxiliary assumption, on average in a worse solvency situation than those paths never ruined, and the former ones are therefore more likely to fall into a state of ruin at t. Hence, introducing the notation (6.9.7), we have $\Delta \Psi_t \leqslant \varphi_{cc}(t)$ which justifies

$$\Psi_T \leqslant \sum_{t=1}^{T} \varphi_{cc}(t). \qquad (6.9.8)$$

For computations Ψ_{t-1} is to be replaced in (6.9.6) by its estimate $\sum_{\tau=1}^{t-1} \varphi_{cc}(\tau)$. Without further analysis it cannot be concluded whether this 'improved upper limit' really is an upper limit any longer because $\varphi_{cc}(t-1)$ decreased in this replacement. However, it can be expected that it is an improved estimate for Ψ_t because the errors in Ψ_{t-1} and in $\Delta \Psi_t$ have the opposite signs, and so the latter corrects the accumulating bias in the former.

Clearly the improved formula (6.9.7) can render a marked improvement in (6.9.6) only when Ψ_T is not very small. In extreme cases where the upper limit of (6.9.6) may exceed 1 the improved formula may still give meaningful values.

The upper limits of the inequalities given can be used for calculation of the finite time ruin probability, particularly when a safe approximation is appropriate:

$$\Psi_T \approx \sum_{t=1}^{T} \varphi_{cc}(t).$$

(e) An integral expression for $\varphi(t-1, t)$ can be derived as a straight-forward application of the d.f. (6.6.17a) of the risk reserve

$$\varphi(t-1, t) = \int_{-\infty}^{u_r(t-1)} G(u, u_r(t); t-1, t)\mathrm{d}_u\, G(u_0, u; 1, t-1),$$

(6.9.9)

where $u_r(t) = U_r(t)/B(t)$ is again the (relative) ruin barrier. The differential term gives the probability that a sample path at $t-1$ is going through the infinitesimal interval $(u, u + \mathrm{d}u]$, and the integrand term gives the conditional probability that it is still under the ruin barrier $u_r(t)$ at time t.

The numerical calculation can be made, for example, by virtue of Simpson's rule substituting the G function by the NP (or gamma) approximations (see items 6.6(f) and (g)). Formulae for the derivative were given in item 3.11(j).

For readers' convenience the formulae needed for calculation of the limits derived are recorded in Appendix D in a form which is readily programmable.

(f) Examples of the limits (6.9.3), (6.9.6) and (6.9.7) are given in Table 6.9.1 for a process illustrated in Fig. 6.9.1.

As the example illustrates the effectiveness of the limit formula, i.e. the closeness of the limits, depended on the fact that the test processes were of a type which dipped down only for a couple of

Table 6.9.1 *Probabilities related to the example given in Fig. 6.9.1* Ψ_{lower} *and* Ψ_{upper} *are the limits for* Ψ_t *as given in the formulae specified in the table.*

	$\varphi(t)$	$\varphi(t-1,t)$	Ψ_{lower}	Ψ_{upper}		
t	(6.9.1)	(6.9.9)	(6.9.6)	(6.9.3)	(6.9.6)	(6.9.8)
1	0.000000	0.000000	0.000000	0.000000	0.000000	0.000000
2	0.000000	0.000000	0.000000	0.000000	0.000000	0.000000
3	0.000007	0.000000	0.000007	0.000007	0.000007	0.000007
4	0.000493	0.000005	0.000495	0.000501	0.000495	0.000495
5	0.003437	0.000390	0.003540	0.003937	0.003542	0.003542
6	0.005709	0.002138	0.007008	0.009646	0.007113	0.007112
7	0.003329	0.002220	0.007008	0.012976	0.008222	0.008220
8	0.000840	0.000700	0.007008	0.013816	0.008363	0.008360
9	0.000124	0.000109	0.007008	0.013940	0.008378	0.008376
10	0.000019	0.000014	0.007008	0.013958	0.008383	0.008380

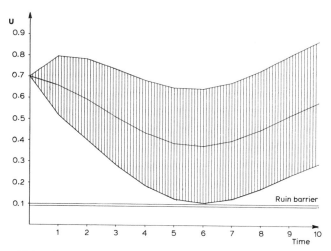

Figure 6.9.1 *An example of the application of the limit formulae.* $\varphi(t)$ *values calculated by the NP method are given in Table 6.9.1. Standard data given in item 7.1(d) except for* $u(0) = 0.7$ *and the amplitude of sinusoidal cycles* $z_m = 0.05$.

years and then recovered. Hence only very few years during the time span were critical in this example. The same is the case in examples given in the figures of Section 6.8. If, on the other hand, the process is of such a type that the lower confidence boundary of the bundle is directed for a long time parallel with the ruin barrier, then the limits may be expected to be more distant from each other. In any case, it is advisable to calculate both the upper and the lower limit to gauge the accuracy of the approximation when the upper limit is used as an estimate for Ψ_T.

A major benefit of the limit formulae is the relative simplicity of the computations compared with other known techniques, and the ability to control the accuracy.

(g) Calculation of the initial minimum solvency ratio The 'finite time' ruin probability derived depends on numerous background variables, parameters and distributions, which will be specified in item 7.1(a). The equation

$$\Psi_T(u) = \varepsilon, \qquad (6.9.10)$$

is mostly employed in the reverse direction in applications, i.e. the ruin probability ε as well as other variables and parameters is

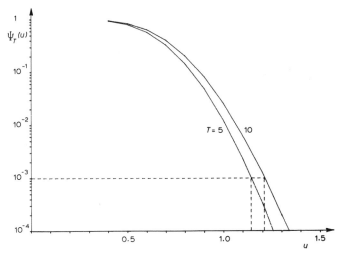

Figure 6.9.2   *The ruin probability* $\Psi_T(u)$ *as a function of u applying the limit* (6.9.8) *for* $T = 5$ *or* 10. *Finding of u when* Ψ_T *is given. Data according to standards given in item* 7.1(d).

given and the initial minimum solvency ratio $u(0)$ (or briefly u) or the corresponding initial risk reserve (solvency margin) $U = uB$ is requested. For the purpose Ψ_T is first calculated as a function of u (Fig. 6.9.2). Then the u values corresponding to any given ε can be read from the figure.

It is convenient to program the computer to seek the required value $u = u_\varepsilon$ directly as a continuation of the calculations producing Ψ_T so that no graphical or other separate determination of u is needed. This approach is precisely what is mostly needed for various applications.

Note that the approximate formulae (6.9.6) or (6.9.8) give still better accuracy than quoted in item (f) when they are used for the calculation of u. This is due to the fact that the curve Ψ_T as a function u is quite steep for larger u values (note the half-logarithmic scale in Fig. 6.9.2), hence inaccuracies in Ψ_T values do not affect u values considerably.

For comparison of the limit formulae and the Monte Carlo method some examples are calculated using both (Table 6.9.2). Generally the direct evaluation dealt with in this section is far more expedient in cases where it is applicable. The benefit of the simulation approach is that it can be employed in very complex models, e.g. when stochastic and dynamic control rules are assumed.

Table 6.9.2 *Examples of the finite time ruin probabilities Ψ_T calculated using the limit formulae and by the Monte Carlo method, $T = 10$ years, ruin barrier = $0.1B$ (Rantala, 1982, pp. 3.1–5).*

u	Limits (6.9.3)	Limits (6.9.6)	Ruins per 1000 simu- lations	Corresponding 95% confidence interval for simulated Ψ_T
0.3	0.79–3.6	0.83–0.88	0.858	0.84–0.88
0.4	0.60–2.3	0.65–0.70	0.644	0.61–0.67
0.5	0.39–1.3	0.42–0.47	0.475	0.44–0.51
0.6	0.21–0.60	0.24–0.26	0.230	0.20–0.26
0.7	0.091–0.24	0.11–0.12	0.107	0.087–0.13
0.8	0.032–0.081	0.042–0.045	0.034	0.023–0.045
0.9	0.0093–0.023	0.015–0.018	0.011	0.0044–0.018
1.0	0.0024–0.0055	0.0040–0.0046	0.001	0.000–0.0030

Exercise 6.9.1. Prove (6.9.6).

CHAPTER 7

Applications related to finite time-span T

7.1 General features of finite time risk processes

(a) Basic variables Many of the considerations presented in Chapter 4 for a one-year time-span can be extended to arbitrary long-time periods, and in addition numerous other applications can now be treated.

The one-year model was characterized by the seven basic variables or parameters listed in (4.1.9). For the finite time version a number of new variables were introduced in Chapter 6; they are as follows (see the notation list or the list in item (d) below).

$$U(\text{or } u), n, \lambda, M, \sigma_{\mathbf{q}}, \gamma_{\mathbf{q}}, z_{\mathrm{m}}, T_z, i_{\mathrm{i}}, i_x, i_{\mathrm{p}}, i_{\mathrm{g}}, t_{\mathrm{p}}, \varepsilon, T. \qquad (7.1.1)$$

Here U is the initial risk reserve and $u = U/B$ the initial solvency ratio (which should be denoted by $u(0)$ if any risk of confusion with the current solvency ratio $u(t)$ exists). In addition the claim size d.f. S underlies all the calculations and the portfolio may be divided in sections $j = 1, 2, \dots, J$. If the time unit is taken as other than one year the parameters must be adjusted accordingly.

In the one year case it was possible to express the interdependence of the basic variables in the form of the fairly simple 'basic equation' (4.1.7), this being applicable except for environments involving very small portfolios. The finite time model is so much more complicated that it seems to be difficult to find any correspondingly simple equation, except for some special problems treated in Section 7.9. Thus numerical computation methods have to be used either by direct analytic calculation or by simulation. The former shall be used, mainly replacing the ruin probability by its upper limit as presented in Section 6.9.

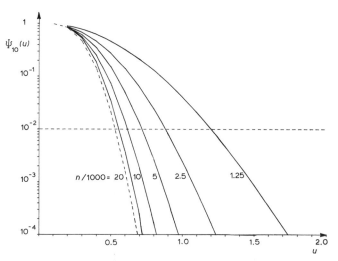

Figure 7.1.1 *The ten year ruin probability as a function of the expected number of claims n and the initial solvency ratio u. Other variables have the standard values given in item (d). The dotted line was obtained by shortening the time-span from* 10 *to* 5 *years in the case* $n = 20\,000$. *Explanation for the slight deviation of* Ψ_5 *from* Ψ_{10} *can be found in the analysis in Section* 7.5.

(b) Types of applications As in Chapter 4, many of the applications of the model are of such a type that some of the variables are calculated as functions of the others. Fig. 7.1.1 gives an example, the ruin probability being calculated by means of the technique presented in Section 6.9 and being plotted letting n and u vary and keeping the other variables fixed.

A more useful approach is often to fix the ruin probability ε to some suitable level, say 0.01 or 0.001, and then to study the relations of the remaining factors either as functions of each other or by introducing some additional conditions, e.g. optimizing profits, volumes, utilities or other outcomes.

(c) Selection of the basic data A number of applications of the finite time technique will be given in this chapter. They are intended to demonstrate the calculation technique. In order to make the sequence of the applications, as far as possible, consequent and mutually comparable the same standard values for the variables (7.1.1) shall be used. They are listed in the next item and follow mainly the material derived in the comprehensive research work (Pentikäinen, 1982 and Rantala, 1982) concerning Finnish non-life insurance. It must be appreciated that the examples given do not claim to give any universally valid conception of the actual risk processes, even if the source data were derived from actual insurance statistics. The environmental conditions and business strategies may be so very different in different countries and different companies that it is completely beyond the scope of this book to try to monitor the great variety of risk processes and their applications appearing in real life, even though the general patterns can be expected to be similar. The purpose of the presentation is essentially to devise tools which can be used for examination of the processes.

(d) Standard data The great number of the variables and parameters involved in the model makes it very difficult to get any insight into the structure of the system and into the interdependence of the variables and background assumptions. One way to get round this difficulty is first to fix average values for the parameters and variables and then to calculate the required analyses for this set of basic values. In other words, a special '*standard insurer*' will be first constructed and examined. Then one or more variables in turn are changed and the resulting reactions calculated. In this way it is possible to get insight into the multidimensional structure of the model. This idea is illustrated in the profile in Section 7.8.

The standard data are as follows:

$n = 10\,000$, the expected average number of claims; see (6.1.9)

$\lambda_p = -0.086$, the premium related safety loading which provides the value 1.71 for the coefficient w, see item 6.5 (h)

$\lambda = 0.040$, the total safety loading; see item 6.5(h)

$M = £10^6$, the maximum net retention; see Section 3.6 and Table 3.6.1

$c = 0.28$, the loading for expenses; see (6.2.8)

$\sigma_q = 0.038$, the standard deviation of the structure variable $\mathbf{q}$; see (2.8.5)

$\gamma_q = 0.25$, the skewness of the structure variable $\mathbf{q}$; see (2.8.5)

$T = 10$, the time-span of the finite time ruin probability

$\varepsilon = 0.01$ ($= \Psi_{10}$), the ruin probability; see (6.7.1)

$i_x = 0.09$, the constant or the average rate of the claims inflation; see item 6.1 (j)

$i_p = 0.09$, the constant or the average rate of the premium inflation; see item 6.2(a)

$t_p = 2$, the time lag between the claims inflation and the premium inflation; see (6.2.2)

$i_g = 0.061$, the rate of the real growth of the premium volume; see item 6.1(c)

$i_i = 0.085$, the rate of the yield of investments; see item 6.3(a)

$z_m = 0.15$, the amplitude of the assumed cycles according to (6.1.3); if the synchronism with the economic cycles is provided as will be presented in item 7.6(d) applying $c_i = 0.5$ in (7.6.2), then z_m is 0.1

$T_z = 12$, the length of cycles; see (6.1.4).

The claim size d.f. is the one given in Table 3.6.1 providing excess of loss reinsurance and the maximum net retention $M = £10^6$. As seen from Table 3.6.1, line 26, the mean claim size is £7302 and the risk indexes $r_2 = 44.1$ and $r_3 = 4465$. In those applications which are directly borrowed from the Finnish research works already mentioned, the d.f. of industrial fire and loss of profit insurance was used (Rantala, 1982, Appendix 1). For moderate retentions the results calculated by either of these d.f. do not deviate notably.

It follows from the above data that:

$B = £90.6 \times 10^6$, the amount of earned premiums net of reinsurance; see (6.2.11);

$r_{igp} = 0.938$, the dynamic accumulation factor; see (6.5.8).

(e) Four types of processes Before going on to detailed consideration of various applications it is useful to characterize some main types of processes. A number of examples of risk processes have already been given in Chapter 6. These showed that the nature of the process is very much dependent on two basic assumptions, namely the dynamic 'discounting factor' r_{igp}, giving the joint effect of interest, growth and inflation (see (6.5.8)), and cyclic behaviour. If $r_{igp} < 1$ then, as stated in item 6.6(c), the process has a finite equilibrium level (6.6.9). If $r_{igp} > 1$, then the stochastic bundle drifts to infinity (if no special control rules are assumed; see item 7.7(f)). An example of the former case is depicted in Fig. 7.1.2(b) and an

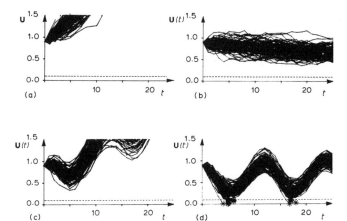

Figure 7.1.2   *The main types of risk processes generated by means of algorithm* (6.5.13) (a) $r_{igp} = 1.027$, *no cycles;* (b) $r_{igp} = 0.938$, *no cycles;* (c) $r_{igp} = 1.027$, *cycles;* (d) $r_{igp} = 0.938$, *cycles.*

example of the latter type in Fig. 7.1.2(a). The algorithm (6.5.15) is the basis of these and the subsequent simulations. It is noteworthy that the breadth of the stochastic bundle of the solvency ratio $u(t)$ (calculated by some given confidence level) in the former case is asymptotically finite but in the latter case tends to infinity. This can be easily verified from (6.6.12).

Illustrations of the effects of the assumption concerning cycles are provided in diagrams (c) and (d) of Fig. 7.1.2 but not in diagrams (a) and (b).

Figure 7.1.2 shows how crucial are the assumptions concerning inflation and cycles. Clearly those processes where both are present may correspond best to practical circumstances. Figure 7.1.2(d) is of this type, even though the assumption concerning cycles was idealized by means of the deterministic sinusoidal formula (6.1.3). The assumption concerning the strictly deterministic form of the cycles can, of course, be relaxed either by taking the phase of the cycle stochastic (Fig. 6.8.6) or by making use of an autocorrelated time series. An example of the latter approach will be given in Section 7.7.

In order to prevent the text from growing too much, the case $r_{igp} < 1$ will be mainly considered in what follows. The proposed technique, however, is applicable also for processes of type $r_{igp} > 1$, as will be shown in items 7.7(f) and 7.10(c).

7.2 The size of the portfolio

(a) Effect of company size As a first example of the use of the technique derived in Chapter 6 the minimum initial solvency ratio $u = u(0)$ is examined as a function of the size of the company in Fig. 7.2.1. The other parameters were kept constant and equal to the standard values listed in item 7.1(d).

In order to get a link with the insurer's records the earned gross premium income B on the insurer's own retention will be used as one of the basic variables instead of the risk premiums P or P_λ (see item 6.2(f)). As an indicator of the financial state of the insurer the risk reserve (solvency margin) U or mostly its relative value, the solvency ratio $u = U/B$ is used and investigated keeping the ruin probability fixed. The reserve $U(= U(0))$ means the smallest initial capital which satisfies the condition

$$\Psi_T(U) \leqslant \varepsilon. \qquad (7.2.1)$$

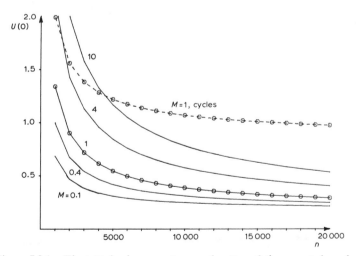

Figure 7.2.1 *The initial solvency ratio as a function of the expected number of claims n and the maximum net retention M given in £ million. Other data as standards in 7.1(d). The dotted curve with circles: cycles assumed, for other cases not.*

Figure 7.2.1 exhibits *u* as a function of the size variable *n* and the maximum net retention *M*. As expected the required initial solvency ratio is higher for small than for large companies because the risk fluctuation is smoothed relatively better in large than in small collectives. Long time cycles were not assumed except in the case $M = 1$ (curves with circles), which was calculated both assuming (dotted line) and not assuming the cycles, in order to demonstrate the effect of this particular assumption.

(b) Joint effect of size and retention In practice larger companies usually apply higher net retentions than smaller ones, because the internal equalization of the claims fluctuation improves the larger the risk collective is. This feature, which is commonly experienced, was clearly seen in the one-year considerations in Section 4.4. It is again confirmed by Fig. 7.2.1. If the solvency ratio $u(0)$ is fixed, the allowed net retention *M* should be considerably smaller for small companies (*n* small) than for large ones. Further examples of the effect of the combinations of the size variable *n* and retention *M* will be given in the form of a profile figure 7.8.2.

(c) Simulation The size of the company can be also examined by means of Monte Carlo simulation. An example is plotted in Fig. 7.2.2 where all data, the retention *M* included, were assumed to be equal to the standards of item 7.1(d) with the exception of the size variable *n*. The stochastic bundle of the smaller company is essentially broader than that of the larger one.

Note that the magnitude of the initial solvency ratio $u(0)$ in these examples as well as in the cases treated later in this chapter is essentially larger than current statutory demands, many standards which are often suggested and the amounts derived in Section 4.4.

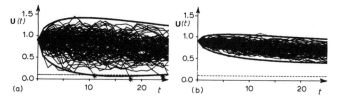

Figure 7.2.2   *A stochastic bundle of (a) a small company (n = 2000) and of (b) a large one (n = 20 000).*

This divergence arises from the long time-span ($T = 10$) and as seen in Fig. 7.21 from the cycles now assumed.

7.3 Evaluation of net retention *M*

As a next example on the application of the finite time technique the net retention *M* is examined as a function of the initial solvency ratio *u* and the expected number of claims *n* in Fig. 7.3.1.

This figure corresponds to Fig. 4.2.4 which was constructed for a one-year time-span; however, the initial solvency ratio $u = U/B$ is now taken as the argument instead of *U*. A striking feature in Fig. 7.3.1 is that *M* curves are located to the right (fairly high values of *u*) for small *M* values. This is due to the fact that the long-term cycles have a dominant effect on the ruin probabilities when the time-span is long, and the conventional reinsurance forms, surplus and excess of loss treaties do not give protection against temporary increases in the number of claims. Such increases are caused by the assumed cycles and the short-term structure variation.

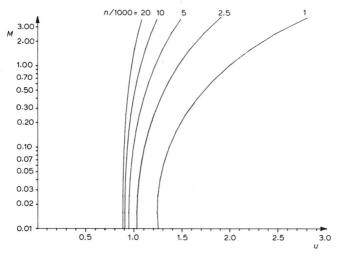

Figure 7.3.1   *The net retention M in £ million as a function of the initial solvency ratio u and the expected number of claims n. Standard data of item 7.1(d), excess of loss reinsurance.*

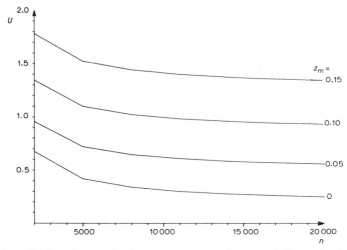

Figure 7.4.1 *The initial solvency ratio u as a function of the amplitude z_m of the cycle waves and the volume parameter n. The values of u are calculated for intervals of length 3000 of n. M = £400 000. Default data according to standards given in item 7.1(d).*

7.4 Effect of cycles

The effect of the cycles which were introduced by the sine formula (6.1.3) has already been demonstrated in Figs 6.8.5 and 6.8.6. The same effect can also be examined by means of the analytical method described in item 6.9(g). Examples are shown in Fig. 7.4.1.

The very significant effect of the cycles is again revealed. The results depend among other things on the length of the cycle, which was chosen to be as long as 12 years according to standards in item 7.1(d). If the cycle length were 6 years, then e.g. u for $n = 11\,000$, $z_m = 0.1$ would drop from the value 0.99 exhibited in the figure to 0.60.

7.5 Effect of the time-span T

The effect of the planning horizon, i.e. the time-span T, is examined in Fig. 7.5.1. It was allowed to grow from 1 to 25. The ruin probability is, of course, an increasing function of T. Here again the effect of the growth factor r_{igp} and the cycles is seen. If the factor is greater than 1, then the process is of the type which is seen in Fig. 7.1.2(a) and (c).

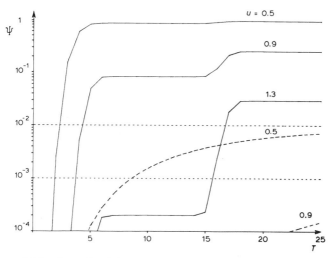

Figure 7.5.1 *Example of the effect of the time span T. Solid lines: processes involved with cycles of type (d) in Fig. 7.1.2. Dotted lines: no cycles, types (a) or (b) in Fig. 7.1.2.*

Then clearly the first few years are critical from the point of view of the solvency effects. When they have passed, the stochastic bundle is soaring high enough that extension of the period T no longer has any noticeable influence on the probability of ruin and hence on the solvency ratio u. The situation is quite different if the growth factor r_{igp} is less than 1. This is seen e.g. in Fig. 7.1.2(d), where also cycles are assumed. Then the stochastic bundle dives down periodically to the critical area. These periods are reflected as upward jumps in the curves of Fig. 7.5.1, which coincide with the beginning of the adverse halves of the cycles.

7.6 Effect of inflation

(a) Two kinds of inflation The technique developed in the previous section can also be used for examination of the effect of inflation on the risk process. It is appropriate first to study steady inflation, keeping the rate $i_x = i_p$ (see item 6.1(j)) constant from year to year and then varying inflation from year to year.

(b) A steady inflation is continually shrinking the already existing solvency margin; this effect was conveniently introduced to the

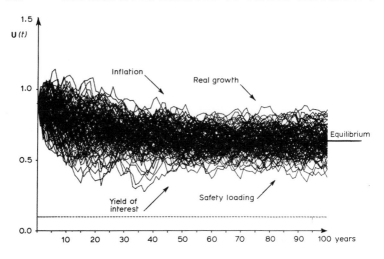

Figure 7.6.1 *Solvency process in the presence of four forces.*

model by means of the factor r_{igp} (6.5.8b). If the nominal growth of the business volume owing to inflation and real growth exceeds the rate of interest then, as stated in item 6.6(c), the stochastic bundle asymptotically tends to a horizontal equilibrium level. If cycles are present, then the bundle fluctuates around this level as exhibited in Fig. 6.6.1. There are in fact four principal forces affecting the asymptotic level of the stochastic bundle as well as its breadth. They are presented in Fig. 7.6.1. The equilibrium level was given by (6.6.9) and an evaluation for the breadth by (6.6.12).

In order to show clearly the asymptotic behaviour, the simulation was extended to 100 years.

(c) Varying inflation has effects which are very different from those of steady inflation. The claims expenditure can be assumed (see items 6.1(j) and 6.2(a)) to be affected nearly immediately, but it is likely that the premium rates are corrected after some time lag t_p. During this time lag a loss occurs which may be compensated later when the adjustment of rates has become effective. The claim inflation and the premium inflation were distinguished in item 6.2(a) for the study of this effect. Let us recall the connecting equation (6.2.2):

$$r_p(t) = r_x(t - t_p). \tag{7.6.1}$$

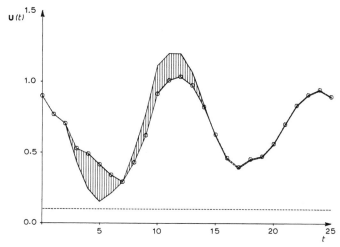

Figure 7.6.2 *Solid line with circles: only a steady inflation rate of* 9% *per annum was assumed. The other line: a shock inflation rate of* 20% *per annum was effective in years* 3 *and* 4. *The shaded area marks the difference between the original and changed flows.*

Furthermore, a special time lag function $D(t)$ was introduced by (6.6.7). The time lag t_p is one of the important control parameters of the model.

First it will be assumed that the inflation has some steady 'normal' level; in the example presented in Fig. 7.6.2 this is $i_x = 0.09$. Then it is allowed to jump up to a higher level (in the example $i_x = 0.2$) for two years, after which it drops down to the original level. In Fig. 7.6.2 first one sample path was generated for the steady inflation and then another for this 'shock inflation'. The figure demonstrates the use of the simulation model as a *sensitivity analyser*. The same random numbers were used for both sample paths. Hence the difference in the flow of the process was caused solely by the changed inflation assumption.

The introduction of a shock inflation into the model produces drastic effects, as can be seen. Owing to the assumed time lag $t_p = 2$ years, the loss accumulates first in two consecutive years until the change in premium rates becomes effective. Furthermore, the inflation shock affects the solvency ratio also via the factor r_{igp} of (6.5.13). Owing to the various model assumptions, above all the factor r_{igp}, the two curves of Fig. 7.6.2 do not coincide completely even in the long run. In fact, the correction of rates according to (7.6.1) overcompensates the losses.

In the example the inflation shock caused an extra loss of some 20% of the premium income and is consequently one of the factors to be taken into account when the dimensioning of solvency margins is deliberated.

(d) Correlation with economic cycles A question of importance is whether or not the inflation variations are *correlated with the general economic booms and recessions*, which is one of the main reasons for the cycles of the claim frequencies. Some past experience has been that a boom also gives rise to increased inflation and a recession to low inflation. This is quite natural because during the boom the demand for commodities is high. This increases the demand of manpower which can cause pressure for increased wages and salaries, and hence in turn people have more money available to buy commodities. All these features are apt to provoke inflation. Tendencies are reversed during a recession. If, as this experience suggested, booms and recessions are synchronized with inflation, then these factors reinforce each other in a way which is significant for solvency considerations. In the figures, which will be given as examples in the following, this kind of correlation was assumed. The experimental formula

$$i_x(t) = \max(i_x + c_i z(t), \tfrac{1}{2}i_x), \qquad (7.6.2)$$

was introduced, where $z(t)$ is the cyclic variable determined as presented in items 6.1(d)–(f). The auxiliary condition $i_x(t) \geqslant i_x/2$ can be justified by the experience that the rate of inflation may not totally disappear even in a period of recession. c_i is another model parameter, subject to free selection.

It must be appreciated, however, that the correlation between inflation and the economic climate of the national economy mentioned above has been considerably disturbed in recent years following the well-known 'oil crisis'. In contradiction to the old rules recession and high inflation have appeared simultaneously in some countries; this is so-called 'stagflation'. Because the purpose of this book is only to present risk-theoretical techniques, further discussion of national economic phenomena is beyond the scope of this book. The models obviously must be capable of working with any assumption according to the choice and judgement of the user. It is, of course, often advisable to experiment with different assumptions in the evaluation of the numerous background features, and to alter among other things the level and character of inflation.

(e) **Effect of the length of the time lag** t_p was studied assigning to it values 0, 1 and 2 years respectively; a sample path was driven for the each of them, keeping the sequence of random numbers the same (Fig. 7.6.3). The change of inflation was now programmed according to (7.6.2) with $c_i = 0.5$.

As expected, the time lag gives rise to considerable loss when inflation is in its increasing phase in this case also. The loss is compensated during the decreasing phase. The assumed synchronism enlarges the amplitude of the cycles, as concluded easily from (7.6.2) and as seen in Fig. 7.6.3. In effect, about the same outcome as given by the synchronization (7.6.2) can be achieved by taking $c_i = 0$ and by making the amplitude z_m larger, which procedure somewhat simplifies the considerations. This was given as another alternative for z_m in the standard list of item 7.1(d). More details on this relationship can be found in Pentikäinen (1982, item 4.2.6.4).

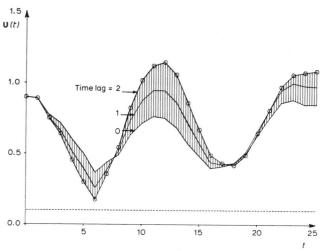

Figure 7.6.3 *A sample path driven for three inflation time lags. The rates of inflation were synchronized according to (7.6.1) and (7.6.2).*

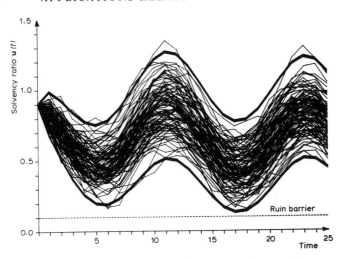

Figure 7.6.4   *For examination of the effect of the time lag t_p it is here removed from the process that was exhibited in Fig. 6.8.5; otherwise the two processes are the same.*

The effect of the time lag is examined also by simulating the stochastic bundles, first assuming the time lag and then omitting it. The former case has already been given in Fig. 6.8.5, where $t_p = 2$ years. The latter is depicted in Fig. 7.6.4. As expected, the waves of the stochastic bundle were clearly smoothed. This is reflected also in the number of ruins, which was reduced from 18/100 to 0/100.

7.7   Dynamic control rules

(a) Market pressures and self-control It was stated conclusively in Section 2.7 that claim frequencies are subject to trends, periodic variations and 'pure' random fluctuation. The trends were incorporated into the model in item 6.1(c). The periodical variations were approximated by sinusoidal waves (6.1.3) in the previous sections. Furthermore it was stated in Section 6.2 that the biases and inaccuracies in premium rates are another source of variations in underwriting results. The third source of variation is the yield of interest, which was incorporated in the model, amalgamating it to the joint control coefficient r_{igp} together with inflation and growth in item 6.5(g). Ultimately the different effects are concentrated in the modified (total) safety loading λ as defined by (6.5.12).

The somewhat schematic assumptions accepted in the foregoing can now be improved, taking λ as a central control variable. In principle it is under the control of the insurer in premium rating. However, in practice this control may be hampered and delayed by competitive market pressures, by the uncertainty of the actual level of profitability and by the technique involved in the rate calculation and their implementation. If the rates are controlled by supervising authorities, still further delays and restrictions may arise.

The evidence of market pressures can be revealed when the business flow of all insurers operating in the same market is analysed. A quite clear synchronism of the profitability waves is frequently observed, resulting in waves also in joint statistics of the total amounts of claims and underwriting profits or losses (see Pentikäinen, 1982, Fig. 2.2.4). This is a general feature of the insurance market – as the markets of other industries – that tends to generate cyclic variation. If the profitability is good for a certain period, intensified competition is provoked, marketing costs increase and reductions in the rates are used as a competitive tool. As a consequence profitability is rapidly worsened and safety loadings, even if possibly still positive, are no longer adequate to provide increases in the solvency margin in keeping with the growing volume of business, the growth being caused by inflation and real growth together. Then solvency ratios $u(t) = U(t)/B(t)$ are generally decreasing, and this continues until eventually the presence of too many insurers becomes critical. Competitive pressures are then reduced and amendments of rates become inescapable, so giving rise to an upswing and to a new cycle wave.

(b) Dynamic control This reasoning suggests an extension of the model by rules which simulate the assumed behaviour of the market and insurers. This is done by letting the safety loading λ depend on the current level of the solvency ratio $\mathbf{u}(t)$.

An example of a rule realizing this idea is given in Fig. 7.7.1 and formulated as follows

$$\lambda(t) = \begin{cases} \lambda_0 - c_2(u(t - t_1) - R_2)^+ \\ \lambda_0 + c_1(R_1 - u(t - t_1))^+. \end{cases} \tag{7.7.1}$$

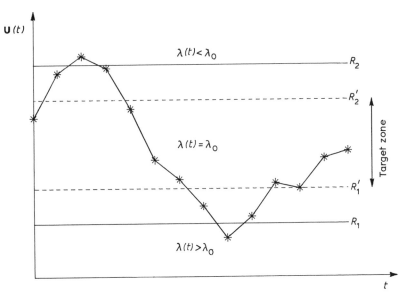

Figure 7.7.1   *Dynamics of the safety loading.*

If the solvency ratio $\mathbf{u}(t)$ exceeds a given limit R_2 then the safety loading is reduced after a time lag t_1. On the other hand, if $\mathbf{u}(t)$ drops below another limit R_1 then the safety loading is enhanced. Here λ_0 is a target value of the safety loading and c_1 and c_2 free parameters. The changed safety loading is valid either until (according to the rules (7.7.1)) another change is coming, the absolute value of which is larger than the previous one, or until the solvency ratio falls in the normal zone, defined by limits R_1', R_2'. In this zone the safety loading has the target value λ_0.

The rule described is an example of the so-called *dynamic* or adaptive processes. The process is made self-correcting by means of 'autoregressive' rules (7.7.1).

The rule suggested was made fairly simple because the aim is mainly to illustrate the control technique. The applied simulation procedure also allows, without serious complications, more sophisticated systems; e.g. the programmed changes in λ (and possibly in other control variables, too) may depend on the profits or losses of the previous accounting years or on some joint combination of the profitability and solvency position. For example, the works of

Frisque (1974), Pentikäinen (1978), Bohman (1979), Martin-Löf (1983) and Balzar and Benjamin (1980, 1982) can be referred to. Of course, the actual possibilities and ways of controlling the rates and other relevant factors should be considered when models are planned.

(c) Sensitivity tests Experiments to show the effect of the dynamic rule are illustrated in Figs 7.7.2 and 7.7.3, where first the lower control limit and then the upper one were introduced.

The limits of the normal zone were assumed to be

$$R'_1 = 0.7R_1 + 0.3R_2$$
$$R'_2 = 0.3R_1 + 0.7R_2. \tag{7.7.2}$$

(d) Simulation The effect of both rules is illustrated in Fig. 7.7.4. It exhibits the same process as Fig. 6.8.5, but the dynamic rules are now incorporated into the model, the limit values being as presented in the caption to the figure. The number of ruins is expectedly essentially reduced, being only 1 against 18 of the total number of 100 sample paths in Fig. 6.8.5. The effect of the dynamic control can also clearly be seen in the form of the stochastic bundle. In

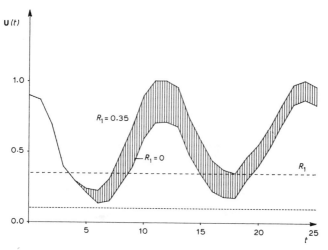

Figure 7.7.2   *Effect of the lower limit R_1 which is either 0.35 or 0. The coefficient $c_1 = 0.3$.*

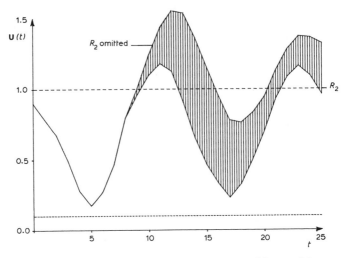

Figure 7.7.3   *Effect of the upper limit $R_2 = 1.0$; $c_2 = 0.3$.*

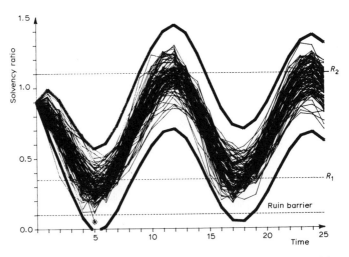

Figure 7.7.4   *A Dynamically controlled process; $R_1 = 0.35$, $R_2 = 1.1$, $c_1 = c_2 = 0.3$, $t_1 = 1$.*

Fig. 7.7.4 the bundle for larger t values is significantly narrower than the bundle in Fig. 6.8.5. The confidence boundaries were calculated disregarding the dynamics.

(e) Comparison of the deterministic and dynamic control In order to study the effect of the foregoing dynamics the deterministic cycles were relaxed (the cycle variable $z(t)$ was put $\equiv 0$) and the standard data was changed to make $r_{igp} > 1$. Figure 7.7.5 exhibits a case where one sample path was generated by providing the dynamics (7.7.1) and by omitting it. Furthermore, 100 samples of a similarly dynamically controlled process are generated in Fig. 7.7.6 to give an idea of the character of the process concerned. It is seen that the dynamic control of the safety loading results in a cyclic variation of the solvency ratio $\mathbf{u}(t)$, as has already been anticipated in item 6.2(e).

It can be expected that processes being mixtures of the above types, i.e. allowing outside impulses such as those caused by the cycles of the national economy, the profitability waves of the insurance market and the current status of the insurer concerned, may be best suited to describe the behaviour of the flow of the

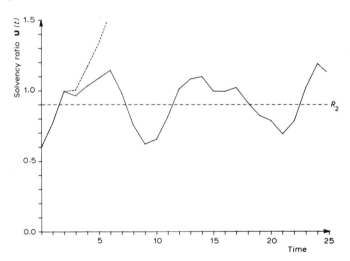

Figure 7.7.5 *A sample path generated by providing the dynamic control* (7.7.1) *(solid line) and by omitting it (dotted line).* $R_1 = 0.3$, $R_2 = 0.9$, $r_i = 1.1$, $r_x = 1.05$, $r_g = 1$, $z_m = 0$, $\lambda_p = -0.05$; *these parameter values result in* $r_{igp} = 1.048$ *and* $\lambda = 0.11$.

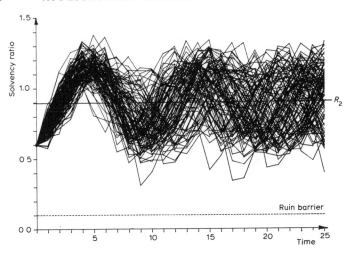

Figure 7.7.6   *A stochastic bundle exhibiting a similar process to Fig. 7.7.5.*

trading result and the solvency ratio. The simultaneous application of the approaches discussed offers frameworks for this. Figure
7.7.4 illustrates an example where both the (deterministic) cycles
of the basic probabilities and the cyclic control (7.7.1) are present.

(f) The case $r > 1$ In most of the foregoing examples the important
accumulation factor r_{igp} was < 1 according to the standard bases
given in item 7.1(d). In essence, the same simulation technique and
many of the straightforward calculations as employed earlier are
equally applicable for processes where $r_{igp} > 1$, i.e. in cases of low
inflation and low real growth of the portfolio. This is demonstrated
in Figs 7.7.5 and 7.7.6. As seen in Fig. 7.7.5, the uncontrolled flow
of $\mathbf{u}(t)$ tends to infinity (dotted line). This is, of course, an unrealistic
situation in view of the applications. Hence, additional assumptions
are unavoidable to make the model workable in those cases where
$r_{igp} > 1$. The rules (7.7.1) suggest an approach for the purpose. More
sophisticated models will be discussed in Chapter 10.

7.8   Solvency profile

(a) Purpose of profiles The structure of the model developed in
Chapter 6 was studied in the previous sections, selecting sets of two,

three or four variables in turn as moving variables and investigating their interdependences and tie-ins. Owing to the large number of variables, it is, however, difficult to get an idea of the model's structure *as a whole* in that way. Therefore an attempt is now made to find a general view about the properties of the model. For this purpose the minimum initial solvency ratio u will be calculated for numerous combinations of the model variables and then plotted as horizontal columns in one and the same graph. Thus it is possible to show in a single picture the sensitivity of the solvency to the different background factors. The idea is the same as in Fig. 4.2.7 where only the one-year time-span was considered.

(b) The influence of the basic assumptions of the model is illustrated in Fig. 7.8.1.

First only the number of claims is assumed to be a random variable; claim sizes and all other aspects are constant. As expected, the necessary minimum solvency ratio can be quite small – in this example, 8.5%.

The next step is to randomize also the claim size. After that the short-span variations of basic probabilities are introduced and then the long-term cycles. Finally inflation and all the other assumptions are introduced as standards in item 7.1(d). The 10-year ruin probability of 1% is assumed.

The figure again shows how significant is the assumption concerning

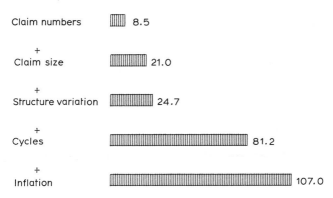

Figure 7.8.1 *The dependence of the minimum solvency ratio on the different basic assumptions.*

cycles. The rate of inflation also has a marked effect on the solvency condition.

(c) A comprehensive profile The sensitivity of the minimum initial solvency ratio $u(0)$ to numerous other background factors was tested by applying the same technique as above in Fig. 7.8.2. A number of values calculated for the standard insurer (as defined in item 7.1(d)) are exhibited. The text given in the figure details the entries concerned, so no further explanations are necessary.

Because our purpose is only to illustrate the technique of analysing and presenting the effects of various backgrounds, more details are not dealt with. They can be found in Pentikäinen (1982, Sections 4.2.15 and 4.2.2).

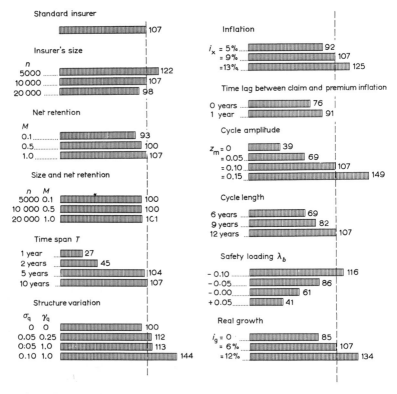

Figure 7.8.2 *Values of the minimum initial solvency ratio $u(0)$ for different parameter sets. $T = 10$ years. B and M given in £ million.*

7.9   Evaluation of the variation range of $u(t)$

(a) The problem setting It is useful to have at least an approximate idea of the dimensions of the fluctuations of the solvency ratio $\mathbf{u}(t)$. Every insurer must have the capacity and technique to meet fluctuations, i.e. some kind of buffer is needed in the form of hidden or book reserves or an opportunity to make use of flexibility in the valuation of the assets and liabilities. In some countries, e.g. in Finland, Germany and Sweden, this is taken into account in legal regulation in the form of a special fluctuation (equalization) provision or margin inside the technical underwriting reserves.

Two ways of setting the problem can be distinguished:

(i) The limits are to be found between which a stochastic bundle like that shown in Fig. 6.8.5 can be expected to be located. The range R_v in Fig. 7.9.1 illustrates the idea.
(ii) The maximum probable plunge during some period of length T will be taken as a measure for the solvency margin. The range R_s in Fig. 7.9.1 is an example.

Approach (i) is meaningful only when the stochastic bundle is limited from above, i.e. is not tending towards infinity. This is the case if $r_{igp} < 1$ as was seen in item 7.1(e) or if some rule is assumed

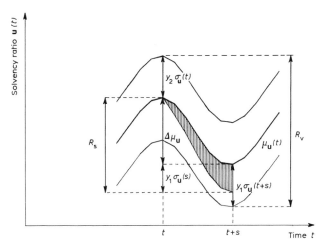

Figure 7.9.1   *Two ways of defining the range R of fluctuation.*

according to which the solvency ratio $\mathbf{u}(t)$ is kept under some finite limit, e.g. by suitable application of bonus or dividend policies.

(b) The variation range R_v is composed of the variation $(= \Delta\mu_\mathbf{u})$ of the midline $\mu_\mathbf{u}(t)$ of the bundle and of the breadth of the confidence area of the bundle of the fluctuating $\mathbf{u}(t)$. The time t corresponds to a peak of the bundle and $t + s$ to the next minimum. The midline can be obtained from (6.6.8) and is mainly due to the cyclical waves. The breadth of the bundle can be expressed as multiples of the standard deviations $y_1\sigma_\mathbf{u}(t + s)$ and $y_2\sigma_\mathbf{u}(t)$, where y_1 and y_2 are the confidence coefficients and the sigmas can be evaluated from (6.6.11). Owing to the skewness of the process and to the time difference (s in Fig. 7.9.1), y_1 and y_2 may deviate from each other even though they are both usually approximately equal to $y = N^{-1}(1 - \varepsilon)$. Hence

$$R_v \approx \Delta\mu_\mathbf{u}(t, t + s) + 2y\sigma_\mathbf{u}(1, t + s). \tag{7.9.1}$$

The notation introduced in Chapter 6 is made up by writing out, if necessary, the ends of the periods concerned. It is appropriate to choose s as half the cycle length (see (6.1.4))

$$s = T_z/2. \tag{7.9.2}$$

The calculations can be made by means of the formulae of Chapter 6 in a way similar to that illustrated in the next item. Note that the outcome depends on the time t in (7.9.1). It is natural to take t fairly large so that the breadth of the bundle is already close to its steady state dimensions (see (6.6.12)). Approximate rapid rules are presented in Rantala (1982, Chapter 4). They are intended to define a limit up to which a fluctuation buffer (equalization reserve) can still be reasonably deemed to be a technical rather than a free reserve.

(c) Solvency margin can be understood as the capital which an insurer should have to meet adverse periods. Its minimum amount, denoted by R_s in Fig. 7.9.1, must obviously be high enough to cover by a safe probability the loss which may arise during the unfavourable half of a cycle. This can be expressed in the terms of the preceding item as follows

$$R_s = \Delta\mu_\mathbf{u}(1, T) + y\sigma_\mathbf{u}(1, T). \tag{7.9.3}$$

The limit R_s depends on all the basic variables (7.1.1) of the model.

Table 7.9.1   *The minimum solvency margin* (7.9.3) *as function of some basic parameters* (7.1.1), $T = T_z$.

Z_m	T_z	λ	r_i	r_x	r_g	t_p	C_i	M	R_s
0.10	12	0.040	1.085	1.090	1.061	2	0.50	1.00	0.91
0.00		0.040	1.085	1.090	1.061	2	0.50	1.00	0.43
0.10	6	0.040	1.085	1.090	1.061	2	0.50	1.00	0.65
0.10	12	0.176	1.085	1.090	1.061	2	0.50	1.00	0.35
0.10	12	0.210	1.200	1.090	1.061	2	0.50	1.00	0.33
0.10	12	0.044	1.085	1.050	1.061	2	0.50	1.00	0.82
0.10	12	0.047	1.085	1.090	1.000	2	0.50	1.00	0.75
0.10	12	0.040	1.085	1.090	1.061	0	0.50	1.00	0.68
0.10	12	0.040	1.085	1.090	1.061	2	0.00	1.00	0.61
0.10	12	0.040	1.085	1.090	1.061	2	0.50	0.40	0.86

It can be investigated by programming it using the formulae of Chapter 6, which have already been specified in the previous item. The time horizon T should be at least equal to half of the cycle length (s in Fig. 7.9.1). If cycles are not assumed or if they are weak, the breadth of the bundle is decisive and R_s can be determined as the difference of the initial level $u(0)$ and the lowest point of the lower boundary of the bundle in time $(0, T]$. Depending on the type of process the outcome may be affected very much by the choice of T, as demonstrated in Fig. 7.5.1.

Some examples are set out in Table 7.9.1. On the topmost line is the standard set of values of the variables data as given in item 7.1(d). Then each variable is changed in turn to ascertain the sensitivity.

(d) Legal stipulations for the solvency margins were considered already in Section 4.4, deriving some rules on the basis of a one-year planning horizon. The background of the short horizon is the view that public intervention to control the insurance industry can be limited mainly to safeguarding the interests of those insured. Therefore only that margin is necessary which is needed to protect the financial state of a possibly weak insurer from direct bankruptcy for a 'warning period' during which the weakened solvency is to be restored on pain of winding up. On the other hand a short planning period is, of course, not sufficient from the point of view of the insurer. The objective should be a safe continuation of the existence of the institution, which provides a long time horizon. Then understandably also the dimension of the minimum solvency margin increases substantially, as already seen. Another reason for the divergence of the outcomes given from conventional approaches is the fact that the model assumptions applied in this and in the preceding section are less restrictive than has been the case in many of the previous studies; in particular, the introduction of cycles and inflation proved significant.

Further discussion on the solvency margins and equalization reserves can be found in Karten (1980) and Pentikäinen (1982, Chapter 5).

7.10   Safety loading

(a) Minimum condition The technique described can also be used for evaluation of a minimum requirement for the safety loading λ. The principle is demonstrated in Fig. 7.10.1. An obvious condition for solvency is that the stochastic bundle does not intersect the ruin barrier u_r. The position of the bundle depends on the safety loading λ, understood as an aggregate loading including also the yield of interest earned for the technical reserves as defined in item 6.5(h). If λ is too small, the bundle falls down with fatal consequences. The problem is to find the lowest value for λ which still prevents the bundle from hanging below u_r. It is necessary to distinguish

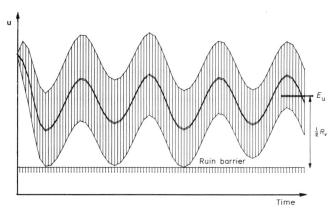

Figure 7.10.1   *The lowest still solvent positions of the stochastic bundle;* $r_{igp} < 1, r_g > 1$.

between the cases when the 'dynamic discount factor' r_{igp} (see item 6.5(g)) is either < 1 or > 1.

(b) The case $r_{\text{igp}} < 1$. The flow of the midline of the bundle was given by (6.6.8) (see Fig. 6.6.2). Assuming a constant rate for interest, inflation and growth it tends towards an equilibrium level $E_{\mathbf{u}}$ (6.6.9). Furthermore, the measure for the breadth of the bundle is required. It was studied in the previous section and denoted by R_v. Clearly $E_{\mathbf{u}}$ must be at a distance at least $\frac{1}{2}R_v$ from the ruin barrier, or in terms of the quantities given

$$E_{\mathbf{u}} > u_r + \tfrac{1}{2}R_v.$$

Substituting (6.6.9) for $E_{\mathbf{u}}$ and solving an inequality for λ, the following is obtained

$$\lambda \geqslant (1 - r_{\text{igp}})(\tfrac{1}{2}R_v + u_r). \tag{7.10.1}$$

Assuming that $u_r = 0.1$, $R_v = 1.2$ (see item 7.9(c)) and (according to the standards in item 6.1(d)) $r_{\text{igp}} = 0.938$, a numerical value is found for the lower limit of $\lambda \geqslant 0.043$.

Another way to study minimum conditions for the safety loading is to use the asymptotic expressions (6.6.9) and (6.6.12). This is done in Exercise 7.10.1.

The interpretation of this outcome is as follows. A minimum amount of safety loading is necessary to counteract the eroding effect of inflation and to increase the solvency margin in keeping with the real growth of the business volume, in so far as the yield of interest is not sufficient for these purposes, as is the case when $r_{\text{igp}} < 1$. The situation is more complicated if the insurer can acquire fresh capital to reinforce the solvency margin U, as may be possible at least in the case of proprietary companies. Then the demand of the safety loading which is needed to compensate the eroding capital is smaller, but on the other hand the stockholders expect a return for their investment, which increases the need for margins or loadings in rates.

It will be recalled that the safety loading, as defined above, is an aggregate quantity composed of the yield of interest earned for the underwriting reserves and of the 'ordinary' loading accrued from premiums according to (6.5.12). Furthermore, for the above considerations the *total* amount of the safety income λB is relevant, as was discussed in item 4.1(c), without paying any attention to the problem of how it is divided between different policies and policy groups. In essence, the solvency considerations discussed only provide conditions for just this aggregate amount, not for the individual rates, which are subject to aspects such as those dealt with in Section 5.3.

(c) The case $r_{igp} > 1$ According to (6.6.8) a safety loading of

$$\lambda > - (r_{igp} - 1)u(0)$$

is sufficient to ensure that the midline of the stochastic bundle tends to infinity. Note, however, that the presence of cycles may cause irregular and even unlimited oscillations. If the lower confidence boundary grows toward infinity and has a minimum, the value of the solvency ratio $\mathbf{u}(t)$ at this minimum point depends among other things on the safety loading, as shown in Fig. 7.10.2. The required solvency condition is now that λ or rather its premium related component λ_p should be larger than the critical value giving the minimum ($\lambda_p = - 0.09$ in the figure).

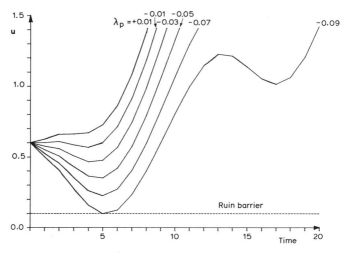

Figure 7.10.2 *The lower confidence boundary of the stochastic bundle as a function of safety loading λ_p. The standard data, given in item 7.1(d), was changed by putting $r_i = 1.1$, $r_x = 1.05$ and $r_g = 1$ resulting in $r_{igp} = 1.048$. Note that despite the assumed negative values of λ_p, the total safety loading according to (6.5.12) is strongly positive.*

As discussed in item 7.7(f), the uncontrolled flow of the $\mathbf{u}(t)$ when $r_{igp} > 1$ is an oversimplification of the processes concerned and the model should necessarily be supported by some control rules. Then the problem may become more complicated than before, but the same idea, i.e. finding the lowest safety loading that still prevents the stochastic bundle from intersecting the ruin barrier, can be expected to be applicable.

Some necessary conditions for the unlimited growth of the lower confidence boundary of the stochastic bundle are dealt with in Exercise 7.10.2.

Exercise 7.10.1 Find a lower limit for λ in the case where $r_{igp} < 1$ by using the limit expressions (6.6.9) and (6.6.12) and applying a similar method as in item (b). What is its numerical value calculated for the standard data of item 7.1(d)?

Exercise 7.10.2 Assume constant rates of interest, inflation and growth so that $r_{igp} > 1$, $\rho = r_{igp}^{-2} r_g^{-1} < 1$ and omit the cycles and the structure variation. Find a condition where the lower confidence boundary of the stochastic bundle, defined as in Section 6.6., grows asymptotically and without limit when t tends to infinity.

CHAPTER 8

Risk theory analysis of life insurance

8.1 Cohort analysis

(a) Special character of life insurance The foregoing analysis
methods were developed to fit, as far as possible, all kinds of
insurance classes, although most examples were chosen from
non-life insurance. There is no doubt that risk theory, as it stands
today, can find its most rewarding applications in just that environment, but the fluctuation of life insurance business can also
be studied by the same technique. Of course, the individual risk
sums Z are the amounts payable S less the policy reserve V, i.e.
$Z = S - V$. There are, however, crucially different features in life
insurance, pension insurance included. Conventionally life insurance
contracts are issued to continue decades up to some termination
age or even lifelong without the possibility of adjusting the original
premiums upwards (unless according to some specified rules in the
case of indexation), whereas non-life premiums are normally valid
only for short terms. The special risk involved in life insurance
is the chance of future adverse development in bases relevant for
the solvent flow of the business, such as mortality, invalidity,
interest rate, inflation etc. As a protection against them the premium
rates are calculated with safe margins. If the margins are not needed
to cover losses, they can be returned as bonuses for instance as
premium rebates, additional benefits (to profit participating
policies) or they can be used to compensate inflation in case of
index-linked policies. It can be said that the practice in life insurance
is to have *implicit solvency margins* in the form of safe calculation
bases, whereas the solvency margins of non-life insurers are mainly
explicit, either shown in balance sheets or possibly also constituted

in underestimations of assets or overestimations of liabilities ('hidden reserves').

In the foregoing considerations the portfolio development was approximated by the trend factor $r_g(t)$ and by the inflation factors $r_x(t)$ and $r_p(t)$. In fact, this was justified only by assuming that the rates are continually, even if after some time lags, adjusted for changing risk structures and inflation. When the life insurance business is dealt with then it may be necessary to accept the fact that the old policies are frozen at their original level or at least cannot fully follow the changing relevant circumstances. If changes occur, for instance, due to inflation or other circumstances or due to the action of the insurer, e.g. revision of premium rates, they may affect old and new policies in significantly differing ways. This suggests a more sophisticated modelling of the portfolio development.

It is beyond the scope of this book to discuss the solvency problems of life insurers as a whole. Only some hints will be given as to how the risk theory technique described in the previous sections may be modified for the analysis of life insurance. It is also possible to link the presentation to the classical individual risk theory which was developed specially for life insurance.

(b) Cohort approach A simplified problem is first considered, which can then be used as a building block for more advanced considerations. Consider that group of policies which have the same entry year, entry age x, policy type and face sum. The scaling will be made taking the entry year equal to 0 and the face sum equal to 1. Endowment insurance will be considered as an example where the same sum, now equal to 1, will be paid at death or at maturity, after w years. Let $l(0)$ be the number of policies (= policyholders) of this group at the beginning of the entry year. Such a group is commonly called a *cohort*, and it will now be followed from year to year assuming that the only way of exit from the cohort is death. Then according to conventional life insurance mathematics the cohort size is obtained from the algorithm

$$l(t + 1) = l(t) \times (1 - q(t)) \qquad t = 0, 1, \ldots, w - 1, \qquad (8.1.1)$$

where $q(t)$ is the mortality rate, i.e. the expected proportional number of deaths in year t. A basic idea of life insurance mathematics is to construct a policy (or premium) reserve $V(t)$, where the difference between incomes and expenditures related to the cohort are accumulated according to the algorithm

$$l(t + 1) \times V(t + 1) = r_i \times l(t)$$
$$\times [V(t) + B - C(t)] - l(t) \times q(t), \tag{8.1.2}$$

where $V(t)$ is the policy reserve per living cohort member at the beginning of year t, B is the premium calculated per cohort member, $C(t)$ is the expense loading, and $r_i = 1 + i_i$ is the (actuarial) rate of interest.

For simplicity of notation it is assumed that the premiums are received and the expenses paid at the beginning of each year and the benefits are paid at the end of the year. The sum 1 is paid at the end of year $w - 1$, or what is the same, at the beginning of the year w, to cohort members still alive. Then conditions

$$V(0) = 0 \text{ and } V(w) = 1, \tag{8.1.3}$$

determine the premium B (see exercise 8.2.1) and the reserve $V(t)$ uniquely.

This conventional deterministic calculation rule can now be readily made stochastic by, as a first step, letting the annual number of deaths

$$d(t) = l(t)q(t), \tag{8.1.4}$$

be a random variable (with the expectation $n = E(\mathbf{d}(t))$). Then also the number of the cohort members obtained by algorithm

$$\mathbf{l}(t + 1) = \mathbf{l}(t) - \mathbf{d}(t) \qquad (\mathbf{l}(0) \equiv l(0)), \tag{8.1.5}$$

will be stochastic. Furthermore, we can define the *random profit* (or loss) $\mathbf{Y}(t)$ resulting from this cohort in year t and the interest calculated up to the end of the year as follows

$$\mathbf{Y}(t) = r_i \mathbf{l}(t)[V(t) + B - C(t)] - \mathbf{d}(t) - \mathbf{l}(t + 1)V(t + 1)$$
$$= \mathbf{l}(t)[r_i V(t) + r_i B - r_i C(t) - V(t + 1)]$$
$$- \mathbf{d}(t)[1 - V(t + 1)]. \tag{8.1.6}$$

As seen from (8.1.2), $\mathbf{Y}(t) \equiv 0$ if $\mathbf{d}(t) \equiv d(t)$. Hence $\mathbf{Y}(t)$ has arisen from the random deviations of $\mathbf{d}(t)$ from those values (8.1.4) which were preassumed in the calculation bases when the premiums were determined.

Furthermore it is useful to follow the accumulated cohort result

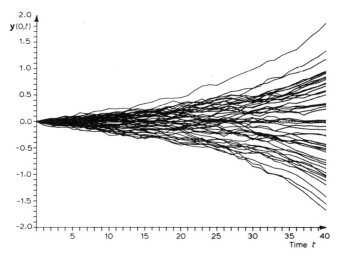

Figure 8.1.1 *The cohort random process* (8.1.7b) *calculated using the following assumptions and data:* $q(t) = 0.0006 + \exp[0, 115t - 8.125]$, $l(0) = 10\ 000$, $r_i = 1.05$, $w = 40$, $\mathbf{d}(t)$ *simple Poisson variable with expectation* $\mathbf{n} = l(t)q(t)$. *Expense loading* $C(0) = 0.02$; $C(t) = 0.002$ *for* $t \geqslant 1$.

$$\mathbf{Y}(0,t) = \sum_{\tau=0}^{t} \mathbf{Y}(\tau)r_i^{t-\tau}. \tag{8.1.7a}$$

The random processes introduced can be handled using the Monte Carlo method in the same way as considered in the previous sections. An example is given in Fig. 8.1.1, where the ratio

$$\mathbf{y}(0,t) = \mathbf{Y}(0,t)/\mathbf{B}(t), \tag{8.1.7b}$$

i.e. the accumulated profit in relation to the premium income $\mathbf{B}(t) = l(t)\mathbf{B}$ is displayed.

The spreading of the bundle in the figure is striking. It is due to the interest calculated according to (8.1.7) accumulating to the randomly arisen profit or loss. Introduction of inflation, real growth and lapses will fully change the character of the process, as will be seen later.

This approach can be extended to any other type of policy, and also to take account of the fact that the face sums are different inside a cohort and that also bases other than the number of deaths are varying, as will be shown later. As expected, the variation range is considerably larger e.g. for cohorts consisting of pure death risk policies (temporary life insurance), and in particular when sickness or disablement benefits are involved.

8.2 Link to classic individual risk theory

The cohort approach was the basis for the consideration of the classic, often called individual, risk theory, which is reviewed for instance by Bohlmann (1909) and Cramér (1930). The practice was to discount all the expected fluctuations to the entry time of the cohort

$$\mathbf{Y}_0 = \mathbf{Y}(0, w - 1)v^w = \sum_{t=0}^{w-1} \mathbf{Y}(t)v^{t+1}, \qquad (8.2.1)$$

where $v = 1/r_i$ is the discounting factor. The uncertainty involved in the business was measured by the standard deviation of $\mathbf{Y}_0$ and the normal approximation was assumed applicable, when the d.f. of $\mathbf{Y}_0$ was introduced.

The consideration is restricted in this section only to the net incomes and outgoings, omitting the expenses and loading (term $C(t)$ in (8.1.2)). Furthermore, only the number of deaths is assumed stochastically varying; all the other bases of calculations, such as interest rate, are assumed to be set exactly according to the deterministic assumptions which were used for premium calculations.

The variance $\sigma_c^2 = \text{var}(\mathbf{Y}_0)$, which was a central characteristic of individual risk theory, is readily deduced from the above issues. Note that the annual terms $\mathbf{Y}(t)$ in (8.2.1) are not mutually independent because the number of deaths in each year controls the cohort size of subsequent years. Therefore the required variance is not directly obtainable as a sum of the variances of the terms.

In order to get a more general result a hypothetical single premium policy is considered, on the basis of which are paid to the cohort members still living both an annuity a at the beginning of years $0, 1, \ldots, w - 1$ and, in case of death or of maturity, a sum S at the end of the relevant year. The single risk premium, i.e. the discounted sum of the expected future outgoings, is then according to conventional life insurance mathematics and adopting a discrete calculation method

$$P_1 = \frac{a}{l(0)} \sum_{t=0}^{w-1} l(t)v^t + \frac{S}{l(0)} \sum_{t=0}^{w-1} l(t)q(t)v^{t+1}$$
$$+ S\frac{l(w)}{l(0)} v^w. \qquad (8.2.2)$$

The last term is due to the maturity at the end of year $w - 1$. The terms related to expenses (see (8.1.6)) do not appear, because the consideration is now limited to risk premiums only.

Note that putting $P_1 = 0$ and $a = -P$ the conventional endowment treaty with all term risk premium P is obtained as a special case, and putting $S = 0$ the capital value of an annuity a.

Now consider one policy entering into the cohort at $t = 0$. There are $w + 1$ different ways it can terminate, i.e. either death in one of the years $t = 0, 1, \ldots, w - 1$ or maturity at the beginning of the year w. These events can be described letting the termination time t be a discrete random variable with frequencies

$$p(t) = \text{prob}\{\mathbf{t} = t\} = \frac{d(t)}{l(0)} = \frac{l(t)q(t)}{l(0)} \qquad (t = 0, 1, \ldots, w - 1)$$

$$= \frac{l(t)}{l(0)} \qquad (t = w).$$

The second line represents the case of maturity. Noting that $l(w) = l(w - 1) \times (1 - q(w - 1))$, and combining the events related to the end of the last policy year $w - 1$ and the beginning of the next year, these expressions can be rewritten as follows

$$p(t) = \frac{d(t)}{l(0)} = \frac{l(t)q(t)}{l(0)} \qquad \text{for } t = 0, 1, \ldots, w - 2$$

$$p(w - 1) = \frac{d(w - 1)}{l(0)} + \frac{l(w)}{l(0)} = \frac{l(w - 1)}{l(0)}. \qquad (8.2.3)$$

Next a profit (or loss) $Z(t)$ arising from termination at year t can be introduced

$$Z(t) = P_1 - a \sum_{\tau = 0}^{t} v^{\tau} - Sv^{t+1} \qquad (t = 0, 1, 2, \ldots, w - 1)$$

$$= P_1 - a\frac{1 - v^{t+1}}{1 - v} - Sv^{t+1} \qquad (8.2.4)$$

$$= P_1 - \left[\frac{a}{1 - v} + \left(S - \frac{a}{1 - v}\right)v^{t+1}\right].$$

The different profit outcomes can be understood to constitute another discrete random variable $\mathbf{Z}$, obtaining values (8.2.4) by probabilities (8.2.3). Its moments about zero are, according to the standard definitions

$$E(\mathbf{Z}^i) = \sum_{t = 0}^{w - 1} p(t)Z(t)^i. \qquad (8.2.5)$$

Since P_1 in (8.2.4) is the pure risk premium, $E(\mathbf{Z}) = 0$, the variance is

$$\sigma^2 = \operatorname{var}(\mathbf{Z}) = E(\mathbf{Z}^2). \qquad (8.2.6)$$

Introducing the notation

$$A(v) = \sum_{t=0}^{w-1} p(t)v^{t+1}, \qquad (8.2.7)$$

the single risk premium can be written

$$
\begin{aligned}
P_1 &= \sum_{t=0}^{w-1} p(t)\left[a\, \frac{1 - v^{t+1}}{1 - v} + Sv^{t+1} \right] \\
&= \sum_{t=0}^{w-1} p(t)\left[\frac{a}{1 - v} + \left(S - \frac{a}{1 - v} \right)v^{t+1} \right] \\
&= \frac{a}{1 - v} + \left(S - \frac{a}{1 - v} \right) \sum_{t=0}^{w-1} p(t)v^{t+1} \qquad (8.2.8) \\
&= \frac{a}{1 - v} + \left(S - \frac{a}{1 - v} \right) A(v),
\end{aligned}
$$

and the following classic expression for the variance σ^2 can be derived by some algebra (exercise 8.2.2)

$$\sigma^2 = \left(S - \frac{a}{1 - v} \right)^2 \times (A(v^2) - A(v)^2). \qquad (8.2.9)$$

Because the discounted cohort profit $\mathbf{Y}_0$ is the sum of the profits $(\mathbf{Z})$ of all the $l(0)$ cohort members, and since these can be assumed mutually independent, 'the cohort variance' is

$$\sigma_c^2 = \operatorname{var}(\mathbf{Y}_0) = l(0)\sigma^2. \qquad (8.2.10)$$

The following special results are now obtained from this general formula:

(i) In the case of the endowment policy with whole term premiums, put $a = -P$ where P is the pure annual risk premium (B without expense loading C); now $P_1 = 0$.
(ii) In the case of single premium endowment treaty put $a = 0$.
(iii) In the case of a single premium annuity ($= a$) put $S = 0$.

For other types of life policies similar formulae can be derived.

The standard deviation σ and the ratio $\sigma/A(v)$ or preferably the per cohort calculated values σ_c and A_c may be used in evaluation of the need of safety loading in premiums and reserves.

In the example given in Fig. 8.1.1 $\sigma = 0.103$, $A = 0.168$ and $\sigma/A = 0.613$. If the cohort size is $l(0) = 10\,000$, then the corresponding cohort characteristics are $\sigma_c = \sigma\sqrt{10\,000} = 10.3$ and $A_c = 10\,000A = 1680$, and hence the 'relative' standard deviation $\sigma_c/A_c = \sigma/A\sqrt{l(0)} = 0.006$.

Exercise 8.2.1 Write down the formula for risk premium P (without loadings) of the endowment policy.

Exercise 8.2.2 Prove (8.2.9).

8.3 Extensions of the cohort approach

(a) Generalized profit algorithm The classic model can be developed to consider and to test the effects of a great number of disturbances, basic variations, impulses, trends etc. other than those arising from the simple fluctuation of the number of deaths considered in Section 8.2.

The gross premium basis is returned to again, and the profit definition (8.1.6) will now be written in a more general form

$$\mathbf{Y}(t) = \mathbf{l}(t)\left[r_i(t)V(t) + r_i(t)B - V(t+1)\right]S(t) \qquad (8.3.1)$$
$$- \mathbf{d}(t)\left[1 - V(t+1)\right]S(t) - \mathbf{l}(t)C'(t)r_i(t).$$

The current insurance sum is now $S(t)$ (hence no longer normed to unity but still the same for all the cohort members). However, the reserve V and gross premium B still have the values which are calculated per unit sum by the primary actuarial bases. The sum $S(t)$ can change from year to year by virtue of bonus or indexation. The interest factor $r_i(t)$ should represent the evaluated or anticipated actual yield of investment, and it is normally greater than the primary actuarial rate r_i. Also the number of deaths $\mathbf{d}(t)$ can be simulated in a way which corresponds to the anticipated actual level.

The variable $C'(t)$ represents the anticipated actual expenses per policy in force. It can be expected to change in pace with inflation.

(b) Second-order bases Formula (8.3.1) now offers an instrument for investigation of the consequences of deviations of the actual relevant factors like interest rate, mortality and many others from those values which were primarily assumed when the premiums were determined at the entry of the cohort.

(i) *The actual yield of investment* can be taken into account in (8.3.1) by the rates $r_i(t)$ which are fitted to the actual average yield of investments. If, as is usual, $r_i(t) > r_i$, 'interest profit' results.

(ii) *Mortality* deviations from the calculation bases can be incorporated into the model, choosing the simulation rule for the generation of the number of deaths $\mathbf{d}(t)$ accordingly. If, for example, the Poisson law is assumed, then the parameter n, the expected number of deaths, should be defined by means of some function $q'(t)$ which is fitted to the actual or anticipated mortality more accurately than the calculation basis $q(t)$. If $q' < q$, then mortality profit arises.

(iii) *Cancellations* of policies will be introduced next, defining a 'lapse ratio' $\rho(t)$. It indicates the proportion of the cohort size $\mathbf{l}(t)$ which cancels its policies at year t before the maturity age. Then the algorithm (8.1.5) is replaced by the following

$$\mathbf{l}(t + 1) = \mathbf{l}(t) - \mathbf{d}(t) - \mathbf{l}(t)\rho(t). \tag{8.3.2}$$

The lapse ratios should be given as input data. Of course, the stochastic definition is also feasible. Furthermore 'a lapse profit' $(\pm)$

$$(V(t) - V_s(t))S(t), \tag{8.3.3}$$

is to be added to the profit equation (8.3.1). $V_s(t)$ is the surrender value per unit, i.e. the amount $V_s(t)S(t)$ is to be paid, if positive, when the policyholder breaks the contract before maturity. Then the reserve $V(t)S$ is released and the difference (8.3.3) constitutes the profit or loss arising.

(iv) *Inflation* will be introduced next, denoting its rate by $i_x(t)$. Perhaps the most crucial point is that the expenses increase in keeping with inflation, but the premiums are either fixed or – according to the practice in some countries – they may be increased by virtue of index linkage but possibly with a time lag. It may be useful to define separately a 'premium inflation' rate $i_p(t)$ for life insurance as was the case for general insurance in item 6.2(a). Of course, if no indexation of the policies is applied, then i_p is zero.

Now the sum insured S in (8.3.1) should be made time dependent according to the algorithm

$$S(t + 1) = r_p(t)S(t), \tag{8.3.4}$$

where $r_p(t) = 1 + i_p(t)$. An example of the definition of rate $i_p(t)$ will be given in point (vi).

The expenses are naturally linked with the 'general inflation' (see item 6.1(k))

$$C'(t) = C(t) \prod_{\tau=1}^{t} r_x(\tau), \tag{8.3.5}$$

where $r_x(t) = 1 + i_x(t)$. Again prognoses or assumptions about the inflation rates are needed to make the algorithm (8.3.1) operable.

(v) *Bonuses* are commonly given to the policyholders when the safely determined calculation bases provide excess profit. Definition for them can be added to the 'profit algorithm' (8.3.1). A simple example may be a rule according to which a bonus is given, if the accumulated profit $Y(0, t)$ (see (8.1.7a)) exceeds some barrier. The amount of bonuses should be deducted from the r.h.s. of (8.3.1).

The bonus barrier controls the allocation of the annual profits between their reservation for future use, to cover any adverse period of the business, and the return of a part of them as bonuses to the policyholders (or as dividends to the shareholders). What is left of the reserve up to the maturity as an accumulated not a distributed profit is the final profit (or loss if negative) arising from the cohort concerned.

(vi) *Indexation* Another practice is to use investment and other profits to support index linkage. This is the case in some so-called equity-linked or similar policies. The idea is to use that part of the accumulated profit $Y(0, t)$ that exceeds some limit for enforcement of the policy reserves, and the insurance sum and the current premiums are simultaneously increased accordingly. This is conveniently implemented by ruling some suitable increment for the insurance sum in (8.3.1)

$$S(t + 1) = r_p(t)S(t), \tag{8.3.6}$$

where $r_p(t) = 1 + i_p(t)$ is a growth factor, which should be determined so that the financial balance is preserved. In fact this means that the increment of the policy reserve $l(t + 1)V(t + 1)(S(t + 1) - S(t)) = l(t + 1)V(t + 1)i_p(t)S(t)$ of the cohort should be equal to the amount which is released from the accumulated profit $Y(0, t)$. The latter amount can be programmed into the system assuming a *bonus barrier* the excess of which will be given away from $Y(0, t)$. It can be introduced by a constant b which defines the bonus barrier in proportion to the premium income of the cohort. Hence we have, given that $S(t)$ and $i_p(t)$ are now stochastic

$$l(t + 1) \times V(t + 1) \times i_p(t) \times S(t)$$
$$= Y(0, t) - bB \times l(t + 1) \times S(t), \qquad (8.3.7)$$

from which $i_p(t)$ is obtained by solving if the right hand side is positive, otherwise put $i_p(t) = 0$. Note that $i_p(t)$ is a direct analogy for the 'premium inflation' rate which was introduced in item 6.2(a).

The above ideas are illustrated in Figs 8.3.1, 8.3.2 and 8.3.3. In order to get a general idea about the effect of the background assumptions, first the process was made deterministic in Figs 8.3.1 and 8.3.2. Explanations can be found in the captions of the figures. Figure 8.3.2, demonstrates how the model can be used to test what degree of inflation the supposed secondary bases still tolerate.

Then one of the processes was selected for Monte Carlo simulation in Fig. 8.3.3. Both the deterministic average flow without bonus barrier and the bundle of stochastically varying flows provided with bonus barrier are exhibited. The hypothetical example set out in Fig. 8.3.3 illustrates a case where the accumulated profit was not sufficient to cover the adverse development at the final phase before maturity. It arose in this example mainly due to the fact that owing to inflation the 'actual' expenses widely exceeded the loading calculated for them.

It is seen that the system is sensitive to changes in the primary bases, whereas the stochastic variation of the number of deaths has a minor though noticeable effect.

The steepness of curves 1 and 3 confirm the well-known experience that in particular the interest rate and inflation are of crucial significance for the long-range balance of that type of life

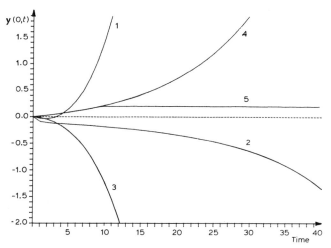

Figure 8.3.1 *Deterministic flows of accumulated cohort profit when the basic assumptions given in the caption of Fig. 8.1.1 are changed one at a time the others being the originals.* (1) *Interest rate* $r_i(t) = 1.09$; (2) *lapses are assumed* $\rho(1) = 0.16$, $\rho(2) = 0.11$, $\rho(3) = 0.06$ *and* $\rho(t) = 0.01$ *for* $t > 3$, $V_s(t) = V(t)$ *if positive, otherwise* 0; (3) *inflation* $r_x = 1.05$; (4) *mortality rates q are lowered by* 20%; (5) *assumption 4 combined with a bonus barrier* $b = 0.2$.

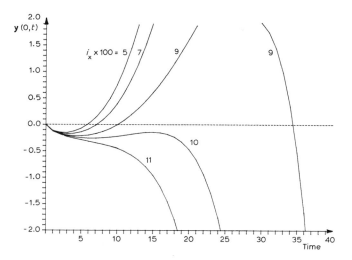

Figure 8.3.2 *Deterministic flows of the accumulated cohort profit. Interest, mortality and lapses as in Fig. 8.3.1, and the rate i_x of inflation varying as depicted in the figure.*

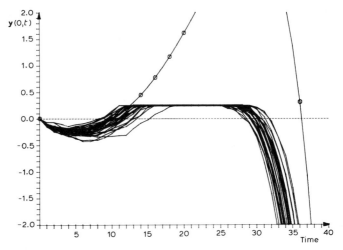

Figure 8.3.3   *Flows of the accumulated cohort profit. The curve with circles is deterministic, assuming no bonus barrier. The other curves are simulated letting deaths be randomly varying according to the Poisson law and adopting a bonus barrier $b = 0.2$, $r_i = 1.09$, $r_x = 1.09$, mortality and lapses as in Fig. 8.3.1.*

insurance which involves a substantial saving element, such as the endowment insurance shown in Fig. 8.3.1.

8.4   General system

(a) Portfolio as a sum of cohorts   The life insurance portfolio is, of course, always composed of a number of cohorts of the type defined in the previous sections. The technique drafted earlier can be applied separately for each of them and then the data for the whole business can be obtained summing the cohort outcomes.

The cohorts are specified by

(i) the entry year t_c
(ii) the entry age x
(iii) the type of the policy including also the maturity age
(iv) the initial insured sums S_c.

In other words, policies having (at least approximately) the same characteristics constitute a cohort, which will be followed up for the whole time they are in force.

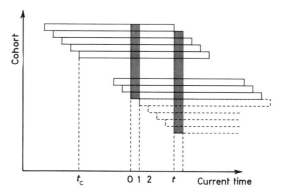

Figure 8.4.1   *A portfolio consisting of cohorts (horizontal pillars). For clarity in the figure it is assumed that all the policies entering in each year t_c constitute only one cohort. The total portfolio profit is obtained by summing the profits emanating from all the cohorts in force that year. Every year a new cohort is assimilated into the portfolio and the oldest one passes away.*

The current time will be denoted by t, putting the order number of the starting year of the analysis at 0. Then the entry years t_c of the cohorts emanating from earlier years have negative values.

For the portfolio analysis it is necessary to have the number of the members of each cohort as an initial datum for $t = 0$. Preferably these numbers can be derived from the actual files. In theoretical considerations they and the initial sums S can also be derived making some assumptions concerning the original initial sizes (for $t = t_c$) of the cohorts, past lapse rates, inflation, bonuses or the index i_p.

When the initial data are obtained, then each cohort can be operated for $t = 0, 1, 2, \ldots$ as before and the results related to each year t are summed in order to get the *underwriting profit* of the year t. Furthermore, each year a new set of cohorts will be assimilated into the portfolio and another set of cohorts is removed due to maturities. For new cohorts some assumption of the acquisition of new policies is needed, possibly characterized by a growth factor $r_g(t)$. Furthermore, the average values and distributions of the sums insured for all the entering policies are needed. Possibly the distributions can be assumed to be unchanged in shape from year to year, but the average sum and equally the scale of the variable S will be changed according to some index, perhaps to the same inflation rate $i_x(t)$ as already introduced above. This means that the sums $S(t + 1)$ of the policies entering the portfolio in year $t + 1$ are equally distributed as the sums $S(t)$ of entries of year t, but so that on an average the sums are increased in the ratio $r_x(t) = 1 + i_x(t)$.

Practical difficulties may arise because the number of cohorts to be constructed and followed has the tendency to grow quite large if the characteristics listed are very strictly applied. It is likely that, without loss of validity of the model, the number of cohorts can be kept reasonable by combining into one and the same cohort, policies having similar characteristics, like entry age, sums S, etc., i.e. dividing the portfolio into classes according to the characteristics and applying a fairly coarse class interval. A further rationalization may be to combine in one and the same cohort all the policies of equal type irrespective of the size of the insured sum S and to introduce the sum d.f., as shown in the next item.

(b) Examples The idea outlined is illustrated in Figs 8.4.2 and 8.4.3. The examples are still simplified in so far as all the new policies of each year are assumed to be of endowment type having the same entry and maturity age, but variation of insurance sums inside the cohort was allowed according to the Pareto law (see Section 3.5.8) with $\alpha = 3$. It was further supposed that the original d.f. of the sums with original parameter α will be preserved inside the cohorts from year to year, but so that the average sum $S(t_c, t)$ is changing and the S scale is set accordingly. The parameter Z_0 in (3.5.20) was determined by the condition that the average insurance sum should coincide with the assumed cohort mean value $S(t_c, t)$, i.e. $Z_0 = [(\alpha - 1)/\alpha] S(t_c, t)$, where t is the current year and t_c the entry year of the cohort. The mean sums of new cohorts compared with the next preceding year were assumed to be increasing in pace with inflation and the sums of 'old cohorts' were increased by the factor $r_p = 1 + i_p$ defined by (8.3.7). Hence, by these assumptions we have

$$S(t_c, t) = S(0, 0) \times r_x^{t_c} \times \prod_{\tau = t_c + 1}^{t} r_p(\tau), \qquad (8.4.1)$$

where $t_c = -w + t, -w + t + 1, \ldots, t$, being the termination time of the cohort concerned (see (8.1.3)).

Furthermore the initial cohort sizes were assumed to grow by the factor r_g from year to year. That means that the policies entering or having entered the portfolio in year t_c have the initial size $l(t_c, t) = l(0, 0)r_g^{t_c}$, and after that the cohort size $l(t_c, t)$ is changed according to algorithm (8.3.2), i.e. members are departing from the cohort before maturity owing to either death or lapse.

These assumptions imply that the example considered is still rather simplified. All the policies were assumed to be of endowment type having the same entry age and maturity age. All the new policies of each year were combined in one single cohort but the spread of insurance sums S was allowed inside the cohort. The initial values of cohorts were obtained by making assumptions about the (past and future) acquisition of new policies, inflation and indexations.

First again some deterministic flows of the accumulated solvency ratio are displayed in Fig. 8.4.2. This figure demonstrates how the model can be used to test how serious an inflation the system still tolerates. For this purpose different values are assigned for the inflation rate i_x as seen in the figure.

The case $i_x = 9\%$ and bonus barrier $b = 0.2$ is simulated in Fig. 8.4.3.

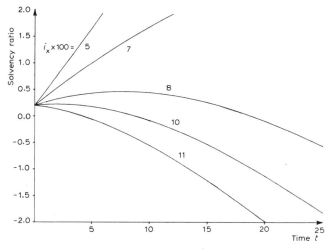

Figure 8.4.2 *Deterministically calculated flow of solvency ratio. The rate of inflation $i_x = r_x - 1$ is varying, the interest rate is 0.075, other data are as in Fig. 8.3.1. The bonus barrier b is not adopted.*

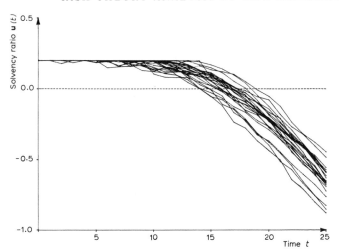

Figure 8.4.3   *Simulation of the case inflation rate* $i_x = 0.09$ *and the bonus barrier* $b = 0.2$. *Other data are as in Fig. 8.4.2.*

These examples are still simplified such that the study of the effect of the differing entry ages and different types of policies was omitted. However, it can be expected that these examples already reveal typical features in life insurance structures. As is well known from earlier experience and already stated in Section 8.3 on the basis of an analysis of one single cohort, the long-range validity of the basic data like interest rate, mortality, loading and the effects of inflation are crucial, whereas the 'ordinary' random fluctuation has minor, even though not negligible, dimensions compared with the effects of the basis aspects. For pure risk insurance (temporary life insurance) and disablement benefits the latter variation range is expected to be larger than in the present examples.

The model can be further developed regarding all the aspects which specify a cohort. Furthermore, time-dependent changes in relevant factors, for instance inflation, interest rate, mortality, lapse rates, etc. can be programmed and the sensitivity of the outcomes of each can be investigated in a similar way to the case of general insurance in the foregoing chapters. Also dynamic rules can be incorporated into the model to simulate possible measures taken by management, e.g. in the case of adverse development.

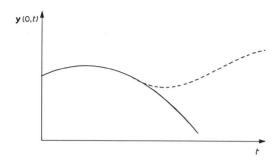

Figure 8.4.4 *Demonstration of the effect of remedial action when an adverse flow of the solvency margin is imminent. The solid line shows the flow if no special measures are taken; the dotted line shows the rectified flow.*

Figure 8.4.4 shows an example. Note that the control mechanism generates cyclic variation as seen also in the analysis of the general insurance (see Fig. 7.7.5). However, owing to the difficulties in rendering rapid improvements in relevant factors affecting the solvency, it can be expected that the wavelengths of the cycles are considerably longer than in the case of non-life business.

In more detailed analyses, of course, features can arise such as the necessity to reinforce the reserves of current policies if the primary calculation bases are weak compared with current experience, and these can bring about enormous stresses for the continuation of the business. It can be expected that the stochastic dynamic model outlined can provide a useful service in the analysis of such kinds of situation, supplementing the conventional deterministic approaches which are traditionally in use in life insurance practice and widely employed in general management information systems as well as in conventional prognosis and budgeting models.

A further dimension for the use of the model provides the possibility of analysing the behaviour of the components of the portfolio, e.g. the profitability of the different cohorts. This is shown in Fig. 8.4.5 where the flows of both the whole portfolio and some of its cohorts are displayed. Even if strongly simplified the example may be realistic in so far as the profitability owing to inflation and other circumstances may differ considerably inside the portfolio.

(c) **Link with general risk theory** If the planning horizon is short or if the portfolio is already more or less in a state of equilibrium,

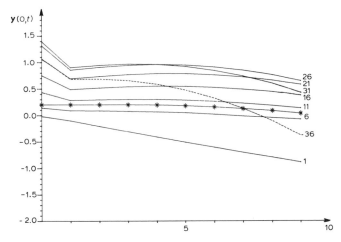

Figure 8.4.5 *Examples of the profit (or loss) flow of a supposed portfolio and eight of its cohorts having the duration from the entry* 1, 6, 11, ... , 36 *years respectively. Interest rate* 7%, $r_g = 1.04$ *and other data are as in Fig.* 8.3.1. *The curve with asterisks represents the joint result of all the cohorts.*

the behaviour of the life insurance business can be studied, without essential modifications, using the same technique as was developed in the foregoing chapters mainly for general insurance. Now, if we follow closely the decomposition idea dealt with in Section 3.7, the expected number of claims is readily obtained from (8.3.1), specifying the cohorts by their entry years t_c and denoting the current year by t.

$$n(t) = \sum_{t_c = -w+t}^{t} E\left(\mathbf{d}(t, t_c) \right)$$
$$= \sum_{t_c = -w+t}^{t} l(t, t_c) q(t - t_c). \tag{8.4.2}$$

The argument $t - t_c$ should be adjusted to correspond to the age of the cohort members in year t, i.e. the current age $x = x_c + (t - t_c)$ where x_c is the age at entry.

Furthermore, the d.f. of the claim sizes, i.e. the risk sums $Z = S(t)(1 - V(t - t_c))$ can be obtained as weighted averages from the cohort distributions, or more simply they can be found by statistical methods directly from the records of paid claims.

The basic difference between the 'general approach' and the 'life insurance approach' outlined in this chapter is that the latter makes it possible to forecast the time-dependent changes in the basic data for the long run, in particular possible distortions in the claim size distributions and expense loadings. On the other hand, very similar models are attainable as for the general system by using the decomposition of the portfolio into parts, as was presented in Section 3.7, and by programming suitable growth and other transition rules for each of them.

CHAPTER 9

Ruin probability during an infinite time period

9.1 Introduction

(a) Passage $T \to \infty$ In the previous chapters a survey was given of methods of determining numerical values of the ruin probability for finite time periods $(0, T]$. It is of interest to examine the behaviour of the risk process when T tends to infinity. For example in applications where the solvency of the insurer is a premise, conservative estimates can be obtained if the planning horizon is not limited to any finite time. This approach forms the basis of the traditional risk theory, resulting in the well-known infinite time formula for ruin probability, which will be presented in Section 9.2.

(b) Examples Some conception of different outcomes of the infinite time problem can be found in the figures of Chapters 6 and 7. In particular, Fig. 7.1.2 is illustrative. In the case exemplified in part (a) of the figure the stochastic bundle drifts into infinity. When the process passes the critical point where the lower boundary of the stochastic bundle (confidence region) has its minimum, the sample paths with increasing probability are more and more remote from the ruin barrier and the probability of ruin at large t values rapidly vanishes. This is seen also from Fig. 7.5.1 where the two lowest curves represent just this type of process. If the lower boundary of the stochastic bundle drifts upwards fast enough the infinite time ruin probability is < 1, as will be shown in item (c). The same is the case also when the cycles are assumed as in part (c) of Fig. 7.1.2.

The drift to infinity of the solvency ratio $\mathbf{u}(t)$ for $t \to \infty$ is not a necessary condition for $\Psi_\infty < 1$. There are cases where the bundle

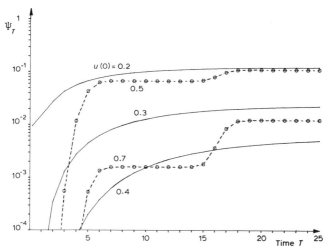

Figure 9.1.1 *Examples of the asymptotic behaviour of the ruin probability* $\Psi_T(u(0))$ *as a function of T calculated for some fixed values of the initial solvency ratio u(0). Solid lines, no cycles assumed; dotted lines with circles, deterministic cycles assumed.*

gets narrower and narrower when T grows, so that (see (6.6.12)) the standard deviation of the solvency ratio $\mathbf{u}(t)$ tends to zero, making $\Psi_\infty(u)$ still less than one (see exercise 9.1.3).

If the process has a finite equilibrium (see (6.6.9)) and $\lim \sigma_{\mathbf{u}}(1, T) > 0$ for $T \to \infty$ (see (6.6.12)) as in parts (b) and (d) of Fig. 7.1.2 then the ruin is usually certain, i.e. $\Psi_\infty = 1$, as further analysis can prove (see exercise 9.1.1). This can be anticipated also from the topmost curve of Fig. 7.5.1.

Figure 9.1.1 exhibits some typical flows of Ψ_T.

(c) A condition for non-zero survival probability It must be appreciated that these examples do not exhaust all the types of processes; nor are the referred conditions always sufficient to keep $\Psi_\infty(u) < 1$. The crucial fact is the speed with which the cross-cut ruin probability $\varphi(t)$ (see (6.6.19)) decreases when $t \to \infty$. This regulates the increment

$$\Delta\Psi_t = \Psi_{t+1} - \Psi_t, \tag{9.1.1}$$

and makes the sum

$$\Psi_\infty = \sum_{t=1}^{\infty} \Delta\Psi_t, \qquad (9.1.2)$$

equal to one or less than one. It follows directly from (6.9.3) that the condition

$$\sum_{t=t_0}^{\infty} \varphi(t) < 1, \qquad (9.1.3)$$

is sufficient for non-zero survival probability at least for $t_0 = 1$. This can be extended to any t_0 by some auxiliary conditions (see exercise 9.1.2).

Another method of evaluating $\Delta\Psi_t$ can be obtained by means of the truncated convolution algorithm (6.7.9) or (6.7.11). It can, for instance, be seen (exercise 9.1.1) that if any finite limit, however large, is assumed for the 'wealth' of the insurer, i.e. a finite upper limit for $U(t)$, then Ψ_∞ is always equal to 1 by quite general conditions. Such an upper limit is called the reflection barrier. It can be supposed that any possible excess of $U(t)$ is divided as bonuses, dividends, etc. In fact a non-zero survival probability can then be obtained only by letting U exceed all limits which, indeed, is a rather unrealistic condition from the point of view of applications. This is a well-known *paradox of classical risk theory*. The nice problem of seeking conditions for non-zero survival probability cannot be dealt with in this book other than by an example in exercise 9.1.3 (see also Ruohonen (1980)).

Exercise 9.1.1 Assume that the underwriting process satisfies the equation $U(t) = r_i U(t-1) + P_\lambda - X(t)$, $U(0) \equiv U_0$, for $t = 1, 2, \ldots$, where the variables $X(t)$ are mutually independent. Further, assume that the variables $U(t)$ have an upper limit of some bound U_{max} (e.g. possible excesses being given away as bonuses or dividends), and that the ruin barrier is $U_r(t) \equiv 0$.

(i) Show that if $M = r_i U_{max} + P_\lambda$ and if

$$\text{prob}\{X(t) > M\} \geq \varepsilon > 0 \text{ for every } t, \qquad (9.1.4)$$

then $\Psi_\infty = 1$. P_λ and r_i are constant (they could be allowed to vary, however, having some finite upper limits).

(ii) Show that $\Psi_\infty = 1$ still applies when (9.1.4) is replaced by the weaker condition

$$\sum_{t=1}^{\infty} \text{prob}\{\mathbf{X}(t) > M\} = \infty. \tag{9.1.4'}$$

Note that (9.1.4) holds, for example, in the case where the variables $\mathbf{X}(t)$ have a d.f. of the compound Poisson type.

**Exercise 9.1.2 Prove that (9.1.3) is a sufficient condition for $\Psi_\infty < 1$ provided that the condition $\Delta \Psi_t \leqslant \varphi_{cc}(t)$ holds for $t > t_0$ (see (6.9.7)) and that $\Psi_{t_0} < 1$.

**Exercise 9.1.3 Assume that in the u-process dealt with in item 6.6(b) the parameters r_i, r_g, r_p and λ are constants and $r_{igp} < 1$, $r_g > 1$, $\sigma_q = 0$ and $u_r(t) = 0$. Prove that if the condition $\Delta \Psi_t \leqslant \varphi_{cc}(t)$ is satisfied for $t > t_0$, then $\Psi_\infty < 1$. (Make use of the Tchebyshev inequality.)

9.2 The infinite time ruin probability

(a) Special assumptions The famous formula for the infinite time ruin probability Ψ_∞, often briefly denoted Ψ and called 'ruin probability', is discussed in this chapter. Consideration is limited to the very special case, where the risk process is *stationary* and *no fluctuations* in basic probabilities, either short term or long term, are present. Also the safety loading λ, and thus implicitly the rating, is never changed; furthermore, interest and inflation are omitted and the continuous checking of the state is adopted (see item 1.4(b)).

The assumption concerning stationarity can be replaced by a more general assumption allowing a preprogrammed deterministic change of the parameter n, the expected number of claims. Anyway, the independence of the stochastically defined increments is assumed.

Hence it will be assumed that the distribution function F of the total amount of claims during one year remains unchanged, or at least that its changes are generated merely by changes in the size of the portfolio giving rise to changes in the expected number of claims each year. However, it will always be assumed that the distribution of the size of a claim is independent of time.

The detailed treatment of the problem is deferred to Appendix C.

(b) Ruin probability Summarizing the main results of Appendix C it can be stated that the probability that the company will be ruined is:

$$\Psi(U) = C(U)e^{-RU}, \tag{9.2.1}$$

where $U(=U(0)=U_0)$ is the initial solvency margin (risk reserve) and $C(U)$ is an auxiliary function having values less than 1. The coefficient R is a positive constant, termed the 'adjustment coefficient' or 'insolvency coefficient' or Lundberg's coefficient. In the Poisson case R is the root of

$$1 + (1 + \lambda)mR = \int_0^\infty e^{RZ}\, dS(Z), \tag{9.2.2}$$

and in the Polya case the root of

$$1 + \frac{h}{n}(1 - e^{-(1 + \lambda)mnR/h}) = \int_0^\infty e^{RZ}\, dS(Z). \tag{9.2.3}$$

The auxiliary function $C(U)$ depends on the special characteristics of the process concerned, among other things on the claim size d.f. S. If the claim sizes have an upper limit M, i.e. $S(M) = 1$ then

$$e^{-RM} < C(U) < 1,$$

as will be proved in Appendix C, equation (C.16). Hence we have

$$e^{-RM} e^{-RU} < \Psi(U) < e^{-RU}, \tag{9.2.4}$$

M may be the retention limit applied in reinsurance. Normally it is small compared with the initial solvency margin U, which makes the limits of the above equalities close to each other as will be shown in exercise 9.2.2. Also more generally the function C is often close to 1 and consequently $\Psi(U) \approx e^{-RU}$ usually gives a satisfactory approximation for the infinite time ruin probability.

Equations (9.2.2) and (9.2.3) can be solved by means of well-known numerical or graphical methods. Using the exponential expansion of e^{RZ} and integrating term by term, (9.2.2) is transformed into the form

$$24m\lambda = 12a_2 R + 4a_3 R^2 + a_4 R^3 + \cdots,$$

from which R can be found by a few trials. By using the first or first two terms and the risk indexes r_2 and r_3 (see (3.3.8)) the following approximations are obtained:

$$R = \frac{2\lambda}{r_2} \frac{1}{m} \tag{9.2.5a}$$

$$R = \frac{1}{m} \sqrt{\left[\frac{6\lambda}{r_3} + \frac{9r_2^2}{4r_3^2} \right]} - \frac{3r_2}{2r_3 m}. \tag{9.2.5b}$$

(c) **Applications** Many of the problems considered in the previous chapters can also be treated by making use of (9.2.1). In fact it fully corresponds to the basic equation (4.1.7a) and its counterpart (7.2.1) for the finite time planning horizon. Some examples will be given in the following items and in the exercises of this section.

(d) Ψ **as function of U and λ** First the ruin probabilities for the claim size distribution given in Table 3.6.1 with $M = £$ million are presented on a semi-logarithmic scale (Fig. 9.2.1). It is seen how

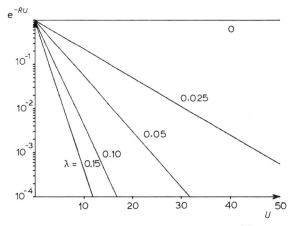

Figure 9.2.1   The (approximate) ruin probability $\Psi \approx e^{-RU}$ as a function of U and λ. The default data are the standards defined in item 7.1(d) (semi-logarithmic scale).

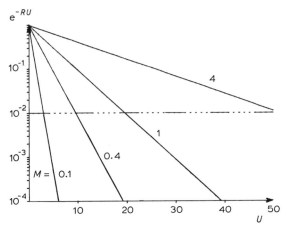

Figure 9.2.2   *The (approximate) ruin probability as a function of U and M; default data as standards of item* 7.1(*d*) (*semi-logarithmic scale*).

closely the value of Ψ/C is linked to the safety loading λ and the initial reserve U. If $\lambda = 0$, it can be proved that $\Psi = 1$, i.e. ruin is certain.

(e) Ψ as a function of U and M   is computed in Fig. 9.2.2. Fixing the value of Ψ the maximum net retention M as a function of U can be read from the figure (dotted line). This figure is a counterpart of Fig. 7.3.1. The crucial difference in the numerical values is due to the fact that cycles of the basic probabilities were assumed in Section 7.3 but are omitted in the present Chapter 9.

(f) Indifference to the size of the portfolio   A strange feature of the e^{-RU} approximation is that it depends only on the distribution function of one claim and the safety loading λ. This statement means, paradoxically, that the size of the company plays no part in calculating, for example, the initial reserves U when the Poisson model is used. This may be difficult to appreciate, especially as for example in Fig. 4.2.2 or in Fig. 7.2.1 it was specifically stated that the reserves should depend on the size of the company. However, the contradiction is only apparent and is due to the assumption that the state of the process is checked continually at every time t. The process $U(t)$ is constituted, independently of the size of the company, as the difference of the incoming premium flow and the outgoing claims flow. The difference between a small company and a large one is that in the latter case more premiums and accordingly more claims are coming and going in a time unit. This can be expressed in another way: it takes perhaps ten years for a small company to experience all that could happen in one year in a large company. But because the state is tested continuously and the time-span is infinite this does not affect the final ruin probability.

If, however, testing for Ψ is only at the end of each fiscal year even if the observations are continued without limit, then a large company has the smaller probability of insolvency, i.e. the function $C(U)$ (see (9.2.1)) deviates more from 1. Since companies are, in general, mainly interested in the measurement of insolvency at the end of each fiscal year, it can thus be expected that the e^{-RU} method leads to larger reserves than necessary, especially for large companies.

(g) Short-cut formulae can be derived for the rapid use of (9.2.1) by applying techniques similar to those employed in Section 4.2.

Exercise 9.2.1 Calculate e^{-RU} for $U = £10^7$ and data given in item 7.1(d).

Exercise 9.2.2 Evaluate the relation of the limits (9.2.4) assuming that $M \leqslant 0.02U$ and that e^{-RU} is either 0.01 or 0.001.

9.3 Discussion of the different methods

(a) One-year approach In this section some further comments will be made concerning the main lines of approach to risk theory problems, as viewed at the beginning of the book in Section 1.4 and implemented in the preceding chapters.

The great advantage of considerations limited to one year only (or any other finite period with a single test point) is that the formulae can be obtained in a form which lends itself to easy computation and which provides a good guide to the interdependence of the main variables n, λ, ε, M, σ_q and U. The trends and variations of basic probabilities have no conclusive influence during short periods and they can therefore be estimated in a rather crude way. The great disadvantage of the short-period method is that it does not directly deal with the long-term continuation of the company's life. From the point of view of the company's management it is not sufficient to arrange reinsurance, different reserves, etc. so that the company will still have a minimum degree of solvency after one year. On the contrary, it is necessary to plan all the security measures affecting the company's existence for an unlimited number of years in the future. Attention was paid to this aspect in the applications of Chapter 4, recommending the cautious choice of the variables, particularly by taking only a part of the actual free reserves as the initial capital U. Often it may be intuitively possible to estimate what part of the reserves the company's management is prepared to lose in one year taking the worst possible view, and to take for this purpose, for example, one-third of the actual reserves. Should this amount really be lost, then reinsurance and other security measures must be re-evaluated and necessary amendments made immediately.

(b) Finite time approach For elimination of the arbitrariness in regard to the choice of the variable U, long-term considerations are developed. This is especially so because the variations in basic probabilities, like trends and cycles as well as inflation, are of crucial importance and necessarily demand a long planning horizon. For this purpose the formula apparatus was extended to an arbitrary time period $(0, T]$ in Chapters 6 and 7. The rather complicated structure of the model restricted consideration mainly to numerical techniques, which are scarely manageable without at least modest computers. The interconnection of the numerous model variables could not be given in any simple analytic form. Fortunately the graphic presentation of the results, which can conveniently be produced even by small computers, effectively provides a survey over the structure of the model. A great merit of the finite time technique is that it can be kept workable without restrictive preconditions and special assumption, for example concerning the variations – both short and long – of the basic probabilities, inflation or the claim size d.f.

(c) Infinite time approach The extreme alternative for the future safety of the company is to take an infinite period. For this reason the e^{-RU} technique has been given considerable attention in actuarial literature. It can be used for evaluation of conservative limits for finite time probabilities providing, however, assumptions are made about the specified stationarity of the process. Unfortunately, elaboration of the calculations and the necessity to keep the ruin probability from becoming equal to one seems to lead to serious restrictions in the choice of model assumptions.

This method also has some other obscure points. In particular, the results, as is seen in Fig. 9.2.1, are all very sensitive to the size of λ and in other respects the method also involves assumptions concerning all future time. Even if it were possible to estimate λ for a few future years, it is very difficult to say what it will be subsequently. In fact, experience shows that different kinds of trends, amendments of premium tariff and also other circumstances are always changing λ, often cyclically. On the other hand, it is sometimes observed that only the very beginning of the process affects the value of e^{-RU} (see Figs 7.1.2, 7.5.1 and 9.1.1). When the dangerous part of the process is passed then the longer future has no significant influence; this would suggest the infinite time ruin probability as an acceptable upper limit for finite time approaches. This seems, however, to be true only as a consequence of rather restricted conditions and by letting the *reserves grow to infinity*. In practice this is clearly an unrealistic situation, indeed. This is 'the paradox' mentioned in item 9.1(c): if it is assumed that there exists some upper limit for the accumulated profit, however large it may be, over which the company will not increase its reserves, then $\Psi = 1$. In other words, all the companies subject to this assumption will sooner or later be ruined.

It is true that some of the trends have no fatal influence on the insolvency probabilities, perhaps no influence at all. This is so as regards the growth in volume, which is indicated by the increase in the annual number of claims n. In fact, it only means that the process runs more rapidly as stated in item 9.2(f). Unfortunately, however, other trends and long-term oscillations seem to have an influence which is difficult to estimate, and, as noted above, some of the future changes can have such serious consequences that simple methods become of no value.

One point in the e^{-RU} method was the assumption of continuous checking which can give excessively large values for large companies. Another arbitrariness exists in the selection of a suitable insolvency probability $\varepsilon = e^{-RU}$. The same selection is also certainly necessary for short-period systems, but as regards infinite or long periods the problem has another dimension. This is a rather nice question which may be seen by considering the alternatives of whether to allow an insolvency in one year with probability $\varepsilon = 10^{-4}$ or over ten years with probability $\varepsilon = 10^{-3}$ or over an infinite period with $\varepsilon = 10^{-2}$.

(d) An optimum choice may be available between two extremes, i.e. between the one-year system and the infinite system, taking into consideration some finite number of fiscal years. As shown in Chapters 6 and 7 it is feasible, at least if computers are available, to study the insolvency problem attached to a suitable series of consecutive years in a very flexible way and to experiment with different assumptions concerning the behaviour of the basic variables and the claim size d.f. S. In this way it may be possible to utilize methods which are known from operational research studies. Different kinds of assumptions and operational rules can be experimented with; for example it may be possible to program rules of procedure which are to apply if the profit is rapidly accumulating excessively, or vice versa if it is diminishing, as will be referred to in Chapter 10. These rules can concern bonus systems, amendments of tariffs, interest yield on the accumulated reserves, changes of the maximum net retention as a function of the accumulated solvency margins, etc. It also seems necessary to include conditions concerning special circumstances like competition and taxation.

The question of which of the different methods is suitable and which is superior to the others is, of course, very much dependent on the special circumstances and the way in which the question is asked. It may often be advisable to apply the different methods and ways of proceeding in parallel, and it will probably prove both interesting and illustrative to compare the results reached.

CHAPTER 10

Application of risk theory to business planning

10.1 General features of the models

(a) The purpose of the model The many applications of the theory of risk described in the previous chapters, such as the estimation of a suitable level for the maximum net retention, the evaluation of stability, the safety loading and the magnitude of the funds, have been treated as isolated aspects of an insurance business. In this chapter an endeavour will be made to build up a picture of the management process in its entirety and to place the risk theoretical aspects in the context of other management aspects, many of which are not of an actuarial nature. In this way many of the applications previously dealt with can be integrated with the concepts of modern business planning, in particular the techniques of long-range planning and dynamic programming.

The object is to describe the actual management process of the insurance business by means of a mathematical model.

(b) Corporate planning The construction of the model depends on the objectives of the user. If it is aimed at corporate planning it may be very rich in details simulating all the actions of an insurance office which may be relevant for the trading result. It is used e.g. to forecast the future flow of business and to help in evaluation of different policy alternatives. A corporate planning model can analyse the business structures and answer questions of the type 'what ... if ...'. To be successful it should be closely incorporated with the conventional accounting and statistical functions extracting the necessary data basis from them. Pioneering work in the building of insurance models is credited to McGuinness (1954). Descriptions of models have been recently published for instance by Heubeck (1971), Galitz (1982, so-called ASIR model) Gelder and Schauwers (1981), Geusau (1981) Reischel (1981) and Roy (1981).

(c) **Risk theory models** Model building is useful also for the study of risk-theoretical behaviour of portfolios, e.g. for analysis of the solvency conditions. It can be developed as a natural extension to the conventional risk theory, with the purpose of giving a comprehensive view over the structures as a whole and of trying to find tie-ins between the numerous aspects involved. Then it is sufficient to select from the very numerous variables and details which are needed in comprehensive corporate models only those which are most relevant for solvency properties. This line will be followed in the sequel. A model of this type was experimented with in a Finnish solvency study (Pentikäinen, 1982 and Rantala, 1982).

In order to facilitate the reading only the main lines will be drawn. For example, the decomposition of the portfolio in sections is omitted; even though it would not be difficult in principle to accomplish using the technique described in Section 6.4, its implementation can be laborious. Furthermore, problems concerning rate-making, technical reserves and many other aspects which are relevant for corporate planning are not dealt with, because it has been necessary to limit the scope of this book to aspects which are suitably handled by the technique of risk theory. For the same reason 'non-stochastic risks' like failures in investments, political risks, consequences of misfeasance or malfeasance by management are not discussed, notwithstanding the fact that they may be quite important and can seriously jeopardize the solvency of insurers (see Pentikäinen, 1982, Section 2.9).

The presentation will be limited to approaches which are best fitted to non-life insurance. However, life insurance can also be handled in a similar way, in particular if the planning horizon is fairly short. For the long-range consideration of life insurance, modifications and attention to the special features along the lines discussed in Chapter 8 are necessary. It is a matter of course also that generally, in all kinds of business, the capability of models of producing reliable analyses rapidly deteriorates when the time-span grows because most of the basic distributions and data distort in a way which is barely predictable, and because the environment where the future insurers operate is likely to be very different from the present one. However, prognoses extended to cover rather long future periods may also be of interest. Despite the fact that they may be of little value in giving a reliable view of the true total situation, the models can illustrate the structures and properties of insurance undertakings and help to understand underlying tie-ins. Of course, the models can be improved by further developing and refining the basic assumptions – which were made in the preceding chapters and will now be adopted as building blocks for the more comprehensive approaches we are going to deal with in this chapter – but discussion about them is beyond the scope of the presentation, which is necessarily to be limited to monitor mainly general features of the risk theory and its applications.

(d) General structure of the models Revenues and expenditures will be incorporated in the model as displayed in Fig. 10.1.1. The difference between the incoming and outgoing money flows is accumulated into the risk reserve – or as it is nowadays called – the solvency margin U.

The schedule is essentially the same as is conventionally used in the accounting of profit and loss statements and balance sheets. This basic setting also constitutes the framework of various prognoses and business analysis schemes according to the current practice of insurers. The conventional prognoses are mostly deterministic. The major contribution of risk theory is that the forecast can be made *stochastic*. The apparatus developed in previous chapters can now be incorporated into the schedule. Then a model is achieved which gives the future state as a *distribution* of the relevant variables, i.e. a range in which for example the solvency margin can be expected to lie after some time interval, whereas a deterministic model gives only one single value. This approach makes it possible to deal with problems where solvency is also involved, an aspect which is mostly not adequately possible in deterministic systems.

Another advantage of the risk-theoretical approach is that planning schemes can be made *dynamic*, i.e. the system can be made self-controlling or, as is often said, adaptive. For example, if the solvency during the planning horizon T is weakening, special rules can be programmed which provide restoring measures such as increases in premium rates, economies in cost, etc. This idea was exemplified in Section 7.7 and can be benefited from in model building.

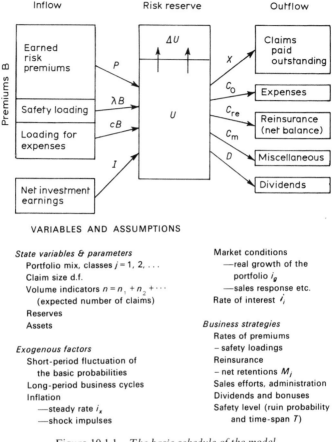

Figure 10.1.1   *The basic schedule of the model.*

10.2   An example of risk theory models

(a) Synthesis of submodels The idea displayed in the schedule of Fig. 10.1.1 can be readily written, using the notation shown in the figure, in the form

$$\mathbf{B} + \mathbf{I} = \mathbf{X} + \mathbf{C}_0 + \mathbf{C}_{re} + \mathbf{C}_m + \mathbf{D} + \Delta \mathbf{U}. \qquad (10.2.1)$$

The variables involved need detailed definition in order to make the model operative. In fact, each of them represents the outcome of corresponding submodels, as will be seen in the following, and (10.2.1) represents a synthesis of these submodels.

All the variables may be stochastic (printed in bold letters) even though it may be necessary often to simplify the model by assuming that many of the elements involved are deterministic. For example, it is convenient to concentrate the stochasticity of the premium income into the safety loading λ defining (see (6.2.11))

$$\mathbf{B} = P/(1 - c - \lambda_b),$$

where the risk premium should be found deterministically by using the technique developed in Chapter 6. Methods to implement the the stochasticity of λ_b (or λ) were discussed in item 6.2(e) and in Section 7.7.

(b) Three ways of handling ceded reinsurance One way to construct the basic schedule is to calculate the premium income $\mathbf{B}$, claims $\mathbf{X}$ and other variables *gross of reinsurance*. It is illustrative to unite all transactions concerning the ceded reinsurance as one single entry, the 'reinsurance cost'

$$\mathbf{C}_{re} = \mathbf{B}_{re} - \mathbf{X}_{re}, \tag{10.2.2}$$

where $\mathbf{B}_{re}$ is the amount of the ceded reinsurance premiums accounted as earned amount and net of commissions and bonuses and $\mathbf{X}_{re}$ is the reinsurers' share of claims including the outstanding claims.

Another approach can be used when the trading result on the insurer's own account, i.e. net of reinsurance, is concerned. Then the premiums and claims are decomposed in the shares which are due to the insurer's net retention and due to the reinsurers:

$$\mathbf{B} = \mathbf{B}_o + \mathbf{B}_{re} = \mathbf{B}_o + P_{re}(1 + \lambda_{re})$$
$$\mathbf{X} = \mathbf{X}_o + \mathbf{X}_{re},$$

where the subscripts 'o' and 're' refer to the insurer's own account and to the reinsurers. P_{re} is the ceded part of the risk premiums and λ_{re} the loading including net compensation of the reinsurers' expenses, safety margin and profit margin. Substituting in (10.2.1), the reinsurance terms offset each other and the equation is transformed in the following *net of reinsurance* form

$$\mathbf{B}_o + \mathbf{I} = \mathbf{X}_o + \mathbf{C}_o + \mathbf{C}_m + \mathbf{D} + \Delta\mathbf{U}. \tag{10.2.3}$$

In fact this formulation is used conventionally in risk theory, and that was the case also in the foregoing chapters.

Formula (10.2.3) has, however, the inconvenience that the re-insurance cost is hidden in the calculation rules and in the rates of B_o and X_o. A *compromise* would be to decompose $\mathbf{X}_{re}$ into its expectation P_{re} and stochastic variation $\Delta\mathbf{X}_r(=\mathbf{X}_{re}-P_{re})$ and then to substitute into (10.2.2) and (10.2.1) $\mathbf{X}_{re} = P_{re} + \Delta\mathbf{X}_{re}$, $\mathbf{X} = \mathbf{X}_o + P_{re} + \Delta\mathbf{X}_{re}$ and $\mathbf{B}_{re} = (1 + \lambda_{re})P_{re}$

$$\mathbf{B} + \mathbf{I} = \mathbf{X}' + \mathbf{C}'_{re} + \mathbf{C}_o + \mathbf{C}_m + \mathbf{D} + \Delta\mathbf{U}, \qquad (10.2.4)$$

where

$$\mathbf{X}' = \mathbf{X}_o + P_{re} \qquad (10.2.5)$$

$$\mathbf{C}'_{re} = \lambda_{re}P_{re}. \qquad (10.2.6)$$

This approach is based on the fact that $\Delta\mathbf{X}_{re}$ does not affect the trading result $\Delta\mathbf{U}$ because it is included, with the $+$ sign in $\mathbf{X}$ and the $-$ sign in $\mathbf{C}_{re}$. Hence, when the outcome on the insurer's net retention only is concerned it is unnecessary to simulate the stochastic value of $\mathbf{X}_{re}$ because the net result is the same as if it is replaced by its expected value.

The benefit of the version (10.2.4) is that the reinsurance cost is expressly shown, which is particularly useful when different reinsurance policies are investigated and compared (see the example given in item 4.5(d)). The type of the reinsurance treaty as well as its parameters like the retention limits M and the target level of the loading λ_{re} are model parameters.

A more detailed analysis should necessarily concern also *the effect of the yield of interest* earned for the shares of reserves or for the agreed depositions.

In what follows the choice of the approach is left open: the user can understand the basic variables either as gross amounts or net amounts and in the latter case drop the term $\mathbf{C}_{re}$ from the equations, if it is taken into account in the definition of the variable values calculated on the insurer's net retention. It is also dependent on the application concerned whether λ_{re} and consequently $\mathbf{C}_{re}$ are to be assumed stochastic or deterministic.

(c) Premiums have already been defined in Sections 4.1 and 6.2, and the technique to handle stochastic control was discussed in connection with (10.2.4). The growth of the premium income is controlled by the trend factor $r_g(t)$ (6.1.2), 'premium inflation' factor $r_p(t)$ (6.2.1) and safety loading $\lambda(t)$ (6.5.12).

Because the earned premiums, which are provided in the equations, are calculated by deducting from the written premiums the increment of *the reserve of unearned premiums*, the aspect related to the reserve calculations is also to be considered in advanced comprehensive models. However, because the relation of this reserve to the premium volume is fairly constant and not seriously sensitive to inflation and other disturbances, it was suggested in item 6.5(h) that the interest earned for the reserve could be amalgamated into the safety loading, after which this reserve may not be needed any more as a special entry. The case is essentially another in the long-term analysis of life insurance, where it may be necessary to follow the flow of the policy reserves for instance by means of the technique outlined in Chapter 8.

(d) Investments have already been discussed in Section 6.3. In advanced models different investment strategies can be assumed and their outcomes analysed and optimized.

A major difficulty is to find realistic assumptions concerning the future returns earned for the investment, i.e. for the entry $I(t)$ in (10.2.1). The interest yield or the concept of rate of return, which includes also movements in the capital value of the investments, depends on varying conditions of the general investment markets of the country and on the investment strategies which the management has chosen. Some suggestions have been made that $I(t)$ could also be taken to be stochastic in order to take into account the often quite great variations in the rate of interest and of security values. A major difficulty is, however, to find any meaningful distributions. The rate of interest notoriously depends very much on the political decisions which are in the hands of governments or the national central banks. There is also some correlation between the variation in different countries. The 'genuine' random fluctuation in the interest rates seems to be of a smaller order of magnitude than the long-term political and economic changes. The examples given in Figs 6.3.1 and 6.3.2 illustrate the situation.

As was seen in previous chapters, a more relevant feature of the interest rate is its relation to the simultaneous inflation rates and also to the real growth of the portfolio, all three effects being combined in the important growth factor r_{igp} or, in a more general case, in $r(t_1, t_2)$ (see (6.5.8) and (6.6.1)). In advanced models it may be appropriate to treat the rate of interest $i_i(t)$ and the inflation rates $i_x(t)$ and $i_p(t)$ as separate variables, trying to find appropriate assumptions for their combinations. Experience has convincingly shown that all these quantities are subject to long-term major variations and, in addition, to short-term oscillations having a minor amplitude. The abundant econometric literature may suggest ideas for the construction of proper submodels for these features. At present there are no well-developed theoretical disciplines available for insurance applications. As has already been suggested in item 6.3(b), the sensitivity of the model outcomes to the investment entries may be tested by making varying optimistic and pessimistic deterministic (or semi-deterministic) assumptions about the anticipated future level of the return rates and their relation to inflation and growth.

In risk theory models the investment earnings can be handled in different ways. They can be kept as a separate variable or they can be divided between the underwriting reserves and the solvency margin as was suggested in Section 6.5 (see (6.5.2) and (6.5.12)).

(e) Underwriting result and claims   As a next step, terms relating to the underwriting profit will be united

$$\mathbf{Y}(t) = (1 + \lambda(t))P(t) - \mathbf{X}(t), \qquad (10.2.7a)$$

where $\mathbf{Y}$ means the result of the underwriting business on the insurer's net retention. The variables P and $\mathbf{X}$ have already been defined above. The safety loading λ can conveniently include also the income gained on the technical reserves following the technique put forward in item 6.5(h). The definition of this loading depends also on the handling of reinsurance as discussed in item (b).

In fact, the results derived in Chapter 6 are now directly applicable.

The claims $\mathbf{X}$ in the above formula, as generally in the foregoing, include both paid and outstanding items. As mentioned already in item 3.1(c) this involves an idealization: it is supposed that any claim is paid immediately when it occurs. It was stated that factually the inaccuracies in the evaluation of outstanding claims, including also effects of inflation, do not escape from the model. Their effect is to move possible profits or losses only from year to year and should be allowed for in the basic data of the model when these are derived from actual records. However, for advanced models, which are constructed for corporate planning, it is highly advisable to consider the outstanding claims as a set of separate variables, in particular in the case of long-tail business. A shock inflation especially can give rise to adverse effects which should not be ignored. An extra reinforcement of the reserve may be necessary, as has already been discussed in item 6.1(l).

The adequacy of the outstanding claims reserves is commonly checked *a posteriori* by means of 'run-off triangles' or by otherwise comparing the actual claims amounts with the reserve estimates made earlier. If the deviations appear noticeable compared with the total business volume and with the 'normal' fluctuation of the underwriting business a simple way to amend the model is to take the estimation error of the outstanding claims as a special entry $\mathbf{O}(t)$ into the model replacing (10.2.7a) by

$$\mathbf{Y}(t) = (1 + \lambda)P(t) - \mathbf{X}(t) + \mathbf{O}(t). \qquad (10.2.7b)$$

The variable $\mathbf{O}(t)$ should be defined and calibrated in a way which fits with observed experience and with the reasonably anticipated future development. It can be expressed in terms of a random component (so-called pure 'noise') and cyclical and trend components if necessary. Special attention to inflation can be focused in particular in case of long-tail business. The standard methods of mathematical statistics are available as well as the recent rapid development of the theoretical and practical consideration of the problems about the outstanding claims. The discussion of further details falls, however, outside the scope of this book. Reference to the research work of the Insurance Technical Laboratory of the University of Copenhagen (a comprehensive report was expected around 1983) as well as the proceedings of the XVI ASTIN Colloquium in Liège 1982 can be made.

(f) Expenses Usually the insurers also use special accounting for their expenses. Its outcomes can be linked with the model as a special entry through the terms C_o and C_m. C_o represents all the sales and operating expenses the insurer may have. C_m includes different kind of miscellaneous entries in the loss and profit account. These items may be either stochastically or deterministically defined. Probably it will be convenient to keep them deterministic and move the uncertainties to the safety loading λ (see item 6.2(d)). This is supposed to have been done in the present considerations, and these variables are denoted accordingly (no longer using bold letters).

It is convenient to divide the expenses C_o into two parts. On the one hand every insurer has some *normal* costs which cannot be controlled much by the insurer, at least not in any radical way in the short term. Some of these costs are related to the volume of sales of new policies, some to the number of policies in force and some to the number of claims. On the other hand, some other costs, e.g. those related to the sales, are very much under the control of the management, and it is advisable to introduce a special variable Q for them. Hence the total costs are composed of a normal amount C_1 and a *moving* part Q as follows.

$$C_o = C_1 + Q.$$

As will be seen in Section 10.3, Q can be one of the key issues in a dynamic program, because e.g. sales campaigns and other similar operation policies can be introduced into the model by using it. Furthermore, alternative actions concerning personal, office facilities, etc. can be considered. For example, investments in new buildings and inventories will obviously first cause a rise in expenses but later on will reduce them.

The normal costs C_1 should be programmed to depend on the forecasted business volume. Often a sufficient approximation for a risk theory model may be to assume them proportional to the premium income $P(t)$, as was presented in item 6.2(f), i.e. $C_1(t) = c'P(t)$, where c' was adopted as a coefficient related to unloaded risk premiums P instead of the coefficient c which was used in (6.2.8). In fact, $c' = c/(1 - c - \lambda_b)$ as seen from (6.2.11). It is natural in this connection to base the supposed actual costs on a quantity which is not stochastically varying. This was the rationale for the change of the definition.

Tax is one of the relevant items of the model. Its consideration and programming depends on local legislation and practice. We assume it to be included in expenses in one way or other. Some actuaries have suggested it as a separate entry in the basic equation (10.2.3) and provided rules on its dependence on the book profit (and dividends).

(g) Dividends is another entry in the basic schedule. It is supposed that this concept consists of the 'ordinary dividends' divided between the stockholders of proprietary companies, as well as bonuses given possibly to the policy-holders. It depends essentially on the business objectives. The topic will be discussed in Section 10.4. If the underwriting business is considered on the basis of the interest of an outside investor, i.e. the stockholder of the insurance company or a private underwriter, then a natural idea is to search for strategies that maximize the dividends. Another approach, natural for bonuses of mutual companies and also for dividends of many proprietary companies operating in modern environments, is to consolidate them to some suitable level preferably in one way or another related to the volume of the business

$$\mathbf{D}(t + 1) = d \times \mathbf{B}(t), \tag{10.2.8}$$

where again $\mathbf{B}$ is the premium income and d is a constant which is one of the free parameters of the model.

(h) Modified basic equation It is often useful to rearrange the terms of the original schedule (10.2.1) in a way in which the net results of the different operational sections are entries instead of the incoming and outgoing money flows

$$\mathbf{Y}_x(t) + \mathbf{Y}_i(t) + Y_c(t) - C_{re}(t) = \mathbf{D}(t + 1) + Q(t + 1) + \Delta\mathbf{U}(t), \tag{10.2.9}$$

where $\mathbf{Y}_x(t)$ is the underwriting profit (or loss) (10.2.7b); $\mathbf{Y}_i(t)$ is the net income gained on investments; $Y_c(t) = cB - C_1 - C_m$ is the net surplus of the expense budget, which is equal to the loading minus the actual operating expenses, the term Q being excluded (item (f)); $C_{re}(t)$ is the (consolidated) reinsurance cost (10.2.6); $\mathbf{D}(t + 1)$ are the dividends, e.g. according to (10.2.8); $Q(t + 1)$ are the specified extra sales or other expenses as defined in item (f); and $\Delta\mathbf{U}$ is the increment of the risk reserve, equal to the amount allocated to enforce the financial status of the insurer, equal to the balancing term of the equation (10.2.9).

Only four of the variables in (10.2.9) were assumed stochastic (bold letter), despite the fact that the other variables can also be modelled stochastic. For example, they can indirectly via the technique of dynamic programming depend on the outcomes of 'primarily' stochastic variables like the underwriting profit $\mathbf{Y}_x$.

Equation (10.2.9) is a direct extension of the basic equation (6.5.1) which constituted the basis for finite time considerations. The l.h.s. gives the resources available and the r.h.s. their allocation.

The same simulation technique as applied in the foregoing chapters can be used also for this generalized model as well as many of the analytic evaluations and short-cuts derived above. However, the new features introduced require special attention. They are dealt with in the subsequent sections.

10.3   Stochastic dynamic programming

(a) Theory and practice of dynamic programming It is useful to note that the model drafted above is along the same lines as the approach which was originally called *industrial dynamics*, due to Forrester (1972). It is mostly concerned with the flow of work, decision-making and other kind of operations *inside* factories and organizations. An attempt to apply the idea to insurance environments was reported by Veit (1976). The industrial dynamics method has been widely used for operational research and planning and its name has recently changed to '*system dynamics*'. A comprehensive survey of this discipline is edited by Roberts (1978).

Our model also has features similar to so-called *dynamic programming*, which is a tool much used in the operational research applied to many industries. A well-developed mathematical discipline exists for these topics; pioneering work was published by Bellman (1957) (see also Nemhauser (1966) for example).

The idea of dynamic programming is to provide the calculation algorithm with rules which control the flow of subsequent steps in a way which depends on the outcome of the preceding steps. An example of the dynamic control rule has already been given in Section 7.7, where the *premium rates* were changed according to the level of the solvency ratio via the safety loading. The actual change in safety loading can be obtained either by adjusting the premium rates or, at least in emergency cases, by economizing in administration and possibly in other costs as well.

Another way to introduce dynamics into the model is to control the *level of net retention* as a function of the solvency ratio. If the solvency is good, then the company can take more risks in net retention and in that way gain by a reduction in reinsurance costs. If the solvency is getting weak, then as one of the protective measures perhaps the net retentions can also be lowered. This approach was investigated by Pentikäinen (1975) and (1982).

Further dynamics can be introduced by linking some relevant entries with outside impulses like the growth of the national economy. An example was given in item 6.1(f).

(b) Terminology Using the practice of the dynamic programming theory the variables and rules involved in the model can be characterized as follows.

State variables define the state of the system (insurer's fiscal status) at times $t = 0, 1, 2, \ldots$. Volume parameters n, assets, liabilities, solvency margin U, etc. are examples.

Transition equations like (10.2.9) determine the increments of the state variables from each time t to the next $t + 1$.

System parameters are needed to define both the state and transitions. Some of them, such as inflation, depend wholly or at least mainly on the outside circumstances and environment. Some others, so-called decision parameters or rather *decision variables*, can be controlled at least to some degree by the management of each insurer, e.g. premium rates, net retentions and allocation of resources like dividends D and sales efforts Q. Some parameters are of mixed character, being partially dependent on exogenous factors and to some degree on the insurer's own policy decisions. Rate of interest is an example. A set of the numerically assigned decision variables is called *a strategy*. Examples of the variables and factors involved with the model are listed in Fig. 10.1.1.

Aspects of the strategies and business objectives will be discussed in Section 10.4, but before that the idea of dynamic programming is illustrated in the remaining items of this section.

(c) Return functions The strategies mentioned can concern various policy options. In order to get the model operative special rules, so-called return functions, are needed to make possible the evaluation of the consequences of the policy options. As an example the situation is considered when the management decides to attempt to expand the business volume, the market share, launching a sales campaign and allocating money Q (see item 10.2(f)) for the purpose. The problem is to find in one way or another an estimate of the premium increment ΔB which can be expected to be received as a return of the marketing cost – or in other words 'investment' – Q.

There are available a number of textbooks concerning these so-called *sales response functions*, e.g. Kotler (1975).

A sales response function can be, of course, constructed and calibrated only on the basis of experience. Depending on environments and special circumstances Kottler suggests two basic types of functions. The first is *linear*

$$\Delta B = qQ, \tag{10.3.1}$$

where q is a so-called elasticity factor. If, as frequently happens, the return is spread over more than one year, this can be suitably programmed.

Another alternative function is *exponential*. Assume that the extra marketing costs are again Q and in addition that a reduction of p 100% is made in premium rates as another competitive measure. Then the normal formula of the annual premium increment (see (6.5.7)) is changed as follows

$$B(t + 1) = B(t)r_g r_p \left(1 + \frac{Q}{C_o}\right)^\alpha (1 - p)^{-\beta}. \tag{10.3.2}$$

The exponential coefficients are to be found empirically. By a logarithmic differentiation approximate partial effects can be derived

$$\frac{\Delta B_Q}{B} = \alpha \frac{Q}{C_o}, \tag{10.3.3a}$$

and

$$\frac{\Delta B_P}{B} = \beta p. \tag{10.3.3b}$$

Owing to the form of these equations α and β are called 'elasticities'.

A more accurate treatment of the problem is to provide for the situation where the effect is spread over several years. Furthermore, the sales campaign is likely to be concentrated only on some special type of policies and the return can be expected to concern mainly the same type of insurance. However, experience shows that if a new customer is acquired, e.g. owing to lowered rates of motor third-party insurance, his other insurance cover is often moved to the same company irrespective of whether or not any special benefit concerning other classes is offered. This is an extra complication in finding sales responses.

Furthermore, the return of a sales campaign can quite crucially depend on the reactions of the competitors in the same market. For example, the effect of premium reduction will be completely missed if the competitors follow suit. Aspects like this will be discussed in Section 10.5.

An example of sales responses and market reactions is displayed in Fig. 10.5.2.

(d) Algorithm When all the assumptions are settled and values for the model parameters determined, then the model can be operated by means of the Monte Carlo method, just as was presented for the simple underwriting processes in Chapters 6 and 7. The difference is that the number of model variables may be greater and, in addition to the claims, other stochastic variables, e.g. the yield of interest and premiums, via the response functions can also now be stochastic. For different state variables, and above all for the solvency margin U, 'a random walk' can again be obtained as is illustrated in Fig. 10.3.1. In principle it fully corresponds to the simulation figures of the previous chapters, e.g. Figs 6.8.3 and 6.8.4; however, now only the boundaries of the confidence region are plotted.

(e) Characterization of business strategies A major difficulty in the use of models like that just drafted is that the number of variables, distributions and aspects involved can be very great. It is quite difficult for the user to obtain any insight into the structure of the

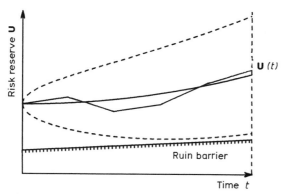

Figure 10.3.1 *An outcome of a stochastic model.*

model which, in fact, is a more or less complicated configuration in a multidimensional parameter space. It is still more difficult to explain successfully the properties and outcomes of the model to any outsider, e.g. to the members of the management team who are not familiar with the technique of dynamic programming and the risk theory. A quite useful approach is graphic data processing. Some of the most relevant variables should be displayed in a way which reveals the essential features of the properties of the process concerned. By changing different strategy parameters new outcomes are obtained, which can usefully be plotted in the same figure to get an idea of the behaviour of the structure. In fact, the graphic display of the result has been amply used already in the foregoing, and it will be still further exemplified in the following.

The variable **U**, the solvency margin, can be selected as one of the main variables. It represents the 'wealth' of an insurer. Another important feature to be followed and analysed is the *volume*. This can be suitably described by the gross premium income on the insurer's net retention **B**, and it will be accepted as the second main variable. It is useful to give a survey of the total situation by plotting the variables **B** and **U** in the same plane. This is done in Fig. 10.3.2, where now instead of time (see Fig. 10.3.1) the premium volume B is displayed on the x-axis.

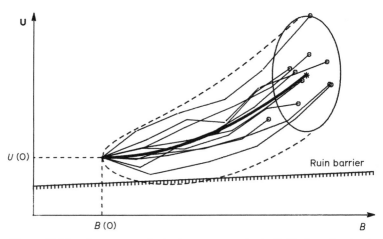

Figure 10.3.2 *An outcome of a business strategy in the B, U plane. Stochastic bundle and its confidence region.*

Each simulation step generates for the variable pair B, U a new outcome which represents the state of business at time t, and the next step at time $t + 1$, etc. A sample path in the B, U plane is a broken line, a 'random walk' as seen in Fig. 10.3.2. The repetition of the simulation generates a bundle of sample paths and the final points represent a sample of the situation at the end of the planning horizon T. For Fig. 10.3.2 it was assumed that not only the solvency margin U but also premium income B is stochastic. Then at a given confidence level the final points are two-dimensionally distributed over a region which is approximately elliptical in shape.

Graphic configurations like that in Fig. 10.3.2 give an idea of the assumed flow of business and properties of chosen strategy options. The more the distribution ellipse is situated to the right, the more expansive, i.e. volume increasing, is the strategy option. The vertical position of the ellipse indicates the solvency situation. If the ellipse or the bundle intersects the ruin barrier, it is an indication of a risky situation.

(f) Comparison of strategies The purpose of the model is above all to give a tool for the evaluation of business strategies and for their comparison. This is illustrated in Fig. 10.3.3, where the outcomes of two strategy options I and II are plotted.

For clarity only the mid-lines (solid lines) and the lower confidence

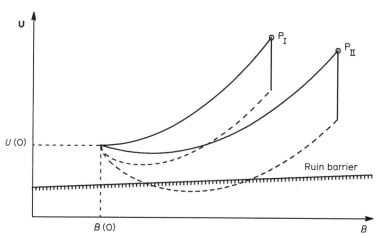

Figure 10.3.3 *A conservative strategy, I, and a risk-taking one, II.*

boundary (dotted lines) of the stochastic bundles are plotted. The endpoints P_I and P_{II} represent the expected average outcomes of the strategies. The lower boundaries make it possible to evaluate the risks involved. The strategy option I is intended to exemplify a conservative policy, not accepting any solvency risks. The strategy option II is an expansive one. At the beginning of the planning period money is invested in marketing which is reflected in a faster growth of the volume B but in a lower growth, even a temporary reduction, of the solvency margin U until the invested costs are regained. However, the stochastic bundle B intersects with the barrier. This can be interpreted as a solvency risk w with this expansive strategy option.

(g) Ruin probabilities can be found as a by-product of the Monte Carlo simulation, as presented in Section 6.8.

(h) Straightforward technique It must be appreciated that, instead of the Monte Carlo simulation, the direct calculation of the final state and the evaluation of ruin probability may often be feasible and advantageous following the ideas presented in Section 6.9. The computation time can thereby be radically shortened. On the other hand if dynamic rules are provided, their handling in direct calculations may be out of the question. Then probably no technique other than simulation can be tractable. Fortunately a fairly small number of sample paths, when plotted appropriately, may be sufficient to give quite a satisfactory visual picture of the process concerned, as was stated in item 6.8.1(d).

10.4 Business objectives

(a) Strategies The above model gives as output the distribution of the final state of the business at the end of the planning period, and as a by-product it can also give an appreciation of the ruin probability during this period. When the strategy assumptions are changed, a new outcome is obtained. A very interesting problem is to try to find 'the best strategy' among the infinitely many options. Is it for instance better to be 'great but poor' or 'smaller but wealthier'? To answer these kinds of questions it is necessary to define the *business goals*, or the objectives which the management will use as a guideline for its decision-making.

(b) Strategic triangle In the earlier literature a business goal often used was the maximization of profit. As recent literature on business behaviour now indicates, this goal is nowadays too narrow. Substantial private entrepreneurs have disappeared and most large enterprises are led by professional managers. Galbraith (1973) describes how the interest of professional managers may be not so much the maximization of the dividends to an often large and diffuse group of stockholders, but rather the safeguarding of the stability and continuity of the enterprise and often – a common status symbol – the achievement of a strong expansion in sales volume. Hence it seems necessary to assume multiple goals. For example, dividends, growth in sales, and growth in net worth can be alternative business goals which must be weighted in some way. These three items correspond to the three r.h.s. terms in (10.2.9). They constitute a 'strategic triangle' as depicted in Fig. 10.4.1. The three goals are mutually contradictory and the problem is to find in one way or another a balance between them.

(c) Selection between the goals One reasonable way is first to provide the solvency constraint ($\Psi_T \leqslant \varepsilon$) to be fulfilled, then to fix some acceptable level for dividends or bonuses (so that the stockholders and/or policyholders are sufficiently satisfied, as

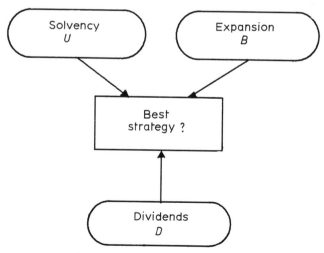

Figure 10.4.1 *The strategic triangle.*

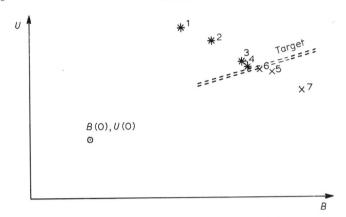

Figure 10.4.2   *Search for an optimal strategy. The labelled points represent outcomes of different strategies.*

Galbraith notes). After that the available resources are to be divided between expansion in sales and net worth, i.e. between the terms Q and ΔU in (10.2.9).

There are at least two approaches here: (i) the 'looking-at-the-chart' method and (ii) the utility function method. The latter will be discussed in items (d)–(h). The former operates simply with a figure like Fig. 10.4.2, where the outcomes of different strategies are points in the plane. They correspond to the average end points P_I and P_{II} in Fig. 10.3.3, the strategy options being specified by the numbers 1, 2, ... For clarity the confidence boundaries of the stochastic bundles (dotted in Fig. 10.3.3) are not plotted. Instead information about the solvency aspect is given by marking with an asterisk the cases where the solvency condition $\Psi_T \leqslant \varepsilon$ is satisfied and with a cross the cases where the solvency risk is imminent, suggesting rejection of the strategy concerned.

It is the insurer management's task to define a suitable business goal from the chart. In Fig. 10.4.2 a straight line is taken as the goal. It balances B and U and optimization means finding a point on the target line as far to the right as possible.

(d) The concept of utility   The choice of the strategy options in the approach described was left very much to the subjective weighting between the contradictory alternative outcomes. Attempts to find more objective criteria can be made by introducing the so-called *utility functions.* This concept derives from the well-developed theories of games and economic behaviour due to von Neumann and Morgenstern (1947).

Karl Borch has pioneered the application of the idea of utility to the insurance environment (1961, 1962, 1963 and 1970).

Utility functions are widely used in the literature to describe the economic behaviour of individual persons as well as of institutions. They constitute a useful way of clarifying situations in which the decision-making is to be done. To illustrate the concept a simplified example is given which describes a potential policy-holder who is deliberating whether or not to take insurance cover for a particular risk object, and if yes, what level of deductible claim, if available, ought to be chosen (this presentation follows an idea given by Jewell in his lecture in the Oberwolfach seminar, 1980).

Let a person have an initial capital U_0 and let his property be subject to the incidence of a loss causing event with probability p. For the sake of simplicity, assume that one risk sum X only is possible if a claim occurs. Then he has to choose between two alternatives (Table 10.4.1):

(I) Take an insurance to cover the risk and pay a premium B.
(II) Save the premium B and take the risk of loss of the amount X.

The utility function $G(U)$ is now constructed to describe the decision-making situation and to give the problem a mathematical formulation. It attempts to weigh how desirable the different outcomes are for the decision-maker. Clearly it can be expected that it is the better for him the larger is his wealth U. It is, however,

Table 10.4.1 *Decision options of a potential policyholder*

	The wealth if	
	I *Insurance* *taken*	*II* *Insurance* *not taken*
In case of		
(i) no incidence of loss	$U_0 - B$	U_0
(ii) incidence of loss	$U_0 - B$	$U_0 - X$

reasonable to assume that the 'desirability' is not directly proportional to U. If for some reason or another the decision-maker loses a substantial part of his wealth, rather great inconveniences can entail. As a consequence may be e.g. the loss of home or loss of ability to afford school education for the children. Hence a special weight should be given to the outcomes where wealth becomes very low (not to say negative). The desirability of such chances is best described by negative values. On the other hand, growth of wealth is generally accepted as a positive event, but the more wealth is received, probably the less weight can be assumed for the interest to get still more wealth. These personal aspects, conveniences and inconveniences will be described by constructing a function $G(U)$ to give numerical evaluations for the desirability or, as it is called, 'utility' of different outcomes. It can be assumed to be an increasing function of U and the aspects discussed furthermore suggest that it should be a concave function as illustrated in Fig. 10.4.3.

Expressed by means of formulae the above conditions are

$$G'(U) > 0; G''(U) < 0, \tag{10.4.1}$$

assuming the existence of the derivatives.

The simplified example concerning the decision alternatives of the potential policyholder related to a hypothetical utility function is depicted in Fig. 10.4.3. It seems natural to characterize the two decision alternatives, i.e. to insure or not, by considering on one hand

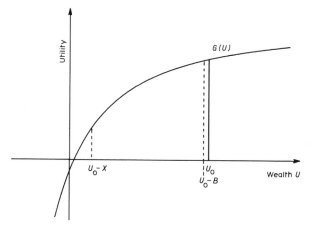

Figure 10.4.3 *Schematic presentation of the options of a policyholder.*

the value of the utility function G and on the other hand the probability that just the outcome in question may occur. The weighted utility of the option I is then

$$G_I = (1 - p)G(U_0 - B) + pG(U_0 - B) = G(U_0 - B),$$

and that of the option II, i.e. not to insure, is

$$G_{II} = (1 - p)G(U_0) + pG(U_0 - X).$$

Insurance should be taken if $G_I > G_{II}$, otherwise not. This depends on the selection of the utility function G and also on the initial state U_0 and on the values of p, X and B.

Note that in the particular case in which G is linear, equal to $aU + b$ (against the axioms (10.4.1)),

$$G_I - G_{II} = -aB + apX.$$

Now $pX = E(X)$ is the risk premium. Hence, if the rating is correct, i.e. the gross premium B is greater than the risk premium P, this expression is always negative. This means that strictly statistically the policyholder is losing. Insurance is, however, meaningful if the possible loss X is large compared with U_0 and its consequences harmful, maybe extremely, for the policyholder if not compensated by insurance. Therefore a linear utility is not suitable to describe the actual situation and a concave function is rational. Then $G_I - G_{II}$ may be positive, suggesting that insurance cover should be taken. However, if X is very small compared with the initial wealth U_0, then the conclusion may be the opposite, i.e. it is not useful to cover quite modest risks by insurance. Perhaps a suitable deduction would then be appropriate.

Another interesting situation arises if the probability p of a large loss is very small, in which case $G_I - G_{II}$ can also be negative. This is the classical dilemma of whether or not to take insurance cover for risks with a remote but positive chance of occurrence. (The more so because the lack of experience in these cases may result in a prohibitive safety margin in premium B.) The outcome depends, in any case, on the subjective choice of the utility function, i.e. whether or not and to what degree the person in question has a risk-taking or risk-averting attitude.

The above example was simplified so that only two outcomes were assumed, namely the loss of fixed amount occurs or does not. A more general situation is where several, perhaps continuous,

outcomes are present. It may concern the decision situation of
insurance management, e.g. the choice between policy strategies
like those illustrated in Fig. 10.3.3. Then the probability numbers
p and $1 - p$ are to be replaced by a distribution function $F(U)$ and
the utilities can be expressed in the form of an integral

$$\bar{G} = E(G(\mathbf{U})) = \int_{-\infty}^{+\infty} G(U)\mathrm{d}F(U), \qquad (10.4.2)$$

which is called the utility of a variable U having a distribution F.
The simplified Fig. 10.4.3 is now replaced by Fig. 10.4.4.

The one-variable utility function is often suggested also for
analysis of the insurer's decision-making when strategy options are
considered on the lines illustrated in Fig. 10.4.4. One of the difficulties, when the construction of a concrete utility function is
attempted, is the diffuse problem of the numerical values that ought to
be assigned to the possibility of ruin, i.e. for the values of U which drop
below the ruin barrier. However, this dilemma may be circumvented

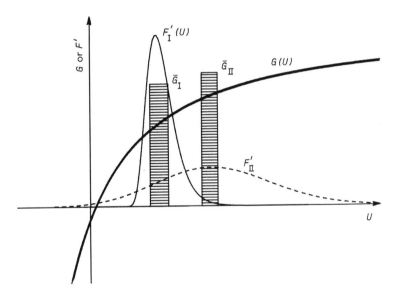

Figure 10.4.4   *The idea of utility applied in a decision situation of insurance
management. Two strategy options I (conservative) and II (risk-taking) and
their distributions. The utilities $\bar{G}_I$ and $\bar{G}_{II}$ are obtained weighting U values by
the respective densities according to* (10.4.2) *and are depicted by vertical bars.*

by separating the ruin problem from the utility definition. For this purpose every strategy which does not satisfy the condition

$$\Psi_T \leqslant \varepsilon, \qquad (10.4.3)$$

is to be rejected. Then the definition of the utility function is needed only for the values of U which exceed the ruin barrier (option II in Fig. 10.4.4 was chosen so that (10.4.3) obviously is not fulfilled, and consequently it is not acceptable regardless of whether or not $\bar{G}_{\mathrm{II}} > \bar{G}_{\mathrm{I}}$).

(e) Multivariate utilities A serious restriction is the limitation of the business objectives to one goal only (mostly solvency margin or equivalent), which is an obvious oversimplification of the real world situation. This can be helped (see Kotler (1975)) by introducing *multivariable utility functions* where at least the three goals of Fig. 10.4.1 are present. However, a subjective evaluation can never be avoided. Firstly, the often diffuse business objectives have to be expressed in the form (or guise) of some mathematical function. Secondly, values for parameters involved with the formula have still to be found and this may not be done without a more or less intuitive selection; on the other hand, subjectivity is always involved with a decision judgement irrespective of which kind of formal methods are applied. A benefit of the utility function approach is that it makes the management procedure more consequent than decision-making case by case. Similar situations can be handled in a similar way and different situations can be put in a logical badge of rank.

Even if the utility function approach is, no doubt, mathematically appealing and elegant, and can be used for many considerations, the 'looking-at-the-chart' method may be more practical and more easily understood for persons who are involved in decision-making but do not have sufficient training in the mathematics of risks and utility theory. Mathematically, the difference between the approaches need not be significant; it may even be semantic. In any case, the model should allow a choice and the user should then decide which of them (or some other method) is accepted.

(f) Optimal strategy Irrespective of which of the approaches is chosen, the search for an optimal strategy leads to intricate problems of how to find extreme values of a multivariate function, i.e. a

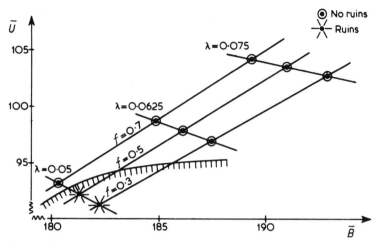

Figure 10.4.5   *Example of the search for favourable strategies presented by Pentikäinen (1976). λ is the safety loading and f is a parameter that allocates the sales efforts between the two classes of insurance presented in the example. The midpoints only for each outcome are plotted. An acceptable or not acceptable level of the risk of ruin is indicated by circles or asterisks respectively.*

maximum for the utility G or an optimal position of the final state in the B, U plane. A simple procedure is to experiment with different parameter sets and by trial and error move in the multidimensional parameter space towards a region where better and better outcomes can be found. Fig. 10.4.5 illustrates the method. One or two of the variables in turn are changed whilst the others are held fixed. The target functions seem to be approximately linear in that fairly narrow region which is allowed by resources or other limitations. This observation essentially facilitates the search operation.

More sophisticated techniques can be found in standard textbooks on dynamic programming, e.g. Nemhauser (1966).

Exercise 10.4.1   Prove that if a utility function G is linearly transformed to another

$$H = aG + b \qquad (a > 0),$$

then any relation $\bar{G}(F_1) > \bar{G}(F_2)$ defined by (10.4.2) implies $\bar{H}(F_1) > \bar{H}(F_2)$.

10.5 Competition models

(a) Multi-unit models The foregoing consideration was mainly limited to an isolated insurer. A brief reference to the dynamics connected with competitive measures was given in item 10.3(c) in the form of sales response functions. In reality, however, the market situation can affect the business flow in a rather more complicated way than was assumed for the isolated case. It is possible, in fact likely, that an acceleration in sales efforts very soon leads to a reaction from competitors. It is necessary therefore to extend the model by bringing in the relevant insurance market, incorporating consideration of the behaviour of competing insurers. In principle, this can be done by constructing a model, similar to that drafted above, separately for each of the companies of the market and then adjusting their interactions. This is illustrated in Fig. 10.5.1, where, for brevity, only three companies I, II and III are presented.

It is first supposed that no special competitive activity is being undertaken by any of the companies. Then the flow of the business of the three companies may be as plotted by thick curves 1. Each of the companies has a normal growth both in volume and solvency margin. Next it is supposed that company I launches a sales campaign making use of the premium reductions, advertising, etc. If the other two companies do not react, the outcome can be as plotted

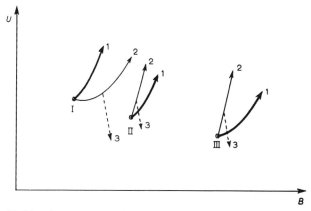

Figure 10.5.1 *Competitive market of three insurers I, II and III. The curves represent the flow of the average outcome EB(t), EU(t) as functions of time for respective insurers (see Figs 10.3.2 and 10.3.3).*

by curves 2. Company I benefits by a considerable growth in volume. The solvency margin may first be decreased due to the campaign expenses, but the increased portfolio later leads to a recovery. On the other hand, assuming that the market concerned is relatively small and almost saturated and that each of the insurers has a fairly sizable share of it, the action of insurer I is reflected in a reduction of the volume growth of the competitors.

Alternative 3, plotted by the dashed lines, describes the possibility that after some time lag companies II and III react with a similar campaign, reducing rates and increasing sales activity. It can be expected that the sales efforts of all three companies neutralize each other and equilibrium is again reached after some fluctuations. As a consequence no extra growth in volume is gained by any of the companies. Instead, however, the campaign expenses remain thus giving rise to a negative return. Clearly continuation of the situation soon leads one or more of the companies to a critical situation and necessitates stabilizing changes in business strategy. Just this kind of market mechanism was supposed to be one of the major causes for the cyclic variation introduced to the model in Section 6.1. The example could be continued, e.g. by speculating on the consequences if one or more of the companies first amends its rates and stops the other competitive efforts.

(b) Simulation of competition To make the multi-unit model workable information is needed for each of the market unit and also formulae for the behaviour of the market shares. It is appropriate to adjust the response functions as exemplified by (10.3.2) so that first some kind of average level of premium rates is determined and then the possible deviation of each insurer from this level. These deviations are just those relevant in competition. In this connection the premium reduction variable p in (10.3.2) is to be understood as such a deviation from the average market level.

Although models using general marketing theories are well developed and frequently applied to other industries, a near complete lacuna concerning insurance applications surprisingly seems to exist, as e.g. Jewell in his model survey (1980) stated. Even if difficult it may, however, be possible to gain experience, perhaps by trial and error methods, to get some idea of this very complicated reaction mechanism. Possibly one reason for the lack of reports is the tendency not to publish this kind of data. Annual company reports

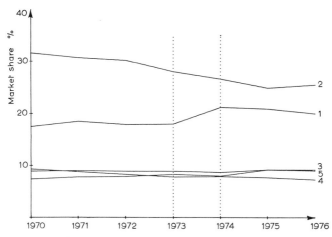

Figure 10.5.2 *Third-party motor insurance. Trend in market shares of the five companies as percentages of the whole market (Pentikäinen, 1979).*

and general insurance statistics may possibly be of use as one of the sources of information. For illustrative purposes reactions of Finnish motor third-party liability markets are depicted in Fig. 10.5.2.

In years 1973 and 1974 company 1 applied rate reductions and gained in its market share until the rates were equalized.

The market reactions depend among many other things also on the degree of saturation of the market. Extreme cases are mandatory insurance classes such as third-party liability insurance. Because no market effort can increase the joint volume of the insurance, any growth of market share is possible only at the cost of other insurers. In the case of most voluntary classes market efforts can be expected to discover objects which otherwise may have been left outside insurance cover. In such a situation an accelerated sales activity partially increases the national volume of insurance and is likely in addition to move market shares from competitors. Only experience can give guidance for the construction of suitable response formulae.

(c) The analysis of multi-unit markets belongs to the large realm of *multiplayer games* and theories of economic behaviour. For instance theories of oligopolitic markets can be referred to (Friedmann, 1977) where problems related to collusions, equilibriums, etc. are examined. If the strategy changes are made in short time intervals the scenario is much akin to systems which are treated by the theory of *differential games*, a survey of which theory is edited by Grote (1975).

Both for staff training and for business planning so-called *business games* have been developed. Special teams play the role of the management of different enterprises and their decisions are simultaneously put into a computer programmed to give as output the market reactions. These are then fed back to the playing teams for the next step. Obviously the models drafted in this chapter can well be used for such purposes. If stochasticity is programmed into the model, it can give a new dimension to conventional game models, which may mostly be deterministic.

Derivation of the Poisson and mixed Poisson processes

A.1 Poisson process

Let $\mathbf{k}(t)$ be the number of claims in the half-closed interval $(0, t]$ $(t > 0)$. Define $\mathbf{k}(0) = 0$, and let $s > 0$ and $0 \leqslant t_1 < t_2 \leqslant t_3 < t_4$. The following conditions are assumed to be valid:

(i) The variables $\mathbf{k}(t_2) - \mathbf{k}(t_1)$ and $\mathbf{k}(t_4) - \mathbf{k}(t_3)$ are independent.
(ii) The variables $\mathbf{k}(s + t) - \mathbf{k}(t)$ and $\mathbf{k}(s)$ have the same distribution.
(iii) The probability that more than one claim occurs at the same time or that an infinite number of claims occur in a finite interval are both zero.

A somewhat weaker condition can be substituted for condition (ii):

(ii)′ $\qquad \text{prob}\{\mathbf{k}(s + t) - \mathbf{k}(t) = 0\} = \text{prob}\{\mathbf{k}(s) = 0\}.$

Let $\pi_k(t) = \text{prob}\{\mathbf{k}(t) = k\}$. According to (i) and (ii)

$$\pi_0(s + t) = \text{prob}\{\mathbf{k}(s + t) = 0\} = \text{prob}\{\mathbf{k}(s) = 0, \mathbf{k}(s + t) - \mathbf{k}(s) = 0\}$$
$$= \text{prob}\{\mathbf{k}(s) = 0\}\,\text{prob}\{\mathbf{k}(t) = 0\} = \pi_0(s)\pi_0(t)$$

or

$$\pi_0(s + t) = \pi_0(s)\pi_0(t), \tag{A.1}$$

for every $s, t > 0$.

Hence $\pi_0(t)$ is everywhere a non-increasing function. Let s and t be positive rational numbers. Then according to (A.1)

$$\pi_0(st) = [\pi_0(s)]^t = [\pi_0(t)]^s,$$

giving the result $[\pi_0(t)]^{1/t} = \text{const.} \leqslant 1$. This non-negative constant cannot be 0, since, if $\pi_0(t) = 0$ *for every rational* t, then according to

(ii) any interval should contain at least one claim with the probability 1; thus the interval $(0, t]$ would contain an infinite number of claims with the probability 1, contrary to (iii). Consequently the constant can be denoted $e^{-\rho}(\rho \geqslant 0)$ giving

$$\pi_0(t) = e^{-\rho t} \qquad (\rho \geqslant 0), \tag{A.2}$$

This is true for any positive rational number t. Further, since $\pi_0(t)$ is everywhere non-increasing, $\pi_0(t)$ cannot have steps and is accordingly continuous. Thus (A.2) is also true for irrational ts.

In order to calculate $\pi_k(t)$ for $k > 0$ let h be an integer such that $n = 2^h > k$ and write down the disjoint partition

$$I_i = \left(\frac{i-1}{n}t, \frac{i}{n}t\right] \qquad (i = 1, 2, \ldots, n),$$

of the interval $(0, t]$.

This partition has the property that when h increases then the pre-existent division points remain division points. From the set of all possible realizations of the process (both the number of claims k and their placement in $(0, t]$ vary) two subsets are now selected for a fixed h as follows:

A_h is the set of all realizations (sample functions) such that at least one claim occurs in exactly k intervals I_i; that is to say, realizations for which exactly $n - k$ intervals remain without claims (now $\mathbf{k} \geqslant k$)

B_h is the set of all realizations such that at least in one interval I_i at least two claims occur (hence $\mathbf{k} \geqslant 2$)
Evidently

$$\{\mathbf{k}(t) = k\} \subset A_h \cup B_h,$$

since, in order that exactly k claims occur, it is necessary that either k different intervals must include claims or some interval must have at least two claims. On the other hand,

$$A_h - B_h \subset \{\mathbf{k}(t) = k\},$$

since the left-hand side includes only realizations where claims occur in exactly k intervals and nowhere more than 1. Thus

$$\mathrm{prob}(A_h - B_h) \leqslant \pi_k(t) \leqslant \mathrm{prob}(A_h \cup B_h)$$

or, a fortiori

$$\mathrm{prob}(A_h) - \mathrm{prob}(B_h) \leqslant \pi_k(t) \leqslant \mathrm{prob}(A_h) + \mathrm{prob}(B_h) \tag{A.3}$$

To prove that $\text{prob}(B_h) \to 0$ let $h \to \infty$ and let ω be an arbitrary realization. There are two possibilities:

(1) ω is such that from a certain value of h every interval contains at most one claim.
(2) ω is such that independently of h there is always at least one interval where at least two claims occur.

Clearly $\lim \text{prob}(B_h)$ can be > 0 only if realizations of type (2) have positive probability. There are two ways of belonging to category (2). Either some division point must contain two (or more) claims, or the claim points have to have an accumulation point. These two possibilities both have probability 0 according to condition (iii).

Returning to (A.3) it remains to calculate $\pi_k(t) = \lim \text{prob}(A_h)$. The probability that in a fixed I_i at least one claim occurs is, according to (A.2),

$$1 - \pi_0(t/n) = 1 - e^{-\rho t/n}.$$

Thus the probability that claims occur in exactly k fixed intervals is

$$(1 - e^{-\rho t/n})^k (e^{-\rho t/n})^{n-k}.$$

These k values can be chosen in $\binom{n}{k}$ different ways, so that

$$\text{prob}(A_h) = \binom{n}{k}(1 - e^{-t/n})^k (e^{-t/n})^{n-k}$$

$$= \frac{1}{k!} e^{-\rho t}(1 - e^{-\rho t/n})^k n^k (e^{\rho t k})^{1/n} \left(1 - \frac{k-1}{n}\right) \cdots \left(1 - \frac{1}{n}\right)$$

$$= \frac{e^{-\rho t}}{k!} \left(\frac{1 - e^{-\rho t/n}}{1/n}\right)^k \left(1 + O\left(\frac{1}{n}\right)\right)$$

$$\to e^{-\rho t} \frac{(\rho t)^k}{k!}.$$

Hence,

$$\pi_k(t) = e^{-\rho t} \frac{(\rho t)^k}{k!} \qquad (\rho \geqslant 0). \tag{A.4}$$

According to (A.2) this is also true for $k = 0$. The process $\mathbf{k}(t)$ is called a *Poisson process*.

A.2   Extensions

The theory of Poisson processes can be extended by replacing one or more of the assumptions (i) to (iii) by weaker ones. The new claim number processes obtained in this way play a central role in the advanced theory of risk.

As has been seen, the conditions (i), (ii) – or (ii)′ – lead to (A.2), which gives $\pi_0(t)$ as an exponential function of t. Suppose now that condition (ii) is substituted by a weaker condition assuming only that:

(ii)* $\pi_0(t)$ is a continuous function of t tending to 0 for $t \to \infty$.

Obviously $\pi_0(t)$ – which certainly cannot be anywhere increasing – can also be denoted by $e^{-\rho \tau(t)}$, where $\tau(t) = -(1/\rho) \log \pi_0(t)$ is another continuous function, tending to $+\infty$ for $t \to \infty$, and being nowhere decreasing. The constant ρ can be chosen so that $\tau(1) = 1$. For every positive τ there exists at least one t so that $\tau = \tau(t)$. The original process $\mathbf{k}(t)$ can be considered as a random process of a new variable τ, denoted $\mathbf{k}'(\tau)$, defining simply $\mathbf{k}'(\tau) = \mathbf{k}(t)$, where t is any such number, that $\tau = \tau(t)$.

(*Note*: If $\pi_0(t)$ is absolutely decreasing in point t, the correspondence between τ and t is a one-to-one correspondence. Now let (t_0, t_1) be an interval, where $\pi_0(t)$ is constant. Then for any t within this interval $\pi_0(t_0) = \pi_0(t) = \text{prob}\{\mathbf{k}(t) - \mathbf{k}(t_0) = 0\} \text{prob}\{\mathbf{k}(t_0) = 0\} = \text{prob}\{\mathbf{k}(t) - \mathbf{k}(t_0) = 0\}\pi_0(t_0)$. Thus $\text{prob}\{\mathbf{k}(t) - \mathbf{k}(t_0) = 0\} = 1$, and accordingly, with probability one, $\mathbf{k}(t) = \mathbf{k}(t_0)$, so that $\mathbf{k}'(\tau)$ is also uniquely defined in this case.)

Now let $\tau_1, \tau_2 > 0$, and let t_1, t_2, and t be such that $\tau_1 = \tau(t_1)$, $\tau_2 = \tau(t_2)$, and $\tau_1 + \tau_2 = \tau(t)$. Then according to condition (i)

$$\text{prob}\{\mathbf{k}'(\tau_1 + \tau_2) = 0\}$$
$$= \text{prob}\{\mathbf{k}'(\tau_1 + \tau_2) - \mathbf{k}'(\tau_1) = 0\} \, \text{prob}\{\mathbf{k}'(\tau_1) = 0\},$$

and hence, because $\text{prob}\{\mathbf{k}'(\tau) = 0\} = e^{-\rho \tau}$

$$\text{prob}\{\mathbf{k}'(\tau_1 + \tau_2) - \mathbf{k}'(\tau_1) = 0\} = e^{-\rho \tau_2} = \text{prob}\{\mathbf{k}'(\tau_2) = 0\}.$$

This proves that the process $\mathbf{k}'(\tau)$ satisfies the condition (ii)'.
  Accordingly

$$\text{prob}\{\mathbf{k}(t) = k\} = \mathrm{e}^{-\rho\tau(t)} \frac{[\rho\tau(t)]^k}{k!}. \tag{A.5}$$

  It can be said that the process $\mathbf{k}(t)$ is a Poisson process in the transformed new time scale τ, in so-called *operational time*.
  Conditions (i) to (iii) lead to a process where only the constant
ρ remains to be estimated in applications. The weakened condition
(ii)* instead of (ii) leads to a process where the function $\tau(t)$ remains
as a 'parameter' to be estimated or assumed in applications. The
product $\rho\tau(t)$ gives, in this case, the expected number of claims in
the interval $(0, t]$. The derivative $\tau'(t)$ can be called the intensity
of the process. In applications the intensity can be assumed to be,
for example, increasing in accordance with some prognosis concerning the future volume of the insurance collective in question or,
perhaps, due to the anticipated changes in the frequencies of claims.
The process (A.5) gives an example of *processes with non-stationary
increments*, also called *heterogeneous in time*, whereas the Poisson
process (A.4) is a *process with stationary increments*, also called
homogeneous in time.
  A further extension of risk processes is obtained if the constant
ρ is thought of as a random variable $\boldsymbol{\rho}$, which varies due to some
outer factors, e.g. random effects of weather conditions. Suppose
that the claim number $\mathbf{k}(t)$ satisfies the conditions (i), (ii)*, and (iii)
on condition that $\boldsymbol{\rho}$ has a given value ρ. Then the conditional distribution of $\mathbf{k}(t)$ is again a Poisson distribution.
  A more general case is obtained, which is also more realistic,
if $\boldsymbol{\rho}$ is dependent on time, hence being a general stochastic process
$\boldsymbol{\rho}(t)$. In order to give a short survey, let $\rho(t)$ be a realization, i.e. a
sample function of this process, and suppose that, for the fixed $\rho(t)$,
conditions (i) (ii)*, and (iii) are satisfied. Then again, for any value
of t, $\text{prob}\{\mathbf{k}(t) = k\}$ (on condition that this sample function $\rho(t)$
of the process 'occurs') is evidently dependent only on the expected
value of the number of claims in the interval $(0, t]$, i.e. of the product
$\rho\tau$, where ρ is the value which the sample function takes for t, but
it is not dependent on the values that the sample function takes
for other values of time. Generally, since the operational time τ
is calculated separately for different realizations $\rho(t)$, it is dependent

on the value ρ as well; thus the notation $\tau = \tau(t, \rho)$ is used in the following. Hence for the unconditioned process:

$$\text{prob}\{\mathbf{k}(t) = k\} = \int_0^\infty e^{-\rho\tau(t,\rho)} \frac{[\rho\tau(t, \rho)]^k}{k!} \, d_\rho V(\rho, t),$$

where the 'structure function' $V(\rho, t) = \text{prob}\{\boldsymbol{\rho}(t) \leqslant \rho\}$ is in general dependent on time.

Finally the integration variable is changed by introducing $q = \rho\tau(t, \rho)/t$ and solving ρ from this equation. Then the solution is placed in $V(\rho, t)$ and a new structure function $H(q, t) = V(\rho(q, t), t)^*$ is constructed. The probability can be rewritten:

$$\text{prob}\{\mathbf{k}(t) = k\} = \int_0^\infty e^{-qt} \frac{(qt)^k}{k!} \, d_q H(q, t). \tag{A.6}$$

A process which satisfies condition (A.6) is called a *mixed Poisson process in the wide sense* or, especially if the structure function H is independent of time t, a *mixed Poisson process* (in the narrow sense). It might happen that a mixed Poisson process in the wide sense in time t is a mixed Poisson process in the narrow sense in a suitably chosen operational time τ. (An example of this is the process satisfying condition (A.5), which can be modified into the form (A.6) and which is thus a mixed Poisson process, leading to a structure function dependent on time. In fact if, for clarity, the integration variable is denoted by x, $H(x, t) = \varepsilon(x - \rho\tau(t)/(t)$, where $\varepsilon(x)$ denotes the degenerated distribution function.)

For further information see for example Philipson (1968) and Thyrion (1967).

A process with property (A.6) no longer obeys conditions (i) and (ii) in general. It should be remarked that (A.6) does not yet define all properties of the process $\mathbf{k}(t)$, since, for example, it displays only the distribution of random variables $\rho(t)$ for various values of t, but not the way that these variables are dependent on each other. So it might happen that two processes have the same distribution (A.6) for every t, but that the probabilities that k claims occur in the time interval $(0, t]$, on the condition that i claims have occurred in the time interval $(0, t/2]$, are different.

---

* More rigorously, $H(q, t) = \int d_\rho V(\rho, t)$ where the integration is taken over all such values of ρ for which $qt > \rho r(t, \rho)$.

Edgeworth expansion

If all derivatives of the function G exist and if $G^{(k)}(\pm\infty) = 0$ for all $k \geqslant 1$, then:

$$\varphi_k(s) = \int_{-\infty}^{+\infty} e^{isx} dG^{(k)}(x) = \left[e^{isx} G^{(k)}(x) \right]_{-\infty}^{+\infty} - is \int_{-\infty}^{+\infty} e^{isx} dG^{(k-1)}(x)$$

$$= (-is)\varphi_{k-1}(s) = \cdots = (-is)^k \varphi_0(s).$$

Since the normal distribution

$$N(X;m,\sigma) = \frac{1}{\sqrt{(2\pi)}\sigma} \int_{-\infty}^{X} \exp\left[-\frac{1}{2}\left(\frac{z-m}{\sigma} \right)^2 \right] dz$$

$$= N\left(\frac{X-m}{\sigma}; 0, 1 \right) = N\left(\frac{X-m}{\sigma} \right),$$

clearly satisfies these conditions, the characteristic function of its kth derivative is

$$\varphi_k(s; m, \sigma) = (-is)^k \varphi_0(s; m, \sigma), \tag{B.1}$$

where

$$\varphi_0(s; m, \sigma) = \exp(ism - s^2\sigma^2/2), \tag{B.2}$$

is the characteristic function of $N(x; m, \sigma^2)$. Evidently,

$$N^{(k)}(X; m, \sigma) = \sigma^{-k} N^{(k)}\left(\frac{X-m}{\sigma} \right). \tag{B.3}$$

The characteristic function of the simple compound Poisson function is

$$\varphi(s) = e^{n\psi(s)-n},$$

where ψ is the characteristic function of the claim size d.f. It has the following expansion, according to (B.2)

$$\varphi(s) = e^{n\psi(s)-n} = \exp\left\{n\sum_0^4 \psi^{(k)}(0)\frac{s^k}{k!} + nO(s^5) - n\right\}$$

$$= \exp(isnm - \tfrac{1}{2}s^2 na_2)$$

$$\times \exp\left\{n\psi^{(3)}(0)\frac{s^3}{3!} + n\psi^{(4)}(0)\frac{s^4}{4!} + nO(s^5)\right\}$$

$$= \varphi_0(s; nm, \sqrt{(na_2)})\left\{1 + \frac{na_3}{6}(is)^3 + \frac{na_4}{24}(is)^4\right.$$

$$\left. + \frac{n^2 a_3^2}{72}(is)^6 + nO(s^5) + n^2O(s^7) + n^3O(s^9) + \cdots\right\}$$
$$+ \text{remainder.}$$

Hence by inverting the characteristic function, according to (B.1):

$$F(X) = N(X; nm, \sqrt{(na_2)}) - \frac{a_3}{6}n N^{(3)}(X; nm, \sqrt{(na_2)})$$

$$+ \frac{a_4}{24} n N^{(4)}(X; nm, \sqrt{(na_2)}) + \frac{a_3^2}{72}n^2 N^{(6)}(X; nm, \sqrt{(na_2)})$$

$$+ \cdots + \text{remainder,}$$

where the terms omitted are of the form $Cn^i N^{(j)}(X; nm, \sqrt{(na_2)})$
with $j/2 - i \geqslant 3/2$, C being independent of n. Hence, if $x = (X - mn)/\sqrt{(na_2)}$, according to (B.3),

$$F(X) = N(x) - \tfrac{1}{6}a_3 n(\sqrt{(na_2)})^{-3}N^{(3)}(x)$$
$$+ \tfrac{1}{24}a_4 n(\sqrt{(na_2)})^{-4}N^{(4)}(x)$$
$$+ \tfrac{1}{72}a_3^2 n^2(\sqrt{(na_2)})^{-6}N^{(6)}(x) + \cdots + \text{remainder,}$$

where the terms omitted are of the form

$$C'n^i(\sqrt{(na_2)})^{-j}N^{(j)}(x) = C'' n^{i-j/2} N^{(j)}(x) = C'' n^{-k} N^{(j)}(x),$$

with $k \geqslant 3/2$. Hence

$$F(X) = N(x) - \tfrac{1}{6}a_3 a_2^{-3/2} n^{-1/2} N^{(3)}(x) + \tfrac{1}{24}a_4 a_2^{-2}n^{-1}N^{(4)}(x)$$
$$+ \tfrac{1}{72}a_3^2 a_2^{-3}n^{-1} N^{(6)}(x) + O(n^{-3/2}).$$

APPENDIX C

Infinite time ruin probability

C.1 Assumptions

We are now going to extend to a special case the consideration of the risk processes related to a finite time interval as considered in Section 6.5, letting the length of the time interval grow to infinity. The assumptions and notation are modified as follows.

Let Δ denote a time unit. It is assumed that the state of the risk process is tested at times $\Delta, 2\Delta, \ldots, t\Delta, \ldots$.

The aggregate claims amount during the period $((t-1)\Delta, t\Delta]$ is denoted by $X(t)$ and the underwriting profit (or loss if negative) will be defined for each period by the equation

$$Y(t) = (1 + \lambda)P - X(t), \qquad (C.1)$$

where P is the risk premium $E(X(t))$ and $\lambda > 0$ is a safety loading. It is assumed that the variables $Y(t)$ of the consecutive periods are mutually independent and have the same d.f. G. The only assumption concerning G is that the integrals needed later are convergent. Without loss of generality it can also be assumed that $Y(t)$ assumes negative values with positive probability; otherwise the probability of ruin would be always zero.

It is assumed that the risk premium income P and the safety loading λ are constant. However, it would be possible to extend the consideration for cases where the business volume is growing according to some deterministic rule as presented in Section A.2, where the concept 'operational time' was introduced, but for simplicity this is not provided in the following.

Next, the accumulated profit is defined by

$$W(t) = Y(1) + \cdots + Y(t). \qquad (C.2)$$

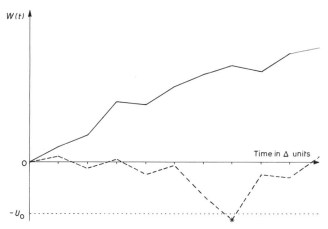

Figure C.1.   *Two realizations of the accumulated profit* $\mathbf{W}(t)$ *with* Δ *as length of test period. For the other realization a ruin (asterisk) is observed.*

Then the ruin probability related to the time period $(0, T\Delta]$ is

$$\Psi_T = \Psi_T(U_0)$$
$$= 1 - \mathrm{prob}\{\mathbf{W}(t) \geqslant - U_0 \text{ for } t = 1, 2, \ldots, T\} \qquad (C.3)$$

where U_0 is the initial risk reserve (see Fig. C.1.1).

Note that in terms the notation of Chapter 6 $\mathbf{W}(t) = \mathbf{U}(t) - U_0$ (if $\Delta = 1$).

The *infinite time ruin probability* $\Psi = \Psi_\infty$, which is obtained when T tends to infinity, depends, as well as on the risk process, on the choice of the time unit Δ: the smaller Δ is the larger Ψ becomes. When $\Delta \to 0$ the testing is carried out continually at every time point.

In general the assumptions given above concerning the variables $\mathbf{Y}(t)$ do not remain valid if Δ is replaced by some other time unit Δ', unless $\Delta' = k\Delta$, where k is some positive integer. However, if the risk process under consideration is a simple compound Poisson process, it is obvious that the assumptions remain valid for any positive Δ.

C.2   Estimation of Ψ

Estimation is based on a technique which makes use of the joint moment generating function

$$M(s) \equiv M_{\mathbf{Y}(t)}(s) = E\{\exp(s\mathbf{Y}(t))\}, \tag{C.4}$$

of the variables $\mathbf{Y}(t)$.

Suppose first that $T < \infty$ is given. Then the m.g.f. M_T of $\mathbf{W}(T)$ satisfies

$$M_T(s) = E\{\exp[s(\mathbf{Y}(1) + \cdots + \mathbf{Y}(T))]\} = M(s)^T. \tag{C.5}$$

The idea is to derive yet another expansion for this function, which then directly gives the result sought. It is obtained by introducing the concept 'the time of (first) ruin' (Δ as time unit), denoted by $\mathbf{t}_1$. Then the realizations of the process are separated into two groups. The first group consists of all the realizations that lead to ruin during the first T periods. The probability of getting a realization belonging to this group is, by (C.3), Ψ_T. All the other realizations are left in the second group, that is to say, realizations which lead to ruin subsequently, i.e. after the period $(0, T\Delta]$ or do not lead to ruin at all (referred to $\mathbf{t}_1 = \infty$). Now the expansion in question can be partitioned into two conditional expectations

$$\begin{aligned} M_T(s) = &\Psi_T E\{\exp(s\mathbf{W}(T)) | \mathbf{t}_1 \leqslant T\} \\ &+ (1 - \Psi_T)E\{\exp(s\mathbf{W}(T)) | T < \mathbf{t}_1\}. \end{aligned} \tag{C.6}$$

Making use of the definition of $M(s)$ and the independence of the variables $\mathbf{W}(T) - \mathbf{W}(t)$ and $\mathbf{W}(t)$, $t \leqslant T$, one obtains

$$\begin{aligned} &E\{\exp(s\mathbf{W}(T)) | \mathbf{t}_1 \leqslant T\} \\ &\quad = E\{\exp(s\mathbf{W}(\mathbf{t}_1)) \exp[s(\mathbf{W}(T) - \mathbf{W}(\mathbf{t}_1))] | \mathbf{t}_1 \leqslant T\} \\ &\quad = \sum_{t=1}^{T} \mathrm{prob}\{\mathbf{t}_1 = t | \mathbf{t}_1 \leqslant T\}E\{\exp(s\mathbf{W}(t))M(s)^{T-t} | \mathbf{t}_1 = t\} \\ &\quad = E\{\exp(s\mathbf{W}(\mathbf{t}_1))M(s)^{T-\mathbf{t}_1} | \mathbf{t}_1 \leqslant T\}. \end{aligned} \tag{C.7}$$

Hence (C.6) can be rewritten as

$$\begin{aligned} M_T(s) = &\Psi_T E\{\exp(s\mathbf{W}(\mathbf{t}_1))M(s)^{T-\mathbf{t}_1} | \mathbf{t}_1 \leqslant T\} \\ &+ (1 - \Psi_T)E\{\exp(s\mathbf{W}(T)) | T < \mathbf{t}_1\}. \end{aligned} \tag{C.8}$$

So far the choice of the auxiliary variable s has been open. To obtain convenient values it is given the value which makes

$$M(s) = 1. \tag{C.9}$$

To prove that there really exists a unique negative solution $s = -R$

of (C.9) observe the following facts

$$M(0) = 1$$
$$M'(0) = E(\mathbf{Y}(t)) = \lambda P > 0$$
$$M''(s) = E(\mathbf{Y}(t)^2 \exp(s\mathbf{Y}(t))) > 0 \qquad \text{for every } s.$$

Hence M is a strictly convex function which is increasing at the origin where it assumes the value 1. In order to prove the existence of the desired solution $-R$ it is sufficient to prove that $M(s)$ is greater than 1 for some negative s. But by the assumption that $\mathbf{Y}(t)$ also assumes negative values there exists a constant $s_0 < 0$ such that $p = \text{prob}\{\mathbf{Y}(t) \leqslant s_0\} > 0$. Hence, for $s < 0$

$$M(s) = E(e^{s\mathbf{Y}(t)}) \geqslant pE(e^{s\mathbf{Y}(t)}|\mathbf{Y}(t) \leqslant s_0)$$
$$\geqslant pe^{ss_0} \to \infty \qquad \text{as } s \to -\infty,$$

and the existence of the solution $s = -R$ of (C.9) follows. Combining (C.5) and (C.8) and substituting the solution $s = -R$ of (C.9) the following equation is obtained

$$1 = \Psi_T E\{\exp(-R\mathbf{W}(\mathbf{t}_1))|\mathbf{t}_1 \leqslant T\}$$
$$+ (1 - \Psi_T)E\{\exp(-R\mathbf{W}(T))|T < \mathbf{t}_1\}. \qquad (\text{C.10})$$

Two approximations are now made. First the second term is omitted, as it is known to be positive or zero. For the second approximation note that from the definition of $\mathbf{t}_1$ the quantity $\mathbf{W}(\mathbf{t}_1)$ in the first term indicates the ruining value of the (negative) profit; hence it is always $\leqslant -U_0$. If then $\mathbf{W}(\mathbf{t}_1)$ is replaced by $-U_0$ the first term of the right-hand side of the equation is decreased. Hence

$$1 \geqslant \Psi_T e^{RU_0}, \qquad (\text{C.11})$$

or

$$\Psi_T \leqslant e^{-RU_0}. \qquad (\text{C.12})$$

This formula is one of the main results of the theory of risk. In it T can be any positive integer and therefore it holds also when T tends to infinity.

Before developing the theory further it is of great interest to get some idea as to how much $\Psi = \Psi_\infty$ differs in reality from the upper limit e^{-RU_0}, i.e. would it be feasible to use the approximation

$$\Psi(U_0) = C(U_0) e^{-RU_0} \approx e^{-RU_0}, \qquad (\text{C.13})$$

where $C(U_0)$ is an unknown function being ≈ 1; by (C.12) it is known that necessarily $C(U_0) \leqslant 1$.

The evaluation of the error in this approximation has been the subject of intensive studies and has been solved separately for different definitions of the function G, for finite and infinite time intervals and for different configurations of the ruin test points. These details are not considered here because it would be beyond the scope of an elementary textbook and especially because it has not yet been possible to derive simple general formulae which would be useful in practical applications. An extensive survey of the results has been given by Segerdahl (1959). The following shows however that as a rule the approximation is not too rough, at least not when Δ is relatively small.

Let T tend to infinity in (C.10). To find the limit obtained by the second term on the right-hand side another partition will be made denoting for brevity $\mathbf{W} = \mathbf{W}(T)$

$$(1 - \Psi_T)E(e^{-R\mathbf{W}} \,|\, T < \mathbf{t}_1) = \psi_1 E(e^{-R\mathbf{W}} \,|\, \mathbf{W} < B, \, T < \mathbf{t}_1)$$
$$+ \psi_2 E(e^{-R\mathbf{W}} \,|\, B \leqslant \mathbf{W}, \, T < \mathbf{t}_1), \quad \text{(C.14)}$$

where $\psi_1 = \text{prob}\{\mathbf{W} < B, \, T < \mathbf{t}_1\}$, $\psi_2 = \text{prob}\{B \leqslant \mathbf{W}, \, T < \mathbf{t}_1\}$, and B is a number which will shortly be fixed. The object is to prove that both terms vanish when $T \to \infty$. To show this it is sufficient to prove that when B and T are chosen large enough, both terms are $\leqslant \varepsilon/2$ where ε can be fixed in advance to be arbitrarily small. This is so as regards the latter term if $B = -\log(\varepsilon/2)/R$ because then $e^{-R\mathbf{W}} \leqslant e^{-RB} = \varepsilon/2$ in this term. As regards the first term the well-known Tchebychev's inequality $\text{prob}\{|\mathbf{W} - E(\mathbf{W})| \geqslant k\sigma_{\mathbf{W}}\} \leqslant 1/k^2$ is applied for $k = T^{1/4}$ and gives

$$\text{prob}\{|\mathbf{W} - E(\mathbf{W})| \geqslant \sigma T^{3/4}\} \leqslant T^{-\frac{1}{2}},$$

where $E(\mathbf{W}) = T\lambda P$ and σ is the joint standard deviation of the variables $\mathbf{Y}(t)$. Now taking T large enough to satisfy both inequalities $T \geqslant (4/\varepsilon^2)\exp(2RU_0)$ and $T\lambda P - T^{3/4}\sigma \geqslant B$ it follows that

$$\psi_1 \leqslant \text{prob}\{\mathbf{W} \leqslant B\}$$
$$\leqslant \text{prob}\{|\mathbf{W} - T\lambda P| \geqslant T^{3/4}\sigma\}$$
$$\leqslant T^{-\frac{1}{2}} \leqslant \frac{\varepsilon}{2}e^{-RU_0}.$$

Noting that, by the definition of $\mathbf{t}_1$, $\mathbf{W} = \mathbf{W}(T)$ in the first term of the partition (C.14) is $\geqslant - U_0$ and hence $\exp(-RW) \leqslant \exp(RU_0)$, it follows that this term $\leqslant \varepsilon/2$ and so the proof is completed.

The second approximation when obtaining (C.12) was the replacement of e^{-RW} by e^{RU_0}. This means in fact that ruin is always assumed to occur only by exactly reaching the ruin barrier $W = - U_0$. In reality this is, of course, not true as a rule and the barrier is exceeded more or less. But in the case when Δ is relatively small the effect of this approximation is generally not very great.

Since the second term in (C.10) vanishes when $T \to \infty$, it follows that

$$E(e^{-RW(t_1)}|t_1 < \infty)\Psi(U_0) = 1 = \frac{\Psi(U_0)}{C(U_0)\,e^{-RU_0}},$$

from which

$$\frac{1}{C(U_0)} = E(e^{-R(W(t_1) + U_0)}|t_1 < \infty). \tag{C.15}$$

From this formula it can be directly seen that $C(U_0)$ is close to 1 if the absolute value of the ruining loss W is in general only relatively slightly in excess of U_0. This is the case, for example, when the test period Δ is very short or equals 0 and reinsurance cuts off the large claims. When $\Delta \to 0$, only one claim can with probability 1 cause the 'final ruin'. If, due to the reinsurance, the size of one claim is limited by some upper limit M, then also $|W(t_1) - U_0| < M$ and a limit formula

$$C(U_0) > e^{-RM}, \tag{C.16}$$

is obtained, which holds when $\Delta \to 0$ provided that the assumptions introduced in Section C.1 remain in force (this is the case if the risk process is a simple compound Poisson process).

It should further be noted that even if $C(U_0)$ were as low as 0.5 and e^{-RU_0} is of the order of magnitude of 0.01, then in replacing the true Ψ by the approximation (C.13), the original U_0 would be replaced by $1.15U_0$, the adjusting figure compensating for the uncertainty of $C(U_0)$. If C were greater than 0.5 the error arising from the use of the approximate formula would be still smaller. Cases where this type of margin in U_0 is significant will seldom arise in practical actuarial work since the choice of the permitted magnitude of the ruin probability is itself arbitrary. From numerical examples presented in this book it is seen that the safety loading and, in many cases, the net retention, are factors which have considerable influence on the insolvency function, far more, in fact, than the uncertainty of $C(U_0)$. Of course, in certain critical cases the study of the exact theory as developed in the papers referred to may be desirable.

As has been shown, (C.12) holds for every length of the test period Δ (if the **Y**s remain independent and stationary) and also when $\Delta \to 0$, i.e. when testing is carried out continually at every time. At the same time the ruin probability $\psi(U_0)$ increases. This is easily seen since the ruin probability is less when the solvency is tested once a year, for example, as compared with continuous testing. The former case allows temporary insolvency during the observation years provided solvency is regained at the end of each year.

Equation (C.9) (with $s = -R$) is inconvenient for computation and it is useful to develop it in a more suitable form.

According to the definition (C.4)

$$1 = M(-R) = E(e^{-R\mathbf{Y}(t)}) = e^{-(1+\lambda)PR}E(e^{R\mathbf{X}(t)}),$$

i.e.

$$e^{(1+\lambda)PR} = M_{\mathbf{X}(t)}(R). \tag{C.17}$$

In the particular case when the risk process is a simple compound Poisson process the m.g.f. (C.17) can be expressed in terms of the m.g.f. M_Z of the claim size d.f. S

$$M_{\mathbf{X}(t)}(R) = \exp\left[nM_Z(R) - n\right].$$

By taking logarithms and by using (C.17) this gives the formula

$$n + (1+\lambda)PR = n \int_0^\infty e^{RZ} \, dS(Z).$$

Noting that $P = E(\mathbf{X}(t)) = nm$ where m is the mean claim size, it follows that

$$1 + (1+\lambda)mR = \int_0^\infty e^{RZ} \, dS(Z). \tag{C.18}$$

From this it is seen that 'the insolvency constant' R, the opposite of the non-trivial root of (C.9), is not dependent on the choice of the time unit but solely on the distribution function S of the amount of one claim. Thus it will again be appreciated that the inequality (C.12) is valid independently of how frequently the insolvency measurements are made, and thus it will hold good even if the possibility of insolvency is measured at every time.

A formula corresponding to (C.18) can also be obtained when the fluctuating basic probabilities are assumed to be in accordance with the distribution (2.9.9). In this case the m.g.f. in (C.17) is given by (3.4.4), and thus the equation

$$e^{(1 + \lambda)mnR} = \left[1 + (n/h)\left(1 - \int_0^\infty e^{RZ} \, dS(Z) \right) \right]^{-h},$$

may be written down. This equation may be expressed as

$$\int_0^\infty e^{RZ} \, dS(Z) = 1 + \frac{1 - e^{-(1 + \lambda)nmR/h}}{n/h}, \qquad (C.19)$$

from which the insolvency constant R may be found.

In this formula the reservation made on item C.1 must be kept in mind. It is valid only when the structure process $\mathbf{q}$ and the test period are synchronized, i.e. when a new value for $\mathbf{q}$ is drawn at the end of each period.

It can be noted that (for $h \neq \infty$) there is an essential difference between (C.18) and (C.19). In the latter the constant R depends on the size of the company.

Consider the case of a simple compound Poisson risk process with test period $\Delta \to 0$. In order to estimate $C(U_0)$ in (C.15), define

$$\mathbf{V} = \mathbf{W}(\mathbf{t}_1 - 1) + U_0,$$

where the values corresponding to the realizations having $\mathbf{t}_1 = \infty$ are not under interest, and it is defined $\mathbf{V} = \infty$ for those realizations. Denoting $\mathbf{Z}_1 = -\mathbf{Y}(\mathbf{t}_1)$ (define $\mathbf{Z}_1 = 0$ when $\mathbf{t}_1 = \infty$) it is quite obvious that the conditional probability $\text{prob}\{\mathbf{Z}_1 \leqslant Z | \mathbf{t}_1 < \infty\}$ approaches to the probability that the size of one claim is greater than $\mathbf{V}$ but not greater than Z, when $\Delta \to 0$ (see Fig. C.2.1).

Thus, when testing is carried out continually, i.e. $\Delta \to 0$, one gets the limit formula

$$E(e^{RZ_1} | \mathbf{V} = V, \mathbf{t}_1 < \infty) = \frac{1}{1 - S(V)} \int_V^\infty e^{RZ} \, dS(Z), \qquad (C.20)$$

for all $V \geqslant 0$. Denoting, for brevity, by

$$E_1(\cdot) = E(\cdot | \mathbf{t}_1 < \infty),$$

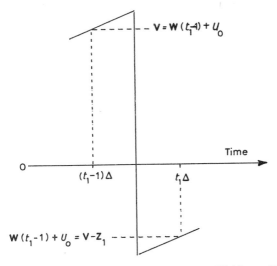

Figure C.2.1 *If Δ is small and $t_1 < \infty$, then $V - [V + Y(t_1)] = - Y(t_1) = Z_1$ is approximately the size of one claim under the condition that the claim is larger than V.*

the expected value operator related to the set of all realizations having $t_1 < \infty$, it follows from (C.15) that

$$
\begin{aligned}
\frac{1}{C(U_0)} &= E_1(e^{-R(W(t_1) + U_0)}) \\
&= E_1(e^{-RV + RZ_1}) \qquad\qquad (C.21) \\
&= E_1\{E_1(e^{-RV} e^{RZ_1} | V)\} \\
&= E_1\{e^{-RV} E_1(e^{RZ_1} | V)\}.
\end{aligned}
$$

This formula together with (C.20) can be used when $C(U_0)$ is approximated.

Consider, as an example, the case that the claim sizes are exponentially distributed, i.e. $S(Z) = 1 - \exp(-aZ)$, $a > 0$, $Z \geqslant 0$. In this special case it is easily seen from (C.15) that (note $m = 1/a$)

$$
R = \frac{\lambda}{1 + \lambda} a, \qquad\qquad (C.22)
$$

especially $R < a$. Using (C.20) it is seen that

$$e^{-RV} E(e^{RZ_1} | \mathbf{V} = V, \mathbf{t}_1 < \infty)$$

$$= e^{-RV} \frac{1}{1 - S(V)} \int_V^\infty e^{RZ} \, dS(Z)$$

$$= e^{(a-R)V} \int_V^\infty a \, e^{-(a-R)Z} \, dZ = \frac{a}{a - R} = 1 + \lambda,$$

is now independent of the value V. Therefore (C.21) can be calculated directly:

$$\frac{1}{C(U_0)} = E_1 \{ e^{-RV} E_1(e^{RZ_1} | \mathbf{V}) \} = E_1(1 + \lambda) = 1 + \lambda.$$

Hence, for exponential claim size d.f.

$$C(U_0) = \frac{1}{1 + \lambda} \qquad \text{and} \qquad \Psi_\infty(U_0) = \frac{e^{-RU_0}}{1 + \lambda},$$

where R is given by (C.22).

It should be noted that in this example $C(U_0)$ does not depend on the parameter a. It is quite clear that $C(U_0)$ does not depend very strongly on the shape of the claim size d.f. in the general case either. In fact it can be shown that the value of $C(U_0)$ is also of the same order $1/(1 + \lambda)$ for many other claim size distributions.

Computation of the limits for the finite time ruin probability according to method of Section 6.9

D.1 Given quantities

n, M, $m = a_1, r_2, r_3$, T are given, where the moments are functions of the net retention M as provided in Section 3.6.

Furthermore, the following *deterministically* defined time-dependent functions are to be given: $r_i(t)$, $r_g(t)$, $r_x(t)$, $r_p(t)$, $z(t)$, $\lambda(t)$, $U_r(t)$. The process is constituted by the algorithm dealt with in Chapter 6 in form (6.7.7) and the ruin probability as given by (6.9.1). The NP approximation will be used, and for convenience of notation (see 3.11.14a) $N_y(x)$ will be denoted by $N(x; \gamma)$.

D.2 Calculations

$$n(t) = n \prod_{\tau=1}^{t} r_g(\tau)$$

$$\mu_X(t) = \mu_X(t-1)r_g(t)r_x(t)(1 + z(t))/(1 + z(t-1)),$$

where $\mu_X(0) = nm$.

$$P_\lambda(t) = \mu_X(t)(1 + \lambda(t))/(1 + z(t))$$
$$B(t) = P_\lambda(t)/(1 - c)$$
$$\mu_U(t) = r_i\mu_U(t-1) + P_\lambda(t) - \mu_X(t).$$

For brevity the subscripts U or X are omitted in the following expressions of the standard deviation, third moments, and skewness.

Note that by the conditions given the standard deviations are the same for U and X but the third moments and skewness have opposite signs.

$$\sigma^2(t) = (r_2/n(t) + \sigma_q^2)\mu_X(t)^2$$
$$\sigma^2(1, t) = \sigma^2(1, t - 1)r_i^2 + \sigma^2(t)$$
$$\mu_3(t) = (r_3/n(t)^2 + 3r_2\sigma_q^2/n(t) + \sigma_q^3\gamma_q)\mu_X(t)^3$$
$$\mu_3(1, t) = \mu_3(1, t - 1)r_i^3 + \mu_3(t)$$
$$\gamma(t) = \mu_3(t)/\sigma^3(t)$$
$$\gamma(1, t) = \mu_3(1, t)/\sigma^3(1, t)$$
$$\varphi(t) = 1 - N\left[\frac{\mu_U(t) - U_r(t)}{\sigma(1, t)}; \gamma(1, t)\right]$$
$$\varphi(0) = 0$$
$$\varphi(t - 1, t) = \int_{-\infty}^{U_1} D(t)\,dU,$$

which can be evaluated by Simpson's rule

$$\approx \frac{h}{3}[D(U_1) + 4D(U_1 - h) + 2D(U_1 - 2h) + 4D(U_1 - 3h) + \cdots],$$

where

$$D(t) = [1 - N(x_1, \gamma(t))]\frac{d}{dU} N(x_2; \gamma(1, t - 1))$$
$$U_1 = U_r(t - 1)$$
$$x_1 = (r_i U + P_\lambda(t) - U_r(t) - \mu_X(t))/\sigma(t)$$
$$x_2 = (\mu_U(t - 1) - U)/\sigma(1, t - 1)).$$

Furthermore $(d/dU)N(x_2; \gamma(1, t - 1))$ is (3.11.18) where σ_X should be substituted for $\sigma(1, t - 1)$ and g for $\gamma(1, t - 1)/6$.

It is appropriate to take as the Simpson's interval $h = \sigma(1, t - 1)/k$, where k is a constant to be selected to determine the length of integration step. From experience, values 2 or 3 are sufficient. Note that now $\sigma(1, t - 1)$ is reduced from the Simpson's sum, because it is in the numerator of h and in the denominator of dN/dU.

Finally, the lower limit of Ψ_T is

$$\Psi'_T = \max_t \left[\varphi(t - 1) + \varphi(t) - \varphi(t, t - 1)\right],$$

and the upper limit

$$\Psi''_T = \sum_{t=1}^{T} [\varphi(t) - \varphi(t-1, t)],$$

regarding $\varphi(0, 1) = 0$.

If (6.9.7) is required, the algorithm should be applied

$$\Psi'''_t = \Psi'''_{t-1} + \frac{1 - \Psi'''_{t-1}}{1 - \varphi(t-1)}(\varphi(t) - \varphi(t, t-1)).$$

APPENDIX E

Random Numbers

E.1 Uniformly (0, 1) distributed (pseudo) random numbers

0.6296	0.2398	0.4581	0.3662	0.4208	0.9293	0.0621	0.0482	0.3030	0.4816
0.8251	0.4668	0.9510	0.7583	0.8647	0.8345	0.7651	0.9910	0.2975	0.7888
0.3556	0.0782	0.0987	0.5638	0.7772	0.6325	0.7109	0.9119	0.5130	0.7772
0.4041	0.7764	0.2097	0.6930	0.3849	0.7126	0.1610	0.9153	0.6557	0.0600
0.5427	0.3808	0.6239	0.8641	0.3968	0.2245	0.4621	0.5486	0.3656	0.3263
0.2164	0.3367	0.1768	0.6085	0.6667	0.4235	0.8771	0.0819	0.9354	0.8975
0.8170	0.6431	0.8471	0.4127	0.3852	0.6215	0.0381	0.6105	0.4928	0.0758
0.8154	0.2912	0.8076	0.8412	0.7663	0.3364	0.7387	0.3261	0.1178	0.3806
0.1709	0.0589	0.8460	0.2330	0.9489	0.9852	0.5352	0.0496	0.1115	0.5144
0.9877	0.2549	0.8766	0.3164	0.5828	0.2138	0.3750	0.8691	0.3863	0.6536

E.2 Normally (0, 1) distributed random numbers

0.6211	−1.1983	−0.5891	1.8947	1.2064	0.9722	−0.7708	0.1443	−0.3138	0.9395
−1.3769	−0.6988	−0.9492	−0.9243	0.2836	−0.6349	−0.3449	−0.0277	0.3379	−0.1070
0.9971	−0.3024	−0.5235	−0.0315	0.2423	0.3936	−0.3664	−1.4520	−0.2174	−2.0894
0.1015	−1.1994	−2.0946	1.1515	2.6083	1.0364	−0.3801	−0.7835	−1.3011	−1.1076
0.3792	−0.1713	−1.2002	−0.6104	0.4016	−0.2125	−0.8872	0.5802	1.2419	0.5373
0.2474	0.7294	0.6982	0.6237	0.6423	−1.3561	−0.1343	0.4261	0.0666	−0.9646
−0.1009	−0.2162	−0.5640	−1.4068	−0.1834	0.0118	−0.3795	−1.9057	0.7346	−1.7216
1.2772	0.3481	0.6472	0.3538	0.4539	−0.0924	−0.3890	1.4981	0.8572	−0.7642
−1.0352	−0.2686	−1.4689	−0.3880	−1.4175	0.3399	1.7439	−1.7855	3.0626	−0.0526
1.9466	−0.6060	−0.2452	0.6367	−0.8552	0.2417	0.3301	0.4039	0.6269	−1.4241

E.3 NP(0, 1, γ) distributed random numbers
(a) γ = 0.5

1.7366	0.3073	0.5520	−0.7275	−1.0791	0.1868	−1.2969	2.1834	−0.0579	1.1571
−1.7942	0.9956	−0.4829	−1.1483	−0.4519	−0.5708	0.1116	−0.2678	−1.6752	1.8835
0.3308	0.1720	0.0786	1.0786	−0.1472	1.2757	−0.2711	−0.5553	−0.3948	0.0301
−0.1475	2.4209	0.5093	2.8619	0.2556	0.6315	−0.0934	0.1079	0.0994	0.2971
0.0998	−1.9343	1.2952	−1.3509	−0.2523	1.0017	−0.8328	−0.2878	0.2090	1.3646
−0.4914	−0.6692	−1.8089	0.3057	0.2782	0.1107	−1.0372	0.1593	0.1673	−0.4022
−1.5223	−0.5254	−0.8486	−0.0634	−0.8544	−1.5779	−0.8696	1.0558	−0.5158	0.6833
−1.4123	1.8236	−1.6554	0.0246	0.9758	−1.0005	0.0056	−0.1732	−0.7792	0.1885
−1.3262	−0.5699	0.6259	2.2760	0.3705	0.5842	−1.2739	−1.2732	−0.5890	−0.4409
1.3115	0.0324	0.2220	1.0291	−0.9462	−0.1104	0.2320	0.6383	0.1168	1.3788

(b) $\gamma = 1.0$

0.6947	-0.4526	-1.4981	2.3178	-0.1857	-0.4655	-1.4804	-1.0227	-1.2948	-0.2342
0.3982	0.1092	1.8420	-1.1016	-1.4655	-0.1568	-0.4998	-1.0772	-0.4776	0.3044
-1.9760	0.3013	-1.0754	2.2538	0.2810	1.0067	3.8306	-0.1465	-0.2595	-1.1833
1.2749	-1.3010	-0.8147	0.2485	-1.5294	0.2597	-0.3160	-0.7570	3.2355	-0.2540
-1.1806	-0.1517	-0.6264	-0.3259	-0.2138	0.2344	-1.4570	1.0950	0.2183	0.1515
-1.1553	2.2340	-0.5611	-0.5717	-0.9523	-0.2603	-0.3859	-0.0134	-0.2194	-0.8178
4.2132	-0.6998	0.8881	-0.7762	-0.2138	-0.1504	-0.4196	2.0429	-1.0294	0.2643
0.3140	-0.4378	3.7994	-1.2701	-0.4573	-0.3335	1.0099	-0.6327	0.1963	-0.1462
-0.8154	-0.3648	1.4191	-0.8595	-1.1017	1.7996	-0.0024	0.4220	-0.3136	-1.2075
-0.8118	0.1803	0.3486	2.5939	0.5823	-1.0132	-0.5640	-0.5312	-1.1353	0.0013

Solutions to the exercises

F.1 Chapter 2

2.4.1

$$\alpha_2 = \sum_{k=0}^{\infty} k^2 e^{-n} \frac{n^k}{k!} = n e^{-n} \sum_{k=1}^{\infty} \frac{n^{k-1}}{(k-1)!} k \qquad \text{(substitute } k = k - 1 + 1\text{)}$$

$$= n e^{-n} \left[n \sum_{k=2}^{\infty} \frac{n^{k-2}}{(k-2)!} + \sum_{k=1}^{\infty} \frac{n^{k-1}}{(k-1)!} \right]$$

$$= n^2 + n.$$

2.5.1 $E(\mathbf{k}) = n = 0.01 \times 1000 = 10$, $P_\lambda = n(1 + \lambda)S = 11S$. The total claims amount is $\mathbf{X} = \mathbf{k}S$. The minimal value of the required security reserve U_0 is the smallest U which satisfies

$$\text{prob}\{U + P_\lambda - \mathbf{X} \geqslant 0\} = \text{prob}\{\mathbf{X} \leqslant U + P_\lambda\}$$
$$= \text{prob}\{\mathbf{k} \leqslant (U + P_\lambda)/S\} \geqslant 0.99.$$

(a) prob $\{\mathbf{k} \leqslant 17\} = 0.986$ and prob $\{\mathbf{k} \leqslant 18\} = 0.993$. Hence, rounded upwards to the next integer value of k

$$U_0 = (18 - 11)S = 7S = 7000.$$

(b) If $N((k - n)/\sqrt{n}) = 0.99$, then $k \approx 17.4$ and therefore again $U_0 = 7000$.

(c) $U_0 = 7000$.

2.5.2 54 300

2.5.3
$$P/1000 = \sum_{k=3}^{\infty} (k-2)\frac{e^{-1}}{k!}$$

$$= e^{-1}\left[\sum_{k=3}^{\infty}\frac{1}{(k-1)!} - 2\sum_{k=3}^{\infty}\frac{1}{k!}\right]$$

$$P = £104.$$

A shorter way to get the solution is to observe that

$$P_{reins} = P_{tot} - P_{cedent} = 1 \times 1000 - 1000\left[p_1 + 2(1 - p_0 - p_1)\right]$$

2.6.1

$$M(s) = \exp\left[n(e^s - 1)\right] = \exp\left[ns + ns^2/2! + \cdots\right]$$
$$= 1 + [\ ] + [\ ]^2/2! + \cdots$$
$$= 1 + ns + (n + n^2)s^2/2! + (n + 3n^2 + n^3)s^3/3!$$
$$+ (n + 7n^2 + 6n^3 + n^4)s^4/4! + \cdots$$

2.6.2 For $t > 0$

$$F_k(t) = \text{prob}\{\mathbf{W}_k \leqslant t\} = 1 - \text{prob}\{\mathbf{k}(t) < k\}$$
$$= 1 - \sum_{i=0}^{k-1} e^{-\rho t}(\rho t)^i/i!.$$

By differentiation it follows that

$$f_k(t) = F'_k(t) = \frac{\rho^k}{(k-1)!} e^{-\rho t} t^{k-1}.$$

Note that $\mathbf{W}_k/\rho$ is $\Gamma(t; k)$ distributed; see (2.9.1).

2.6.3 Conditions (i) and (ii) are obvious. For proof of condition (iii) define a variable $\mathbf{W}_k^j$ ($j = 1, 2; k = 1, 2, \ldots$) which gives the time when the kth event of the process j occurs. The variables $\mathbf{W}_k^1$ and $\mathbf{W}_h^2$ are independent and their distribution functions continuous (see exercise 2.6.2). Then $\mathbf{W}_k^1 - \mathbf{W}_h^2$ is also continuously distributed. Hence, $\mathbf{W}_k^1 \neq \mathbf{W}_h^2$ by probability 1, i.e. the probability of a multiple event is zero.

2.8.1 The proof is straightforward when the relevant expressions are substituted for $E(\mathbf{X}|\mathbf{Y} = Y)$.

2.9.1

$$\alpha_i = \frac{1}{\Gamma(h)} \int_0^\infty z^i e^{-z} z^{h-1} \, dz = \frac{1}{\Gamma(h)} \int_0^\infty e^{-z} z^{i+u-1} \, dz = \Gamma(h+i)/\Gamma(h)$$
$$= h(h+1)\ldots(h+i-1).$$

If the d.f. of $\mathbf{q}$ is $H(q) = \Gamma(hq; h)$, then the d.f. of $h\mathbf{q}$ is $\Gamma(x; h)$ and hence

$$\alpha_i(\mathbf{q}) = \alpha_i/h^i.$$

Substituting into the expressions defining the relevant characteristics, and noting (1.5.6), the requested formulae are obtained.

2.9.2

$$M_\Gamma(s) = \int_0^\infty e^{sz} \frac{1}{\Gamma(h)} e^{-z} z^{h-1} \, dz .$$

Substitute $u = (1-s)z$

$$M_\Gamma(z) = \frac{1}{(1-s)^h} \times \frac{1}{\Gamma(h)} \int_0^\infty e^{-u} u^{h-1} \, du$$
$$= (1-s)^{-h}.$$

2.9.3 Substitute $u = q(h+n - n e^s)$ in

$$M(s) = \frac{1}{\Gamma(h)} \int_0^\infty e^{nq(e^s - 1)} e^{-hq} (hq)^{h-1} h \, dq.$$

Note that the condition of convergence is $h + n - n e^s > 0$ or $s < \ln(1 + (h/n))$.

2.9.4

$$\binom{h+k-1}{k} \left(\frac{h}{n+h}\right)^h \left(\frac{n}{n+h}\right)^k$$
$$= \frac{(h+k-1)(h+k-2)\ldots(h+1)h}{k!} \times \frac{1}{\left(1+\dfrac{n}{h}\right)^h} \times \frac{n^k}{(n+h)^k} \to e^{-n} \frac{n^k}{k!}.$$

2.9.5

k	0	1	2	3	4	5	6	7	8	9	10	11	12	13	14	15
$p_k (\times 10\,000)$		67	337	842	1404	1755	1755	1462	1044	653	363	181	82	34	13	5	2
$\tilde{p}_k (\times 10\,000)$		173	578	1060	1413	1531	1429	1191	907	643	428	271	164	96	54	30	14

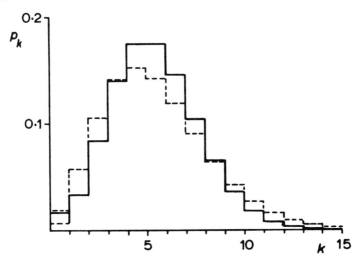

Figure F.1.1 *Poisson probabilities (solid line) and Polya probabilities;*
$n = 5, h = 10$.

2.9.6 See Fig F.1.1

$$\bar{M}(S)^2 = \left[\frac{h}{h + n(1 - e^s)} \right]^{2h} = \left[\frac{2h}{2h + 2n(1 - e^s)} \right]^{2h}.$$

2.9.7 Apply repeatedly integration by parts and note that k is a positive integer

$$1 - \Gamma(n, k + 1) = \frac{1}{\Gamma(k + 1)} \int_n^\infty e^{-z} z^k \, dz = \frac{e^{-n}}{k!} \sum_{v=0}^k n^v \frac{k!}{v!},$$

$$= F(k, n),$$

(see exercise 2.6.2).

2.9.8

$$\bar{p}_k / \bar{p}_{k-1} = \frac{h + k - 1}{k} \times \frac{n}{n + h} \geq 1,$$

when $k \leq n(1 - (1/h))$ (providing $h > 1$).

F.2 Chapter 3

3.3.1

$$n = 100 \times 0.01 = 1$$

It is convenient for the computations to take £100 as the monetary unit. S is a step function having a step $2/3$ at 1 and $1/3$ at 2. The total amount of the claims can be only a non-negative integer $X = 0, 1, 2, \ldots, N, \ldots$. Constructing all the possible combinations of the sums 1 and 2 which can lead to N, the following expansions are obtained making use of the abbreviation $p_k(1) = p_k$ (the difference compared with (3.2.3) is that N, not k, is taken as the variable):

$$
\begin{aligned}
F(X) &= p_0 = e^{-1} = 0.37 & \text{when } 0 \leqslant X < 1 \\
F(X) &= p_0 + p_1(\tfrac{2}{3}) = 0.61 & \text{when } 1 \leqslant X < 2 \\
F(X) &= F(1) + p_2(\tfrac{2}{3})^2 + p_1(\tfrac{1}{3}) = 0.82 & \text{when } 2 \leqslant X < 3.
\end{aligned}
$$

The following steps are constructed in a similar way: $F(3) = 0.92$, $F(4) = 0.97$, $F(5) = 0.99$, $F(6) = 1.00$.

3.3.2

$$
\begin{aligned}
E(\mathbf{X}) &= 1 \times (1 \times \tfrac{2}{3} + 2 \times \tfrac{1}{3}) = 1.33 \text{ or } £133 \\
\sigma &= \sqrt{\left[1 \times (1^2 \times \tfrac{2}{3} + 2^2 \times \tfrac{1}{3})\right]} = 1.41 \text{ or } £141.
\end{aligned}
$$

3.3.3

$$
\begin{aligned}
\bar{F}(X) &= \sum_{k=0}^{\infty} \bar{p}_k(n) S^{k*}(X) = \sum_{k=0}^{\infty} \left(\int_0^{\infty} e^{-nq} \frac{(nq)^k}{k!} \, dH(q) \right) S^{k*}(X) \\
&= \int_0^{\infty} \left(\sum_{k=0}^{\infty} e^{-nq} \frac{(nq)^k}{k!} S^{k*}(X) \right) dH(q) = \int_0^{\infty} F_{nq}(X) \, dH(q).
\end{aligned}
$$

3.3.4

$$
\begin{aligned}
\mu_3\!\left(\sum_j \mathbf{Z}_j\right) &= E\!\left(\sum_j (\mathbf{Z}_j - E\mathbf{Z}_j)\right)^3 \\
&= \sum_j E(\mathbf{Z}_j - E\mathbf{Z}_j)^3 + 3 \sum_{i \neq j} E(\mathbf{Z}_i - E\mathbf{Z}_i) E(\mathbf{Z}_j - E\mathbf{Z}_j)^2 \\
&\quad + 6 \sum_{h<i<j} E(\mathbf{Z}_h - E\mathbf{Z}_h) E(\mathbf{Z}_i - E\mathbf{Z}_i) E(\mathbf{Z}_j - E\mathbf{Z}_j).
\end{aligned}
$$

The assertion follows from the fact that at least one of the factors included in the last two sums is always zero.

3.3.5

$$\sigma_X^2 = \beta_2 - \beta_1^2 = na_2 + n^2 m^2 a_2(\mathbf{q}) - n^2 m^2.$$

Substituting $a_2(\mathbf{q}) = \sigma_\mathbf{q}^2 + 1$, (3.3.7) follows. The skewness is obtained in a similar way by using the connecting equations between the central moments and the moments about zero.

3.3.6 Let $q_1, \ldots, q_k$ be the jump points of H. Then H can be written as

$$H(q) = \sum_{i=1}^{k} h_i \varepsilon(q - q_i), \qquad \sum_{i=1}^{k} h_i = 1, h_i > 0.$$

Let F_n be the simple compound Poisson d.f. with the same claim size d.f. as $\mathbf{X}$ and having n as expected number of claims, and let G_n be the corresponding standardized d.f., i.e.

$$G_n(x) = F_n(Px).$$

Then (see (3.3.17))

$$\bar{G}_n(x) = \bar{F}_n(Px) = \int_0^\infty F_{nq}(Px)\,dH(q) = \sum_{i=1}^{k} F_{nq_i}(Px)h_i = \sum_{i=1}^{k} G_{nq_i}(x)h_i\,,$$

and, by (3.3.15),

$$G_{nq_i}(x) \to \varepsilon(x - q_i) \qquad \text{as } n \to \infty.$$

Therefore

$$\bar{G}_n(x) \to \sum_{i=1}^{k} h_i \varepsilon(x - q_i) = H(x) \qquad \text{as } h \to \infty.$$

3.4.1 Expand first (3.4.1) in powers of s according to (1.6.4) and denote

$$E \equiv nq(M_Z(s) - 1) = nqms + nqa_2 s^2/2! + nqa_3 s^3/3! + nqa_4 s^4/4! + \cdots.$$

Then the integrant in (3.4.2) can be expanded as follows

$$e^{nq(M_Z(s) - 1)} = 1 + E + E^2/2! + E^3/3! + E^4/4! + \cdots.$$

Substituting the expressions of E, arranging according to the powers of s, substituting in (3.4.2) and integrating, the requested moments β_j are obtained, applying again (1.6.4), as the coefficients of the terms $s^j/j!$

$\beta_1 = mn$

$\beta_2 = na_2 + n^2 m^2 a_2(\mathbf{q})$

$\beta_3 = na_3 + 3n^2 m a_2 a_2(\mathbf{q}) + n^3 m^3 a_3(\mathbf{q})$

$\beta_4 = na_4 + 4n^2 m a_3 a_2(\mathbf{q}) + 3n^2 m^2 a_2 a_2(\mathbf{q}) + 6n^3 m^2 a_2 a_3(\mathbf{q}) + n^4 m^4 a_4(\mathbf{q}),$

where

$$a_j(\mathbf{q}) = \int_0^\infty q^j \, dH(q).$$

The requested formulae (3.3.7) are obtained by passing from the moments β_j and $a_j(\mathbf{q})$ about zero to the central moments.

3.4.2 Now $M_Z(s) = e^s$.

3.4.3 The proof is the same as for exercise 2.9.3 when e^s is substituted by $M_Z(s)$.

3.5.1 Denote the unknown rate of death by q. Then the following values for the step function S follow from (3.5.1)

$$S(100) = \frac{5000q}{5000q + 1000q + 2 \times 2000q} = 0.5; \; S(250) = 0.6 \text{ and}$$

$$S(500) = 1.$$

3.5.2 Assuming the formula valid for $k - 1$ the next step is verified by substituting (3.5.4) and the expression of S into:

$$S^{k*}(X) = \int_0^X S^{(k-1)*}(X - Y) \, dS(Y),$$

and integration by parts. Verify still the validity for $k = 2$.

$$\mu_X = na_1 = n/c; \sigma_X = \sqrt{na_2} = \sqrt{(2n)/c}$$

$$F(2) = 0.82.$$

3.5.3 From (2.9.17) and the general moment rule

$$a_j(a\mathbf{z} + b) = a^j a_j(\mathbf{z}) + \binom{j}{1} a^{j-1} b a_{j-1}(\mathbf{z}) + \cdots + b^j,$$

it follows

$$a_1(a\mathbf{z} + b) = a a_1(\mathbf{z}) + b = \alpha$$
$$a_2(a\mathbf{z} + b) = a^2 a_2(\mathbf{z}) + 2aba_1(\mathbf{z}) + b^2 = \alpha(\alpha + 1)$$
$$a_3(a\mathbf{z} + b) = a^3 a_3(\mathbf{z}) + 3a^2 b a_2(\mathbf{z}) + 3ab^2 a_1(\mathbf{z}) + b^3 = \alpha(\alpha + 1)(\alpha + 2).$$

Substituting the moments $a_1(\mathbf{z}) = 0$, $a_2(\mathbf{z}) = 1$ and $a_3(\mathbf{z}) = \gamma$ of the standardized variable $\mathbf{z}$, the coefficients of (3.5.8) and (3.5.9) are obtained as solution.

3.5.4 For $z > 0$ (see (3.5.7))

$$1 - \Gamma(w, \alpha) = \frac{e^{-\alpha} \alpha^\alpha}{\Gamma(\alpha + 1)} \int_w^\infty e^{\alpha - u} \left(\frac{u}{\alpha}\right)^{\alpha - 1} du$$

$$= \frac{h}{3} C(q(w) + 4q(w + h) + 2q(w + 2h) + 4q(w + 3h) + \cdots),$$

where q is the notation for the integrand

$$q(v) = e^{\alpha - v} \left(\frac{v}{\alpha}\right)^{\alpha - 1},$$

and h is the integration step of the Simpson formula. Furthermore, applying the Stirling formula to the constant C, preceding the above integral, we have

$$1/C = \sqrt{(2\pi\alpha)} \left(1 + \frac{1}{12} \frac{1}{\alpha} + \frac{1}{288} \frac{1}{\alpha^2} + \cdots \right).$$

The series should be extended until the terms vanish within the required limits of accuracy. The integration step h can be taken as $h = (1/k)\sqrt{\alpha}$, where k is another coefficient; e.g. $k = 10$ seems to give a satisfactory accuracy. For $z < 0$ the integral can be taken from w to $-\infty$ giving $\Gamma(w, \alpha)$ and h should be negative.

3.5.5

$$\text{prob}\{\mathbf{Z} \leqslant Z\} = \text{prob}\{\mathbf{Y} \leqslant \ln(Z - a)\}$$

$$= \frac{1}{\sigma\sqrt{2\pi}} \int_{-\infty}^{\ln(Z-a)} e^{-(1/2\sigma^2)(y-\mu)} \, \mathrm{d}y,$$

$S'(Z)$ is the derivative of this function.

3.5.6 (i) For $a = 0$ we have $\mathbf{Z} = e^{\mathbf{Y}}$, where $\mathbf{Y}$ is a normally $N(\mu, \sigma^2)$ distributed variable. Its moments about zero are

$$a_j^0 = E(\mathbf{Z}^j) = E(e^{j\mathbf{Y}}) = M(j) = e^{\mu j} \, e^{\frac{1}{2}j^2\sigma^2}.$$

(ii) Passage from $\mathbf{Z}$ to $\mathbf{Z} - a$ transforms the first moment a_1^0 to $a_1^0 + a$ but does not change the variance and skewness. The requested formulae are obtained expressing the central moments by means of the above moments.

(iii) Choose $\eta = \sqrt{(e^{\sigma^2} - 1)}$ and use (ii).

3.5.7

$$a_j = \frac{\alpha}{\alpha - j} Z_0^j \qquad \text{for } j < \alpha.$$

3.6.1

$$S_M(Z) = \begin{cases} S\left(\dfrac{1}{1-r} Z\right) & \text{for } Z < M \\[2mm] 1 & \text{for } Z \geqslant M. \end{cases}$$

3.7.1 Clearly $\mu_{\mathbf{X}} = nm = Nn_j m = 1840$ in both cases. In case (i)

$$\sigma_{\mathbf{X}} = \sqrt{(na_2 + n^2m^2\sigma_{\mathbf{q}}^2)} = 383,$$

and in case (ii) each risk unit forms a section, and therefore

$$\sigma_{\mathbf{X}} = \sqrt{\left[\sum_j (n_j a_2 + n_j^2 m^2 \sigma_{\mathbf{q}j}^2) \right]} = 105.$$

3.8.1

$X =$	0	1	2	3	4	5	6
$F =$	0.162	0.215	0.441	0.521	0.695	0.760	0.858

3.11.1 $\gamma = 0.6364$, $x = 2.828$; (a) 0.0023, (b) 0.0094; (c) 0.0093.

3.11.2

$$\text{prob}\left\{x < -\frac{nm}{\sqrt{(na_2 + n^2m^2\sigma_\mathbf{q}^2)}}\right\} = \text{prob}\{\mathbf{X} < 0\} < \varepsilon.$$

This implies

$$nm/\sqrt{(na_2 + n^2m^2\sigma_\mathbf{q}^2)} > -x_\varepsilon \qquad \text{where } x_\varepsilon = N_\gamma^{-1}(\varepsilon).$$

The condition is obtained from this inequality.

For calculation of x_ε the skewness $\gamma = \gamma_\mathbf{X}$ is needed. However, this depends, according to (3.3.7), on the unknown n. Hence an iteration is necessary.

Note that a conservative evaluation is obtained by taking $x_\varepsilon = N^{-1}(\varepsilon)$. In this case $x = N^{-1}(10^{-4}) = -3.72$ which can be taken as an initial value for iteration. It follows from (3.11.15) that $n = 143$. Furthermore, substituting in (3.3.7) this value and the given value $\gamma = 0.531$ are obtained. Then according to (3.11.15) and (3.11.16) $x = -3.01$. Repeating the iteration loop four times more the final evaluation $n = 85$ is obtained.

If the initial ε were 10^{-3}, then $n = 60$ would result.

3.12.1 According to the conditions of the exercise and (2.9.17),

$$a_1 = \alpha/a = \mu_\mathbf{X}$$
$$a_2 = \alpha(\alpha + 1)/a^2 = \sigma_\mathbf{X}^2 + \mu_\mathbf{X}^2 .$$

Solving these equations the following is obtained

$$a = \mu_\mathbf{X}/\sigma_\mathbf{X}^2, \alpha = \mu_\mathbf{X}^2/\sigma_\mathbf{X}^2 \quad \text{and} \quad \gamma_\mathbf{X} = 2\sigma_\mathbf{X}/\mu_\mathbf{X}.$$

3.12.2

$$y = \gamma/6 - 6/\gamma + 3(2/\gamma)^{2/3}(2/\gamma)^{1/3}[1 + \gamma z/2]^{1/3}.$$

Develop the term $(\ \ )^{1/3}$ as a Taylor series

$$y = z - \frac{\gamma}{6}(z^2 - 1) + \frac{5}{108}\gamma^2 z^3 - \cdots.$$

F.3 Chapter 4

4.2.1

$U = y\sqrt{(na_2)} - \lambda P$; $U + \Delta U = y\sqrt{(0.9na_2)} - \lambda P$. Hence $\Delta U = (U + \lambda P)(\sqrt{0.9} - 1) = (20 + 0.05 \times 100)(\sqrt{0.9} - 1) = -1.28$

4.2.2 If £100 is taken as the monetary unit and the unknown frequencies of the sums 1 and 2 are denoted by p and $1 - p$ then

$$m = p + 2(1 - p) = 2 - p$$
$$a_2 = p + 4(1 - p) = 4 - 3p$$
$$U = y\sqrt{[(4 - 3p)n]} - \lambda(2 - p)n,$$

U as a function of p reaches its maximum for

$$p = \frac{4}{3} - \frac{3y^2}{4n\lambda^2} \approx 0.52,$$

and the maximum $U = 1.5 = £150$.

4.2.3

$$U = y\sqrt{(r_2/n + \sigma_{\mathbf{q}}^2)P} - \lambda P = 0$$
$$\lambda = y\sqrt{(r_2/n + \sigma_{\mathbf{q}}^2)}$$
$$a_1 = \int_0^\infty Z e^{-Z}\,dZ = 1; a_2 = \int_0^\infty Z^2 e^{-Z}\,dZ = 2; r_2 = a_2/a_1^2 = 2$$
$$\lambda = 2.33\sqrt{(2/1000 + 0.04^2)} = 0.14.$$

4.2.4 Substitute

$$a_i = \frac{\alpha}{\alpha - i} - \frac{i}{\alpha - i}M^{-\alpha + i},$$

into

$$U = y_\varepsilon\sqrt{(na_2)} - \lambda na_1 = 2.33\sqrt{(100a_2)} - 0.1 \times 100a_1,$$

and calculate U for suitably chosen M values. After some trials the requested value is obtained: $M = 2.0$.

4.2.5 Put into the NP formula $X = U + (1 + \lambda)P$ where U is $15.72£10^6$ according to item 4.2(b). $\bar{F}$ is 0.0015, 0.0042 and 0.0302 respectively for $X_c = 5$, 10 and $20£10^6$.

4.4.1 Substitute the values related to the company C_1 into (4.1.7) and solve $y = 2.816$. Then modify (4.1.7) for the merged company applying (3.7.6), (3.7.9) and (3.7.12). $U = £512\,000$.

4.5.1 Substitute $a_i'(M) = iM^{i-1}(1 - S(M))$ into

$$U'(M) = \tfrac{1}{2}y\sqrt{(n/a_2(M))} \times a_2'(M) - \lambda na_1'(M)$$

4.5.2 Prove first $\lim_{M \to 0} a_2(M)/M^2 = 1$. It follows that $U'(M)$ tends to a negative limit as $M \to 0 +$ if $n > (y/\lambda)^2$.

4.5.3 Write (4.5.8) in the form

$$U'(M) = \lambda n(1 - S(M)) \frac{M}{\sqrt{a_2(M)}} \left[\frac{y}{\lambda\sqrt{n}} - \sqrt{\frac{a_2(M)}{M^2}} \right].$$

Let Z_0 be the lowest point for which $S(Z) = 1$. Z_0 may be infinite. Then in the interval $[0, Z_0)$ the expression in brackets determines the sign of $U'(M)$. Note that $a_2(M)/M^2$ is in this interval a non-increasing function of M (proof!). Hence if $U'(0) > 0$ (see exercise 4.5.2), $U(M)$ is in this same interval an increasing function. If $U'(0) < 0$ and $a_2(M)/M^2 < y^2/(\lambda^2 n)$ at Z_0 then $U(M)$ has a minimum inside the interval, otherwise it is a decreasing function.

4.5.4 Reading from Fig. 4.5.1 one finds $M \approx £0.5$ million. The approximate value is £0.45 million.

4.5.5 $\Delta U = U'(M)\Delta M$ and $\Delta P = P'(M)\Delta M$ and the return $R = \lambda\Delta P$. The required rate is

$$i_r(M) = R/\Delta U = \lambda_r P'(M)/U'(M).$$

$U'(M)$ was calculated for exercise 4.5.1 and

$$P'(M) = na_1'(M) = n(1 - S(M)),$$

(see exercise 4.5.1). Then after some reductions and interpolating from Table 3.6.1 we obtain

$$i_r = \frac{\lambda_r}{yM/\sqrt{(na_2)} - \lambda} = 0.25.$$

4.5.6 Let M move upwards until the rate of $i_r(M)$, calculated in the previous exercise, reaches i_0. It is convenient to solve M^2/a_2 from the equation. From the given data the value 1130 is found for it. The line most nearly corresponding to it in Table 3.6.1 is $M = £2.512$ million. Then $P = £80.8$ million and $U = £18.4$ million are obtained from (4.1.8).

4.5.7 Consider the new policy as another 'portfolio' to be merged to the original one. The premium income of it is qM and variance $q(1-q)M^2 \approx qM^2$. Then

$$U = y\sqrt{(na_2)} - \lambda P = y\sqrt{(na_2 + qM^2)} - \lambda(P + qM).$$

Solving this:

$$M = 2\lambda(U + \lambda P)/[(U + \lambda P)^2/na_2 - q\lambda^2] \approx 2\lambda na_2/(U + \lambda P).$$

4.5.8 For $M > 1$

$$a_1 = \frac{4}{5} - \frac{1}{5}\frac{1}{M}\,; a_2 = \frac{7}{15} + \frac{2}{5}\ln M\,.$$

Substituting these expressions and the given data into (4.1.8) the equation

$$20 = \sqrt{(253.3 + 217.2\ln M)} - 4 + \frac{1}{M}$$

follows. By standard methods (or more easily by a few trials) the solution $M = 4.2$ is obtained.

4.7.1 Applying (3.3.7) and counting also the cases $Z_{re} = 0$ into n we have

$$\sigma_{re}^2 = na_{2(re)} + P_{X/L}\sigma_q^2,$$

where

$$a_{2(re)} = \int_A^B (Z - A)^2\, dS(Z) + (B - A)^2(1 - S(B)).$$

Decomposing these expressions in terms and substituting the moments (3.6.3) for $M = A$ and $M = B$ the required formula is obtained.

4.7.2

$$\frac{nbZ_0^\alpha}{\alpha - 1}\left[\frac{1}{A^{\alpha - 1}} - \frac{1}{B^{\alpha - 1}}\right].$$

4.7.3 Calculate the first moment according to (3.6.3)

$$a_1(M) = 0.6\,Z_0 - 0.05Z_0^3/A^2.$$

Then $P = na_1(\infty) = n0.6Z_0$ and $P_{X/L} = n \times 0.05 \times Z_0^3 \times (A^{-2} - B^{-2})$. Putting $Z_0 = 1$, $A = 2$ and $B = 5$ we have $P_{X/L}/P = 1.75\%$.

For evaluation of inflation replace Z_0 by $1.1Z_0$; then the correct risk premium percentage is increased in the ratio $1.1^2 = 1.21$.

4.7.4

$$S_{re}(Z_{re}) = (S(M + Z_{re}) - S(M))/(1 - S(M))$$
$$= 1 - e^{-cZ_{re}}$$

$$\text{var } \mathbf{X}_{re} = \frac{2n}{c^2} \times e^{-cM} + \frac{n^2}{c^2}e^{-2cM}\sigma_q^2.$$

4.8.1 Substitute into (4.8.1a) $dF(X) = dN(y)$ and $X = \mu_\mathbf{X} + \sigma_\mathbf{X}(y + \gamma_\mathbf{X}y^2/6 - \gamma_\mathbf{X}/6)$ which follow from (3.11.14) (lowest line) and (3.11.16). In manipulating the integrand, note that $yN'(y) = -N''(y)$ and $y^2 N'(y) = N'''(y) + N'(y)$ (see (3.11.4)).

4.9.1 7 years.

4.10.1

$$\sigma_P^2 = \frac{1 - (1 - Z)^{2t}}{1 - (1 - Z)^2}Z^2\sigma^2.$$

For proof of the second part of the exercise replace the individual variances by their joint upper limit.

4.10.2

$$E(\mathbf{G}) = k\int_0^B (B - X)\,dF \leqslant B - P$$
$$= \int_0^\infty B\,dF - \int_0^\infty X\,dF = \int_0^\infty (B - X)\,dF.$$

Hence $k \leqslant 1$, equality being valid only in the case $F(B) = 1$.

4.10.3

$$Z = \frac{0.1}{2\sqrt{(10/200)}} = 0.224$$

$$P_1 = 0.224 \times \frac{180\,000}{1000} + 0.776 \times 300 = \pounds273.$$

F.4   Chapter 5

5.1.1 (i) is obvious and (ii) is simply the formula $E(E(\mathbf{Y}|\mathbf{X})) = E(\mathbf{Y})$ given in exercise 2.8.1. To prove (iii) note that quite generally

$$V(\mathbf{Y}) = V(E(\mathbf{Y}|\mathbf{X})) + E(V(\mathbf{Y}|\mathbf{X})) \geqslant V(E(\mathbf{Y}|\mathbf{X})),$$

where $V(\mathbf{Y}|\mathbf{X}) = E[(\mathbf{Y} - E(\mathbf{Y}|\mathbf{X}))^2|\mathbf{X}]$ is the conditional variance of $\mathbf{Y}$. In fact, since $E(\mathbf{Y}|\mathbf{X}) = R(\mathbf{X})$ is a function of $\mathbf{X}$, it is seen that

$$
\begin{aligned}
V(\mathbf{Y}) - V(E(\mathbf{Y}|\mathbf{X})) &= E(\mathbf{Y}^2) - E(R^2(\mathbf{X})) \\
&= E[E(\mathbf{Y}^2 - R^2(\mathbf{X})|\mathbf{X})] \\
&= E[E(\mathbf{Y}^2 - 2R(\mathbf{X})\mathbf{Y} + R^2(\mathbf{X})|\mathbf{X})] \\
&= E\{E[(\mathbf{Y} - R(\mathbf{X}))^2|\mathbf{X}]\} = E[(\mathbf{Y} - R(\mathbf{X}))^2] \geqslant 0
\end{aligned}
$$

(iv) is just (iii) with $\mathbf{Y}$ replaced by $\mathbf{X} - \mathbf{Y}$.

5.2.1 Let $\mathbf{X}_k$ be the original aggregate claim and $\mathbf{Y}_k$ the share of the company k after the exchange, according to the rule given in the exercise, and $\mathbf{Y}'_k$ the share according to the specified rule:

$$\mathbf{Y}'_k = \frac{1}{r}\sum_k \mathbf{X}_k = \frac{1}{r}\sum \mathbf{Y}_k.$$

Then

$$\operatorname{var}(\mathbf{Y}'_k) = \frac{1}{r^2}\sum_{i,k}\operatorname{cov}(\mathbf{Y}_i, \mathbf{Y}_k) \leqslant \frac{1}{r^2}r^2\operatorname{var}(\mathbf{Y}) = \operatorname{var}(\mathbf{Y}).$$

The inequality follows from the general rule

$$\operatorname{cov}(\mathbf{Y}_i, \mathbf{Y}_k) \leqslant \sqrt{\operatorname{var}(\mathbf{Y}_i)} \times \sqrt{\operatorname{var}(\mathbf{Y}_k)},$$

well known in probability calculus and from the assumption of the equality of the company distributions which means $\operatorname{var}(\mathbf{Y}_i) = \operatorname{var}(\mathbf{Y}_k)$.

5.2.2

(i)
$$\rho_0 = \sqrt{\left(\frac{1}{n} + \sigma_\mathbf{q}^2\right)}.$$

(ii)
$$\rho = \sqrt{\left[\frac{1}{n}\frac{a_2}{a_1^2} + \sigma_\mathbf{q}^2\right]},$$

$a_2/a_1^2 \geqslant 1$ follows from $\mu_2 = a_2 - a_1^2 \geqslant 0$.

(iii) $$U = y\rho P - \lambda P.$$

5.2.3 The proof can be found either by straightforward calculations or more easily by observing that a linear co-ordinate transformation, which stretches x co-ordinates in the ratio $\sqrt{(V_2/V_1)}$ and keeps y co-ordinates unchanged transforms the ellipses concerned to circles. Then the assertion becomes evident, because the transformation keeps straight lines straight and tangents as tangents.

F.5 Chapter 6

6.2.1 Denote $\lambda(t) - \lambda_0 = f(t) = Ab^t$. Then

$$f(t) - a_1 f(t-1) - a_2 f(t-2) = Ab^{t-2}[b^2 - a_1 b - a_2] = 0.$$

Equating the expression in brackets with zero, two values are obtained

$$b = \tfrac{1}{2}a_1 \pm \tfrac{1}{2}\sqrt{(a_1^2 + 4a_2)},$$

and the general solution is

$$f(t) = A_1 b_1^t + A_2 b_2^t.$$

The coefficients A_1 and A_2 are determined by initial conditions.
    The solution is oscillating if b_1 and b_2 are complex, i.e. when

$$a_1^2 + 4a_2 < 0.$$

Moving into polar coordinates

$$b_{1,2} = r\,e^{\pm i\varphi},$$

with

$$r = \sqrt{(-a_2)} \text{ and } \varphi = \arctan\left[\frac{\sqrt{(-a_1^2 - 4a_2)}}{a_1}\right] \quad (0 < \varphi < \pi).$$

The general solution can be written in form

$$f(t) = A_1 r^t e^{i\varphi t} + A_2 r^t e^{-i\varphi t},$$

or, since $e^{i\varphi t} = \cos(\varphi t) + i\sin(\varphi t)$ and by some straightforward transformations

$$f(t) = Ar^t \sin(\varphi t + v),$$

where A and v are other coefficients. The oscillation is damped if $r < 1$. The wavelength is directly seen from condition $2\pi = \varphi T$, i.e. $T = 2\pi/\varphi$.

In the particular case given in the exercise

$$f(t) = \lambda(t) - \lambda_0 = -0.10690 \left(\frac{1}{\sqrt{2}}\right)^t \sin(1.93216t - 0.48669),$$

with $T = 3.25$. Verify the result for $t = 1, 2, \dots$ comparing with the values which are obtained directly from the difference equation; the first step being

$$f(1) = -\tfrac{1}{2}f(0) - \tfrac{1}{2}f(-1) = -0.075.$$

Compared with Fig. 6.2.1 the oscillation is now rapidly vanishing as t increases. This shows that the stationary oscillation in Fig. 6.2.1 is maintained by the continued impulses due to the 'noise' $\varepsilon(t)$.

6.4.1 Now

$$n(\tau) = nr_g^\tau(1 + z(\tau))$$
$$\mu_{\mathbf{X}}(\tau) = n(\tau)m(\tau) = nmr_g^\tau r_x^t(1 + z(\tau))$$
$$P(\tau) = \mu_{\mathbf{X}}(\tau)/(1 + z(\tau))$$

where n and m are obtained from (3.7.2) and (3.7.4). Then (see (3.7.9))

$$\sigma_{\mathbf{X}}^2(t_1, t_2) = \sum_{\tau = t_i}^{t_2} (r_2/n(\tau) + \sigma_q^2) P(\tau)^2,$$

and the coefficients (6.4.5) become time independent (and the argument can be dropped from (6.4.5)). Hence, for convenience of calculations, the time dependence is concentrated in the variables $n(\tau)$, $\mu_{\mathbf{X}}(\tau)$ and $P(\tau)$ only.

6.7.1 The second term of the right hand side of (6.7.11) is replaced by

$$-\sum_{t=T_0}^{T-1} \int_{-\infty}^{U_r(t)} G(Y, U; t, T) \, d_Y \, W(U_0, Y; T_0, t).$$

6.8.1 As primary entries in all the following cases are either uniformly $(0, 1)$ generated random numbers $\mathbf{r}$ or normally $N(0, 1)$ distributed numbers $\mathbf{y}$.

(i)

(I) *n small*

First make a program for the calculation of

$$F(k) = \sum_{i=0}^{k} p_i(n),$$

e.g. by using the algorithm (2.5.2). If n is fixed to be the same during the simulation algorithm, then it may be rewarding to calculate $F(k)$ in advance and to save as an array. Then the simulation algorithm is as follows:

(1) Generate r
(2) $k = 0$
(3) If $r \leqslant F(k)$ deliver k
(4) $k \to k + 1$; go to (3).

Note: If n is not very small, it is useful to start the algorithm consisting of steps (3) and (4) at $k = n$ and if $r > F(n)$ to proceed upwards, otherwise downwards (see Rubinstein 1981, Section 3.7).

Furthermore, pay attention to the possibility that owing to the rounding-off inaccuracies the limit value of $F(k)$ may occasionally remain less than 1 when $k \to \infty$, if F is computed repeatedly for every sample.

(II) *n large*

Denote by y the argument of $N[\ ]$ in (3.5.14), substitute (see (2.4.5)) $\gamma = 1/\sqrt{n}$ and $z = (k - n)/\sqrt{n}$ and solve k:

(a) $k = [(y + A)/B]^3 - n - \frac{1}{2}$,

where y is normally $(0, 1)$ distributed and

(b) $A = 6\sqrt{n} - 1/(6\sqrt{n}); B = 3 \times 2^{2/3} \times n^{1/6}$.

Note the correction term $-\frac{1}{2}$ in (a). It is due to roundings and is not obtained directly from (3.5.14).

Then

(1) Generate y
(2) Calculate k from (a).

(ii)

$$X = -\frac{1}{a}\ln(1 - F).$$

(1) Generate r

(2) $X = -\frac{1}{a}\ln r.$

Note that r and $1 - r$ are equally distributed.

(iii)

(1) Generate $r_1, r_2, \ldots, r_h$

(2) $X = \sum_{i=1}^{h} -\frac{1}{c}\ln r_i = -\frac{1}{c}\ln \prod_{i=1}^{h} r_i.$

(iv)

(1) Generate y

(2) $X = a + \exp(y\sigma - \mu).$

(v)

(1) Generate r

(2) $X = X_0 r^{-1/\alpha}.$

6.8.2 Examples are plotted in Fig. F.5.1.

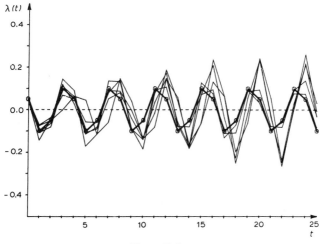

Figure F.5.1.

6.8.3 Example of an outcome of stratified simulation. Sample size 10 000.

X	0	1	2	3	4	5	6	7	8	9
$c(X)$	1352	0	2394	2013	1494	986	703	439	256	159
$F(X)$	0.1354	0.1354	0.3749	0.5763	0.7257	0.8244	0.8947	0.9385	0.9641	0.9800

X	10	11	12	13	14	15	16	17	18	19
$c(X)$	85	40	28	17	15	6	2	3	1	1
$F(X)$	0.9885	0.9924	0.9952	0.9969	0.9984	0.9990	0.9992	0.9996	0.9997	0.9998

The largest X was 29, making $F(29) = 1.0000$.

F.6 Chapter 7

7.10.1 From

$$E_{\mathbf{u}} \geqslant y_\varepsilon \sigma_{\mathbf{u}}(\infty) + z_{\mathrm{m}} + u_{\mathrm{r}}$$

it follows

$$\frac{\lambda}{1 - r_{\mathrm{igp}}} \geqslant y_\varepsilon (1 - c - \lambda_b) \sigma_{\mathbf{q}} (1 - r_{\mathrm{igp}}^2)^{-\frac{1}{2}} + z_{\mathrm{m}} + u_{\mathrm{r}},$$

where z_{m} is the amplitude of the cycles. Substitute according to (6.5.12) $\lambda_{\mathrm{p}} = \lambda - i_{\mathrm{igp}} w$ and solve λ

$$\lambda \geqslant [(1 - c + i_{\mathrm{igp}} w) A + (z_{\mathrm{m}} + u_{\mathrm{r}})(1 - r_{\mathrm{igp}})]/(1 + A),$$

where

$$A = y_\varepsilon \sigma_{\mathbf{q}} \sqrt{\left(\frac{1 - r_{\mathrm{igp}}}{1 + r_{\mathrm{igp}}} \right)}.$$

Substituting the numerical values from item 7.1(d) (note $y_\varepsilon = 2.33$, u_{r} and $w = 1.71$) we have $\lambda \geqslant 0.028$.

7.10.2 Substitute into

$$L = \mu_{\mathbf{u}}(t) - y_\varepsilon \sigma_{\mathbf{u}}(t),$$

first the expression (6.6.8a)

$$\mu_{\mathbf{u}}(t) = u(0) r^t - \frac{1 - r^t}{1 - r} \lambda,$$

where briefly $r = r_{igp}$. According to (6.6.11) and (6.6.6) and denoting $\rho = 1/r^2 r_g = r_g r_p^2/r_i^2$

$$\sigma_u^2(t) = \sum_{\tau=1}^{t} \frac{r_2}{nr_g^{\tau}}(1 - c - \lambda_b)^2 r^{2(t-\tau)}$$

$$= r^{2t}\frac{r_2}{n}(1 - c - \lambda_b)^2 \sum_{\tau=1}^{t} \rho^{\tau}$$

$$= r^{2t}\frac{r_2(1 - c - \lambda_b)^2(1 - \rho^t)\rho}{n(1 - \rho)}.$$

Hence

$$L = r^t \left[u(0) + \frac{\lambda}{r - 1} - y_\varepsilon \sqrt{\left(\frac{r_2(1 - c - \lambda_b)^2(1 - \rho^t)\rho}{n(1 - \rho)}\right)} \right] - \frac{\lambda}{r - 1},$$

which proves that $L \to \infty$ when $t \to \infty$ if $\rho < 1$ and the expression in the brackets is positive.

F.7   Chapter 8

8.2.1

$$P = SA(v) \bigg/ \sum_{t=0}^{w-1} l(t)v^t.$$

8.2.2 All the sums following will run from 0 to $w - 1$

$$\sigma^2 = \sum p(t) \left[P_1 - \left[\frac{a}{1 - v} + \left(S - \frac{a}{1 - v} \right) v^{t+1} \right] \right]^2$$

$$= \sum p(t) \left[\frac{a}{1 - v} + \left(S - \frac{a}{1 - v} \right) A(v) - \frac{a}{1 - v} \right.$$

$$\left. - \left(S - \frac{a}{1 - v} \right) v^{t+1} \right]^2$$

$$= \left(S - \frac{a}{1 - v} \right)^2 \sum p(t) [A(v)^2 - 2A(v)v^{t+1} + (v^2)^{t+1}],$$

from which (8.2.8) follows, noting that $\sum p(t) = 1$.

F.8   Chapter 9

9.1.1 The introduction of the 'bonus barrier' U_{max} means in fact that $U(t)$ is replaced by $U^*(t) = \min(r_i U^*(t-1) + P_\lambda - X(t), U_{max})$, where $U^*(0) \equiv U_0$. Since

$$\{U^*(t) \geqslant 0\} \subset \{X(t) \leqslant M\},$$

and since the variables $X(t)$ are mutually independent it follows that

$$1 - \Psi_\infty = \text{prob}\left(\bigcap_{t=1}^\infty \{U^*(t) \geqslant 0\}\right) \leqslant \text{prob}\left(\bigcap_{t=1}^\infty \{X(t) \leqslant M\}\right)$$

$$= \prod_{t=1}^\infty \text{prob}\{X(t) \leqslant M\} \leqslant \exp\left(-\sum_{t=1}^\infty \text{prob}\{X(t) > M\}\right).$$

The last estimate is an application of the inequality $1 - x \leqslant e^{-x}$.

9.1.2 By making use of the relations derived in item 6.9(d) we have for every $t > 0$

$$\Delta\Psi_t \leqslant \varphi_{cc}(t) = (1 - \Psi_{t-1})\frac{\varphi_c(t)}{1 - \varphi(t-1)} \leqslant (1 - \Psi_{t-1})\frac{\varphi(t)}{1 - \varphi(t-1)}.$$

Obviously Ψ_t is non-increasing. Assuming that (9.1.3) is true, let $t_1 \geqslant t_0$ be such that $\sum_{t > t_1} \varphi(t)/(1 - \varphi(t-1))$ is < 1. Then

$$\Psi_\infty = \Psi_{t_1} + \sum_{t > t_1} \Delta\Psi_t \leqslant \Psi_{t_1} + (1 - \Psi_{t_1})\sum_{t > t_1}\frac{\varphi(t)}{1 - \varphi(t-1)} < 1.$$

9.1.3 Substitute in to the Tchebychev inequality

$$\text{prob}\{|\mathbf{u}(t) - \mu_\mathbf{u}(t)| \geqslant k\sigma_\mathbf{u}(t)\} \leqslant \frac{1}{k^2}$$

$$k = \mu_\mathbf{u}(t)/\sigma_\mathbf{u}(t).$$

Then

(a) $\qquad \varphi(t) < \text{prob}\{|\mathbf{u}(t) - \mu_\mathbf{u}(t)| > \mu_\mathbf{u}(t)\} < \sigma_\mathbf{u}(t)^2/\mu_\mathbf{u}(t)^2.$

Denoting briefly $r = r_{igp}$, it follows from equation (6.6.8a)

(b) $\qquad \mu_\mathbf{u}(t) = u(0)r^t + \lambda\frac{1 - r^t}{1 - r} = A[1 + o(r^t)],$

where A is a constant and the expression $o(\cdot)$ vanishes when its argument tends to zero. Furthermore, according to (6.6.11) (see exercise 7.10.1)

(c) $\qquad \sigma_u^2(t) = \frac{r_2}{n}(1 - c - \lambda_b)^2 \rho r^{2t}\frac{1 - \rho^t}{1 - \rho}.$

where $\rho = 1/r^2 r_g$. This expression can be written in the form

$$\sigma_u^2(t) = [r^{2t} - (r^2\rho)^t]B,$$

and then

$$\varphi(t) < [r^{2t} - (r^2\rho)^t]C,$$

where B and C are constant. Because r and $r^2\rho = 1/r_g$ are by assumption < 1 the premises of exercise 9.1.2 are satisfied which proves the assertion.

9.2.1 According to (9.2.5b) $R = 0.235$ and then $e^{-RU} = 0.095$.

9.2.2
$$e^{-RU}/(e^{-RU}\,e^{-RM}) = e^{RM} = (e^{-RU})^{-M/U}.$$

For $e^{-RU} = 0.01$ and $M/U \leqslant 0.02$ this is $\leqslant 1.096$ and for $e^{-RU} = 0.001$ it is $\leqslant 1.148$.

F.9   Chapter 10

10.4.1 Substituting in (10.4.2) it follows that

$$E(H(\mathbf{U})) = aE(G(\mathbf{U})) + b,$$

from which the assertion follows directly.

Bibliography

$SA = $ Scandinavian Actuarial Journal (earlier Skandinavisk Aktuarietidskrift)

$MS = $ Mitteilungen der Vereinigung Schweizerischer Versicherungsmathematiker

$AB = $ The Astin Bulletin

$CA = $ Transactions of the International Congress of Actuaries

$BARAB = $ Bulletin de l'Association Royales des Actuaires Belges

$GP = $ Geneva Papers on Risk and Insurance

$JIA = $ Journal of the Institute of Actuaries

$JRI = $ The Journal of Risk and Insurance

$PCAS = $ Proceedings of the Casualty Actuarial Society

Abramowitz, M. and Stegun, I. (1970) *Handbook of Mathematical Functions*, (9th print) Doover Publications, New York.

Adelson, R.M. (1966) Compound Poisson distributions, *Operations Research Quarterly*, **17**.

Ammeter, H. (1948) A generalization of the collective theory of risk in regard to fluctuating basic probabilities, *SA*.

Ammeter, H. (1953) The calculation of premium rates for excess of loss and stop loss reinsurance treaties, *CA*.

Ammeter, H. (1963) Experience Rating, *AB*.

Bailey, A.L. (1945) A generalized theory of credibility, *PCAS*, **32**.

Balzar, L.A. and Benjamin, S. (1980) Dynamic response of insurance systems, *JIA*.

Balzar, L.A. and Benjamin, S. (1982) Control of insurance systems, *JIA*.

Beard, R.E. (1947) Some statistical aspects of non-life insurance, *JIA*.

Beard, R.E. (1959) Three R's of insurance – risk, retention, and reinsurance, *JIA*.

Beard, R.E. (1971) On the calculation of the ruin probability for a finite time period, *AB*.

Becker, F. (1981) Analyse und Prognose von wirtschaftlichen Zeitreihen der Deutschen Schaden- und Unfallversicherung, Inaugural-Dissertation, Universität Mannheim, Veröffentlichungen des Instituts für Versicherungswissenschaft der Universität Mannheim, **19**.

Bellman, R. (1957) *Dynamic Programming* (reprinted 1965), Princeton.

Benckert, L-G. (1962) The lognormal model for the distribution of one claim, *AB*.

Benjamin, B. (1977) *General Insurance*, Heinemann, London.

Benktander, G. (1970) Schadenverteilung nach Grösse in der Nicht-Leben-Versicherung, *MS*.

Benktander, G. and Segerdahl, C-O. (1960) On the analytical representation of claim distrubution with special reference to excess of loss reinsurance, *CA*.

Berger, G. (1972) Integration of the normal power approximation, *AB*.

Bertram, J. (1981) Numerischen Berechnung von Gesamtschadenverteilung, *Blätter der Deutschen Gesellschaft für Versicherungsmathematik*.

Bohlmann, G. (1909) Die Theorie des mittleren Risikos, *CA*.

Bohman, H. (1964) To compute the distribution function when the characteristic function is known, *SA*.

Bohman, H. (1979) A mathematical model of insurance business and how it may be used, *Geneva Papers on Risk and Insurance no. 11* (January).

Bohman, H. and Esscher, F. (1964) Studies in risk theory with numerical illustrations concerning distribution functions and stop loss premiums, *SA*.

Borch, K. (1960) Reciprocal reinsurance treaties, *AB*.

Borch, K. (1961) The utility concept applied to the theory of insurance, *AB*.

Borch, K. (1962) Application of game theory to some problems in automobile insurance, *AB*.

Borch, K. (1963) Economic theory and their application to insurance, *AB*.

Borch, K. (1970) *The Mathematical Theory of Insurance*, D.C. Health & Co., Lexington, MA.

Brigham, E.O. (1974) *The Fast Fourier Transform*, Prentiss Hall, Englewood Cliffs, New Jersey.

Bühlmann, H. (1967) Experience rating and credibility, *AB*.

Bühlmann, H. (1970) *Mathematical Methods in Risk Theory*, Springer, Heidelberg.

Bühlmann, H. and Jewell, W.S. (1979) Optimal risk exchanges, *AB*.

Butsic, R.P. (1979) Risk and return for property-casualty insurers, in Total return due a property-casualty insurance company, Casualty Actuarial Society.

Casualty Actuarial Society (1980) Inflation implications for property-casualty insurance, Discussion paper program.

Chatfield, C. (1980) *The Analysis of Time Series*, 2nd edn, Chapman and Hall, London.

Christy, G.A. and Clendenin, J.C. (1978) *Introduction to Investments*, McGraw-Hill, New York.

Chung, K.L. (1974) *A Course in Probability Theory*, 2nd edn, Academic Press, New York.

Cornish, E.A. and Fisher, R.A. (1937) Moments and cumulants in the specification of distributions, *Rev. Int. Statist. Inst.*, **5**, 307.

Cox, D.R. and Miller, H.D. (1965), *The Theory of Stochastic Processes*, Methuen. London.

Cramér, H. (1926) Review of F. Lundberg, *SA*.

Cramér, H. (1930) On the mathematical theory of risk, Skandia Jubilee Volume, Stockholm.

Cramér, H. (1945) *Mathematical Methods of Statistics*, Almqvist and Wicksells, Uppsala.

Cramér, H. (1955) Collective risk theory, a survey of the theory from the point of view of the theory of stochastic processes, Skandia Jubilee Volume, Stockholm.

De Wit, G.W. and Kastelijn, W.M. (1980) The solvency margin in non-life insurance companies, *AB*.

D'Hooge, L. and Goovaerts, M.J. (1976) Numerical treatment of the determination of the structure function of a tariff class, *CA*.

DuMouchel, W.H. and Olsten, R.A. (1974) On the distribution of claim costs, Berkeley Actuarial Research Conference on Credibility.

Eggenberger, F. and Polya, G. (1923) Über die Statistik der vergetteter Vorgänge, *Zeitschrift für angewandte Mathematik und Mechanik*, I.

Ferrari, J.R. (1968) The relationship of underwriting, investment, leverage, and exposure to total return on owners' equity, *PCAS*.

Forrester, J.W. (1972) *Industrial Dynamics*, The MIT Press, Massachusetts.

Friedman, J.W. (1977) *Oligopoly and the Theory of Games*, North Holland Publishing Company, Amsterdam, New York and Oxford.

Frisque, A. (1974) Dynamic model for insurance company's management, *AB*.

Galbraith, J.K. (1973) *Economics and the Public Purpose*.

Galitz, L. (1982) The ASIR model, *GP*.

Gelder, H.v. and Schauwers, C. (1981) Planning in theory and practice with reference to insurance, Delta Lloyd Insurance Group, Amsterdam.

General Electric Company (1962) *Tables of the Individual and Cumulative Terms of Poisson Distribution*, D. van Nostrand Co., Princeton.

Gerber, H.U. (1979) *An Introduction to the Mathematical Risk Theory*, S.S. Huebner foundation monographs, University of Pennsylvania.

Gerber, H.U. (1982) On the numerical evaluation of the distribution of aggregate claims and its stop loss premiums, *Insurance: Mathematics and Economics*, I.

Geusau, A.B.J.J. von (1981) Some applicable actuarial forecasting models, Nederlandske Reassurantie Groep.

Godolphin, E.J. (1980) Specifying univariate models for the Zoete equity index, Maturity Guarantees Working Party.

Gossiaux, A-M. and Lemaire, J. (1981) Méthodes d'ajustement de distributions de sinistres, *MS*.

Grote, J.D. (1975) *The Theory and Application of Differential Games*, D. Reidel Publishing Company, Dortrecht, Holland.

Hammersley, J.M. and Handscomb, D.C. (1964) *Monte Carlo Methods*, Methuen, London.

Heiskanen, J. (1982) Degree of loss and surplus reinsurance of fire insurance, unpublished research work, Helsinki.

Helten, E. (1977) Business cycles and insurance, *GP*.

Heubeck, K. (1971) Optimale Reservepolitik als Markoffscher Entscheidungsprozess, *Blätter der Deutschen Gesellschaft für Versicherungsmathematik*, Band X, Heft 1.

Hovinen, E. (1964) A method to compute convolutions, *CA*.

James, K.D. (1981) Underwriting cycles in property-casualty insurance industry, Discussion papers, Casualty Actuarial Society.

Jewell, W. (1976) A survey of credibility theory, University of California, Berkeley.

Jewell, W. (1980) Models in insurance, *CA*.

Jewell, W. and Sundt, B. (1981) Recursive evaluation of compound distributions, *AB*.

Johnson, N.L. and Kotz, S. (1969) *Distributions in Statistics, 1, 'Discrete Distributions'*, Wiley, New York.

Johnson, N.L. and Kotz, S. (1970) *Distribution in Statistics, 1, Continuous Univariate Distributions*, Wiley, New York.

Johnson, N.L., Nixon, E., Amos, D.E. and Pearson, E.S. (1963) Tables of percentage points of Pearson curves for given $\sqrt{\beta_1}$, and β_2 expressed in standard measure, *Biometrika*, **50**.

Karten, W. (1980) The new 'Schwankungsrückstellung' in annual statements of German insurers. An application of the theory of risks, *GP*.

Kauppi, L. and Ojantakanen, P. (1969) Approximations of the generalized Poisson function, *AB*.

Kendall, M.G. and Stuart, A. (1977) *The Advanced Theory of Statistics*, Charles Griffin & Co., London.

Kimball, S.L. and Pfennigstorf W. (1981) The regulation of insurance companies in the United States and the European communities, a comparative study, International Insurance Advisory Council, Chamber of Commerce of the United States.

Kotler, P. (1975) *Marketing Decision Making, a Model Building Approach*, Holt, Rinehart and Winston, New York.

Landin, D. (1980) Risk accumulation, a lecture paper.

Levine, S.H. (ed.) (1975) *Financial Analysts' Handbook II: Analysis by Industry* (Vol. 2) Dow Jones-Irwin, Inc. Homewood, Il.

Loimaranta, K. Jacobsson, J. and Lonka, H. (1980) On the use of mixture models in clustering multivariate frequency data, *CA*.

Lorie, J.H. and Hamilton, M.T. (1973) *The Stock Market: Theories and Evidence*, Richard D. Irwin, Inc. Homewood, Il.

Lundberg, F. (1909) Zur Theorie der Rückversicherung, *CA*.

Lundberg, F. (1919) Teori för riskmassor, Stockholm (Försäkrings-inspektionen).

Lundberg, O. (1964) *On Random Processes and their Application to Sickness and Accident Statistics* (reprint of thesis 1940) Almqvist and Wiksells Boktryckeri, Uppsala.

Martin-Löf, A. (1983) Premium control in an insurance system, an approach using control theory, *SA*.

Maturity Guarantees Working Party (1980) Report, *JIA*, **107**.

Mayerson, A.L. (1965) A Bayesian view of credibility (discussion) *PCAS*, **52**.

McGuinness, J.S. (1954) *Top Management, Organization, and Control of Insurance Companies*, Stanford University Press, Stanford, CA.

McGuinness, J.S. (1966) *A Feasibility Study of Flood Insurance*, New York.

McGuinness, J.S. (1970) Elements of time-series analysis in liability and property insurance ratemaking, *PCAS*.

Mihram, G.A. (1972) *Simulation*, Academic Press, New York.

Munich Reinsurance Company (1971) The Influence of Inflation on Insurance, Munich.

Nemhauser, G.L. (1966) *Dynamic Programming*, Wiley, New York.

Neumann, J. v. and Morgenstern, O. (1964) *Theory of Games and Economic Behaviour*, Wiley, New York.

Panjer, H.H. (1981) Recursive evaluation of a family of compound distributions, *AB*.

Pearson, K. (1954) Tables of incomplete Γ-function, Biometrika Office.

Pentikäinen, T. (1952) On the net retention and solvency of insurance companies, *SA*.

Pentikäinen, T. (1975) A model of stochastic-dynamic prognosis. An application of risk theory to business planning, *SA*.

Pentikäinen, T. (1976) Stochastic-dynamic prognosis, *CA*.

Pentikäinen, T. (1977) On the approximation of the total amount of claims, *AB*.

Pentikäinen, T. (1978) A solvency testing model building approach for business planning, *SA*.

Pentikäinen, T. (1979) Dynamic programming, an approach for analysing competition strategies, *AB*.

Pentikäinen, T. (1982) *Solvency of Insurers and Equalization Reserves* (Vol. I) Insurance Publishing Company, Helsinki.

Pesonen, E. (1964) Solvency measurement, *CA*.

Pesonen, E. (1967a) On the calculation of the generalized Poisson function, *AB*.

Pesonen, E. (1967b) Magnitude control of technical reserves in Finland, *AB*.

Pesonen, E. (1967c) On optimal properties of the stop loss reinsurance, *AB*.

Pesonen, E. (1969) NP-approximation, *SA*.

Pesonen, M. (1983) Optimal reinsurances, to be published in *SA*.

Philipson, C. (1968) Some compound Poisson processes applicable in the theory of risk, *CA*.

Rantala, J. (1982) *Solvency of Insurers and Equalization Reserves* (Vol. II) Insurance Publishing Company, Helsinki.

Reischel, M. (1981) Dynamische Rückversicherungs- und Ausschuttungspolitik, Inaugural Dissertation, Universität Hamburg.

Revell, J. (1979) Inflation and financial institutions, *Financial Times*.

Roberts, E. (1978) *Managerial Applications of System Dynamics*, MIT Press, Cambridge, Massachusetts.

Roy, Y. (1981) A stochastic simulation model for reinsurance decision-making by ceding companies, dissertation, University of Pennsylvania.

Rubinstein, R. (1981) *Simulation and the Monte Carlo Method*, Wiley, New York.

Ruohonen, M. (1980) On the probability of ruin of risk processes, *SA*.

Seal, H. (1969a) Simulation of the ruin potential of non-life insurance companies, *Transactions of Society of Actuaries*, **21**.

Seal, H. (1969b) *Stochastic Theory of a Risk Business*, Wiley, New York.

Seal, H. (1971) Numerical calculation of the Bohman-Esscher family of convolution-mixed negative binomial distribution functions, *MS*.

Seal, H. (1974) The numerical calculation of $U(w, t)$, the probability of non-ruin in an interval $(0, t)$, *SA*.

Seal, H. (1977) Approximations to risk theory's $F(x, t)$ by means of the gamma distribution, *AB*.

Seal, H. (1978) *Survival Probabilities*, Wiley, New York.

Seal, H. (1980) Survival probabilities based on Pareto claim distribution, *AB*.

Segerdahl, C.-O. (1959) A survey of results in the collective theory of risk. The Harald Cramér Volume, Uppsala.

Shpilberg, D. (1977) The probability distribution of fire loss amount, *JRI*.

Sparre-Andersen, E. (1957) On the collective theory of risk in the case of contagion between the claims, *CA*.

Straub, E. (1978) How to fix retention, *MS*.

Sugars, E.G. (1974) Selected results from a risk theoretic simulation of an insurance company, *JRI*.

Taylor, G.C. (1978) Representation and explicit calculation of finite time ruin probabilities, *SA*.

Thorin, O. (1971) An outline of a generalization – started by E. Sparre-Andersen – of the classical ruin theory, *AB*.

Thyrion, P. (1967) Regards sur le développement récent de la théorie du risque, *AB*.

Veit, K. (1976) The use of system dynamics simulation models for corporate long range strategic planning, *CA*.

Venezian, E.C. and Gaydos, E.M. (1980) The effects of variable size of risk on capital solvency requirements, Research report of Insurance Services Office, New York.

Whitney, A.W. (1909) The actuarial theory of fire insurance rates, *CA*.

Witt, R.C. and Miller, H. (1980) A comparative analysis of relative costs under competitive and non-competitive rate regulatory laws, University of Texas, Austin.

Author index

Subject index

#/